TABLE TALES

◊

THE GLOBAL
NOMAD CUISINE
OF

ABU DHABI

FOR
Steve, Tala, Badr, and
Abu Dhabi, a city we call home.

HANAN
SAYED WORRELL

TABLE TALES

◇

THE GLOBAL
NOMAD CUISINE
OF

ABU
DHABI

PHOTOGRAPHS
Martin Nicholas Kunz
and Heike Fademrecht

Author
Hanan Sayed Worrell

Text, Recipes and Photographs
© Hanan Sayed Worrell

Art Direction and Graphic Design
Eps51 Berlin
Cover Calligraphy
Wissam Shawkat

Recipe Editor
Ruth Hennum Fowler

Copyeditor
Sylvia Adrian Notini

Photography
All photos by **Martin Kunz** and **Heike Fademrecht**
page 12 by **Mohamad Somji**
pages 16, 17, 20, 371 by **Hazem Sayed**
pages 173, 267, 268, 269 by **Rasha Amer**

Libri Illustrati Rizzoli
© 2018 Mondadori Electa S.p.A., Milan
All rights reserved
First edition: October 2018
Third printing, 2020
2020 2021 2022 2023 / 10 9 8 7 6 5 4 3

No part of this publication may be reproduced,
stored in a retrieval system, or transmitted in any form
or by any means, including electronic, mechanical,
photocopying, recording, or otherwise,
without the prior consent of the publishers.

Distributed in English throughout the world
by Rizzoli International Publications Inc.
300 Park Avenue South
New York, NY 10010, USA

ISBN: 978-8-89-181793-8

ISO 9001
Mondadori Electa S.p.A. is certified for the Quality
Management System by Bureau Veritas Italia S.p.A.,
in compliance with UNI EN ISO 9001.
This book respects the environment.
The paper used was produced using wood from forests
managed to strict environmental standards;
the companies involved guarantee sustainable
production certified environmentally.
Printed in Italy

CONTENTS

FOREWORD 13
HE Noura Al Kaabi

INTRODUCTION 15
Hanan Sayed Worrell
      Banana Bread with Crystallised Ginger and Walnuts 21

HOW I MET MY ABU DHABI 24
Dr. Mariët Westermann

THE RECIPES 32
Hanan Sayed Worrell

— 1960s —
START TO SIMMER

Zaki Nusseibeh 38
United Arab Emirates
      Za'atar Chai / Thyme Tea 43

Frauke Heard-Bey and David Heard 46
Germany and United Kingdom
      Apfeltorte ohne Deckel / Apple Tart without a Lid 51

Nicholas Cochrane-Dyet 52
United Kingdom
      Grilled Cheese Sandwich with Marmite 57

— 1970s —
BRING TO A BOIL

Asma Siddiq Al Mutawaa 62
United Arab Emirates
      Tahta Lahem / Emirati Lamb Pilaf 67
      Hamam Mahshi bil Freek / Freekeh-Stuffed Squab 68

Lina Mikati 70
Syria/Canada
      Muhammara / Walnut and Red Pepper Dip with Flax Seed 73
      Circassian Chicken / Syrian Poached Chicken with Walnut Sauce . . 74
      Sambal Udang / Prawn Sambal 77
      Ma'amoul bil Jibn / Cheese-Filled Shortbread Pastries 78

Nira and Vinay Varma 80
India
    Lassie—Spicy or Fruity 83
    Channa Bhatura / Spiced Chickpea Curry with Fried Bread 85
    Lobster Maharaja with Green Rice 86

Mary and Martin Corrado 88
United States
    Polpette con Salsa di Pomodoro / Italian Meatballs and Tomato Sauce ... 93
    Pastiera Napoletana / Italian Easter Cake 94

Maria Angeles Ruiz de Alom 96
Spain
    Fattoush / Bread and Purslane Salad 99
    Tortilla Española de Patatas / Spanish Omelette with Potatoes . 100
    Gazpacho / Chilled Tomato Soup 101
    Paella de Marisco / Seafood Paella 102

Amina Rizk and Bachir Elhaskouri 104
Morocco
    Braised Chicken with Lemons and Olives 108
    Harira / Moroccan Tomato Lentil Soup 109

— 1980s —
LOW AND SLOW

Ahmed Al Bawardi 114
United Arab Emirates
    Chbaab / Emirati Pancakes 118
    Chai Karak / Cardamom Milk Tea 119

Paula Al Askari 120
Lebanon / United States
    Fennel, Beetroot, and Orange Salad with Cumin Dressing 126
    Spiced Sweet Potatoes with Marshmallows 127
    Honey-Basted Turkey with Chestnut Stuffing 128

Reem Al Orfali 130
Iraq / Canada
    Istikan Chai / Iraqi Tea 134
    Tatar Kulaghi / Meat Dumplings with Yogurt Sauce 135
    Klaichat Tamur / Iraqi Date Cookies 136

Nadia Sehweil and Mira Naaman 138
Palestine / United States and Lebanon / Canada
    Trio of Smoothies 142
    Tahini Raw Powerbites 143
    Gluten-Free Nut and Goji Maple Granola 144

Salma Al Riyami and Amin Karim 146
United Arab Emirates and United Kingdom
    Ginger Lemonade 149
    A Trio of Tartines 150

— 1990s —
LIFT THE LID

Raman Khanna 156
India
    Dum Ki Dal / Slow-Simmered Indian Lentils 159
    Portuguese Spiced Hammour 160
    Green Prawn Curry with Fennel Shavings 161
    Blueberry Risotto 162

Reem and Ramzi Ghannoum 164
Lebanon / Canada and Jordan / Canada
    Musakhan Rolls / Sumac and Caramalised Onion Chicken Rolls 167
    Arayes / Lamb-Stuffed Mini Pita Sandwiches 168
    Sheikh al Mukhshi / Stuffed Eggplant with Pomegranate Molasses 169
    Beef Shawarma with Tahini Sauce 170

Salama Al Shamsi 172
United Arab Emirates
    Tuna Tahta / Emirati Spiced Pilaf with Tuna 175
    Sticky Date Pudding with Cardamom Sauce 176

Carolina Collazos and Laurent Depolla 178
Colombia and France
    Tostadas de Platano con Hogao / Fried Green Plantains with Tomato Salsa 182
    Scallop Ceviche with Mango 183
    Pie de Coco / Colombian Coconut Pie 184

Mona Zaki 186
Egypt / United States
    Molokhia / Jute Leaf Soup 191
    Egyptian Konafa with Cream 192

Lana and Hani Baramki 194
Palestine / Canada
    Marinated Beef Tenderloin 199
    Mint and Pine Nut-Crusted Lamb Chops with Black Peppercorn Sauce 200
    Grilled Honey and Mint Strawberries with Mascarpone 201

Nathan Brown 202
New Zealand

    Warm Lentil Salad with Garden Vegetables and Poached Shrimp 205
    Branzino al Sale / Herb and Salt-Crusted Sea Bass
        with Porcini Mushrooms and Purple Potatoes 206

— 2000s —
A NEW COURSE

Shaikha Al Kaabi 212
United Arab Emirates

    Gahwa Arabia / Arabic Coffee 215
    Luqamaat / Fried Dumplings with Date Syrup 216
    Machboos Deyay / Emirati Rice Pilaf with Chicken 218

Ranya and Salim Nasser 220
Palestine / United States

    Crab Cakes with Mango Avocado Salsa 225
    Gemista me Feta / Greek Stuffed Tomatoes with Quinoa, Capers, and Olives 226
    Caramelised Onion and Fig Tart with Manouri Cheese 229
    Mango and Blackberry Coconut Buckle 230

Marjon Ajami 232
Afghanistan / United States

    Borani Banjan / Eggplant with Tomato and Mint Yogurt Sauce 236
    Borani Kadoo / Sautéed Butternut Squash with Saffron and Yogurt 237
    Cauliflower and Roasted Beetroot Salad with Tahini Dressing 238
    Kale Caesar Salad with Yogurt Dressing and Za'atar Croutons 240

Roulana and Muhannad Qubbaj 242
Palestine / Lebanon / Canada and Palestine / Jordan / United Kingdom

    Brussels Sprouts with Mint Yogurt Sauce 246
    Aish al Saraya / Lebanese Bread Pudding 247
    Fattet al Hummus / Chickpeas with Pita and Tahini Yogurt 248

Yunib Siddiqui 250
United Kingdom

    Roasted Pumpkin and Feta Cheese Salad with Yuzu Dressing 253
    Wagyu Burger with Bois Boudran Sauce 254

Nada Akkari 256
Lebanon

    Quinoa Herb Salad 260
    Roasted Eggplant with Avocado, Thyme, and Green Olives 261
    Asian Glazed Salmon 263
    Guava and Pomegranate Salad 264

Buthaina Al Mazrui and Noor Bani Hashim 266
United Arab Emirates
    Spicy Tuna on Crispy Rice 270
    Biscoff Cheesecake with Salted Caramel Sauce 271

Peggi and Alfred Bloom 272
United States
    Bong Bong Gee / Bong Bong Chicken 276
    Chinese 'Strange Flavour' Eggplant 277

Tamu and Amir Al Islam 278
United States
    Couscous with a Trio of Flavours 282

Nazzy Beglari and Peter Scarlet 284
Iran / United States and United States
    Sup-e Pesteh / Pistachio Soup 289
    Kashk-e Bademjan / Eggplant and Yogurt Dip 290
    Albaloo Polow / Sour Cherry Rice 293
    Fesenjan ba Ordak / Duck with Walnut and Pomegranate Sauce 294

— 2010s —
WHAT'S BREWING

Maisa Al Qassimi 300
United Arab Emirates
    Marbled Cheesecake Brownies 303
    Salonat Lahem / Braised Goat and Root Vegetable Stew 304

Rickie Naito and Manami Tominaga 306
Japan
    Nasu Tama Miso / Eggplant Miso 311
    Kyuri to Wakame no Sunomono / Marinated Cucumber and Seaweed
        with Sweet Vinegar Dressing 312
    Gyu-niku no Tataki / Seared Beef with Microgreens 313
    Chirashi Zushi / Garnished Sushi 314

Alia and Adnan Amin 316
Afghanistan / United States and Kenya
    Afghan Aush / Afghan Noodle Soup with Swiss Chard 321
    Chapli Kebab / Afghan Beef Patties 322
    Fondant au Chocolat / Molten Chocolate Cake 324

Manuela Mirkos and John Defterios 326
Greece / Italy and Greece / United States
    Garides me Feta / Shrimp with Feta Cheese 329
    Umbrian Farro and Pearl Barley Salad 330
    Cardamom Spiced Orange Cake 332

Maria Eduarda Grillo and Jaime Van Zeller Leitão 334
Portugal
      Chilled Beetroot Soup with Yogurt. 338
      Chicken Satay with Peanut Sauce 339

Buthaina Kazim and Mishaal Al Gergawi 340
United Arab Emirates
      Chili con Carne with Daqoos 344
      Toasted Pumpkin Seed Guacamole 345

Laila Afridi 346
Pakistan / United Kingdom
      Mirch Machli / Red Snapper with Green and Red Chilies 350
      Keema Matar and Raita / Minced Meat with Peas and Cucumber Yogurt Sauce 351

Fatima and Alyazyah Al Shamsi 352
United Arab Emirates
      Chicken Mac and Cheese 356
      Pecan Pie 357
      Snickerdoodle Cookies 358

Pascale and Alain Sabri 360
Lebanon / France
      Pain Perdu / French Toast with Salted Caramel Sauce 363
      Tabbouleh / Parsley and Bulgur Salad 364
      Tom Yum Goong / Spicy and Sour Shrimp Soup 366

THANK YOU 370

THE AUTHOR 371

INDEX 372

FOREWORD

While growing up in Abu Dhabi during the 1980s, I witnessed my country's rapid transformation. In those formative years, I visited countries where the tales of their development echoed from every street corner. Anyone who has visited the United Arab Emirates since the mid-1980s will know the country has developed at an unfathomable speed. In just twenty years, ours has become one of the most advanced countries in the world. For me, this change would not have been possible without the shared values of hospitality found here, and the incredible people who contributed their skills and talent to building our nation, all of which was encouraged by our late founding father, HH Sheikh Zayed bin Sultan Al Nahyan.

I have met many people over the course of my education and career in Abu Dhabi, and they all have wonderful stories to tell about where they were when skyscrapers began shooting up, or islands became world-class resorts, or when cultural districts came to life. These stories, although diverse, have a shared element: they are all stories of change and impressive adaptation.

One of my favourite conversations is reminiscing about what has been and dreaming of the unlimited possibilities for what will be. These meaningful discussions take place mostly at the table, over a delicious home-cooked meal. As the country continues to grow, it also continues to welcome people, and these people in turn extend their hospitality as they contribute to a thriving collection of narratives that have become the social fabric of Abu Dhabi and the United Arab Emirates.

Table Tales: The Global Nomad Cuisine of Abu Dhabi provides a special glimpse into the different lives that form the fabric of our country. That same hospitality and togetherness that I've met throughout my life is emulated in this book. Reading through each page, through each recipe and story, I felt that I, too, knew these people and had spent time discussing the same topics with them as I do every day with friends. Abu Dhabi is a place of connecting people through shared memories, but also diverse backgrounds, and I appreciate this book for its genuine representation of Abu Dhabi's growth, but also its local flavour.

Just as many have made the United Arab Emirates their home, *Table Tales* shares stories and provides recipes that celebrate Abu Dhabi's enticing culinary culture, from the home to the streets. On this journey of development, food is woven into the fabric of the country. For memories of the past and tales for the future, this book captures the ever-changing tides that form the essence of this great nation.

HE NOURA AL KAABI

◊

Minister of
Culture and Knowledge
Development

INTRODUCTION

HANAN
SAYED WORRELL
◊
LEBANON/EGYPT/
US

I grew up eating dinner at a round table. *Al ma'eda al mustadeera* (the round table), as my father referred to it, was the focal point of our home on the outskirts of Kuwait City. Onyx-topped with a low-hanging chandelier above, it was where we gathered for our daily family meals in the red-brick Villa Hazem that my father built in the 1960s in the barren desert of Surra. My siblings and I would walk home from school and wash up. My mother, a high school history and French teacher, would be home already, supervising the multi-course meal preparations in the kitchen. Hungry, but not allowed to nibble, we would wait for my father to arrive, often late from work — there was no family dinner without my father.

A round table is meant to shift power from the head of the table to everyone seated around it. At our own round table, though, it was clear that my father, Abu Hazem, was the Head of State. He set the tone for the thousands of conversations and meals that took place at our table. He was particular about how we held our utensils, where we placed our hands, when we were allowed to leave the table, and that we finished the food on our plates. He made us taste everything from boiled Brussels sprouts to stuffed quails, which he ate with the bones, proudly pointing out that he had never needed to visit a dentist. He encouraged us to stand up for our opinions and debated politics with us. If you made a mistake, you earned the deep humiliation of his silent treatment! He could be effusive in his praise for our cook, but he also did not mince his words if the *mahshi* (stuffed vegetables) was not prepared the Egyptian way.

When my father sat us down at the round table, he saw more than the food on his plate. He saw his life. His working-class Egyptian parents had doted on him, the long-awaited male child born after a long series of miscarriages and stillbirths. He had grown up in Cairo in the mid-twentieth century, become politically active against colonial rule, gotten exiled from his country, married my Syrian-Lebanese mother, and taken her away from her family to a foreign land where he had established a successful contracting business. He was a proud man and he took deep satisfaction in the good life he had made for himself and his family, much of which was discussed and debated at al ma'eda al mustadeera, as we ate a wide array of Egyptian and Levantine dishes.

A busy working woman, my mother left everyday cooking to our cook. Her baking skills lay dormant until the fasting month of Ramadan, when she would fill the round table with our favourite desserts. She would often try recipes that were exchanged in the teachers' lounge at her school. Her signature dessert, *labneh* cheesecake, made from low-fat strained yogurt instead of cream cheese, was a highlight. Her *kunafa* and *katayef* were irresistible, scented with orange blossom and swimming in a puddle of *atar* (syrup). It was during Ramadan that we truly harvested the culinary delights of our dual heritage — my mother always made two versions of kunafa and katayef, the Levantine with cheese filling, and the Egyptian with spiced nuts, to please my father.

I did not grow up in the kitchen. My parents prioritised education and physical fitness above all, which meant we dedicated our time to studying, getting into top universities, playing sports, and watching our diet. The kitchen was off limits, with the cooks preparing the food under my mother's supervision, unless it was a special occasion such as Eid, when my father would make his favourite Egyptian *fatta*. But food and hospitality were central to our life, be it our family meals, Ramadan *iftars*, summer lunches at my grandmother's, my mother's ladies' gatherings, my father's epic camping trips, or his large dinner parties. There was always space for more people, as the round table expanded to an oval one.

It was at college in California that I learned to cook. My freshman roommate, Sue, from Newport Beach, would return from her weekend trips home with batches of cookies — chocolate chip, peanut butter, and oatmeal and raisins. I studiously copied the recipes and tried them when I went home. I was converted. I remember my college years now by the foods I was introduced to. In my junior year, my roommates and I had our own kitchen and living room. We loved to cook and invite friends over. I returned that fall armed with freshly acquired knowledge on how to roll grape leaves, stuff *kusa*, and flip *maqluba*. Kath had returned from a semester in Paris and was making quiche and fondue, and Bec, the ultimate tri-athlete, was carb loading with different pasta dishes and a mean mocha cake. Hungry not only to try new foods but to learn how to make them, I became an avid recipe hunter. I searched for recipes in newspapers and magazines; I cut, copied, rolled, and stuffed them into my metal recipe box. I started to collect cookbooks, which we did not have growing up. I grew my own sprouts, joined the local co-op in Palo Alto, and bought seeds, nuts, and grains in bulk to make granola. I joined the Dag Hammarskjold cooperative house, where I learned to cook for large numbers, and a gourmet club where we prepared elaborate five-course meals. The bounty of California, the diversity of the people, and the earthy food movements made for a rich culinary education alongside my civil engineering studies.

In fact, in my first concrete lab class, Professor Paulson looked at me, the only female in the lab, and stated: 'When it comes to ensuring proper proportions of a concrete mix, it is a lot like baking. Mess up the contents and you are likely to have a disaster of a cake on your hands'. To help us understand the nature of concrete he likened it to baking a fruit cake. You mix some flour, baking powder, butter, and eggs, add dried fruit and nuts, and pour the whole thing into a cake pan. Heat it in the oven, and voilà — you have something new. The original batter has changed, while the fruit and nuts are pretty much the same — just suspended and held together by the cake. Professor Paulson emphasised that while the design of the concrete mix is a science, good engineers learn to have a 'feel for the mix', as one would with a cake batter. After that course, I had a renewed respect for the alchemy that happens in a kitchen.

That summer, after graduating with a master's in civil engineering, I rewarded myself by enrolling in Le Cordon Bleu, the celebrated Parisian culinary school. My father, concerned that this might signal a career move, reluctantly agreed on the condition that my mother would join me. Paris stood up to every fantasy of mine. We were a small class of eight female students, and two chef instructors with two assistants, all men. Coming from the engineering world, I had expected to see women in the kitchen, but once again, men were in charge. After a morning at the market buying ingredients, we donned our whites and entered the kitchen. Every day, we cooked a three-course meal, using a mixture of cooking and pastry techniques: bundling *bouquet garnis*, preparing stock for sauces, hand-whipping egg whites, and blending fresh mayonnaise. At the end, exhausted from just four hours in the kitchen, we sat down to eat our work. Three afternoons a week I took the patisserie class. We made croissants from scratch, kneading the layers of dough and butter until completely absorbed, then *tarte aux pommes*, and *pâte à choux*. While my pastries did not look as impressive as the instructor's, they tasted fantastic. Each afternoon I proudly took my pastries back to our little apartment and shared them with my mother and aunt. With the first bite, the croissant shattered and then tore into dozens of stretchy layers and strands. Sitting in cafés, taking long walks through the city, stopping at fromageries and sampling their wares, visiting chocolate shops and open markets — I realised what it meant to master a craft, be it croissant or concrete. I also learned that both could coexist in my life.

I joined the workforce in the 1980s, diving into the decade head first, with shoulder pads, Bill Blass suits, aerobics leotards, and leg warmers. Working for CF Braun on an oil refinery project in California, I was climbing the corporate ladder and the San Bernardino mountains. But I also equipped my kitchen with the latest gadgets, spices, and ingredients, ready to test all the recipes I had been collecting over the years. I said yes to everything: frozen yogurt, bran muffins, tricolour pasta salad, Cali-Mex, poppy seed dressing, pesto on everything, Cajun-blackened anything, and white chocolate mousse. I learned to appreciate food and the level of abundance that is unfamiliar in many parts of the world.

A couple of years later, I returned to Kuwait — and my father's ma'eda al mustadeera — when I started working as a field engineer on the Mina Abdulla oil refinery. The new job was demanding, with long hours and a commute to the Saudi Arabian border, so while I missed my California kitchen, I was happy to have someone else cooking. Once again, concrete played a key role in my life. At the pre-tender meeting for the concrete package for the refinery, I met a man who I would bring home to the round table. Steve, a southerner from Virginia, had spent many years working in Saudi Arabia. He was the construction manager on the project and as he taught me about setting up batching plants and curing concrete, I couldn't help notice his chiselled face and rugged demeanor, reminding me of the Marlboro Man. As I got to know him more, I also started enjoying his dry humour and confident candour, which stemmed from an independent spirit and a resilient personality. The oil refinery project was completed in 1989, and Steve and I were married in 1990, just a few months before Saddam Hussein's troops marched into Kuwait on 2 August 1990. We lived under siege for several months, growing acutely aware of the food shortages and the risks to life. Eventually, hopscotching back to New York, Steve's work took us to Santiago de Chile.

During my first Ramadan in Santiago, I felt incredibly homesick. Luckily, just before leaving Kuwait, my colleague, Abdulrazak, had connected me to his parents, the Syrian ambassador and his wife. They introduced us to the thriving Palestinian and Syrian communities in Santiago. Savouring Arabic food so far away from home helped ground me in the new city. But we also enjoyed discovering Chilean cuisine: *assado* (meat roasted on the barbecue), empanadas, and *ensalada de apio* (celery salad). Even then, I knew that I was enjoying the grace of my mother's karma — she had always welcomed people to our home in Kuwait, imagining that someday when her children found themselves to be strangers in a foreign place, Allah would connect them to people who would in turn welcome them.

> Hungry not only to try new foods, but to learn how to make them, I became an avid recipe hunter.

As Gulf War I came to an end, our lives continued to be peripatetic, now with the addition of our children, Tala and Badr. We established a home base in New York City, where my two sisters lived, while Steve returned to Kuwait to work on the reconstruction of the country after the devastation of the war. In 1993, Steve was offered a position in Abu Dhabi developing an onshore gas field. Reluctantly, I agreed to leave our base in New York and my family in Kuwait and move to Abu Dhabi for what was supposed to be a two-year assignment.

Now, twenty-five years later, we still call Abu Dhabi home.

Abu Dhabi is where I realised the power of food to nurture a family and create a community. Steve's first job was in the remote desert of the Western Region where he lived during the week and came home on weekends. While setting up home with two toddlers and navigating a new city, I was determined to pursue my career. I began managing aviation and environmental projects for the government. As I cooked for a young family while juggling long hours at work, memories of my parents came rushing back, comforting and reassuring me. At the end of the day, when I was exhausted and fed up and unsure of everything, food was the only certainty. Remembering the foods of my childhood, I realised that while the food itself was amazing, what was truly nourishing was the steady rhythm of meeting my family and sharing a meal every day at the round table.

At work, my Emirati colleagues introduced me to their culture through the morning office ritual of *rutab* (fresh dates), *gahwa* (coffee), and *bakhoor* (incense*)*, and the mid-morning snack of *chbaab* (Emirati pancakes) and *chai karak* (cardamom milk tea). I joined them for Friday lunches at their farms in Al Ain, falconry training in Sweihan, royal weddings in palaces, Ramadan *iftars*, and Eid feasts. The South Asian workers on my job site shared their tiffin of *channa* with naan wrapped in newspaper, washed down with hot chai. With guest workers making up three-quarters of the population, Abu Dhabi is truly an international community. Over time, I came to realise that the diversity of the city and how it caters to everyone from the labourer to the executive, is special. On a typical day, I would interact with people of a dozen different nationalities.

The Arab world has long cherished hospitality as a central value of its culture. Gratitude for water, so crucial for survival in the desert, is embedded in the Arabic language. Before Islam, the word *sharia*, the path of god, meant the path to a watering hole. *Ain* (spring) is the same word as eye — both are essential; both produce water. To this day, it is a desert tradition to greet visitors with coffee and a glass of water. At work, during a meeting with the municipality on the landscaping of the highway approach to the airport, the chief engineer informed us that the date palms lining the median had to be of a limited height. That was the directive of Sheikh Zayed, the president of the United Arab Emirates, so workers passing by could help themselves to the low-hanging fruit, thus sharing in the bounty of the land.

As I benefited from this hospitality, I also learned to offer it. I began to host Thanksgiving dinners, inviting American and non-American friends to share in this tradition of gratitude, and each year welcoming a newcomer to the city. Ramadan, of course, was a special month in Abu Dhabi, and I enjoyed sharing it with our Muslim and non-Muslim friends. We celebrated Christmas at the Hochar's with turkey, foie gras, and *Bouche de Noel*. We welcomed the new year with Yousef in his verdant garden, with a fresh supply of Beluga caviar from the Caspian Sea, and pungent and addictive French cheese on baguette hunks. Our friend, Alain, an avid outdoorsman who had moved to Abu Dhabi in the 1980s and knew everything about its beaches, islands, desert, and oases, organised epic dhow journeys. Meticulously planned to the last detail, these sailing picnics brought together his friends from different walks of life and their foods. My own contribution was the perennial classic, banana bread, made from rotten bananas that lurked in the icy depths of my freezer.

For most newcomers or visitors to the city, Abu Dhabi can appear impermeable and somewhat generic. Visitors see tall buildings and fast highways. But living here is an experience in connection. Again and again I saw people arrive, leaving behind their countries, creating transitory homes, and then moving on. Yet, at the same time, they leave such a big impression on our lives, on who we are, who we become, and how we see the world. I learned from Emirati friends how the rapid changes had impacted their lives and how their native food and customs had become infused with global flavours and spices. This international vision of hospitality was also evident in the built environment. The architect of the Sheikh Zayed Grand Mosque told me that, according to the brief of Sheikh Zayed, every Muslim in the United Arab Emirates should find something from their own Islamic architectural heritage in the mosque. Today, it is an elegant combination of Moghul domes, Ottoman minarets, Moorish arches, Moroccan *zellige* (mosaic tile work), and Persian carpets.

> The Arab world has long cherished hospitality as a central value of its culture.

The city itself opened its arms to take in my family and me. I shopped with my children at open air markets where we got to know shopkeepers by name. Talented South Asian tailors stitched the Halloween costumes of their dreams each year. The neighbourhood *baqala* (grocery store) was my lifeline. Whatever I needed, food, diapers, or detergent, I would call the shopkeeper and he would deliver what he had and source what he didn't from nearby stores, keeping a tab, which we paid at the end of the month. The American Community School where our children graduated was another oasis of friendships. There were a few restaurants we visited occasionally but mostly our life was built around the tables of our tight-knit community of friends. I could hardly go anywhere in the city without running into someone I knew or had just met.

Of course, Abu Dhabi never stands still. With growth spurts and increased connection to global markets came the influx of more wealth and waves of new people. The announcements of the Saadiyat Cultural

District and partnerships with New York University, Sorbonne University, Cleveland Clinic, and Formula One, put Abu Dhabi on the map, as never before. My own work expanded to new endeavours in education, culture and the arts. Suddenly my phone was ringing with friends and friends of friends wanting to visit Abu Dhabi, so I started hosting dinners for visitors and newcomers. My table was increasing in radius day by day. Today, Abu Dhabi attracts global nomads with a high degree of mobility. The city has become ground zero for the kind of global nomad cuisine that emerges when people from different cultures gather at a round table. A hearty meal from your homeland might help cure homesickness when you are first immersed in a foreign culture, but when you return home, you start missing the foreign dishes that were once exotic: many global nomads in Abu Dhabi know this feeling all too well.

As I started to think about how I could capture these stories, I was beginning to see in action what social anthropologists say: cooking can be a language; a form of narrative that marks our culture. It allows us to weave elaborate culinary stories with which to shape and consolidate our social worlds. Many writers and scholars have suggested that cooking makes us human. But it is not just cooking that distinguishes us, it is also how we share it. According to archaeologist Martin Jones, we are the only creatures who share food with strangers, people not from our family or tribe. Hospitality, whether offered in an elaborate feast, or a cup of coffee, is what makes us civilised.

This is especially true in Abu Dhabi, where a sense of impermanence permeates our lives. In a city where most of the people are foreigners, time often seems to telescope, with the hours merging into each other and the years passing like seasons. We don't know where the merry-go-round of life will deliver us or if home is a real place. So, I began dreaming of a book, with its weight and solidness, that could capture a moment in time. A book that would say, 'We were here, and this is what we ate, and this is who we became'. I also wanted to give something back to a city that has been home for twenty-five years, and show a different face of Abu Dhabi, one the world doesn't often see.

And so, I got back into the kitchen with a vengeance. I started pestering my friends and their friends for recipes. Recipes unfolded into stories, for without a story, a recipe is just a set of bland, boring instructions. It is the stories and the people telling them that give flavour to the recipes. I learned about different cuisines and cultures first hand. I sifted through memories and memorabilia. In the process, I deepened my friendships and made new friends. To watch someone cook is to watch them live. I saw my friends overcome their vulnerabilities and transform in the kitchen. I shared in their loss, their grief, their joy, and separation. With every recipe I tested at home, every story I collected, I excavated another layer of Abu Dhabi.

> Abu Dhabi is where I realised the power of food to nurture a family and create a community.

I also realised that everything about food is luxurious: reading about it, shopping for it, thinking about it, preparing it, and finally eating it. Today in Abu Dhabi, many of us have access to any ingredient we want. What a huge privilege, especially when we are surrounded by countries where people subsist on almost nothing. As I cook, I am conscious of how lucky we are that we can afford to cook so abundantly and how important it is to share that abundance with those less fortunate.

So, I invite you to my Abu Dhabi. Meet Emiratis and expatriates from Syria to Spain, India to Italy, Afghanistan to the Americas, who have made Abu Dhabi home over the last six decades. A simple bowl of meatballs with *salsa di pomodoro*, hearty Afghan *aush*, aromatic Emirati *machboos deyay*, sinfully sweet *luqamaat*, Japanese home sushi, and slow-cooked North Indian *dal*—these are some of the recipes that will take your taste buds on a culinary journey through the kitchens of this city's global nomads. Come join us at Abu Dhabi's ma'eda al mustadeera.

BANANA BREAD
with Crystallised Ginger and Walnuts

HANAN *I was first introduced to quick breads by my mother's friend, Adalat, who had moved to Elgin, Illinois, from Kuwait a few years before I arrived in California for college. One morning, I received a package from her. When I opened it, I found a heavy, rectangular object wrapped in foil, labelled 'Zucchini Bread', with a note welcoming me to the States. That was as foreign as a bread could be! After the first slice — moist, tender, and spotted with walnuts — I was intrigued. I delved into quick breads, and the humble loaf that is banana bread became a college favourite that I have been baking ever since, with variations of nuts, chocolate, coconut, or ginger. The secret is to use extra-ripe bananas because their sugar has naturally caramelised. There is something profoundly reassuring for me to have a bunch of speckled bananas at the ready in my freezer, as if I were hoarding gold bullion.*

—
SERVES
8 TO 10
—

225 g (8 oz) butter, softened

520 g (2½ c) granulated sugar

4 eggs

4 large, ripe bananas, mashed

110 g (½ c) crystallised ginger, chopped

95 g (¾ c) walnuts, chopped

525 g (3½ c) all-purpose flour

2 tsp baking powder

2 tsp baking soda

¼ tsp salt

2 tsp vanilla

240 ml (1 c) buttermilk or laban

Preheat the oven to 190°C (375°F). Grease and flour two 23 x 13-centimetre (9 x 5-inch) loaf pans.

Cream the butter and sugar in a large bowl with an electric mixer, until pale. Add the eggs one at a time, beating well after each addition. Fold in the bananas, crystallised ginger, and walnuts until well blended.

Sift the flour, baking powder, baking soda, and salt into another bowl. Gradually stir the dry ingredients into the banana mixture. Combine the vanilla with the buttermilk. Gradually pour it into the batter, stirring gently with a rubber spatula and scraping down the sides as needed, until just combined. Do not over-mix.

Pour the batter into the pans, using a spatula to smooth the surface. Bake for 50 to 60 minutes or until a toothpick inserted in the centre comes out clean. Transfer to a wire rack to cool completely before removing from the pans.

HOW I MET MY ABU DHABI

DR. MARIËT WESTERMANN
◊
Executive Vice President
Mellon Foundation

The provision of food and entertainment as a mechanism for getting to know the intentions of strangers is a universal phenomenon. Some of the best evidence of this cross-cultural tendency may be found in the accounts of European explorers. In 1792, the Spanish captain Jacinto Caamaño Moraleja, charged to explore today's British Columbia, attended a potlatch ceremony and feast offered by a chief of the Southern Tsimshian people in the village of Ksidiya'ats, on Pitt Island.[1] After spending several weeks exploring the Vancouver estuary and having repeatedly hosted Jammisit, the village chief, on his ship with wine and ship's biscuit, he finally accepted an invitation to come to the chief's house for 'a grand fete…arranged in my honour' as 'they desired to entertain me with a grand ball'. At the event, his host placed him, his officers, and his crew in an arrangement that put him on an approximate par with the position of another guest of honour, Chief Gitejon of a neighbouring village, who appeared to be a shaman. Camaaño reported that Gitejon approached him with bizarre but seemingly kind gestures and showered the guests with feathers. Various dances and songs followed, along with handsome helpings of boiled fish, 'though few of us tried it'.

Encounters like these, between would-be conquerors and wary but polite indigenous leaders appear throughout the literature of exploration between peoples who did not speak each other's languages and had good reason to fear each other. Camaaño was clear about his motivations to accept the invitation: 'Curiosity to see [the village], as well as the fete for which such extensive preparations were being made, induced me to comply with his entreaties'. Curiosity, an intercultural drive often present in even the most rapacious conquistadors,

[1] He called the village Citeyats. Henry R. Wagner and W. A. Newcombe, eds., 'The Journal of Jacinto Camaaño. Part II', *British Columbia Historical Quarterly* II, no. 4 (October 1938), pp. 265-302; for the account of the potlatch and events leading up to it, see pp. 285-293.

[2] Claude Lévi-Strauss, *Le cru et le cuit*, Paris, 1964, trans. by John and Doreen Weightman as *The Raw and the Cooked: Introduction to a Science of Mythology*, vol. 1, New York and Evanston, 1964, p. 1.

surely mattered, but the captain and the chiefs also maintained a symmetry of politeness that might form a basis for a future relationship. Caamaño may have wished to honour Jammisit's offer to reciprocate the hospitality that the captain had offered the villagers aboard his ship. Despite his inability to eat the fish on offer or make sense of the music and dancing, Caamaño recognised that the ceremony was presented as an act of hospitality, and that laws of hospitality required him and his men to accept the vital rituals of the host culture.

No matter how oddly someone else's cooking, eating, and hosting habits, dining décor, or toasting customs may seem to us, rituals around eating and sharing food are part of the human story. Offering a meal both unites and differentiates *Homo sapiens* in all its variety. In the preface to his great study, *The Raw and the Cooked* (1964), the anthropologist Claude Lévi-Strauss asserted that 'certain categorical opposites drawn from everyday experience with the most basic sorts of things — e.g. "raw" and "cooked", "fresh" and "rotten", "moist" and "parched", and others — can serve a people as conceptual tools for the formation of abstract notions and for combining these into propositions'.[2] This densely packed statement amounts to an assertion that a culture's oppositional terms attached to food are grounded in the worldview and social arrangements of the people who live in that culture. Lévi-Strauss could make this claim with great confidence, having derived it from years of analysing hundreds of myths of Amazonian Indian peoples in terms of such binary oppositions. Organising cultural forms into opposites, cognates, or allied terms appears to be something *all* societies do: like shared eating, making art, or telling jokes, it is one of the processes that makes us human. This realisation made

Lévi-Strauss see that the so-called 'primitive' mental set is no less sophisticated than the thought world of the 'Renaissance man', the 'Enlightenment man of letters', or the 'modern avant-garde'.

Even though Lévi-Strauss looked at lots of forms of cultural expression for his study, he was especially interested in culinary terms, and named his book *Le cru et le cuit*, 'The Raw and the Cooked'. The title may be rendered more precisely, 'The Raw and What Is Prepared for Eating'. There are many ways of transforming the raw into something a community will recognise as fit for consumption. This is true for sashimi and sushi, highly ritualised forms of preparing creatures of the sea for eating, even if the protein remains uncooked. In Lévi-Strauss's universe, the *cooked* doesn't necessarily mean roasted, fried, or boiled. 'The cooked' is a culturally mediated form of sustenance that separates human dining from the way a lion, say, might devour its prey raw. The lion may have eating practices that shield the food from rivals who might steal it, but, as far as research has been able to determine, the lion does not slice, dice, or season the meat in a particular way that gives a satisfaction beyond caloric and protein needs. Its meat is not *cuit* the way carpaccio is.

I read *The Raw and the Cooked* and accounts of Northwest Coast feasting when I was in graduate school, and the eye-opening experience came back to me when I first arrived in Abu Dhabi to start the development of the New York University (NYU) campus there. At first, the place seemed somewhat impenetrable, not easy to get to know in the way that people can feel instantly familiar with New York City or sort of at home in Paris or Beirut. And yet within a few weeks, it became evident to me and our Deputy Vice Chancellor Hilary Ballon how personal and professional relations were organised and developed through the sharing of food and drink. Upon entering any office for a meeting, whether with our government partners or a rental car agent, a higher education official or a property broker, we were offered water, dates, and Arabic coffee with cardamom — age-old staples of Bedouin hospitality on the Arabian Peninsula that had clearly been adopted by many newcomers as well. We marvelled that the tiny cups could not be put down on a coffee table and learned quickly how to rock them gently

to decline further servings. Our long days often did not allow for lunch, and I remember a lucky break one late afternoon at the Urban Planning Council when the dates had almonds and orange rinds wedged into them, and we hungrily replenished our energies with those original power bars.

In the early days of planning NYU Abu Dhabi (NYUAD), it became clear to us that Abu Dhabi does not have a public sphere in a familiar European or American sense, with bars and restaurants actively advertising their sociability, or an abundance of sidewalk cafes taking full advantage of the weather in the clement months of the year. I soon realised, however, that hotel lobbies and malls provided vital alternatives to such space, being easily accessible and well provided with a variety of comfortable seating and food and beverage services. Before NYUAD had offices, I used the spacious, light-filled lobby of the Beach Rotana Hotel — the impressive creation of Nasser Al Nowais — for that purpose, and marvelled that the accommodating staff would let me sit there for hours on end as I met with strings of people. Those early conversations were leavened with gorgeously layered fruit mocktails and free nibbles like small green Lebanese olives and fried *kibbeh*.

The hospitality we experienced in our fledgling efforts to get to know Abu Dhabi was amplified in extraordinary dining experiences of a generosity recalling that of Chief Jammisit in the Pacific Northwest. In the fall of 2007, HH Sheikh Mohamed bin Zayed Al Nahyan, Crown Prince of Abu Dhabi, treated the local and international community gathered for the announcement of NYUAD to wonderful meals at the Lebanese restaurant on the pleasant terrace of the Emirates Palace Hotel. At L'Auberge, Mr. Zakariah, the ever-welcoming maître d'hôtel, would personally administer generous helpings of the freshest tabbouleh, and then oversee a parade of dishes overflowing with hummus and *moutabal*, chilled artichoke with lemon, and chicken livers in pomegranate syrup, and, if I could convince others to eat them with me, *assafeer*, those fried tiny larks that provide a burst of game flavour and crunchy texture unmatched in any cuisine. As the *mezze* bowls accumulated on the table, large platters would come around with kebabs of lamb, chicken, and hammour resting on Arabian bread crackling with a smoky oven crust. At the end of such an evening we would waddle up the grand Emirates Palace stairs, leaving the tables covered with dishes so full that it looked as if no one had eaten.

At first this restaurant practice struck me as extravagant and irresponsible. I had grown up the daughter of parents who had known persistent hunger in The Netherlands and Indonesia during World War II, and who insisted that we take only as much as we could eat and empty our plates once we had served ourselves. But I came to see hospitality organised around the copiousness and variety of food on offer as a profound mark of the culture and history of the Emirati people, and a great asset for human interaction. In the 1930s and 1940s, and probably often before, the peoples of Abu Dhabi and the Emirates had known scarcity, if the date harvest was not as full as needed to provide sufficient sustenance and leave a surplus for trade, or after the pearl fishing industry declined once cultured pearls from Japan flooded the world market. And yet, even in years of poverty, the tribes of Abu Dhabi maintained a commitment to sharing food with those in need, and especially with strangers who would come their way in the unforgiving desert. These traditions of care and hospitality, and of sharing whatever your community may have to offer, continue to drive the culture of hospitality in the Emirates today.

In Abu Dhabi, I quickly realised, food in social settings was not meant to be finished: it was intended to be shared and enjoyed for as much as one would like, and then talked over during sustained dinner conversations. This point was first brought home to me when HE Khaldoon Al Mubarak, chairman of the Executive Affairs Authority (EAA), invited about ten members of our leadership team to have dinner at his home. After a lively conversation over fresh fruit drinks, we were invited into the garden on one of those special January evenings, when it is warm at first, but the night soon becomes starry and women wrap themselves in embroidered pashminas and men wish they had brought jackets that seemed unnecessary even an hour before. As we enjoyed dish after dish of Arabic salads, bean preparations, and stewed vegetables before tucking into flank steak, lamb kebabs, and fish fried with Indian spice, I realised that each of the New York guests had been carefully seated next to local dinner partners, who not only told us interesting things about the

history of the United Arab Emirates, but also took seriously their mandate to explain and personally serve every last dish to us. My dinner partner was Ali Frayhat, the talented chief legal counsel for the Executive Affairs Authority, who gave lively insight into what made Abu Dhabi such a welcoming place for him, a Jordanian citizen. Suffused with this generous spirit, the dinner for me was the beginning of important friendships that have lasted.

Over the years, I came to see that this culture of hospitality and sharing food is set at the top and carried through all the layers of Emirati society and into the large and diverse expatriate communities. HH Sheikh Nahyan bin Mubarak al Nahyan, who has served the country so well as Minister of Higher Education and Scientific Research, Minister of Culture and Knowledge Development, and now Minister of Tolerance, regularly invites wide swaths of local and international guests to lunch after the Friday sermon, or to events he hosts to celebrate milestones in the lives of his friends. When my sons joined me at a desert retreat where Sheikh Nahyan offered a wedding celebration for a friend, he invited them to talk about the books they had brought along, while he encouraged two extraordinary henna artists to decorate my hands and ankles with a beautiful design. Those tasks accomplished, Sheikh Nahyan later astounded us as he used his hands to serve us nimble helpings of rice and baby camel, a precious delicacy.

Hummus, tabbouleh or *za'atar* with arugula, slow-roasted lamb, rice, all with lemon and sumac for taste and colour: although these foods are hardly the only ones you will be offered at an Abu Dhabi feast, they are the characteristic ingredients of the meals presented by the finest local hosts. In the anthropological terms of Lévi-Strauss, these choices and combinations seem highly significant. Legume-based dishes such as hummus or *foul medames* are satisfying in taste, and together with rice or bread make a protein-rich and filling meal. No one who has been offered such foods will leave dinner hungry, in the same way that pasta or rice fill out Italian or Japanese dinners. Fresh salads, recalling verdant gardens, are a luxury in a desert climate where the growing of plants is a precarious and expensive undertaking. They were rare treats in many places before refrigeration and modern transportation made produce available in well-off countries most any time of year.

As in most cultures, meat is the main event, as it is the most resource-intensive, most generous food one can put on the table. In traditional Bedouin society, the luxury protein was stretched to feed as many people as possible by cooking small, air-dried chips of lamb into the thick, long-stewed wheat porridge known as *harees*, drenched with a little oil to facilitate ingestion. But roast lamb, the core dish shared with family and community at Eid Al Adha, also known as the Feast of the Sacrifice, is the ultimate expression of hospitality in Emirati culture. By privileging roast meat — whether a baby camel, whole lamb, kebabs, or small cuts layered over biryani — Abu Dhabi hosting practice resembles that of many cultures around the world. When *Homo sapiens* first managed to harness fire to human purpose, some 150,000 to 600,000 years ago, our ancestors appear to have understood that roast meat (and vegetables) are easier to digest than their raw forms, and to many also taste better. Food touched by fire (or its oven equivalent) is often considered the most honorific and greatest treat one can offer a guest. The American Thanksgiving turkey is one of the most widely shared manifestations of this idea, immediately grasped by millions of immigrants who take to the habit as fish to water.

I cannot remember a dinner or lunch without a roast lamb dish whenever my family, students, guests, and I have enjoyed the hospitality of HE Zaki Nusseibeh, usually after a welcoming drink of his beloved za'atar tea. Visits to Zaki's house are enriched immeasurably by conversations about the modern art of the Arab world that he has collected assiduously since the 1970s, and about the books he reads voraciously. His polyglot collection of literature and non-fiction is the finest and widest-ranging private library in the country, arranged with great logic and taste between his homes in Abu Dhabi and Al Ain.

The generosity of Emirati hospitality has been embraced by the country's complex and variegated expatriate community, made up of citizens from more than 110 countries. Only ten percent of the country's population originally hails from the seven emirates that make up the nation. Many of the newcomers who arrived sometime after the country's building boom took off grounded themselves by finding the company of compatriots or other immigrants. Every weekend, numerous picnics in Abu Dhabi's parks along the Corniche or in Khalidiya and Al Bateen — the legacy of Sheikh Zayed bin Sultan Al Nahyan's green urban plan for the capital — bring together the generations for food and games.

For years, however, fostering the mingling of local and expatriate leaders involved in the building of Emirati institutions and economic and cultural sectors has been the special contribution of long-term residents from other Arab, Gulf, and South Asian countries. Members of this diverse and cosmopolitan community hailing from Lebanon, Jordan, Egypt, Oman, India, and elsewhere, have generously made their residences into hubs of sociable networks. The home of Hanan and Steve Worrell and their outgoing children, Tala and Badr, has been one such haven for me. At the first dinner they invited me to, in 2007, I was astounded by the mix of people from eight countries, the lovely food and drink, and the easy flow in and out of house and patio. But what impressed me most was the combination of utterly gregarious banter and vital information exchange. Here I first met American Ambassador Rick Olsen, a great mind with a longstanding dedication to the region, who clearly thought the Worrell home an important place to be. He was to become a friend of crucial importance to NYU's efforts to understand how best to make true common cause with our new Abu Dhabi partners. Also at the table was the incomparably charming Ousama Ghannoum, a citizen of Jordan, who told the story of how he'd arrived at JFK airport the month after 9/11 and told the immigration official that he was on his way to a world trade centre conference. It took a few hours for United States immigration services to process that Ousama was on the board of the international World Trade Centers Association that is based in New York. Ousama told all this without a speck of rancour, and with sympathy for the befuddled officer. And so the evening went. I am used to late dinners and I am a very sociable person, but it was a shock for me to realise that at 1:15 am I was the first to leave.

That dinner introduced me to Paula Al Askari, who entertains with great frequency and elegant care in her 1980s villa (old by the country's standards) on the Corniche. Her menu is always just right for the

> I came to see hospitality organised around the copiousness and variety of food on offer as a profound mark of the culture of the Emirati people.
>
> MARIËT

company and the occasion, whether it is dinner with local friends and international art dealers or lunch with her children, Basil and Mariam. In fact, those casual Saturday lunches, when Paula will serve what she calls simple dishes like lamb chops layered over dolmades followed by freshly baked fruit tart with melting cream, are among my most memorable Abu Dhabi meals.

The sorts of experiences I have described helped undo the prevailing notion among New York colleagues and friends that the United Arab Emirates had neither culture nor history, other than an ambitious plan to build skyscrapers on low-lying sand and to seed cultural institutions in arid soil. As these generous meals extended in leisurely time, dense layers of history unfolded, registered in the lives of people there and in the communities and places they created. It was striking to see how much expatriates brought into Emirati society. For more than forty years, for example, Martin and Mary Corrado have introduced scores of newcomers to their hearty Friday supper of spaghetti and meatballs or their festive Chinese New Year celebrations.

The culinary mixing bowl of Abu Dhabi and the people who make it such a vital social force are on vivid display in the stories, recipes, and photographs gathered in this book. In Abu Dhabi, where so many people are from elsewhere, the connective power of dining provides a measure of cohesion for a country that is a contemporary crossroads but also a place where traditional Bedouin, Arab, and Muslim life can thrive and contribute to a dynamic intercultural community. Hanan Sayed Worrell, hostess and international recipe hunter of the highest order, has done us an incomparable service by capturing these energies with *Table Tales: The Global Nomad Cuisine of Abu Dhabi*.

THE RECIPES

HANAN SAYED WORRELL

On this journey to offer up a taste of Abu Dhabi, I invited forty individuals or couples to share their stories and favourite recipes. As a nod to the city's hundreds of communities that contribute to an immense tapestry of cuisines, I chose forty, which, in many faiths, represents an approximation of a much larger number. It also represents periods of transformation, which this city has certainly seen.

What connects these people and recipes is more than just good food: it is the experience of being a global nomad, the notion of home, the spirit of generosity, the importance of hospitality, and the value of friendships. The individual recipes carry special meaning to each of their owners; some are family heirlooms cooked in the age-old traditions of their place, some are traditional with adaptations to suit their new surroundings, and some are creations inspired by local ingredients or lifestyle. The 106 recipes illustrate the diverse global nomad cuisine of the city and the universal nature of a dish served with generosity and love. I hope that through this eccentric selection of recipes I have succeeded in distilling the spirit of the place that has shaped my family and me for the past quarter century.

This book is not organised in a conventional cookbook format — by main ingredient, course, or region — and it does not include recommendations for pantry contents or equipment. Instead, it is organised by decade, showcasing the people who came to call Abu Dhabi home in that decade, and the recipes they cherish. Since most meals comprise multiple dishes and are served family style, the recipes tend to be generous. Most are not thirty-minute, throw-together efforts, but for the time spent creating these dishes, you will be rewarded with a depth of flavour that only 'the real thing' can offer.

Recipes from my Western friends, with a longer tradition of written instructions, were easy to adapt. For my Arab and Asian friends, where cooking is transferred generationally by showing, it was a challenge to get them to commit to specific measurements. They explained how variable their dishes are depending on their mood, the freshness of ingredients, the potency of spices, the quality of olive oil, or the purity of the orange blossom water, for instance. I joined them in their kitchens with my digital scale and measured as they cooked, meticulously noting the instructions while making sure the cook didn't sneak in a dollop of honey to balance the sweet and sour flavour while I wasn't looking. Fortunately, most of the recipes, except for a few desserts, are forgiving, so adjusting the spices or cooking time will not alter them dramatically.

I, along with my recipe editor, Ruth, and chefs Raman and Michael, have meticulously measured, tested and documented the recipes to make them as clear and easy to follow as possible. I found that the characteristics of flour can vary, so greater accuracy may be achieved by weighing. What is considered a 'large' onion in one country will not be the same in another, so I have given weights for produce in most cases. Ingredients such as onion, garlic, or ginger can be used generously or sparingly as a matter of choice. Spices and seasoning come down to preference and freshness, so start with less, taste, and adjust. The components of the Emirati spice mix, *bzar*, and seven spices, *baharat*, vary from family to family, but recipes to make your own can be found online. Items such as *za'atar*, sumac, red pepper paste, and *achaar* are available in Middle Eastern grocery stores.

What I learned in this process is to taste the food as you make it, adjust, and trust your taste. This is in the spirit of these recipes, which are personal and rich in variations, and this is what cooking is about. No one knows your palate or equipment better than you do. Add a handful of fresh coriander or omit the garlic if that appeals to you. Sear the salmon or fry the tortilla for a few extra minutes if you wish. I encourage you to adapt, do what feels right, and enjoy!

The Recipes

1960s
START TO SIMMER

In the early 1960s, Abu Dhabi was a sparsely populated fishing village, part of the Trucial States, with a special treaty relationship with Britain. It had weathered extreme poverty into the mid-twentieth century, following the crash of the pearling industry. Despite the first export of oil in 1962, Abu Dhabi remained a sleepy village lacking even the basic amenities until later that decade. Except for a few families and the tribal sheikhs, everyone lived in *barasti* houses made from palm fronds, and there was no electricity or fresh water. People drank, bathed and cooked with brackish water until the first desalination plant was installed, although it could not completely support the population.

Life was hard. The local diet included dates from the oases, goat milk yogurt, and fish, with some imported foodstuffs, such as rice. The men fished, and the women sold the catch in the local market or traded it for other products. The women collected driftwood for cooking and fetched water from the well, carrying it back in a goatskin bag. There was one school, but children were expected to help with the daily chores at a young age. The first hospitals were not built until the late 1960s, and before that major milestones were not recorded, leaving many unsure of their actual birthday. Travel was mostly by camel, and the 160-kilometre journey from Abu Dhabi to Al Ain took seven days. When radio was introduced, it provided the first instantaneous link to the world for most Abu Dhabians, although prominent members of society travelled for business or medical reasons, via Bahrain, to the Indian subcontinent, Europe, and the United States. The first hotel, the Beach Hotel, opened in 1964 to accommodate the growing interest in Abu Dhabi, as the oil flowed to international markets.

But, things really started to simmer in 1966, when Sheikh Zayed bin Sultan Al Nahyan became the ruler of Abu Dhabi, and energised the economy, which had lagged significantly behind its neighbouring sheikdoms and countries. Sheikh Zayed believed in growth and development to better the life of his people and he was in a hurry. Immediately, new government departments were set up, cash was distributed, and masterplans developed. Desalinated water and power plants were commissioned, hotels and accommodations built, banks established, roads, ports and airports inaugurated, and schools opened. This brought the first large influx of foreigners from other Arab countries, Africa, Asia, and Europe, to develop the basic infrastructure. Early expatriates found that fresh produce was limited to what could be grown locally, and imported food was mostly canned. Bully beef, minced corned beef in gelatine and a main field ration of the British Army, was often served fried with onions and spices. The British Club, with its Curry Friday lunches prepared by expatriate wives, and the Al Ain Palace Hotel, with its two food and beverage outlets, provided social activities for expatriate workers and their families.

Abu Dhabi's importance as a trading and commercial centre increased as the oil industry expanded, and what was once a small fishing village became a bustling construction site. In 1968, the British announced their intent to withdraw from the Trucial States treaty. The ruler realised the danger, and while building Abu Dhabi at breakneck speed, he set about convincing the other sheikdoms to form a union to prevent being swallowed up by their bigger neighbours. The withdrawal of the British opened the markets to other countries, bringing Japanese, Americans, French, Italians, and Germans. The seeds of a multicultural Abu Dhabi were sown.

ZAKI NUSSEIBEH

MINISTER
OF STATE
◊
UAE

When we want some calm and respite, one of Steve's and my favourite weekend trips is to go to Al Ain, a desert oasis about 160 kilometres east of Abu Dhabi. Al Ain holds a special place in the United Arab Emirates as the traditional summer home to the ruling Al Nahyan dynasty and a historical crossroads for caravans. The highlight of our visit is to have lunch and afternoon tea at Zaki Nusseibeh's home, which is a large, custom-built white villa with pink bougainvillea dotting the fence. Al Ain is where Zaki loves to spend his time when he is not working in Abu Dhabi. He built the house to accommodate his ever-growing library of fifty thousand books and several thousand classical music CDs, in addition to his expanding collection of modern and contemporary Arab art. The city's historical significance and its cool oasis temperatures are a draw for a man steeped in culture, history, and tradition.

Our visit usually begins with a tour of the house and an insightful discussion of any new additions to his collections. I ask Zaki about the fifty books neatly stacked in three piles on the central table, all bearing the word 'Jerusalem' in their titles, and the adjacent collection of keys and locks. 'This section is a tribute to Jerusalem, the city where my forefathers arrived during the seventh century. The Muslim conquest of 637 AD ushered in a period of peaceful coexistence and freedom of worship for the followers of the three monotheistic faiths. To protect the Christian places of worship, the Caliph Omar bin Al Khattab entrusted the custody of the Church of the Holy Sepulchre — the site where Christians believe Jesus was buried and the site of his accession to Heaven — to 'Ubadah ibn al-Samit, a companion of the Prophet, the first ruler of Palestine, and a forefather of the Nusseibeh family. To date, this tradition continues. This collection reminds me and my family of our ancestral home', Zaki explains.

When Zaki left Jerusalem in the early 1960s to attend boarding school in England, he did not know that he would not return. He also did not imagine that he would find a new home in a desert nation that embraced the values of tolerance, respect, and generosity. Having completed his studies at Cambridge University in 1967, and with the outbreak of the June 1967 war, returning to Jerusalem was not an option. His father suggested he work for the family construction company that had recently opened an office in Abu Dhabi, and which he had visited in 1964 on a family trip. 'I moved to Abu Dhabi in 1967 and lived in the prefabricated cabins of the construction company. It was quite primitive. The electrical generators were unreliable, the temperatures were soaring, and we ate minced beef from tin cans', Zaki recalls.

Zaki's evenings were spent at the old Beach Hotel, which was also frequented by foreign correspondents who had started to travel to Abu Dhabi to report on the economic and political developments. Zaki realised he was much more interested in politics and literature than business, which led him to a correspondent's job as a stringer for several foreign news outlets.

In 1968, he had an assignment to interview Sheikh Zayed bin Sultan Al Nahyan, the ruler of Abu Dhabi, for a British TV documentary. This also meant he was translating for the leader, since Zaki was fluent in Arabic and English. This pivotal interview set Zaki's life on an unexpected trajectory, one that combined his passion for culture, languages, politics, and diplomacy. Shortly after his interview, Zaki was invited to work for the Abu Dhabi government and began as a translator for Sheikh Zayed while also translating legal documents for the Civil Service Department. He then moved to the Department of Information (which became a federal ministry after the formation of the union in 1971), where he worked on documentation, research, publications, media, and broadcasting, before joining the Presidential Court, at which time he became the official translator and advisor to Sheikh Zayed.

Over the next half-century, Zaki worked for the president, meeting most of the world leaders and learning to speak eight languages. He shares with me a story of how he came to learn these foreign languages: 'I remember a trip to Spain with Sheikh Zayed in 1969, and we were watching the news on the local TV station of the first man landing on the moon. Sheikh Zayed asked me to translate what they were saying, but I told him that I did not speak Spanish. He grinned and asked me to *ijtahid*, meaning "give it a try", and so I did, using my French and knowledge of Latin to get by'. It was this comment that inspired Zaki to pursue his passion for languages and to become an erudite polyglot.

The Friday lunch buffet at Zaki's home is always generous and varied with a selection of Levantine appetizers and healthy options of grilled meat and vegetables. It is prepared weekly to welcome family and guests, planned or unexpected. Zaki explains that invitations to meals are fundamental aspects of the cultural, social, and political life in the Emirates. Zaki experienced this first hand when he accompanied Sheikh Zayed travelling or receiving world leaders. 'The tradition of hospitality is deeply rooted in the Bedouin culture. It starts from historical times with the harsh desert environment where hospitality was an essential part of a person's nobility and a necessity for survival. Sheikh Zayed always welcomed people to his meals, including breakfast.

> Hospitality was an essential part of a person's nobility and a necessity for survival.
>
> ZAKI

He rarely ate by himself. For Sheikh Zayed, sharing meals with citizens, officials, family members, and his retinue was integral to nation-building. Hosting banquets and feasts that offered Emirati and international cuisine for foreign guests and dignitaries was central to his diplomacy. Sheikh Zayed loved the Omani halva, and he developed his own recipe, one not as rich in sugar, which was prepared at the palace. There was a ritual at the end of the meal in which Sheikh Zayed invited the guests to take at least three spoonfuls of this low-calorie halva to satiate any sweet cravings', Zaki recounts fondly.

After lunch we retire to Zaki's library, and he offers us *za'atar* tea and a selection of dates from the Al Ain palm groves. Zaki tells us: 'Sheikh Zayed planted millions of date palms. He was deeply connected to the land. He used to say that the most important activity a man can do is agriculture, which is the key to survival. If you don't produce any food on your land, then you are a poor person. In the old days dates were the real wealth of individuals and the nation'.

This generosity of spirit continues in the Emirates today along with the tradition of honouring guests and sharing food in an intimate meal or lavish feast. The tolerance and celebration of the different feasts in the United Arab Emirates, such as Christmas, Diwali, Easter, Eid, Holi, and Ramadan remind Zaki of his early years and the flavours of cosmopolitan Jerusalem.

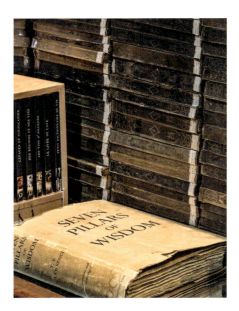

ZA'ATAR CHAI
Thyme Tea

Za'atar is an elemental taste of the Levant. The word refers to both an herb and a spice mix. As a fresh herb, za'atar is the Arabic name for *Origanum syriacum,* also called wild thyme or bible hyssop. The idea that the earth bestows geographically unique charms on its crops is probably most true for the flavourful za'atar of the hills of Jerusalem and the mountains of Lebanon, Syria, and Jordan.

The za'atar spice mix is a harmony of herbs, toasted seeds, and sumac (the dried and ground berry from the plant *Rhus coriaria*). Recipes for this spice mix vary throughout the Levant and individual blends are the pride of many families. The green-coloured Lebanese, Palestinian, or Jordanian za'atar starts with a hyssop base (dried and ground), and a combination of marjoram, oregano, sumac, toasted sesame seeds, and salt. The Aleppo za'atar differs from that of the surrounding region. Its reddish-brown colour comes from its mixture of herbs and sumac, with roasted fennel, anise, coriander, sesame, pomegranate, watermelon seeds, and a kick of Aleppo pepper.

The versatile, flavour-rich spice can be mixed with olive oil to make a delicious *man'oushe* (Arabic pizza), included in a grilled-cheese sandwich, or sprinkled over roasted chicken. Za'atar is an ancient cultural institution, part of a national identity, and in many cases, a family secret.

ZAKI *Thyme is an ancient herb that has been used for medicinal and culinary purposes. It is rich in anti-oxidants, provides essential minerals, relieves indigestion, and soothes a cough. Many associate the herb with the za'atar spice mix, but when thyme is brewed as a tea, it is a healthier alternative to a morning coffee or after-lunch espresso. Many of my guests request za'atar tea moments after they settle into my library.*

SERVES 4 TO 6

2 c water
2 tbsp fresh or **1 tbsp** dried thyme
Sprigs of fresh thyme
Granulated sugar, to taste

Bring the water to a boil in a saucepan. Add the thyme and let it boil for 30 seconds. Turn off the heat, cover the saucepan, and allow it to steep for 5 minutes.

Pour into tea cups or *istikanas* (small tea glasses), straining out the thyme. Add a sprig of fresh thyme to each glass for aroma, if desired. Serve with sugar on the side.

FRAUKE HEARD-BEY AND DAVID HEARD

HISTORIAN ◊ GERMANY

ENGINEER ◊ UK

My request for one of her recipes led Frauke to discover a family treasure. In the summer of 2015, she excavated her mother's belongings that were stored back home in Germany and was surprised to find a brown envelope she had not seen before. The envelope contained a handwritten cookbook with a photograph. The author, Sabine Florentine Raab, had dedicated it to a Florentine Raab upon her birth in 1805. Frauke did not know who these women were and why the cookbook was with her mother's belongings. The historian in her was intrigued and she set out to decipher the old German, which had not been in use since World War I. Her diligence paid off and she traced Florentine Raab as her great-great-grandmother. Delighted at this discovery, she set about translating and testing the recipes on her family. So, although she was more accustomed to contributing scholarly essays to publications, she was more than happy to contribute the *apfeltorte ohne deckel* (apple tart without a lid) recipe for this book.

Frauke grew up in a divided Germany. Born in East Berlin, the second daughter of Rear Admiral Erich Bey and his wife Anneliese, she, her mother, and sister fled to West Germany after her father died in the war. Frauke and her sister wanted to improve their English, since its use was increasing after World War II, so they spent the summer of 1959 at a Christian guesthouse in Bournemouth, England. Here she met David, who was teaching for the summer. The romance grew, and the long-distance relationship blossomed.

David came to Abu Dhabi in 1963 as a petroleum engineer with the Abu Dhabi Petroleum Company, just before the first shipment of oil from onshore Abu Dhabi was exported. 'We worked six days a week in the desert at the oilfields. There were no paved roads and the Gulf Aviation DC 3 from London arrived only once a week. A pipeline to bring fresh water from the oasis in Al Ain to Abu Dhabi was just being built', David recalls.

Frauke completed her Ph.D. just four days before their wedding in September 1967 and joined David in Abu Dhabi two months later. She thought they might stay for two years and then go elsewhere, like their colleagues, or back to Germany. Little did she know their stay would extend for more than half a century!

One of Frauke's striking memories was of her first Christmas in Abu Dhabi. At the time, they were living in one of the oil company bungalows by the sea. She was in bed with the flu and David had offered to prepare a light and health-restoring meal. While she waited, she heard hammering from the kitchen and a little later, David arrived with a pale, yellow, wobbly substance on a plate. 'Scrambled eggs the way my mother makes them', he said. Frauke acknowledges that the eggs were quite tasty, but she was more concerned by the banging. She snuck down to the kitchen a little later to investigate and found David's geology hammer, a small pot, and three empty tins, squashed and sitting in a large pot of tepid water. Since they didn't have a double boiler, David had crafted one to prepare the eggs.

The following weekend, David bought her a record album by Dietrich Fischer-Dieskau, a famous German baritone whom Frauke had heard at the Berlin opera. Feeling homesick, she wondered what she was doing there. 'There weren't any German speakers here at the time, but David was making a valiant attempt at learning German. I was with the oil company ladies mostly, and their Scottish, American, and Greek accents were difficult to decipher', Frauke adds with a smile. On the weekends, David and Frauke would go to the British Club, which was founded in 1962 as a place for British families to socialise. They screened a movie each week and people brought food along. It was there that she had her first taste of Arabic food: tabbouleh. During the summers, most of the wives on the oil company compound would return home. 'I stayed

across the threshold to browse through the collection and was completely surprised by the hidden treasure she found. The small office at the fort and what would become the National Archives was Frauke's second home for the next thirty-nine years.

Frauke and David have borne witness to the Emirates' development through multiple published works, with Frauke focusing on the country's history and David on the early years of oil exploration. In 2000, David was honoured by Queen Elizabeth and made a Commander of the Order of the British Empire for his services to the oil industry and the British community in Abu Dhabi. In 2007, Frauke was honoured with the Abu Dhabi Award by HH Sheikh Mohammad bin Zayed Al Nahyan, Abu Dhabi's crown prince and deputy supreme commander of the United Arab Emirates Armed Forces, for her work in chronicling the life and society of the Arabian Gulf over the past four decades. Now, the renowned historian and the elder statesman enjoy their children and grandchildren at their home in Abu Dhabi, while continuing to give back to the community that welcomed them fifty years ago.

> There was this expectation for me to cook and feed the summer bachelors.
>
> FRAUKE

with David and realised there was this expectation for me to cook and feed the summer bachelors. In my first year here, there were hardly any fresh vegetables. It was mostly tinned food. Then Middle East Airlines established a mercy flight from Beirut bringing fresh fruit and vegetables once a week. The ladies would all meet at Abela's, the recently opened Lebanese supermarket, on Wednesdays to buy the fresh produce and socialise', Frauke recounts.

Instead of focusing on what she missed, Frauke channelled her efforts into learning Arabic and the history of her new home. The British had declared their intent to withdraw from the region in 1968, and there was concern about abrogation of treaties and the exposure of the individual Emirates, which were then collectively known as the Trucial States. Frauke also knew that because of oil exports, there would be a lot of wealth and change. She wanted to find out how society would deal with such political and economic shifts and learn more about the history of the local tribes. Someone suggested she visit Qasr al Hosn (the old fort) located in Abu Dhabi, where historical documents were being collected. In 1969, she stepped

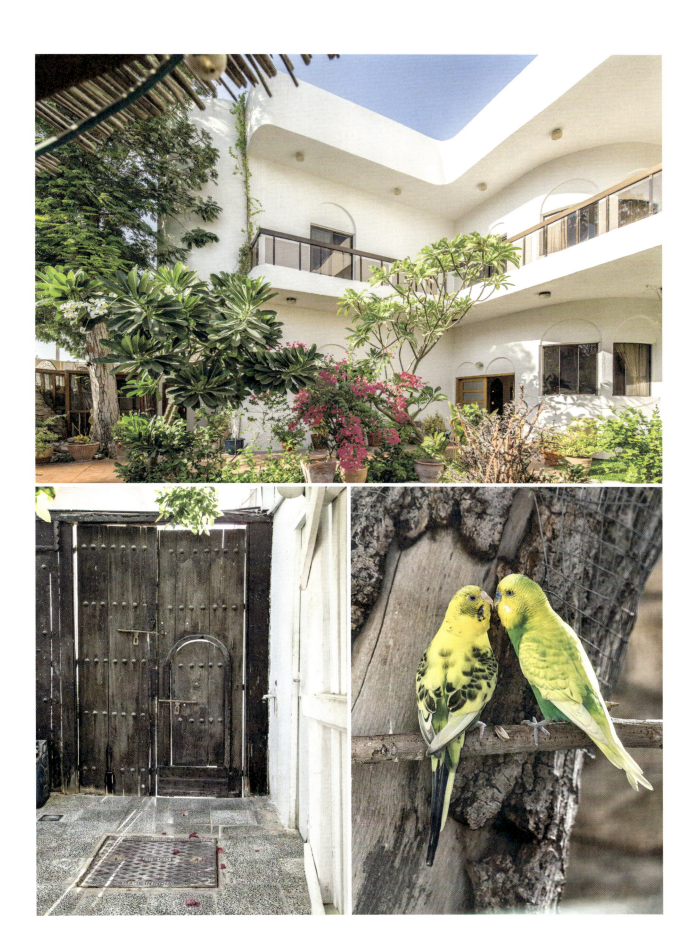

APFELTORTE OHNE DECKEL
Apple Tart without a Lid

FRAUKE *This is the first recipe I translated and updated from the late eighteenth-century cookbook written by Sabine Florentine Raab, my great-great-grandmother. At that time, the size of apples was considerably smaller than now and there were no oven temperature settings. After a few attempts of making this apple tart, I feel that this recipe captures the flavours and textures of eighteenth-century Germany with twenty-first-century techniques!*

—
SERVES
6 TO 8
—

CRUST

- 225 g (1½ c) all-purpose flour
- ¼ tsp salt
- 70 g (⅓ c) granulated sugar
- 1 tbsp grated lemon rind
- 110 g (4 oz) cold butter, cubed
- 1 large egg, beaten

FILLING

- 700 g (1½ lb) tart apples
- 140 g (⅔ c) granulated sugar
- ½ tsp cinnamon
- 1 tbsp grated lemon rind
- 3 eggs, beaten
- 120 ml (½ c) heavy cream
- 125 g (1 c) almond meal

FOR THE CRUST

Combine the flour, salt, sugar, and lemon rind in a medium bowl. Using a pastry cutter or two knives, cut the butter into the flour mixture until the texture resembles coarse crumbs. Add the egg and 2 tablespoons of ice water; mix with a fork just until the dough pulls together. Transfer the dough to a work surface, pat into a ball, and flatten into a disk. Wrap in plastic wrap and refrigerate until well chilled, about 30 minutes.

Place three-quarters of the dough on a floured surface. Roll it into a circle slightly larger than a 23-centimetre (9-inch) non-stick or buttered springform pan. Carefully transfer the dough to the bottom of the pan. Divide the remaining dough into four balls. One at a time, flatten each piece and work by hand to line the sides of the pan with strips of dough approximately 5 centimetres (2 inches) wide, ensuring a good seal where the base and sides meet. Refrigerate for 20 minutes until the dough is firm. Preheat the oven to 180°C (350°F).

Put a piece of wax paper over the crust and cover it with pie weights or any type of dried pulse. Bake it for 10 minutes, until the crust starts to change colour but does not brown; remove from the oven.

FOR THE FILLING

Peel, core, and cut the apples into 2-centimetre (¾-inch) thick wedges. Place in a large bowl and toss with the sugar, cinnamon, and lemon rind. Combine the eggs, cream, and almond meal in another bowl. Pour it over the apples and stir just enough to coat the apples. Spread the apple mixture evenly over the partially baked crust.

Bake the tart for 45 to 50 minutes, until the apples are tender and the top is golden brown. Cover the crust with foil if it becomes too brown before the apples are tender. Transfer the pie to a wire rack and let it cool until it is just slightly warm. Serve with vanilla ice cream or whipped cream.

NICHOLAS COCHRANE-DYET

SPECIAL ADVISOR BP
◊
UK

When Nick was seventeen years old he made a decision that would change the course of his life. He had an acceptance to Oxford University in the United Kingdom, and an invitation to spend a gap year with his godfather in the United Arab Emirates. He was no stranger to the place, having spent summer vacations visiting his father, a British army cavalry officer, who was posted there as a member of the Trucial Omani Scouts in the early 1960s. In the summer of 1975, Nick landed on the newly paved airstrip of Abu Dhabi's Al Bateen Airport. The 180-kilometre drive across the desert to Al Ain took three hours in sweltering heat and blowing sand. His godfather, Colonel Sir John Edmond Hugh Boustead, had been the British political agent in Abu Dhabi in the late 1950s and retired to Mezyad, a small town at the base of Jebel Hafeet on the border of the United Arab Emirates and Oman, to look after the President's Royal Stables. Nick, who learned to ride before he could walk, was eager to work at the stables.

A few weeks after settling into the new job, his godfather said, 'Nick, let's go meet the boss'. Nick accompanied his godfather to the *majlis* of Sheikh Zayed bin Sultan Al Nahyan and was introduced as the new hand at the stables. He greeted Sheikh Zayed and sat to his right, next to his godfather. Sheikh Zayed was speaking to someone on his left in Arabic, and Nick was talking with his godfather in English. Abruptly, Sheikh Zayed turned around and looked straight at Nick with a piercing stare. In surprise, Nick blurted: 'Oh, you speak English, Sheikh Zayed!', since he had been told that he didn't. Sheikh Zayed smiled and turned his attention back to the person on his left. Nick understood the smile to mean: 'Be careful!'

There was no shortage of chores for young Nick to do, breeding Arabian horses and helping his godfather dispense cough syrup and paracetamol to locals to treat common ailments. Soon the gap year turned into four years, with Nick immersing himself in desert life. In 1977, his godfather sent him to live with the Bedu in the desert for three months to learn Arabic. Nick was surprised by the extent of the hospitality extended to him, and found it easier to adapt to life in the desert than his boarding school in England. 'It was embarrassing to me, the generosity of the Bedu who offered me what little they had. On the rare occasions when they cooked meat, they would pick the choice piece and hand it to me ahead of the other family members', he remembers. He adapted quickly to the nomadic desert life and came to admire the amazing faith and trust the Bedu had in God and each other. They trusted that food would be available and that they would be able to handle whatever came their way. There was no anxiety in the harsh desert life despite the infinite uncertainties. There was only contentment, serenity, and a huge amount of gratitude. Even with very little resources, *alhamdulillah* (Praise be to God) was frequently heard as the Bedu spoke.

During these four years, Nick travelled all over the Emirates and ate the local food, the fresh produce, and the dairy products from the experimental farm near Mezyad, where Sheikh Zayed had encouraged the planting of strawberries, tomatoes, and melons. 'There isn't a square inch of this country I haven't seen, from Fujairah to Wigan to Silaa to Wadi Jizzi to Kalba and Dibba and everything in between', Nick remarks. His father, however, was growing impatient with him and pressured him to do something with his life and pursue a career. With the Oxford slot no longer available, Nick reluctantly enrolled at the Royal Military Academy Sandhurst in Surrey, following in his father's footsteps, and left Mezyad, a place he still calls home. Sheikh Zayed, who had kept a close eye on his work at the stables, encouraged him to continue his education and told him he was welcome back any time. 'Sheikh Zayed commanded amazing respect from everyone. He treated everyone the same and with tolerance, from head of state to the *mugahwi* (coffee server)', said Nick, describing the impression this left on him as a teenager.

When Nick returned to Abu Dhabi in the mid-1980s, much had changed. The development boom was in full swing, and many more foreigners were arriving, along with all the conveniences of modern life: paved roads, phones, hospitals, schools, and supermarkets. Life was easier but not richer. He missed the family-like community he had experienced in Mezyad. He came to appreciate even more the privileges he had as a teenager, including working for Sheikh Zayed, living with the Bedu in the desert, and meeting Queen Elizabeth aboard HMY *Britannia* during her first visit to the United Arab Emirates, in 1979.

> Sheikh Zayed commanded amazing respect from everyone. He treated everyone the same and with tolerance, from head of state to the *mugahwi*.
>
> NICK

Today, peering quietly from the wooden bird hide at Al Wathba Wetland Reserve, we see flocks of pink flamingos, black-winged stilts, curlew sandpipers, and Kentish plovers—not what Nick encountered on his early excursions into the desert. Protecting the fragile ecosystem of this manmade wetland is one of the many initiatives Nick is proud to have contributed to during his forty-year career in the United Arab Emirates. He also enjoys going back to the desert with Emirati youth as part of the BP Young Adventurers Programme, which he helped launch. Teaching the young Emiratis life skills and enhancing self-confidence by tapping into the principles of Bedu life, reminds him of what he experienced four decades earlier.

A commitment to the region, to the development of its youth, and to United Kingdom–United Arab Emirates relations are among Nick's passions. He was awarded the Member of the British Empire rank by Queen Elizabeth in 2013 for his services to British business and charitable work in the country. The arrival of his granddaughter in Abu Dhabi marks the fourth generation of his family to reside in the United Arab Emirates. Nick looks forward to sharing his experiences as a youth in the Emirates with her.

GRILLED CHEESE SANDWICH WITH MARMITE

A grilled cheese sandwich may seem so basic that it doesn't warrant a recipe. But to perfect it, one has to consider each basic ingredient carefully. The bread is the foundation of the sandwich, so it should be robust enough to hold its own with the cheese, but not so thick that the cheese doesn't melt. It cannot have too many holes or the cheese will ooze out, but just the right amount will allow the melted cheese to become crispy on the outside. The list of cheeses to use is endless, but a combination is best. One should have a high fat content, so the bread will be coated with a cheesy oil, and the other should be a piquant cheddar. Finally, buttering the bread lends a golden-brown finish to the perfect grilled cheese sandwich.

NICK *Marmite—you either love it or hate it! It is a hundred-year-old British institution and pretty much the Holy Grail of foodstuff, rich in vitamin B. A German scientist accidentally invented it in 1902 in England. It is a thick paste made from concentrated yeast extract, a by-product of brewing. The flavour is so distinctive that it is difficult to describe. For most Britons travelling out of country, all we can think about when we come home is to eat some Marmite on toast. I have combined my favourite English cheddar cheese with toast, Marmite and English mustard to make a unique grilled cheese sandwich. I hope you are willing to try this even if you are not a Marmite fan.*

SERVES 2

---

4 slices hearty white or sourdough bread, about 1 cm (½ in) thick

Butter, softened

2 tsp Marmite, to taste

85 g (3 oz) cheddar cheese, grated

55 g (2 oz) Red Leicester cheese, grated

English mustard

Lightly butter both sides of each slice of bread. Heat a large non-stick skillet over medium heat. Add the bread slices and grill one side for about 2 minutes, until golden brown. Remove the pan from the heat and flip the bread slices so the cooked sides are up. Spread the Marmite on the cooked side of each slice. Arrange the cheese on two slices and place the other slices on top, with the uncooked sides on the outside. Return the skillet to medium heat and cook for 2 to 3 minutes, until golden brown. *[For a lighter version, butter only one side of each slice, keeping the unbuttered sides to the inside of each sandwich.]*

Serve immediately with English mustard on the side. Eat as soon as is comfortably possible.

— 1970s —
BRING TO A BOIL

The beginning of this decade ushered in the formation of the United Arab Emirates, a union of seven sheikdoms, with Sheikh Zayed bin Sultan Al Nahyan as its president. Forming the federation compounded the pace of development in Abu Dhabi, whose development had been slower than that of some of its neighbouring emirates. New federal government entities had to be established and more infrastructure was required to connect the emirates in terms of transportation and communication. Before the establishment of the country, going from Abu Dhabi to Dubai involved going through Customs posts with passport checks. The society also had to transition from tribal loyalty to being citizens of a new country, which itself had to seek international recognition and regional integration. The Emirati college graduates returning from their studies abroad were in high demand and juggled multiple positions as they participated in building their nation.

The Arab oil embargo, following the October 1973 war with Israel, shocked the international markets and led to the quadrupling of oil prices. Suddenly Abu Dhabi was awash with money, and the development projects and large influx of expatriates boiled over to an unprecedented scale, as did the prices of land, commodities, services, and materials. Building codes changed, allowing mid-rise building, which created another construction boom. New hotels opened, catering to expatriates and the growing number of business travellers, who still could not be fully accommodated. Mattresses in the lobbies of some hotels and triple-booked rooms were not uncommon occurrences.

The two-lane, 140-kilometre road between Abu Dhabi and Dubai was completed in 1973 without street lights, making the journey a breezy, yet not without peril, four-hour drive. Camels crossing the new road that bifurcated their habitat were a common danger that drivers had to guard against. Land Rovers were the vehicle of choice, dubbed the 'new ships of the desert'. Traffic lights were introduced. Phone lines between the two emirates were inaugurated, the UAE dirham was coined, and colour TV was broadcast. Electricity and power remained intermittent as the supply simply could not keep up with the skyrocketing demand. Walking up flights of stairs in the newly constructed apartment buildings in sweltering heat and stockpiling water in make-shift bathtub reservoirs, for when the pumps did not have electricity, was a daily chore.

International transportation exploded as well, with more flights connecting Abu Dhabi's Bateen Airport to the world. Fresh produce and meats were flown in weekly from Beirut. Local agriculture and experimental farming on Saadiyat Island was supported by the government and a new souk was built in the heart of the city for produce and freshly caught seafood. Specialty stores and restaurants opened, catering to the different expatriate communities: there was the Lebanese owned Albert Abela and l'Auberge for those from the Levant, Spinneys for Westerners, the Cypriot Greenhouse Stores with its Mediterranean flavours, and a French bistro discreetly serving wine in teapots. The El Dorado Cinema was the first indoor theatre, screening a blend of Hollywood, Bollywood, and Egyptian films.

The rapid boom came to a halt in the late 1970s and Abu Dhabi experienced its first recession. This cycle would continue into the next decades since the economy was tied to a single resource — oil. Nevertheless, the long-term infrastructure programmes to build the transportation networks and sports complex, provide housing for all Emiratis, and expand the education and healthcare systems continued. The locals' hospitality and generosity welcomed the different customs of the Arab, Asian and Western expatriates, yet guarded their traditions against these rapid changes that just a few years earlier were completely alien.

ASMA SIDDIQ AL MUTAWAA

FOUNDER
AL MULTAQA
◊
UAE

Asma struck me as a woman ahead of her time when I first met her in the early 1990s, aboard a private yacht off the shore of Abu Dhabi, at a ladies-only swimwear fashion show. Over the years, I see that Asma is also very much a woman *of* her time. Born and raised in Abu Dhabi, with nine siblings, she learned early on how to negotiate, motivate, accommodate, and provide for others. This sense of community and giving guides Asma in all her endeavours locally and internationally. 'I cannot say no. If I can help, I will do it', affirms Asma.

Of her many activities, *Al Multaqa* (The Gathering) is closest to her heart. She formed this literary salon in 1999 so women could read and discuss books written in Arabic. At that time, the reading groups in Abu Dhabi were in English and led mainly by members of the expatriate community. 'I joined an English reading group and that inspired me to start one in Arabic, so we could explore our rich literature and history. The first word in the Quran revealed to the Prophet Muhammad PBUH was *iqra'a* (read). It was effectively the first command in Islam before prayers or fasting, which shows the importance of reading and knowledge in our faith', Asma explains. When she was young, her love for reading was nurtured by her father, who brought books back from his travels to Cairo. Then, when Abu Dhabi started its first book fair in 1981, Asma became a devotee, stocking up on the year's supply of reading. She went on to earn a bachelor's degree in business administration from the United Arab Emirates University and a master's in contemporary Islam from Zayed University.

As we sit in her home in Al Bateen for an Al Multaqa gathering, surrounded by Orientalist paintings, brocade sofas, and Persian carpets, I am transported to a literary salon of tenth-century Baghdad, animated by authors, poets, and lively debate. In keeping with Arab hospitality, Asma enriches her gatherings with a wide array of savoury and sweet delicacies, elevating the food presentation to an art. The fine linens, iridescent glassware, and porcelain dishes reflect her worldly menu and globetrotting sensibilities.

Every April, Asma transports Al Multaqa to the Abu Dhabi International Book Fair, with a bespoke design complete with plush sofas, embroidered cushions, Persian carpets, and an endless flow of teas, coffees, sweets, and canapés. She invites Arab authors, artists, and thinkers to speak, followed by a moderated conversation, open to the public. Al Multaqa has grown in the past few years and gained influence as a homegrown oasis of thought and dialogue. In November 2016, at the conclusion of the Year of Reading in the United Arab Emirates, Asma was honoured by Sheikh Mohammed bin Rashid for the best personal initiative to encourage reading. She shares her motivation: 'I want to inspire more people to read in Arabic. My language is my identity. We are losing something with the young generation of Emiratis who are educated in English. I hope to contribute to developing a new generation of Arabic readers and thinkers'.

I ask Asma, 'What's next?' She smiles and says, 'I am shifting from the mental to the physical realm. I have partnered with the founder of the Women's Heritage Walk, which follows in the footsteps of our ancestors and honours their way of life'. This annual five-day trek retraces the historic 125-kilometre journey from Al Ain to Abu Dhabi, when the men embarked by sea on their months-long trading trips and the women would head to Al Ain where the weather is cooler. It is also a chance for expatriate women to gain a deeper understanding of local customs and for everyone to get to know each other better and be more active. Asma adds, 'It's important to remember these harsh conditions and share this knowledge with younger generations. It's a celebration of our heritage!'

I want to inspire
more people
to read in Arabic.
My language
is my identity.

ASMA

TAHTA LAHEM
Emirati Lamb Pilaf

SERVES 6 TO 8

1 kg (2¼ lb) lamb shoulder

1 tbsp turmeric, divided

½ tbsp salt

2 tbsp olive oil

1 tbsp ginger/garlic paste

170 g (6 oz) onion, sliced

4 cardamom pods

2 tsp coriander powder

1 tbsp curry powder

1 tsp chili powder

2 tsp cumin

2 tsp Emirati bzar spice mix

2 tsp garam masala

1 tsp black pepper

1-2 bouillon cubes

3 bird's eye chilies

2 tbsp achaar liquid

450 g (1 lb) tomatoes, chopped

Salt and pepper, to taste

6 pieces lime achaar

10 cherry tomatoes

2 tbsp fresh coriander

2 tbsp mint

RICE

500 g (2½ c) basmati rice

1 cinnamon stick

2 bay leaves

1 tsp fennel seeds

4 cardamom pods

5–6 peppercorns

2 tsp ghee

Salt

GARNISH

Fresh coriander

Fresh mint

Saffron

The different influences and spices from South Asia and the Arabian Peninsula have coalesced to produce some fantastic dishes, such as the rice and meat combinations of *tahta*, *machboos*, *biryani*, and *kabsa*. While they are common throughout the Gulf countries, the particulars of these dishes can vary from city to city, from one *fireej* (neighbourhood) to another, and from one family to another.

ASMA *At home, we always have some variation of rice and meat for lunch. This hearty dish is redolent with aromas from the different spices. The meat is layered at the bottom of the pot, thus the name* tahta, *which means 'bottom'. It can be prepared with lamb, beef, or goat. We add lime* achaar *(limes preserved in spicy oil) to our version of* tahta, *which gives it a tangy taste.*

Soak the rice in enough water to cover and let stand until ready to use. Place the meat in a large Dutch oven and add just enough hot water to cover. Bring to a boil, removing any foam that accumulates. Stir in ½ tablespoon of the turmeric and the salt. Lower the heat and simmer for 45 minutes, until the meat is almost cooked. Strain the meat, reserving the stock if desired.

Heat the oil in a Dutch oven over medium heat. Add the garlic/ginger paste, stir for 3 minutes, then add the onion and stir for another 5 minutes, until soft. Add the cardamom pods, coriander, curry, chili powder, cumin, bzar, garam masala, and black pepper and continue stirring until aromatic. Stir in the bouillon cubes, chilies, achaar liquid, and tomatoes; cover. Cook over low heat, stirring occasionally until the oil starts to separate, about 10 to 15 minutes. Add the meat, adjust the seasoning, and cook for 15 to 20 minutes more, until the meat is tender and any liquid has evaporated.

Drain the rice. In a large saucepan, boil 1.2 litres (1¼ quarts) of water. Add the cinnamon stick, bay leaves, fennel seeds, cardamom pods, peppercorns, ghee, and a liberal amount of salt. Scrape the rice into the sauce pan and parboil it for 6 to 8 minutes, until al dente. Gently stir it once so the rice does not stick together; drain.

Grease a large Dutch oven. Spread some of the rice over the bottom. Layer the meat mixture over the rice and cover with the remaining rice. Top with the achaar, cherry tomatoes, fresh coriander, and mint. Seal with aluminium foil, cover, and simmer over very low heat for 20 minutes.

To serve, remove the achaar and set aside. Spread some rice on the serving dish, arrange the meat, and cover with the remaining rice. Top with the achaar and garnish with extra fresh coriander and mint. Combine the saffron with 1 tablespoon of hot water, let stand for 2 or 3 minutes, and drizzle over the rice.

HAMAM MAHSHI BIL FREEK
Freekeh-Stuffed Squab

Freekeh, an ancient grain and a staple of the Middle Eastern diet for centuries, is made from wheat that is harvested while young and green. It is parched and roasted to burn off the husks. The grain on the inside is too young and moist to burn, so the result is a firm, slightly chewy grain with a distinct flavour that is earthy, nutty, and slightly smoky. Aside from its delicious taste, it is full of nutritional benefits.

ASMA *This dish has been considered an Egyptian delicacy since ancient times. I like to serve it to guests alongside an array of Emirati and international dishes. Squab has little meat, so it's not uncommon for guests to enjoy one or two whole squabs. You can make it with poussin or Cornish game hen.*

SERVES 6 TO 8

Ingredients

- **310 g (2 c)** freekeh
- **8** squabs or poussins, with giblets (optional)
- Salt and pepper
- **2 tbsp** oil
- **28 g (1 oz)** butter
- **200 g (7 oz)** onion, chopped
- **110 g (4 oz)** celery, chopped
- **1 tsp** cinnamon
- **1 tsp** cumin
- **1 tsp** coriander powder
- **½ tsp** cardamom powder
- **½ tsp** black pepper
- **1 tsp** salt
- **80 g (½ c)** pine nuts
- **100 g (½ c)** raisins
- **2 bay** leaves
- **4** cardamom pods
- **2 cloves** garlic
- **1** onion, quartered
- **½** orange, quartered
- **Handful** of fresh coriander
- **5** black peppercorns
- **1 tsp** salt
- **2 tbsp** butter, melted
- **Handful** of parsley, chopped

Method

Soak the freekeh in water for 30 minutes; drain. Meanwhile, season the squabs with salt and pepper. Finely chop the giblets, if using.

Heat the oil and butter in a medium saucepan and sauté the onions and celery over medium heat until softened. Add the giblets and sprinkle with the cinnamon, cumin, coriander, cardamom, pepper, and salt. Stir for 2 to 3 minutes until the giblets are cooked through. Pour in the freekeh and stir to combine. Pour in 700 millilitres (3 cups) of water or enough to cover and bring to a boil. Reduce the heat and simmer, covered, for 20 to 25 minutes or until the water is absorbed and the freekeh is soft.

Toast the pine nuts in a small pan and add to the freekeh along with the raisins. Mix well and allow to cool for a few minutes. Stuff each squab with the freekeh mixture and seal the cavities with toothpicks. Reserve the remaining freekeh to serve.

Preheat the oven to 180°C (350°F). Pour 3 litres (3 quarts) of water into a large Dutch oven. Add the bay leaves, cardamom pods, garlic, onion, orange, fresh coriander, peppercorns, and salt, and bring to a boil. Lower the heat to a simmer and carefully place the squabs in the pot. Cover and simmer for 30 to 40 minutes, or until the meat is cooked.

Remove the squab from the broth and allow the excess liquid to drain, reserving the broth for other use, if desired. Place the squabs in a large ovenproof dish and brush with melted butter. Roast for 15 minutes or until golden. Arrange the squab over the reserved freekeh (warmed) on a large serving platter. Garnish with chopped parsley.

LINA MIKATI

MOTIVATIONAL
LEADER
◊
SYRIA / CANADA

It was a hot summer morning in 2003 when the ladies started to arrive at Lina's twentieth-floor apartment on the Corniche for the monthly book club meeting. Lina had invited me to join the recently formed club that included a diverse group of women from Croatia, Iran, Iraq, Lebanon, Palestine, Pakistan, Switzerland, and the United States. The lively discussion that morning was about the books we would read in the fall. It was essential to agree on next year's selections before the summer holiday exodus, so we could buy our books overseas. Bookstores were limited in the United Arab Emirates and Amazon had not yet taken hold. When it comes to pleasing an entire group of women, well, that can be challenging, and a diverse group with different backgrounds, even more so. Fiction, nonfiction, or a combination? Translated or original language? Short stories or poetry? The possibilities were endless. With Lina's calm and light-hearted approach, she guided the discussion and we arrived at a compelling list of books, which we later read and debated for many months, enriched with an array of homemade delicacies.

I ask Lina how she came to be such an accomplished hostess and home chef, having left her parents' home in Syria at a young age. Cuddled next to her husband, Hamed, she gives him the 'I-haven't-forgiven-you' look and says, 'He didn't leave me much choice when he moved to Abu Dhabi'. Hamed had studied architecture in Rome during the early 1970s and had planned to return to Lebanon to join the family contracting business, Arabian Construction Company, which also had a base in Abu Dhabi. His plans took an unexpected turn, however, when his father died. Fuelled by revenues from oil exports, the building boom had begun in Abu Dhabi, necessitating a move to work at that branch of the company. So, in 1975, Hamed left historical Rome and his hometown of Tripoli to toil on the construction sites of Abu Dhabi.

His new home was a corrugated metal caravan on Najda Street, which he did not look forward to returning to in the evening after a long day on site. 'I would come back to my humble dwelling tired, hot, and sweaty. One evening, I was taking my shower when suddenly, a furious sandstorm came up and lifted the entire roof off the caravan! There I was, in my birthday suit, looking up at the night sky! There was not much I could do but laugh. After six years in Rome, I end up in the desert with an open-air shower! As the Arabic saying goes: *sharou al baleyatu ma yudhikou* (the worst of disasters makes one laugh)', Hamed recalls.

Hamed and Lina were married in 1976, and Lina was one of the pioneering women who joined her husband in Abu Dhabi. For Lina, whose father was a diplomat and had moved the family to many parts of the world, nothing Hamed said could have prepared her for those early years in Abu Dhabi. It was a city of practically all men. Many businessmen from the Levant came to Abu Dhabi to set up engineering and construction companies and to take part in the ambitious development of a young nation rising from the sand. Most left their families back home, since the infrastructure was still quite rudimentary with few schools and frequent power and water outages. 'There were many days I wondered what I was doing here, and where my life was going', Lina recalls. Hamed would be at work all day and come home in the evenings with ten colleagues, all single men. She was expected to prepare that home-cooked meal they all longed for.

When she got married, Lina tells me, she literally could not make a cup of coffee, the litmus test for prospective brides in the Arab world. Back home everything was taken care of for her. Hamed hired a young South Asian man to help her, but strong-willed Lina decided the communication and cultural barriers were too much, so she dismissed him and set about figuring out the city, the markets, and the kitchen on her own. The biggest challenge proved not to be the limited choices of produce and meat in the markets, but her limited knowledge of what to do with them. After hauling her

groceries up eight flights of stairs in sweltering 40°C (104°F) heat, often with no elevator, lights, or air conditioning due to the frequent power outages, Lina would find herself alone in the kitchen with her groceries and no one to guide her.

Independently minded, she did not ask for help and started to improvise. One day at the market, she found large heads of cabbage and decided to make *malfouf*, stuffed cabbage, a favourite of her brother-in-law visiting from Tripoli. She concocted a rice-and-meat stuffing flavoured with ketchup and Parmesan, a combination that would make any Arab housewife cringe. She wrapped the raw cabbage leaves in irregular shapes around spoonfuls of stuffing and when they didn't hold in uniform cigar-like shapes, she did the unheard of and secured them with toothpicks. Instead of boiling them with the traditional mint-flavoured tomato sauce, she baked them. After the first bite, the expressions on her guests' faces made her want to crawl down a rabbit hole. As a result, Lina determined not to find herself in such a situation again. She placed a moratorium on having guests and delved into the kitchen, experimenting, looking up recipes in the cookbook from home, and occasionally getting some tips from her sister-in-law.

Today, Lina's dinner table includes a wide array of Levantine and international dishes, as well as many of her own creations, often with a healthy twist on traditional recipes, such as flax seed added to *muhammara*. With similar inventiveness and determination, Lina has pursued her interests in fitness, health, and self-empowerment. She takes great pleasure in inviting motivational speakers, nutritionists, entrepreneurs, authors, ambassadors, and artists to share their passions and knowledge with her diverse circle of friends. After a few years in Canada and Dubai, Lina and Hamed are happy to call Abu Dhabi home again. 'It is the diversity of the communities, the tolerance of the people, the vision of the leadership, the world-class infrastructure, and the lifelong friendships that give us a rich and fulfilling life here', Lina tells me.

> It is the diversity and tolerance of the people, the vision of the leadership, and the lifelong friendships that give us a rich and fulfilling life here.
>
> LINA

MUHAMMARA
Walnut and Red Pepper Dip with Flax Seed

Muhammara, meaning 'reddened', is a nutritious dip usually served as part of a *mezze*. Like many dishes that have been around for centuries, there are probably as many ways to make muhammara as there are people who make it. It originated in Aleppo, known for its wondrous red chili peppers. Aleppo peppers are somewhere between hot paprika and cayenne pepper in terms of spiciness, with a fruity undertone. The traditional method involves making the red pepper paste by drying the fiery chili peppers in the sun, chopping them, placing them in a jar with salt and olive oil, and then leaving them to ferment, which brings out the deep flavours. Some muhammara is made with this red pepper paste and other versions are made with fresh or roasted peppers, red chili flakes, or a blend. Whichever combination you use, the sweetness and spiciness of the peppers, the texture of the walnuts, sourness of the pomegranate molasses, and smokiness of the cumin make for an addictive multi-layered dip.

LINA *My muhammara is a twist on the original Aleppo recipe. Instead of bread, I use flax seed powder, which is high in Omega 3. Muhammara with raw vegetables is a staple in our home. It's a healthy snack after working out and in between meals. Muhammara keeps well and actually improves after a day in the fridge. If it is a bit stiff, soften it with warm water and serve at room temperature. Sahtain (good health)!*

SERVES 4 TO 6

- **125 g (1 c)** shelled walnuts
- **30 g (⅓ c)** flax seed powder
- **2 tbsp** red pepper paste, sweet or spicy
- **55 g (2 oz)** red onion, chopped
- **1 tsp** cumin
- **60 ml (¼ c)** pomegranate molasses
- **60 ml (¼ c)** olive oil
- Parsley

Blend the walnuts, flax seed powder, red pepper paste, onion, cumin, pomegranate molasses, and olive oil in a food processor to form a thick paste. Gradually add 60 millilitres (¼ cup) of water, or more as needed, to achieve the desired consistency, but not so much that the flavour is diluted. The texture should be somewhat coarse.

Garnish with parsley and drizzle with olive oil.

CIRCASSIAN CHICKEN
Syrian Poached Chicken with Walnut Sauce

This dish originates from the historical region of Circassia, which is roughly the area between the Black Sea and what is now Russia and Georgia on the western side of the Caucasus Mountains. The Circassians were displaced in the nineteenth century and settled across the Ottoman lands into what are now Turkey, Jordan, Syria, Palestine, Iraq, and Egypt, which is why so many groups claim this dish. It is still popular today, with variations in each place. In Turkey, for example, Circassian chicken is part of the *mezze*, served as a chicken salad with walnut sauce.

LINA *I learned how to make this dish from my Syrian mother-in-law, who grew up in Latakia; this is one of the region's specialties. It's not too difficult to make once you have tried it the first time. The red chili pepper paste is a key ingredient. It's a staple in Turkish cuisine and you can find it in most Middle Eastern stores. I like to serve this dish at large dinner buffets because it can be made a day ahead of time and served warm or at room temperature, with basmati or vermicelli rice.*

SERVES 6 TO 8

1.5 kg (3½ lb) whole chicken
1 onion, quartered
2 bay leaves
8 black peppercorns
1 cinnamon stick
10 sprigs parsley
450 g (1 lb) shelled walnuts
2 chicken bouillon cubes
1 tbsp coriander powder
3 cloves garlic, crushed
½ tsp cinnamon
⅛ pita
2 tbsp spicy red pepper paste
Salt and black pepper, to taste

GARNISH

3 tbsp walnut oil
3 tsp paprika
Parsley sprigs

Place the chicken in a large Dutch oven. Add 2.5 litres (2½ quarts) of hot water, onion, bay leaves, peppercorns, cinnamon stick, and parsley and bring to a boil. Lower the heat and cook for 45 to 60 minutes, partially covered, until the chicken is very tender and almost falls off the bone. Remove the chicken to cool and reserve the broth. Discard the skin and bones and cut the meat into medium pieces. Prepare the paprika oil for the garnish while the chicken is cooking.

Strain the broth and pour 1.5 litres (1½ quarts) into a large stockpot. Add the walnuts, bouillon cubes, coriander powder, garlic, cinnamon, bread, and red pepper paste; bring to a boil and simmer for 10 minutes.

Allow the walnut mixture to cool, then puree it in batches in a blender. Strain it through a medium sieve back into the pot, using a rubber spatula to press as much of the liquid through. Return the remaining contents of the sieve to the blender, along with 475 millilitres (2 cups) of the remaining broth, and blend again at high speed. Strain the mixture back into the pot and discard the contents of the sieve.

Bring the sauce to a boil, reduce to low heat and simmer, uncovered, for 1½ hours, stirring occasionally. The sauce will thicken slightly and darken to a reddish brown. When the oil starts to separate, the sauce is ready. The sauce should be thick enough to coat the spoon.

Add the chicken pieces to the sauce and simmer for 10 minutes. Season with salt and pepper. Transfer the chicken and sauce to a large serving bowl. Stir the paprika-infused walnut oil (the paprika will have settled) and drizzle it over the chicken. Garnish with parsley sprigs.

FOR THE GARNISH

Heat the walnut oil in a small saucepan over low heat for 1 minute and then stir in the paprika. Remove from the heat immediately and set aside to infuse.

SAMBAL UDANG
Prawn Sambal

LINA — *I first had this dish at a friend's home when I was living in Canada many years ago. It is a popular Malay dish with many variations in the spices and aromas. I love the balance between the sweet prawns and the fiery sambal (the chili mix). When I returned to Abu Dhabi where prawns are plentiful, I adapted the recipe to use the spices that were available at the time. You can infuse the sauce with tamarind, lemongrass, or Thai basil for a more authentic flavour. This is one of my favourite dishes for dinner parties, as it can be prepared well ahead of time and served buffet-style for a large group. I usually serve it with plain basmati rice and sometimes with vegetable fried rice.*

SERVES 8 TO 10

- **2 kg (4½ lb)** large prawns with shell
- **240 ml (1 c)** cooking oil, divided
- **85 g (½ c)** whole cashews
- **4** bird's eye chilies, to taste
- **55 g (2 oz)** ginger, chopped
- **6 cloves** garlic
- **1 tbsp** cumin
- **1 tsp** turmeric
- **285 g (10 oz)** onions, chopped
- **350 ml (1½ c)** coconut milk
- **1 tbsp** sugar
- **60 ml (¼ c)** lemon juice
- **2** chicken or fish bouillon cubes
- **2 tbsp** fresh coriander, chopped
- Fresh coriander sprigs

Shell, devein, and rinse the prawns, keeping the tail. Heat 160 millilitres (⅔ cup) of the oil in a large skillet on high heat. Working in batches, sauté the prawns for 2 minutes, until they start to curl. Remove from the pan with a slotted spoon. You will need this pan and some of the remaining oil, so set it aside.

Dry roast the cashews in a small skillet over medium heat for 2 to 3 minutes to release the aroma. Transfer the cashews to a food processor and add the chilies, ginger, garlic, cumin, turmeric, and remaining 80 millilitres (⅓ cup) of oil. Mix on high speed to form a paste.

Using the same pan and 60 millilitres (¼ cup) of the oil used for the prawns, sauté the onions until translucent. Scrape the cashew paste over the onions and stir for 5 minutes. Add the coconut milk and sugar and continue to stir. Pour in the lemon juice and crumble in the bouillon cubes; bring to a boil and then simmer for 20 minutes, uncovered. Adjust the seasoning to taste. The sauce should coat the spoon. Thin with some warm water if needed.

Fold the prawns into the sauce and simmer for 5 minutes, being careful not to overcook them. Sprinkle with the chopped coriander and toss to combine. Serve in a large bowl and garnish with fresh coriander sprigs.

MA'AMOUL BIL JIBN
Cheese-Filled Shortbread Pastries

Ma'amoul is a delicious Arabic shortbread pastry typically made for religious holidays such as Eid and Easter. As Ramadan draws to an end or on Good Friday, family members of all generations gather at home, kneading the dough, pitting the dates, and shelling and grinding the pistachios and walnuts. The purists prefer to form and decorate each pastry by hand using only a pair of tweezers instead of the traditional wooden moulds. Each region, from Tripoli to Damascus, Jerusalem and Cairo, has its way of making the dough, filling, and shaping the pastry. This recipe is a pleasing variation on the traditional, with its filling of melted *jibn* (cheese) oozing opulence with the first bite.

LINA *Ma'amoul bil jibn is a specialty of Latakia on the Syrian coast, where this pastry is filled with cheese instead of the more common dates or nuts. The traditional Syrian recipe only uses semolina, but I have adapted it to include flour, which is more common with Tripoli's signature ma'amoul bakers. While making ma'amoul is time consuming, the beauty of this recipe is that it can be done ahead of time, frozen for up to one month, and taken immediately from the freezer to the oven for a last-minute dinner party or lunch. Be sure to use good quality akawi cheese. To test it, cut a sliver and heat the edge with a lighter. If it feels stretchy to the touch, it is good to use, because it will melt when heated. You'll always find ma'amoul bil jibn at the Mikati home.*

MAKES 20 TO 24

---

400 g (14 oz) akawi cheese

500 g (3 c) fine semolina

260 g (1¾ c) all-purpose flour

285 g (10 oz) unsalted butter, softened

1–2 tbsp milk, as needed

Icing sugar

FOR THE FILLING

Slice the cheese into thin slivers, rinse under running water for 1 minute and then soak for several hours, changing the water frequently, to remove the saltiness. The duration of soaking depends on the saltiness of the cheese, which can vary greatly, so taste frequently. When the saltiness is gone, strain out the water, pressing the cheese by hand to squeeze out as much as possible.

FOR THE DOUGH

Using a stand mixer, knead the semolina, flour, butter, and milk for 3 to 5 minutes on medium speed until the dough holds together. Test the dough by taking a small amount and patting it flat in your hand to see if it holds together. It will feel slightly rough due to the semolina.

Dredge a ma'amoul mould in flour to lightly coat the interior. Roll a small handful of dough into a ball. Flatten it and press it into the mould, making a cavity in the centre. Fill the cavity three-quarters of the way with the cheese, packing it in. Fold the remaining dough over the cheese to seal it, pressing firmly but not too much, so the dough doesn't stick to the mould. The dough mustn't have any cracks or the cheese will ooze out when baked. Flip the mould over on a lightly greased baking tray, striking it to release the ma'amoul. Repeat this process for all the dough. Place the baking tray in the refrigerator for 30 minutes. The ma'amoul can also be frozen at this stage, covered with plastic wrap, and baked directly from the freezer when needed.

Preheat the oven to 200°C (400°F). Bake the ma'amoul for 15 to 20 minutes, or until lightly golden. Don't allow them to brown or they will harden. Let the ma'amoul stand for 5 minutes before transferring to a serving plate. Sprinkle with a generous amount of icing sugar and serve immediately.

NIRA AND VINAY VARMA

RESTAURATEURS
◊
INDIA

Vinay came to Abu Dhabi from India in 1970, as did many of his compatriots, to seek a better life. Having completed hotelier school, he had just started work at a five-star hotel in Mumbai when his teacher, the well-known Thangam Elizabeth Philip (India's Julia Child), gave him a call. She asked if he wanted to meet a gentleman who was in town recruiting for a catering company in Abu Dhabi. He had not heard of that city but called his sister who had recently moved to Dubai from Basra. Wanting her brother nearby, she encouraged him to come. 'It was my good fortune', Vinay recalls fondly.

Vinay worked for a leading catering and food supply company that serviced the growing oil sector. He lived in the desert near the oil fields of Habshan and Bu Hasa, and as the camp boss, he would get up at 4:00 am, pack the food with his team, and head out to deliver it to the oil rigs. There were no phones or radios, and so, like the Bedu, Vinay learned to read the tracks in the sand, in this case of the Kenwood trucks, to locate where the rig had moved. 'It was one of the best experiences of my life', Vinay enthuses.

Desert life, however, was not suitable for starting a family, so Vinay moved back to Abu Dhabi, where his wife, Nira, joined him in 1975. Keen to branch out on his own, Vinay partnered with the Indian brand, Kwality, and opened his first restaurant in Abu Dhabi in 1985. It was an instant success. After a few years of hard work, Nira challenged her husband with, 'What next?' Vinay remarks, 'I give all the credit to my wife. She said, "Are you going to sit on the laurels of one restaurant and for how long?" She had the foresight to expand and diversify'.

Nira, by then a mother of two toddlers but also a trained chef and confectionery specialist, recognised a need for good quality Indian sweets. After much persuasion, Vinay agreed to venture into this new business, doubting it would last more than six months. Nira flew to Mumbai to hire the best *halwais* (sweet makers). Deeply connected to her Hindu faith, Nira chose an auspicious name for the shop, Chhappan Bhog, meaning 'fifty-six varieties', a reference to the Diwali custom of offering fifty-six varieties of food, both sweet and savoury, to Lord Krishna. When the first Chhappan Bhog restaurant opened in 1996, in a small space next to the Eldorado Cinema, it was an overnight success. On its first Chhoti Diwali, the day before the main festival, it sold out of *mithai* (sweets) by 5:00 pm.

For fifteen years, Nira worked alongside her *halwais* and attended to the needs of her customers, with her husband and children lending a helping hand at crunch time. During Diwali, corporate orders of up to five thousand boxes of sweets had to be made within four or five days of the festival, in addition to the needs of the walk-in customers. Nira reflects on the secret of their success: 'There are hundreds of Indian sweets and snacks appealing to different tastes. At Chhappan Bhog, we keep the prices affordable so even the poorest labourer can buy a few *ladoos* (a round, sweet confection)'.

With several stores and restaurants across the country, Nira and Vinay can now slow down as their children advance the business with new culinary concepts. Nira is most at one in her home temple, which is adorned with her own painstakingly crafted cross-stitched images of Hindu deities. She shares, 'Lakshmi is our goddess of wealth, fortune, and prosperity both in the material and spiritual world. The cosmopolitan city takes you away from the faith. If you reach very high the insecurity of losing the wealth and status is even greater. Praying to our deities protects us and grounds us in eternal life'.

Praying to our deities protects us and grounds us in eternal life.

NIRA

LASSIE – SPICY OR FRUITY

Do you like your *lassie* sweet or salty, spiced, fruity, or plain? This yogurt-based drink is popular throughout the Indian subcontinent, to have before or after a meal, or on its own. It is particularly refreshing in the hot summer months, when some enjoy lassie instead of a meal. Lassie comes in two distinct varieties: sweet and salty. The sweet type includes sugar or honey with some added fruit or cardamom, while the other is subtly flavoured with added salt and spices. Both are utterly refreshing!

—
SERVES 4 TO 6
—

715 g (2½ c) plain yogurt
3 tbsp mint
3 tbsp fresh coriander
1 tsp salt
1 tsp cumin
1 tsp cardamom powder
2 tsp ginger, chopped
1 green chili, chopped
5 ice cubes
Slivered almonds
Slivered pistachios

MASALA LASSIE
Spicy Yogurt Milkshake

Masala lassie is a favourite drink during Holi, the Hindu festival that marks the arrival of spring and celebrates fertility, harvest, and love as a triumph of good over evil. Holi celebrations are filled with fun and colour. People smear each other with paint and throw colourful powdered dye at each other in an atmosphere of good humour, where distinctions of caste, class, age, and gender are suspended. During Holi, masala lassie is spiked with bhang, the leaves and flowers of the female cannabis plant. Any masala lassie offered during Holi should be approached with caution!

Place the yogurt, mint, fresh coriander, salt, cumin, cardamom powder, ginger, and green chili in a blender and whirl until well mixed. Adjust the spiciness to taste. Add the ice cubes and mix for a few seconds. Serve chilled in tall glasses with a sprinkling of slivered almonds and pistachios.

340 g (12 oz) very ripe mango pieces
1 tbsp granulated sugar or honey, to taste
½ tbsp rose water
570 g (2 c) plain yogurt
5 ice cubes
Mint leaves

MANGO LASSIE
Mango Yogurt Milkshake

This refreshing drink is popular during the Indian summers, when mangoes are in season. There are many varieties of mangoes and the colour of the lassie will depend on the variety used. The riper the mango, the tastier the lassie. Some prefer to use frozen mango pulp, which is equally good and allows the drink to be made year-round. This milkshake can be flavoured with cardamom, saffron, or rose water.

Place the mango, sugar, and rose water in a blender and puree. Add the yogurt and ice cubes. Blend for a few seconds until everything is well mixed. Add a splash of water to thin if needed. Serve chilled in tall glasses and garnish with mint leaves.

CHANNA BHATURA
Spiced Chickpea Curry with Fried Bread

Channa bhatura is a typical Punjabi/North Indian breakfast dish made of spicy *channa* (chickpea) curry served with *bhatura* (fried bread) to scoop the chickpeas. Legend has it that when Emperor Shah Jahan was deposed and imprisoned in Agra Fort in 1657 by his son, Aurangzeb, he was allowed to choose only one food that he would eat for the rest of his life. The emperor chose chickpeas for their versatility. For the next eight years, looking out at his beloved Taj Mahal, he would remain in the prison, eating chickpeas prepared by the loyal prison cook, who tried to vary the flavours, thus creating new recipes that would ultimately spread throughout India.

SERVES
6 TO 8

CHANNA

450 g (1 lb) cooked chickpeas

3 tbsp cooking oil

1 tsp cumin seeds

255 g (9 oz) onion, chopped

1 tsp ginger, crushed

1 tsp garlic, crushed

1 tsp turmeric

1 tsp coriander powder

1 tsp cumin

1 tsp chili powder

285 g (10 oz) tomatoes, chopped

2 bird's eye chilies, chopped

1 tbsp tamarind paste

Fresh coriander, chopped

Bird's eye chili, chopped

BHATURA

225 g (1½ c) all-purpose flour

½ tsp salt

½ tsp baking soda

30 g (⅓ c) fine semolina

½ tbsp granulated sugar

½ tbsp oil

85 g (⅓ c) plain yogurt

Cooking oil

NIRA *I developed this recipe to cater to the growing community of South Asian workers who wanted a 'home-cooked' meal at an affordable price. This popular dish is an inexpensive, satisfying, nutritious, and flavourful way to start the workday or for a leisurely Friday afternoon. I encourage you to make your own variation of the channa, adjusting the spices as you like and adding paneer, peas, or potato for a richer curry. You can start with dried chickpeas, soak them overnight and then boil until cooked, or use canned chickpeas for a shortcut. The bhatura can be made in different sizes and you can add nigella, fennel, or ajwain seeds for more flavour.*

FOR THE CHANNA

Boil the canned or soaked and cooked chickpeas in their liquid for 10 to 15 minutes or until soft. Drain and reserve the liquid. Heat the oil in a large skillet. Add the cumin seeds and sauté on high heat until they crackle. Add the onions and sauté for 3 minutes, until golden. Stir in the ginger and garlic and cook for 1 minute. Sprinkle in the turmeric, coriander, cumin, and chili powder and continue to stir for 2 minutes until well blended. Add the tomatoes, lower the heat to medium, and cook for 2 minutes. Stir in the chickpeas, green chilies, and tamarind paste.

Pour in liquid from the boiled chickpeas or water, 60 millilitres (¼ cup) at a time, until the sauce is thick enough to coat the chickpeas. Simmer on low heat for another 10 minutes, adding chickpea liquid or water as needed to attain a thick dry sauce.

FOR THE BHATURA

Sift the flour, salt, and baking soda into the bowl of a food processor or stand mixer. Add the semolina, sugar, oil, and yogurt and mix well. Drizzle in some water a tablespoon at a time, just until the dough holds together and pulls away from the sides of the bowl. The dough will be somewhat elastic. Cover with a damp towel and let it rest for at least 2 hours.

Form the dough into balls that are about 50 grams (1.7 ounces) each. On a floured surface, roll each dough ball into a circle, about 4 millimetres (¼ inch) thick.

In a wok or Dutch oven, heat the cooking oil until it sizzles when a small piece of dough is added. Deep-fry each bhatura for 1 minute on each side, using a flat sieve-like spoon to submerge it intermittently, until golden and bubbly. Remove from the oil and drain on paper towel. Keep the oil at a medium temperature while the bhatura are cooking, but in between, raise the heat before starting the next one.

Garnish the channa with fresh coriander and green chilies and serve *achaar* (pickles) and bhatura on the side.

LOBSTER MAHARAJA WITH GREEN RICE

SERVES 4 TO 6

LOBSTER

800 g (1¾ lb) lobster meat

60 ml (¼ c) olive oil, divided

85 g (3 oz) butter, divided

1 tsp cumin seeds

225 g (8 oz) onion, chopped

1 tsp ginger, crushed

1 tsp garlic, crushed

1 tsp garam masala

1 tsp chili powder, to taste

1 tsp black pepper

700 g (1½ lb) canned tomatoes, diced

1 tsp salt

85 g (½ c) raw cashews

60 ml (¼ c) heavy cream

¼ tsp dried fenugreek leaves

Handful of fresh coriander

RICE

300 g (1½ c) basmati rice

200 g (7 oz) spinach

2 tbsp fresh coriander

2 tbsp cooking oil

1 cinnamon stick

3 cardamom pods, crushed

2 whole cloves

2 bay leaves

55 g (2 oz) onion, chopped

2 tbsp coconut milk powder

1 tsp salt

28 g (1 oz) butter

VINAY *Chef Khalil Mia has been with us since we opened Kwality in 1985. Despite the new highway in front of the restaurant and limited parking, he has been preparing authentic Indian curries, tandoori, rice, and breads for the devoted fans of his 'home-cooked' food. A few years ago, he created this dish for one of his regular Emirati customers who wanted a variation on* murgh makhani *(butter chicken). When paired with the creamy* Nilgiri pulao *(green rice), this dish is fit for a maharajah. You can also substitute jumbo prawns for the lobster.*

FOR THE LOBSTER

Cut the lobster meat into large pieces. (If using prawns, shell and devein.) Heat half the oil and half the butter in a large skillet. Add the lobster and sauté for 3 minutes, until the edges are cooked and the centres are translucent; remove from the skillet.

Add the remaining butter, oil, and cumin seeds to the skillet and stir over medium heat for 1 minute, until fragrant. Add the onions and sauté for 5 minutes, until golden. Add the ginger and garlic with a drizzle of water, reduce the heat, and stir for 1 minute. Sprinkle in the garam masala, chili powder, and pepper, and continue to stir. Add the tomatoes and salt, bring to a boil, and then simmer for about 20 minutes, until the tomatoes are cooked and the oil starts to separate.

Meanwhile, soak the cashews in warm water to cover, for 10 minutes. Drain and puree in a blender with 60 millilitres (¼ cup) of water to make a thin paste. Add the cashew paste to the tomato sauce and cook for another 5 minutes on low heat. Stir in the cream. Return the lobster to the skillet and cook for 3 to 5 minutes. Remove from the heat and crush in the fenugreek leaves. Adjust the seasoning if needed. Garnish with fresh coriander.

FOR THE RICE

Soak the rice in water for an hour; drain. Blanch the spinach and then rinse immediately with cold water to stop the cooking and retain the colour. Place the spinach and fresh coriander in a food processor and blend to form a paste.

Heat the oil in a medium saucepan and add the cinnamon stick, cardamom pods, cloves, and bay leaves and stir for 2 minutes, until fragrant. Add the onion and sauté for 5 minutes, until golden. Combine the coconut milk powder with 120 millilitres (½ cup) of water and shake vigorously. Add the spinach puree, coconut milk, and salt and stir in the rice. Pour 180 millilitres (¾ cup) of hot water over the rice and add the butter, stirring gently to combine all the ingredients. Cover the saucepan and seal the edges with cloth or aluminium foil; simmer on low heat for 40 minutes or until the rice is cooked.

MARY AND MARTIN CORRADO

EDUCATION ◇ US

FINANCE ◇ US

In late 1970, Martin and his wife Mary attended a party at a fellow student's apartment in Greenwich Village, not far from the New York University campus. The eclectic mix of guests included a young student from Abu Dhabi, who later became their neighbour. Little did they know that this encounter would shape the rest of their lives.

The student was one of the first from Abu Dhabi to attend New York University, where Martin was also studying for his MBA. Martin and Mary had met a few years earlier during a study-abroad programme in Cairo, so they knew what it was like to be a student in a foreign land. They immediately took their new neighbour under their wing and enjoyed practising their limited Arabic phrases with him.

Martin had grown up in Greenwich Village, a close-knit, Italian-American neighbourhood with strong vestiges of its immigrant past. The streets of the Village were full of small, mom-and-pop shops, and Martin's mother, who still lived there, took the inquisitive student around to her vegetable man, butcher, and fishmonger, instructing each to 'take care of this kid' and not give him any bad food. And thus, he became a de facto member of a Greenwich Village Italian-American family.

One September evening in 1972, the student hosted an important guest from his nascent country, HE Ahmed Khalifa Al Suwaidi, the first Minister of Foreign Affairs. One year earlier, the United Arab Emirates had become a nation on 2 December 1971, and Al Suwaidi was invited to address the United Nations General Assembly for the first time. The Emirati student wished to honour his guest by preparing a home-cooked meal, as is customary in Abu Dhabi. He invited the Qatari and Kuwaiti ambassadors, along with other students from the Gulf region, and Martin and Mary to his apartment for the celebratory feast. Not having spent much time in the kitchen, the young student had not realised that the leg of lamb he purchased for the occasion was bigger than the tiny oven in his studio apartment. The guests began to arrive around 3:00 pm, and the lamb was jammed into the oven. By 7:00 pm there was still no sign of any food. Martin walked into the kitchen and exclaimed: 'This thing isn't cooking. It's too big for the oven, and with the door open, all the heat is escaping!' But people were in a good mood — a half-cooked leg of lamb was not going to change a momentous occasion. Everyone sat on the floor in the traditional Emirati way, the leg of lamb was placed in the middle, and the guests nibbled on the cooked bits around the edges, enjoying a delicious and festive meal. That evening in Greenwich Village, Martin and Mary became de facto members of the Emirati community.

After graduation, the first group of Emirati students returned to the United Arab Emirates and took prominent positions in the government, and the Corrados moved to Minnesota. Their former neighbour invited them to come and visit. 'We arrived in Abu Dhabi in January 1977, and one of the first places we went was to the public beach in front of the Hilton Hotel. People were stopping their cars to watch these crazy people swimming in January', Mary recalls. They spent two lovely weeks as guests and explored the country. Just before leaving the United Arab Emirates, Martin was invited to meet their host's next-door neighbour, HH Sheikh Suroor bin Mohammed Al Nahyan. Martin did not realise at the time that Sheikh Suroor was a member of the ruling family and held several prominent positions. Sheikh Suroor greeted him warmly and thanked him for 'taking care of my people'. They proceeded to discuss investments and the strength of the dollar, since Martin had been reviewing what he thought was his friend's — and not Sheikh Suroor's — portfolio at the time.

When Martin returned to work in the United States, he found a telex on his desk. It read: 'Please come work for me as my financial advisor — Suroor bin Mohammed'. It was well below freezing in Minnesota, and Martin thought it would be a good time to broach the idea with Mary, who was suffering through the post-vacation blues and a very cold winter. 'How would you like to go back to Abu Dhabi?' Martin asked. Without hesitation, Mary replied, 'I would love to!'

And so began the Corrado's new life in Abu Dhabi. Martin arrived in April 1977 for a one-year contract as financial advisor to Sheikh Suroor, and Mary followed with their daughter a month later. 'The warm and welcoming nature of the Emiratis and their can-do attitude was inspiring. Everyone was trying to contribute to their new nation, especially the recent college graduates', Mary recalls.

Mary has a degree in nursing with an emphasis in international relations. She believes that women in any society need to be educated to protect their families from disease and to contribute to economic growth. 'Education was an area where I felt I could play a part', she tells me. The Emirati women she met were eager to learn, especially English. English-practice conversations broadened to include all kinds of subjects, such as women's health. A commitment to education, health, and culture nurtured Mary's life in Abu Dhabi, as well as raising their three children. She began to advise Emirati students attending universities in the United States on academic, social, and cultural adaptation. In 1996, the American ambassador to the United Arab Emirates, William Rugh, invited Mary to set up the Abu Dhabi office for the non-profit AMIDEAST, where she served as country director for more than twenty years.

Looking out from the fourteenth-floor balcony of the Corrado's apartment, down the brightly lit artery of the city, the Corniche, it is hard to imagine the unpaved roads and open-air markets of the 1970s that Mary describes: 'Grocery shopping was always a surprise. You never knew what products you would find. So, planning for dinner parties was impossible. I would go armed with five different recipes and end up improvising with what I could find'.

Martin and Mary would remind their children of their Italian-American heritage by maintaining their family's food traditions. Sourcing Pecorino cheese was a big concern for Martin, since it was a vital ingredient for many of his Italian dishes. After much searching, Martin discovered Greenhouse, a small shop in what was then known as the Tourist Club area, founded by a Cypriot construction company that imported Mediterranean food products, such as feta cheese and Kalamata olives, primarily for its workforce. Martin would buy an entire wheel of Pecorino cheese and store it in the bottom of the refrigerator.

> Rumours were that I was either CIA or Mafia, or both, which was quite useful. I was an enigma to many, a friend to a few.
>
> MARTIN

Some forty years later, Martin continues to advise Sheikh Suroor on finances and investments. 'Being an American in Abu Dhabi in the 1970s was an amazing experience', Martin reflects. 'Since I was an Italian American from New York, the rumours were that I was either CIA or Mafia or both, which was quite useful. I was an enigma to many, a friend to a few. Thanks to Sheikh Suroor, I met a wide range of people, and always tried to give him the facts'.

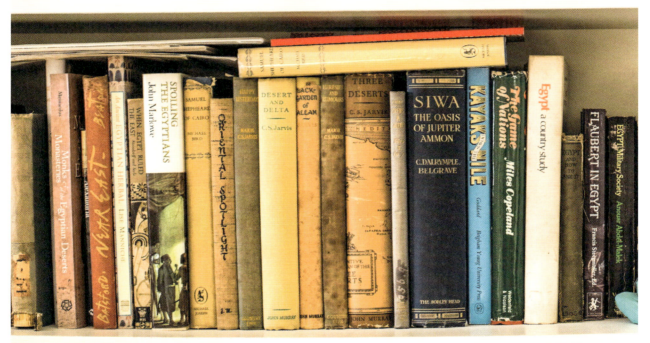
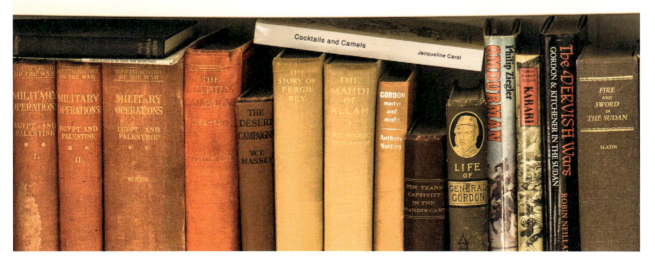

POLPETTE CON SALSA DI POMODORO
Italian Meatballs and Tomato Sauce

In traditional Italian cooking, meatballs are served on their own or in soups. The idea of serving meatballs in tomato sauce over spaghetti is an American variation that originated when many Italian immigrants came to the United States. Their changed personal wealth, the limited availability of Italian food items in American stores in the early part of the twentieth century, and the Anglo-American desire to include a starch with a meal, led to the combination of these separate elements, especially at Italian restaurants.

SERVES 6 TO 8

TOMATO SAUCE

3 tbsp olive oil, divided

225 g (8 oz) yellow onions, chopped

3 cloves garlic, crushed

1 kg (2¼ lb) crushed tomatoes, strained

140 g (5 oz) tomato paste

475 ml (2 c) chicken or vegetable broth

8 g (¼ c) basil, chopped

2 tsp salt

½ tsp black pepper

Pecorino Romano cheese

Packaged spaghetti, uncooked

Basil leaves

MEATBALLS

3 slices white bread

80 ml (⅓ c) milk

450 g (1 lb) minced beef

110 g (4 oz) onions, chopped

2 tbsp parsley, chopped

1 egg

1 tsp salt

1 tsp black pepper

2–3 tbsp olive oil

MARTIN *The staple food of my youth was pasta, dried or freshly made. My Aunt Fay used to serve it with* polpette, *which I helped make by rolling them on my stomach, much to my mother's chagrin. There was a great chef, Vincenzo Corrado, at the Bourbon court in Naples. His book,* Il Cuoco Galante (The Gallant Cook), *written in 1765, was the first recipe book devoted to Neapolitan cooking. He introduced macaroni to the royalty, elevating it from its origin as a street food. He was celebrated for his many innovations with pasta and was the first to combine it with tomatoes. I have been driven to make the perfect tomato-based sauce to match the different types of pasta, as each shape holds the sauce in a different way. With a nod to Vincenzo Corrado, my meatball and tomato sauce recipes are a family tradition.*

FOR THE TOMATO SAUCE

Heat a Dutch oven and add the olive oil and onions; sauté for 5 minutes until soft and lightly golden. Stir in the garlic and sauté for 2 minutes. Add the tomatoes and tomato paste and cook for 5 minutes, stirring occasionally. Pour in the broth and bring to a boil. Stir in the chopped basil, salt, and pepper; simmer uncovered over low heat for 1 hour. Meanwhile, prepare the pasta according to the instructions on the package, and the meatballs.

FOR THE MEATBALLS

Remove the crust from the bread and shred into a bowl; add the milk. Mash with a fork and blend until uniform. Drain any excess liquid. Combine the minced beef, onion, parsley, egg, mashed bread, salt, and pepper in a large bowl. Mix thoroughly by hand.

Shape the mixture into 2-centimetre (¾-inch) balls. Place the completed meatballs on a sheet of wax paper or non-stick baking tray. Cover with a dish towel until ready to cook. *[They can be refrigerated for a day, if necessary.]*

Add the olive oil to a large skillet over medium heat. When the oil is hot, carefully add the meatballs and brown them on all sides. Lower the heat and continue cooking until done. Remove the meatballs from the pan and blot with paper towels if necessary.

Toss with the tomato sauce and garnish with Pecorino Romano cheese and basil leaves. Serve the meatballs on the side or over the pasta.

PASTIERA NAPOLETANA
Italian Easter Cake

MARY *The Easter table would not be complete without* pastiera. *Traditionally, this Neapolitan wheat cake is cooked on Good Friday to allow the ingredients to infuse before Easter Sunday. This recipe has been in the Corrado family for generations. It evolved from the traditional pastiera when Martin's great-grandmother immigrated to the United States from Italy and chose to do without the* grano cotto *(cooked wheat), which she couldn't easily find. I have made this recipe every year since we were married and had my own challenges finding ricotta cheese in Abu Dhabi in 1977. Now I make it with fresh ricotta produced locally in Sharjah, and it has the perfect consistency. Be sure to drain the ricotta of any liquid.*

SERVES 6 TO 8

CRUST

300 g (2 c) all-purpose flour

115 g (1 c) icing sugar

140 g (5 oz) cold butter

3 eggs, seperated

1 tsp vanilla

FILLING

450 g (1 lb) ricotta cheese

210 g (1 c) granulated sugar

3 eggs

2 tbsp orange blossom water

2 tbsp lemon zest

1 tsp vanilla

1 tsp cinnamon

Dash of salt

85 g (3 oz) candied lemon and orange

Icing sugar

FOR THE CRUST

Mix the flour and sugar in a medium bowl. Using a pastry cutter or two knives, cut the butter into the flour mixture until the texture resembles coarse crumbs. Add the egg yolks (reserving the whites for brushing the top of the cake) and vanilla and mix with a fork, just until the dough pulls together. Transfer the dough to a floured surface. Form it into a ball and flatten into a disk. Wrap it in plastic wrap and refrigerate for 1 hour.

Place two-thirds of the dough on a floured surface and roll it into a 30-centimetre (12-inch) circle. Carefully transfer the dough to a 23-centimetre (9-inch) springform pan and press it into the bottom and two-thirds of the way up the sides. Prick the pastry with a fork, cover, and chill while making the filling.

FOR THE FILLING

Preheat the oven to 180°C (350°F). Drain the ricotta well. In a large mixing bowl, blend the ricotta and sugar. Separate the eggs, discarding one of the yolks. Add the 2 egg yolks, orange blossom water, lemon zest, vanilla, cinnamon, salt, and candied fruit and mix thoroughly. Beat the egg whites with a hand mixer until soft peaks form. Fold the egg whites into the cheese mixture and pour into the pastry.

Roll the remaining dough into a rectangle. Cut 7 or 8 long strips, each 2 centimetres (¾ inch) wide. Arrange the strips in a lattice on top of the filling. Brush the pastry strips and edges with the reserved egg whites from the crust.

Bake for 90 minutes, rotating 180 degrees halfway through to ensure even browning. The pastiera is done when a knife inserted in the centre comes out clean. Serve at room temperature, sprinkled with icing sugar.

MARIA ANGELES RUIZ DE ALOM

SPANISH EMBASSY
ABU DHABI
(RETIRED)
◊
SPAIN

Maria was my first neighbour and friendly resource when I arrived in Abu Dhabi. Despite having grown up in nearby Kuwait, the city was sufficiently different that I needed advice: 'Who makes the best *manakeesh*? What about Arabic, I mean, Turkish coffee — which is the best roaster? And spices — is there a spice souk, and where can I order *kunafe* and *katayef* for Ramadan?' My list of questions was endless and Maria was always ready to help. No matter what the panic of the day was, she had been through it in some form or another.

While pursuing a career in interior design in London, Maria met her husband, Kassem Alom, a young Syrian doctor who was training there. Deeply connected to her home in the Cantabria region of northern Spain, yet loving adventure, she followed him to a little-known place called Abu Dhabi, where he was going to set up a medical practice. 'I vividly remember the moment we landed at the old Abu Dhabi International Airport in Al Bateen on a very hot and humid September evening in 1978. Little did I know what lay ahead for us', Maria remarks.

Maria recalls the contrast between 1970s Abu Dhabi and today. Then, even the essential food products, such as fresh milk, meat, and fruit, were not readily available whereas today, our choices are endless. The scarcity of the food products during those early days, however, was overshadowed by the richness of the friendships formed. Maria reflects, 'My fondest memories are how tight-knit we were as an expatriate community. We did everything together; we were a real family away from our own. We spent much of our free time entertaining at home, which meant that as a new bride I had to rapidly learn how to cook a variety of dishes! Luckily, we were forgiving of each other's early experiments; we shared recipes and learned to cook many dishes from international cuisines'. Abu Dhabi was not a tourist destination back then and entertainment, shopping, and dining options were few. A favourite shopping venue was the local souk, with its beautiful fabrics and assortment of South Asian tailors ready to experiment with the latest fashions. Many women's groups formed around reading, cooking, gardening, stitching, and quilting, and these gatherings became the anchor for new people moving to Abu Dhabi.

The leisurely mornings with friends ended once Maria started working at the Spanish Embassy, where she spent the next thirty-five years. During that time, she contributed to the growth of the relationship between the United Arab Emirates and Spain and supported the growing Spanish community. In 1999, Maria was awarded the Cross of the Order of Civil Merit by King Juan Carlos I, and in 2015 with the Cross of the Order of Isabel la Catolica by King Felipe VI, in recognition for her service to her country.

Maria blends, yet honours, the distinct cultural traditions of Spain and her husband's homeland of Syria. She is equally comfortable preparing *fattoush*, *fatayer*, and *ma'amoul* as she is *tortilla de patatas*, gazpacho, and paella. Her Ramadan table includes traditional Syrian drinks and sweets, and family gatherings at Christmas are highlighted by traditional Cantabrian fare.

Maria's garden on Saadiyat Island, with its delightful ambiance, is the perfect place to relax. The Alhambra-inspired fountain is a nod to the historical connections between the Moorish Spain and Arabic cultures. It is also a reminder of the past: 'We had planned for Abu Dhabi to be a two-year adventure, but we have been privileged to call it home for forty years. Here is where our three children were born and raised to become the unique and accomplished individuals we are proud of. Here is where my husband and I have had fulfilling careers and where we have forged many lifelong friendships. Abu Dhabi is where the heart is'.

We had planned for Abu Dhabi to be a two-year adventure, but we have been privileged to call it home for forty years.

MARIA

FATTOUSH
Bread and Purslane Salad

MARIA *Fattoush is one of the first Levantine dishes I learned to make when we got married. It's a salad with a mixture of vegetables, herbs, and bread. It is easily adaptable to personal taste and to what you may have in the fridge that day. The main ingredients are the pita bread, prepared like croutons, purslane, and sumac. It's delicious and nutritious and a daily feature at our* iftar *table during the fasting month of Ramadan. I also like to serve it with paella for Friday lunches.*

—
SERVES
6 TO 8
—

DRESSING

80 ml (⅓ c) lemon juice

120 ml (½ c) olive oil

2 tbsp pomegranate molasses

1 tbsp apple cider vinegar

2 cloves garlic, crushed

Salt and black pepper, to taste

SALAD

Cooking oil, to fry

2 pitas, cut into 2 cm (1 in) squares

1 head romaine lettuce, chopped

100 g (2 c) purslane

10 g (⅓ c) mint, chopped

10 g (⅓ c) parsley

450 g (1 lb) tomatoes, cut into 1 cm (½ in) pieces

340 g (12 oz) cucumbers, sliced

28 g (1 oz) radishes, sliced

2 spring onions, sliced

1½ tbsp sumac

FOR THE DRESSING

Mix all the ingredients in a bottle with a tightly fitting lid and shake well. Set aside until the salad is ready to serve.

FOR THE SALAD

Heat the oil in a skillet and shallow fry the pita bread for 3 to 5 minutes, until golden brown. Remove the bread with a slotted spoon and drain on paper towel.

Combine all the prepared vegetables and herbs in a large bowl and mix well. The quantities are suggestions and can be varied according to taste.

Just before serving, toss the salad with the dressing and sprinkle with the sumac. Scatter the pita croutons over the salad and give it one more toss. The croutons should be added last so they don't get soggy.

TORTILLA ESPAÑOLA DE PATATAS
Spanish Omelette with Potatoes

The culinary tradition of tapas, a variety of snacks served on small plates, originated in Andalusia, Spain. Some diners enjoy tapas with a drink before lunch or dinner, while others prefer tapas bar hopping, known as *ir de tapas*. Tapas can be *cosas de picar* (finger food), such as cured meat and cheese; *pinchas* (skewered with a toothpick), such as olives and tortillas (Spanish potato omelette); or *cazuelas*, something with a sauce such as meatballs, braised chorizo, or calamari sautéed in garlic.

One legend has tapas originating in the late nineteenth century when King Alfonso XIII stopped at a tavern in Cadiz and was served a glass of wine with a piece of cheese on top to protect it from dust and fruit flies. The king enjoyed the cheese as he sipped the wine and then ordered another drink with *una tapa*, literally meaning a lid or cover. As with many culinary trends set by royalty, the tradition of eating small savoury snacks with a drink spread across the country and has become firmly entrenched in the gastronomy of Spain. Now, tapas are served worldwide by many restaurants, from the traditional to the avant-garde.

MARIA *Perhaps the most Spanish of all tapas, this potato omelette makes a satisfying meal on its own. It is much more than the sum of its humble parts. Poaching the potatoes and onions in oil makes them rich and creamy. You can prepare the tortilla ahead of time. It tastes great warm, at room temperature, or cold. Serve it cut into wedges with a green salad for lunch, brunch, or dinner, or cut it into small squares with a toothpick inserted, as tapas.*

SERVES 4 TO 6

800 g (1¾ lb) potatoes

285 g (10 oz) onions, chopped

2 tsp salt

240 ml (1 c) cooking or olive oil

6 eggs

Salt and black pepper, to taste

Peel and cut the potatoes into small cubes. Mix the potatoes and onions in a bowl and add the salt. Heat the oil in a 25-centimetre (10-inch) diameter, deep, non-stick skillet over moderate heat and add the potatoes and onions. Stir occasionally for 15 to 20 minutes, until the vegetables are very tender but not browned. Drain in a colander, reserving the oil. Return 1 tablespoon of the oil to the skillet and save the rest to reuse for another tortilla at a later time. Allow the potatoes and onions to cool for 5 minutes.

Beat the eggs in a large bowl and season with salt and pepper. Gently stir in the potatoes, being careful not to mash them. Heat the oil in the skillet and add the potato mixture, pressing gently with a wooden spoon to create an even layer. Cook for 5 to 8 minutes, until the eggs are completely set at the edges and the omelette easily slips around in the pan when you shake it. Invert the omelette onto a large rimless plate and slide it back into the skillet, pushing any stray potatoes back under the omelette. (This may be a bit challenging and takes some practice.) Use a wooden spoon or spatula to fold the edges down between the omelette and sides of the skillet to create a rounded edge. Cook over low heat for another 5 to 8 minutes, until the tortilla is still moist.

Slide the omelette onto a serving platter and let it cool for 5 minutes. Cut it into wedges or squares to serve.

GAZPACHO
Chilled Tomato Soup

Gazpacho is a cold soup originating in Andalusia in southern Spain but is now served around the world. It is sometimes referred to as a 'liquid salad'. The traditional soup is prepared by using a pestle to push the vegetables through a metal sieve and includes bread, although eliminating the bread produces a lighter soup and the blender version is just as good.

MARIA *Gazpacho is most refreshing in the summer months, but we enjoy it all year round. It's best to use juicy, vine-ripened tomatoes. Some prefer to peel the tomatoes before blending, but if you have a high-powered food processor or blender, there is no need to peel. The diced vegetable garnish gives the soup extra body.*

SERVES 6 TO 8

SOUP

- **1 kg (2¼ lb)** tomatoes
- **1 small** green bell pepper
- **1 small** red bell pepper
- **2 small** cucumbers, peeled
- **110 g (4 oz)** onion
- **1 slice** bread (optional)
- **1 clove** garlic, more to taste
- **60 ml (¼ c)** olive oil
- **3 tbsp** red vinegar
- **3 tbsp** lemon juice
- Salt and black pepper

GARNISH

- **1 small** cucumber
- **1 small** green pepper
- **1 small** tomato
- **1** spring onion

CROUTONS

- **28 g (1 oz)** butter
- **1 clove** garlic, crushed
- **6 slices** bread, crust removed, and cubed

FOR THE SOUP

Coarsely chop the tomatoes, peppers, cucumbers, and onion and place in a food processor. Add the remaining soup ingredients and blend at high speed until the vegetables are well pureed. Pass through a sieve, pressing to extract as much liquid as possible. Taste and correct the seasoning, adding more salt, vinegar, or lemon as needed. Chill well, preferably overnight.

FOR THE GARNISH

Finely dice the vegetables and place in separate bowls.

FOR THE CROUTONS

Melt the butter in a large, heavy skillet and add the garlic. Stir in the bread cubes and coat them with the butter and garlic. Continue to cook over low heat, stirring occasionally for 30 minutes or until the bread cubes are golden and crunchy.

Serve the soup and pass the garnish and croutons.

PAELLA DE MARISCO
Seafood Paella

Paella is known worldwide as a Spanish rice dish that includes a variety of seafood or meats, with vegetables. However, the word 'paella' in Latin originally referred only to the pan in which the food was cooked. Paella originated in Valencia, thousands of years ago, with the confluence of the Roman introduction of the irrigation system and the Arab's contribution of rice. Purists insist that Valencia is the only place to eat paella, but Maria's is a close second.

—
SERVES
6 TO 8
—

MARIA *I have been making this seafood paella for many years — in Spain on an open fire, in Syria at my mother-in-law's, and in Abu Dhabi. The name always prompts a discussion about its origin. Some friends insist it originates from the Arabic word* baqayah, *meaning leftovers, as the servants of the Moorish kings mixed rice with leftovers from the royal banquets in large pots to take home. You can vary the recipe as you wish, including other fish or eliminating the shellfish, but keep the basic proportions of fish to rice the same.*

8 tbsp olive oil, divided

285 g (10 oz) shrimp, shelled and deveined

450 g (1 lb) king prawns, shelled, deveined, and cut in half lengthwise

450 g (1 lb) lobster tails, cut in 4-cm (1½-in) thick circles, including the shell

450 g (1 lb) monkfish or other firm white fish, cut into chunks

285 g (10 oz) calamari, cut into rings

140 g (5 oz) onion, chopped

2 cloves garlic, crushed

110 g (4 oz) green bell pepper, chopped

225 g (8 oz) tomato, peeled and chopped

A few threads saffron, crushed

1 tsp paprika

1 tsp coarse salt, to taste

2 l (2 qt) fish broth

600 g (3 c) short grain rice

130 g (1 c) peas

130 g (1 c) broad beans

255 g (9 oz) clams

255 g (9 oz) mussels

GARNISH

2 pimentos, cut in strips

Lemon wedges

Parsley, chopped

Aioli

Heat 6 tablespoons of olive oil in a large paella pan with a base of about 38 centimetres (15 inches). Separately sauté the shrimp, prawns, and lobster just until pink; use a slotted spoon to transfer each to a large platter. Separately sauté the fish and calamari until lightly browned; remove to the platter.

Add 2 tablespoons of olive oil to the pan, along with the onion, garlic, and bell pepper; cook until the vegetables are soft. Add the tomato and cook for two minutes until any liquid has evaporated. Sprinkle in the saffron, paprika, and salt and adjust the seasoning. Bring the reserved fish broth to a boil.

Stir in the rice and 1.5 litres (1½ quarts) of the heated fish broth; bring to a boil and stir for 5 minutes over medium heat. Add the peas and beans. Distribute the clams and mussels, pushing them into the rice. Add extra broth if needed. Add the fish, shrimp, and calamari and cook for 10 to 15 minutes, until the rice is no longer soupy but some liquid remains.

Arrange the prawn and lobster pieces over the rice and continue to cook, uncovered, for 10 minutes or until the rice is al dente. Cover with aluminium foil, reduce the heat, and cook for 10 minutes. Remove the pan from the heat; let it rest covered for 10 minutes.

Garnish with pimento strips, lemon wedges, and parsley. Serve immediately with aioli on the side.

AMINA RIZK AND BACHIR ELHASKOURI

DESIGNER ◊ MOROCCO

ECONOMIST ◊ MOROCCO

During Ramadan, the holy month when Muslims fast from dawn to dusk, *iftar,* the sunset meal that breaks the fast, is a big social event. Hosting iftars in the Moroccan tradition is Bachir and Amina's hallmark. Bachir explains, 'We introduced iftar gatherings at our home as an ecumenical way to share our culture. We invite diplomats and long-time friends, both Muslim and non-Muslim'. Bachir strives to include diplomats on his guest list, as he believes they are culinary lore carriers, preserving and handing down recipes from the different cultures they experience.

Culinary traditions are deeply rooted in Bachir's family. His father was the chief of staff and chief of the civil household for the vice regal palace of Spanish Morocco. He managed many cooks and hosted many important politicians, serving the most exquisite Moroccan food and creating his own recipes. Bachir remarks, 'Unfortunately, many of his recipes were never documented. His most treasured creation was a whole fish stuffed with *kufta* (minced meat with spices). I have been trying to track down this recipe and may be getting close!' Bachir recalls a special visitor to their home in London: 'Winston Churchill, a great lover of Moroccan food, would come into the kitchen to inspect how his favourite dish was being prepared. He particularly liked my father's smoked entrails of lamb prepared with chickpeas'.

As a young boy growing up in Morocco in the 1970s, the kitchen was off limits to men. The staff working there were all women and any visit by a man, especially a young bachelor, signalled interests that were not just culinary. However, as a foreign student in the United States, Bachir could finally come into his own in the kitchen. At Oberlin College and later at Johns Hopkins University, he prepared what became his signature dish, lemon chicken with olives. It was a hit, especially amongst a group of Emirati students, and eventually led him to a job in Abu Dhabi. Bachir recalls, 'I made my name amongst the Emirati students in the Washington, D.C. area through food. One day they mentioned that Abu Dhabi Investment Authority was in town recruiting. I was one of the lucky few to be picked to join the bonds and equity department of the newly formed sovereign wealth fund'.

Bachir moved to Abu Dhabi in 1979, bringing his culinary enthusiasm and Moroccan spices. He lived in a two-bedroom apartment on Hamdan Street and hosted colleagues for dinner at weekends. As oil revenues rolled in, the influx of foreigners to Abu Dhabi increased and the aromas and food of the city took on new scents and diverse flavours. It was a close-knit community of expatriates and locals. Bachir explains, 'Food was central to the social relationships and people were keen to discover other foods and cultures, which was done only in homes. The only time we used to go to a restaurant was when we tired of Arab and South Asian food, and then it was to the Chinese restaurant at the Center Hotel'.

Happily working as an interior designer with no plans of leaving the United States, Amina met Bachir on one of his trips back to Washington, D.C. He proposed via an unregistered letter, leaving something to fate. And as fate would have it, the letter arrived. They were married in 1987 and Amina moved to Abu Dhabi. By then, Bachir held a diplomatic position and it was important for them to entertain frequently. So, Amina began to experiment in the kitchen, often asking her mother in Casablanca to send spices and recipes. She recalls, 'My cousin was a purser with Royal Air Maroc, so with every flight from Casa to Abu Dhabi, my mother would send over *bastilla* (pigeon pie dusted with icing sugar), *djaj muhamar* (roasted chicken) stuffed with dried fruits, *mshabakiya* (a syrupy pastry), and other Moroccan sweets'. Bachir and

Amina began to schedule their weekly dinner parties around the Air Maroc flights so they could serve their guests authentic, freshly made Moroccan dishes catered directly from Casablanca.

Now, Amina cooks for the family and Bachir cooks for guests. The one exception is during Ramadan, when Bachir hosts all-male iftars. Amina prepares the food and Bachir serves as the major-domo, coordinating between the chef and the guests. My husband, Steve, was a guest at a recent iftar and shared how the four-hour gathering unfolded. After the traditional firing of the cannon at *maghreb* (sunset), followed by the *azan* (call to prayer), Bachir offered everyone a variety of dates, dried figs, and apricots, along with fresh juices and water to break the fast. After the maghreb prayer, they moved to the dining area and sat down at a long table. There was a bit of confusion when they realised a seat was missing for the host. Bachir calmly explained the tradition in the old homes of Morocco and in Arab hospitality: 'The host does not eat with his guests, but honours them by serving them. When you serve someone, you are subordinating yourself socially, which is an honour to the guest'.

The meal began with Bachir serving everyone a hearty *harira* soup, along with *sambousek*, a stuffed meat pastry. He went on to serve bastilla and two more tajine-based entrées. Steve found the discussion about food and libations, religion, economics, and geopolitical events lively. India, Pakistan, Lebanon, Palestine, Morocco, Spain, Belgium, and America were all represented at the table. The evening ended with Bachir serving the traditional Moroccan tea and sweets. At the end of these memorable Ramadan evenings, Bachir brings out the *bakhoor* (incense) burner and circulates it around the living room. This is a signal that the major-domo has completed his duties and will now relax. The guests are welcome to stay but they know the service is done.

While much has changed in the city, with a wide array of restaurants and cuisines, cultural events, and entertainment on offer, the intimate gatherings at Bachir and Amina's home are a treasured culinary tradition. We hope they will continue and will one day include the fish stuffed with kufta.

> When you serve someone, you are subordinating yourself socially, which is an honour to the guest.
>
> BACHIR

BRAISED CHICKEN
with Lemons and Olives

BACHIR *I first made this traditional Moroccan dish as a student at Oberlin College in the 1970s. I was living in Third World House, where most of the foreign students and people of colour lived. It was a close-knit community and we helped each other academically, politically, and culturally. I wrote to my mother and asked her to send me the recipe for my favourite dish, chicken with olives and preserved lemons. After a few attempts, I was confident about sharing it with my housemates. It was an immediate hit and I have been serving this dish ever since for friends, family, business associates, artists, and diplomats.*

I vary the spices depending on my guests and their palettes. For Moroccans, the coriander and cumin are dominant; for South Asians, I add some red chili peppers; and for Southeast Asian guests, I spike it with more ginger. Many diplomats, when leaving Abu Dhabi, request this recipe, and I share it as a parting gift, minus one spice, so they can experiment and make it their own. So, experiment with your own combination of spices or try mine. I marinate the chicken overnight, which makes for a more flavourful dish, but if you are short on time, try to marinate it for at least two or three hours before cooking.

—
SERVES
6 TO 8
—

1.5 kg (about 3 lb) chicken pieces

285 g (10 oz) yellow onions, finely chopped

4 cloves garlic, crushed

28 g (1 oz) fresh ginger, crushed

1 tbsp cumin

2 tsp coriander powder

1½ tsp turmeric or Moroccan yellow colourant

1 tsp black pepper

1 tsp salt

120 ml (½ c) olive oil, divided

3 preserved lemons, finely chopped

15 g (½ c) parsley, chopped

15 g (½ c) mint, chopped

255 g (9 oz) green or red olives

2 preserved lemons, quartered and deseeded

Skin the chicken pieces and cut any large pieces in half. In a large bowl, mix the onions, garlic, ginger, cumin, coriander powder, turmeric, pepper, salt, and half of the olive oil. Add the preserved lemons, parsley, and mint and mix well. Rub the chicken pieces with this marinade, cover tightly, and refrigerate overnight or at least 2 to 3 hours.

Add the remaining olive oil to a Dutch oven over medium heat. Arrange the chicken in the bottom and distribute the onion/spice marinade. Cover and cook the chicken over medium-low heat for 30 minutes, gently stirring and turning the chicken halfway through. If needed, add about 80 millilitres (⅓ cup) of water and turn the heat to low. The chicken will braise in its own juices. Add the olives and preserved lemon quarters and cover. Cook without lifting the lid for another 10 minutes, until the chicken is tender. If there is too much liquid, remove the chicken to a plate and cover it with aluminium foil. Increase the heat and reduce the mixture until most of the liquid has evaporated. Return the chicken to the sauce and let it simmer for another few minutes.

Serve the chicken in a tagine with crusty bread to soak up the sauce.

HARIRA
Moroccan Tomato Lentil Soup

Harira can be considered the national soup of Morocco, prepared in unending variations in every city, street, and home. It is comforting, nourishing and a religious institution unto itself. It feeds the soul as well as the stomach. During Ramadan, every family in Morocco breaks the fast at sunset with a bowl of harira accompanied by a couple of dates and *chebakia*, flower-shaped cookies sprinkled with sesame seeds.

SERVES 8 TO 10

- **2 tbsp** olive oil
- **28 g (1 oz)** butter
- **340 g (12 oz)** yellow onions, finely chopped
- **450 g (1 lb)** lamb or beef, in small cubes, or portobello mushrooms
- **225 g (8 oz)** celery stalks with leaves, finely chopped
- **15 g (½ c)** parsley, finely chopped
- **50 g (1 c)** fresh coriander, finely chopped
- **1 tbsp** salt
- **1 tbsp** cumin
- **1 tbsp** coriander powder
- **1½ tsp** paprika
- **1 tsp** cinnamon
- **1 tbsp** ground ginger
- **1 tsp** white pepper
- **1 tsp** turmeric or Moroccan yellow colourant
- **255 g (9 oz)** cooked chickpeas
- **100 g (½ c)** lentils, washed
- **900 g (2 lb)** tomatoes, peeled and pureed, or canned
- **2 tbsp** tomato paste
- **40 g (¼ c)** all-purpose flour
- **3 tbsp** vermicelli, uncooked
- **60 ml (¼ c)** lemon juice

AMINA *There are many ways to prepare harira, some with more herbs and others with a rich tomato base. Harira can be made with lamb, beef, or chicken. For our vegetarian guests, I replace the meat with portobello mushrooms and they love it. The consistency of the soup is a personal taste, with some cooks preferring to thicken it with the* tadouira *(in Moroccan cuisine, a flour-based thickener), as I do, which gives it a velvety texture. As with most soups, it is even better the next day. You can thin it with water when reheating. Enjoy harira as a hearty meal with some bread and a salad.*

In a large Dutch oven, heat the oil and butter over medium heat; sauté the onions for 2 to 3 minutes. Add the meat, stirring until it is browned on all sides. *[If using mushrooms instead of meat, heat the oil and butter and sauté the onions for 2 to 3 minutes. Add the mushrooms and continue with the next ingredients.]* Add the celery, parsley, fresh coriander, salt, cumin, coriander powder, paprika, cinnamon, ginger, white pepper, and turmeric or colourant; stir well for 2 minutes. Add the chickpeas and 1 litre (1 quart) of water and bring to a boil. Add the lentils and simmer for 30 minutes. Add the tomato puree, tomato paste, and 1 litre (1 quart) of hot water and simmer for 45 minutes. Check the liquid occasionally and add more water if needed.

While the soup is cooking, make the tadouira by mixing the flour with 120 millilitres (½ cup) of water. Stir or whisk the mixture occasionally. The flour will eventually blend with the water. If the mixture still has lumps, pass it through a sieve.

When the lentils and chickpeas are soft, sprinkle the vermicelli into the soup and let it simmer for another 10 minutes. Drizzle the tadouira into the soup in a steady stream while continuously stirring so the flour doesn't stick to the bottom of the pan. Simmer for 5 to 10 more minutes. Remove from the heat and stir in the lemon juice.

Serve in individual soup bowls with a lemon wedge on the side and a couple of dates in the tradition of breaking the Ramadan fast.

— 1980s —
LOW AND SLOW

The 1980s saw the United Arab Emirates become more regionally integrated, with the launch of the Gulf Cooperation Council at the newly built Abu Dhabi Intercontinental Hotel. The turbulent politics of the Middle East had moved closer to home with the start of the Iran-Iraq War in 1981. Tankers exporting oil from the Arabian Gulf were targeted and forced to go through the Strait of Hormuz in groups for protection against attack. Oil prices doubled, and the country found itself strategically placed, with the Jebel Ali port transporting goods to both sides. This increase in oil revenue was short-lived, however, as non-OPEC production increased and oil prices plummeted, remaining low for the rest of the decade.

Nevertheless, Abu Dhabi continued to pursue its long-term development goals, with several of the major infrastructure projects initiated the previous decade reaching completion, including the Cultural Foundation, Zayed Sports City, and the new Abu Dhabi International Airport. These brought more travellers, workers, families, and goods to the city. Similarly, investment in the oil industry continued to grow, reaching its apex, with predictions that the country's oil reserve would be the second largest in the world. Multinational oil companies solidified their presence and more embassies were established in what was, at that time, the provisional capital city.

As the expatriate communities grew, the food and social culture began to change with more hotels, restaurants, and shops. Fast food outlets such as Dairy Queen, Pizza Hut, and KFC were the novelty, along with the highly caloric fruit juice cocktail stands. Westerners found more food products they were familiar with, but availability was erratic, so buying in quantity was common. For those who had experienced the previous decades, this was a time when the different expatriate communities began to segregate themselves, trying to recreate a sense of home and the familiar. Community schools, cultural clubs, and faith groups expanded to support the expatriate groups. The Emiratis became more involved with their growing responsibilities, while continuing with their traditional family and majlis gatherings. For newcomers, the city felt intimate and welcoming, with a diversity of people and a sense of affluence and generosity.

Oil executives, who had large villas and generous entertainment budgets, threw lavish dinner parties, inviting diplomats, businessmen, and Emiratis. They sponsored cultural programmes, music, art, ballet, and cinema, in collaboration with country diplomatic missions. The Abu Dhabi chapter of Chaîne des Rôtisseurs, an international gastronomic society, was founded in 1981, bringing together those who appreciated wine, cuisine, and fine dining. Arab contractors were an anchor of the economy, employing a large workforce, establishing residential compounds to accommodate them, and setting up the supply chain for foodstuffs, leisure, and recreation. With Abu Dhabi's archipelago of islands, activities like boating, fishing, swimming, water-skiing, and camping were favourite pastimes for many families.

Towards the end of the decade, as the Iran-Iraq War ended, the economy picked up with increased liquidity and expanding businesses. More reconstruction was on the horizon as the government drew up plans for rebuilding many of the commercial and residential concrete buildings that had been slapped together quickly in the previous decade. For Abu Dhabi, government spending fuelled the economy and the late 1980s ushered in another cycle. With a vibrant social and business life, the city came into its own in this decade.

AHMED AL BAWARDI

ENTREPRENEUR
◊
UAE

Early one December morning, in the midst of hunting season, I set out to meet Ahmed and his friends in the Sweihan desert. Daily falcon training during the season is important to keep the falcons in shape. Ahmed's bird, a *sakr* falcon about 50 centimetres high, speckled brown, with sharp talons, stands hooded on a wooden perch. The early morning mist hangs low, hugging the red sand dunes. Before the training begins we gather around a crackling wood fire to prepare breakfast. One of the men heats the water while another whisks a saffron yellow batter. The light breakfast of *chai karak* (sweet milk tea) infused with saffron threads and *chbaab* (Emirati pancakes) drizzled with date molasses gives the men just the right amount of energy for the training session.

With breakfast complete, Ahmed gently transfers his falcon from its perch onto his gloved wrist, stroking her breast and softly murmuring her name, the affection between the two palpable. Ahmed removes the bird's hood, revealing its piercing round eyes, like shiny black marbles. The bird bolts skyward in search of prey. In the distance, one of the men whirls a feathered, baited lure, and yanks it away as the bird dives for it. The falcon reels and dives in again, and once more, the lure is snatched away. Then, a pigeon with clipped wings is released. The falcon bolts at lightning speed, its appetite sufficiently whetted by the lure, and closes in from behind for the kill. Ahmed joins his falcon and quickly covers the quarry, offering the falcon just enough meat to reward her. He takes a drink of water and shoots a thin stream into the falcon's open beak, repeating a few times until her thirst is quenched.

Ahmed was introduced to falconry and nature at a young age: 'I started to go on hunting trips with Sheikh Zayed when I was three years old. Sheikh Zayed had a vast knowledge of nature and an intuitive understanding of falcons and the prey. He taught us to train and care for our falcons, to be patient, and to show compassion in the hunt'. Arabs have hunted with falcons for thousands of years in an unbroken tradition passed down across generations. This tradition evolved from their deep understanding of the desert and its wildlife, and their respect for the nobility and bravery of falcons.

Ahmed also loved to visit his grandmother, who preferred tending to her camels and salukis in the Al Ain desert to the comforts of her home in the city. He recalls, 'Everything I learned from my grandmother played a big role in who I am today. I watched the camels follow her everywhere in the desert. She could name every plant we walked past and knew every wind that blew by'. He continued to nurture his love for nature, even as he shuttled between east and west.

Ahmed spent his early years in San Antonio, Texas, where his father was sent by the military for training, and then in Washington, D.C., but there were frequent trips back home to Abu Dhabi. While away from the United Arab Emirates, his parents ensured he wouldn't forget his roots by cooking Emirati food and teaching him to speak Arabic. He explains, 'My parents are very traditional, and they taught us the Bedouin ways of being close to nature, loyal, and hospitable'.

Since moving to Abu Dhabi, I have been intrigued by the simplicity of desert life and the clarity it affords those who choose to dwell in it. 'The beauty of a culture like ours is that it is humbling and close to the ground. You always come back to who you are, no matter how far away you go', Ahmed remarks. For him, maintaining his Bedouin culture, as he hunts for innovative ideas in New York, San Francisco, and Los Angeles, is about being part of a progressive nomadic culture. Ahmed refers to this as 'the neo-tribe — connoisseurs of nature — global nomads connected by a love for wildlife and sun-touched food'. Ahmed appreciates the mystical nature of the East, which he feels is reflected in certain ingredients used regionally, such as saffron, rose water, and *za'atar*. 'They feed the soul', he tells me.

I am part of the neo-tribe—
global nomads connected by a love for wildlife and sun-touched food.

AHMED

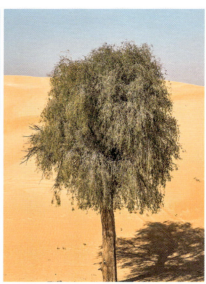

CHBAAB
Emirati Pancakes

Pancakes are one of mankind's oldest prepared foods, which is why there is some version of them in most cuisines around the world. The first iteration probably began with wild grains pulverised between heavy stones, then mixed with water to make a paste before cooking on greased rocks over an open fire. These quick-cooking staples (can we consider them Paleolithic fast food?) have evolved into a myriad of forms, such as the delicate French crepes, sour Ethiopian *injera*, chewy Japanese *okonomiyaki*, fluffy American flapjacks, crispy Indian *dosa*, and Russian blini, to name a few. Around the world, they are served at different times of the day. Start the day with an American breakfast of a short stack with a pat of butter melting under a flow of maple syrup, enjoy a snack of French crepes filled with Nutella and bananas, or for *kvedlsmat*, evening food, in the Scandanavian tradition, top them with lingonberries, fruit compote, or a sprinkling of sugar. A pancake can be a lens through which to view the world, and with that we invite you to savour the Emirati *chbaab* and a day in the desert.

AHMED *Chbaab is our pancake, spiced with cardamom and saffron, which gives it a golden colour. It can be made thin like a crepe or thick like an American pancake. I prefer the thinner batter, which brings out the artist in me and allows me to create abstract shapes on the griddle instead of the conventional round chbaab. This is my favourite breakfast before setting off for a morning in the desert. The batter is prepared at the farmhouse and we then make the chbaab fresh at the campsite over a fire on the multipurpose metal disk known as a tabi. The chbaab can be eaten sweet with honey and date molasses or savoury with cheese. It is also one of the staples at* suhoor, *the meal before dawn during the fasting month of Ramadan.*

MAKES 8 TO 10

- **150 g (1 c)** all-purpose flour
- **1 tbsp** granulated sugar
- **½ tsp** yeast
- **½ tsp** baking powder
- **¼ tsp** salt
- **½ tsp** ground cardamom
- **1 egg**, lightly beaten
- **240 ml (1 c)** milk
- **1 tbsp** cooking oil
- **Pinch** of saffron
- Butter or ghee

Mix the flour, sugar, yeast, baking powder, salt, and cardamom in a small bowl. Whisk the egg, milk, oil, and saffron in a medium bowl. Whisk the dry ingredients into the milk mixture just until moistened. For a thinner pancake, add more milk. Cover with plastic wrap and keep in a warm place away from drafts for 30 to 45 minutes.

Heat a griddle or large skillet over medium-high heat. Add 1 tablespoon of butter or ghee and distribute it as it melts. Pour about 60 millilitres (¼ cup) of batter onto the griddle for each pancake. Cook until bubbles form and a few have burst, about 1 to 2 minutes. Flip with a thin spatula and let the other side brown for another 1 to 2 minutes. Repeat for all of the batter.

Serve hot with honey, date molasses, brown sugar, or cheese.

CHAI KARAK
Cardamom Milk Tea

Chai karak has gained popularity in the *Khaleej* (Arabian Peninsula) recently, with several drive-through cafés and vending machines along the Abu Dhabi-Dubai highway offering this spiced tea. Karak is also a common morning drink at the workplace. Its humble origins can be traced to South Asia, where workers coming to the Gulf brought their love for strong, milky, sweet tea. The main difference between the chai karak in the Gulf and masala tea in South Asia is that the Khaleeji variation uses only one spice, cardamom, and sometimes sprigs of saffron for a special touch. Masala tea, as the name implies, is a mixture of spices such as ginger, cloves, cardamom, and peppercorns.

AHMED *Chai karak is my favourite morning drink before setting out on a hunt. It gives me warmth and energy, and the fragrant flavours linger well after the first cup. It is easy to prepare and quite satiating when served with* chbaab *(Emirati pancakes) for breakfast.*

SERVES 4 TO 6

- **700 ml (3 c)** hot water
- **6** cardamom pods, crushed
- **3–4 tsp** loose-leaf black tea
- **180 ml (¾ c)** evaporated milk
- **2 tbsp** granulated sugar, to taste
- **Pinch** of saffron

Combine the water, cardamom pods, and loose-leaf tea in a medium saucepan. If using teabags, discard the bag and use the loose tea.

Allow the mixture to boil on high heat for 5 to 8 minutes or until aromatic, stirring regularly. Turn the heat down to medium and add milk and sugar to taste. Increase the amount of milk for a creamier tea. Stir the chai karak until heated thoroughly but don't let the milk boil. Remove from the heat, cover it and let it steep for 5 minutes. Strain the chai karak into a thermal carafe or teapot. As an option, add a few sprigs of saffron either to the carafe/teapot or the tea glasses.

Serve hot in small tea glasses or teacups.

PAULA AL ASKARI

HOSTESS EXTRAORDINAIRE
◊
LEBANON / US

Despite having known Paula for two decades, I still marvel at the environment she has created in her home each time I visit. Crossing her threshold is like entering a world that is part Venetian *Settecento*, part Ottoman luxe — a rich mélange of dazzling patterns, luxurious textures, and enticing perfumes, stimulating all the senses. It was dubbed 'Palazzo Paula' by my friend, Derek Moore, an architect and art historian, when he first visited in 2007, in homage to a lost world of East-West syncretism. Imagine floating in on a gondola on the Grand Canal and ascending to her *piano nobile* in candlelight. Lofted amongst the fluttering cherubim and saints of Paula's oil paintings, and the cavaliers and ladies of her tapestries, complemented by gilded furnishings in the Baroque style, one soon realises the décor is much more varied and layered than that of *La Serenissima* — although that moniker suits our hostess. One is tugged to the East, to a land enriched by finely woven fabrics, rich carpets, silks, brocades, and burnished woods found in the grand houses of Damascus merchants in a time now lost.

I ask Paula how she assembled this profusion of objects into such a warm and welcoming home. She vividly recounts her first impressions of a city she now fondly calls home: 'I arrived in Abu Dhabi in 1985 from Paris, where I lived in the 7th arrondissement, the antique quarter. I remember looking out my window and seeing a "greige" sky, the colour of the desert. Many areas were not paved yet. I would step out of the car into a pile of sand. I thought, how am I going to live here?' Her sensitivity to colour led her to create a domestic environment that would speak to her many senses and balance what the external elements could not offer at the time. It was not unusual for a summer holiday in Istanbul, London, or Peru to result in a container full of antiques destined for Abu Dhabi. 'The metamorphosis of my home happened organically. With my impulsive desire to collect, my passion to combine pieces in unexpected ways, and to entertain, I created what you see around us today', Paula explains as she gestures to the seventeenth-century Flemish tapestries in the living room, the array of Turkmen, Uzbek, and Moroccan coats in the dining room, and the eighteenth-century Japanese porcelain vases in the foyer.

Paula presides with radiant beauty on the stage she has created, inviting friends and family to partake in carefully curated feasts and gatherings. Resplendent in an antique kaftan chosen for the occasion, Paula greets her guests and ushers them into her salon. She sets the scene in motion. She ignites the ceremonies, fires the conversation with challenging queries, and has a penchant for penetrating aperçus. Hold your own, if you can. 'The richness of Abu Dhabi is the people from all over the world. Sometimes we are ten different nationalities at the dinner table speaking in four different languages on a wide range of topics. Perhaps I am channelling an eighteenth-century French salon', Paula muses.

The pièce de résistance on this stage is the meal itself, prepared with the same masterly bravura as the surroundings. 'I come up with menus that are a fusion of flavours with unexpected combinations, to reflect my sensibilities', Paula tells me. A product of different influences and cultures, Paula adds her own verve and flare to a rich selection of dishes prepared for her guests. Beyond the table setting of exotic china, iridescent glassware and antique textiles, each course — the *amuse-bouches*, the sensuous mains, the fragrant sides, and delectable desserts — takes you to a new place. I invite you to recreate some of these culinary treasures for your holiday festivities. Enjoy the blend of sweet and savoury, and delight in the complementary colours.

Perhaps I am channelling an eighteenth-century French salon.

PAULA

FENNEL, BEETROOT, AND ORANGE SALAD
with Cumin Dressing

—
SERVES
6 TO 8
—

PAULA *This salad is visually as pleasing as it tastes. The festive colours make it perfect for Christmas dinner. The dressing brings unusual flavours together and is inspired by my love for Moroccan cuisine. It is important to select beetroots and oranges that have similar sizes so they can be more beautifully layered.*

SALAD

3 large beetroots

Coarse salt

3 large oranges

3 large fennel bulbs

30 g (¼ c) dried cranberries

65 g (½ c) pecans, whole

DRESSING

1½ **tbsp** walnut oil

1½ **tbsp** hazelnut oil

3 **tbsp** olive oil

3 **tbsp** balsamic vinegar

2 **tsp** Dijon mustard

1 **tsp** orange zest

½ **tsp** cumin

½ **tsp** coriander powder

½ **tsp** cayenne pepper

Salt and black pepper, to taste

Preheat the oven to 200°C (400°F).

Sprinkle each beetroot with the salt and wrap individually in aluminium foil. Bake for 1½ to 2 hours, until tender when pierced with a fork. Test them periodically. Unwrap and set them aside to cool.

Measure the dressing ingredients into a jar with a tight-fitting lid. Shake well to combine and chill until ready to use.

Peel the oranges and remove as much of the white thread-like material as possible. Slice them into 1-centimetre (½-inch) thick circles, discarding the small circles. Peel the beetroot and slice into 1-centimetre (½-inch) thick circles, discarding the small end pieces. If the beetroots are bigger than the oranges, use a round cookie cutter to make them a similar size. Remove the outer leaves of the fennel and slice thin.

When ready to serve, arrange the beetroot and orange circles in alternating layers on a large, round serving platter. Pile the fennel in the centre and sprinkle with dried cranberries. Decorate with the whole pecans.

Lightly drizzle the dressing over the salad and serve the extra dressing on the side.

SPICED SWEET POTATOES WITH MARSHMALLOWS

Ancient Egyptians were the first to savour the gooey marshmallow, derived from the sap of the marsh dwelling mallow plant. It was used for medicinal purposes and mixed with nuts and honey as an offering to royalty and the gods. In the nineteenth century, French confectioners whipped the mallow sap with egg whites and corn syrup to create the marshmallow. The recipe now uses gelatine instead of mallow and the time-consuming manual production process has given way to an automated process that produces the shape we are familiar with today.

The marshmallow confection was introduced to the United States in the early twentieth century and it soon became very trendy, inspiring sweet treats like moon pies and marshmallow cream. Housewives were encouraged to become 'modern' and substitute the time-saving marshmallow for meringue and whipped cream, both more labour intensive. The first recipe with sweet potatoes and marshmallows dates back to 1917 when Angelus Marshmallows, the first company to mass-produce marshmallows, commissioned a booklet with marshmallow-themed recipes to encourage housewives to embrace the candy in everyday meals. Sweet potatoes with marshmallows is one of the few recipes that survived and spread across the nation. Perhaps it is a way for adults to continue to eat marshmallows beyond their summer camp years.

PAULA *This is a deliciously decadent seasonal treat from the American South that I am probably genetically predisposed to, having been born in Vicksburg, Mississippi. I make it once a year at Christmas and indulge in the aroma of the holiday spices. I recently added the gingersnaps, which give the mashed potatoes and gooey marshmallows a crunchy texture. I use the Indian sweet potatoes because they are not too fibrous and watery. When I can find it, I add a teaspoon of Marks & Spencer Mixed Spice blend.*

SERVES 8 TO 10

2 kg (4½ lb) sweet potatoes

8–10 gingersnap cookies

1 tbsp grated orange peel

55 g (2 oz) butter, melted, divided

50 g (¼ c) brown sugar, to taste

1 tsp ginger

2 tsp cinnamon

½ tsp cloves

½ tsp freshly grated nutmeg

½ tsp salt

140 g (5 oz) small marshmallows

Preheat the oven to 180°C (350°F).

Wash the potatoes, wrap each one in foil, and bake until done, about 1½ hours. While the potatoes are baking, break the gingersnaps in pieces and sauté in a small skillet with 1 tablespoon of the melted butter. Leave the oven on after the potatoes are baked.

Peel and mash the potatoes while warm, preferably with a hand masher. Drain off any excess liquid. In a large bowl, add the mashed potatoes, orange peel, the remaining melted butter, brown sugar, ginger, cinnamon, cloves, nutmeg, and salt. Mix well. Transfer to a 26 x 18-centimetre (11 x 7-inch) oven-proof dish and spread evenly.

Decorate the sweet potatoes with the marshmallows and cookie pieces. Bake for 20 minutes. Turn on the broiler for the last few minutes so the marshmallows are toasted.

HONEY-BASTED TURKEY
with Chestnut Stuffing

The roast turkey was first served in Victorian England on the aristocrats' tables, replacing roast beef and goose at Christmas. Contrary to popular belief, the Pilgrims did not eat turkey at their first feast of thanksgiving. However, once Lincoln declared Thanksgiving a national holiday in 1863 as a means of unity during the Civil War, turkey became popular, mainly because of its feast-worthy size.

SERVES 12 TO 14

PAULA — *I love the fusion of savoury and sweet flavours, so I glaze the turkey with a generous amount of honey. It is important to use premium quality honey, both for the taste and to get a beautiful golden brown finish.*

STUFFING

- **450 g (1 lb)** chestnuts, boiled and peeled
- **285 g (10 oz)** unsalted butter, divided
- **450 g (1 lb)** yellow onions, chopped
- **520 g (5 c)** breadcrumbs
- **2 tbsp** marjoram, dried
- **2 tbsp** sage, dried
- **2 tbsp** rosemary, chopped
- Salt and black pepper
- Chicken broth

TURKEY

- **10 kg (22 lb)** turkey, thawed
- Salt and black pepper
- **170 g (6 oz)** melted butter
- **240 ml (1 c)** honey
- **255 g (9 oz)** potatoes, peeled and quartered

GRAVY

- Cornstarch
- **2 tsp** gravy browning

FOR THE STUFFING

Quarter the prepared chestnuts. In a large skillet, add 100 grams (3 ounces) of the butter and sauté the onions until golden. Stir in the remaining butter, chestnuts, breadcrumbs, marjoram, sage, and rosemary. Add salt and pepper to taste and stir until well combined. Add some broth to bind.

FOR THE TURKEY

Preheat the oven to 200°C (400°F). Remove the giblets and neck and set aside. Pat the turkey dry and rub the inside and outside with salt and pepper. Combine the butter and honey in a small saucepan over medium heat until the butter melts and the mixture is evenly blended.

Place the turkey on a wire rack in a large roasting pan, breast up, tucking the wingtips underneath the body. Fill the neck cavity with some of the stuffing and then pull any excess neck skin over the opening and tuck under the turkey. Fill the large cavity with the remaining stuffing and close the opening. Tie the legs together with kitchen twine. Baste generously with some of the honey mix. Scatter the giblets and potatoes around the turkey.

Roast the turkey uncovered for 30 minutes, basting two or three times with the honey mix. Reduce the temperature to 180°C (350°F) and continue roasting for 30 minutes, basting frequently. Cover the turkey tightly with a double layer of aluminium foil and roast for 4½ hours (depending on size), until the juices run clear. Regularly uncover the turkey and baste with the honey mix, rotating the pan as necessary so the turkey browns evenly. If needed, add 240 millilitres (1 cup) of broth to keep the pan juices from drying out. The turkey is done when an instant-read thermometer inserted in the thickest part of the thigh reads 83°C (180°F) or 74°C (165°F) when inserted into the stuffing or breast. Uncover for the last 15 minutes and baste again. Transfer to a serving platter, loosely tent with foil, and let it rest for 20 to 30 minutes.

FOR THE GRAVY

Pour the pan drippings, giblets, and potatoes into a saucepan, skimming and discarding most of the fat. Add 240 millilitres (1 cup) of water; bring to a boil and cook for 10 minutes. Remove the giblets but keep the potatoes and puree in a blender. Strain the gravy through a sieve. Add salt and pepper to taste. To thicken, add 1 to 2 tablespoons of cornstarch diluted in a small amount of cold water. Add the gravy browning and cook for 5 minutes, until thickened.

REEM
AL ORFALI

HIGHER
EDUCATION
◊
IRAQ / CANADA

Reem arrived in Abu Dhabi in 1982, a year after the start of the Iran-Iraq war, to join her fiancé, who was working in the oil sector. Their extended families could not travel from Iraq because of the war. Unlike the large, family-filled celebrations of Baghdad, only her mother, sister and mother-in-law attended Reem's *kateb el ketab* (marriage ceremony) at the Intercontinental Hotel. Although she was surrounded by many new friends, Reem longed for the celebration to have been in Baghdad, where she would be feted by her family and childhood friends. At that time, many friends of Reem's family were among the established Iraqi community in Abu Dhabi — prominent diplomats, lawyers, doctors, engineers, and educators who had come in the 1960s to help Sheikh Zayed bin Sultan Al Nahyan establish the new nation. This core group of friends helped ease her longing for home, and over the past thirty-five years they have become an extension of her family.

Reem grew up in a home that was open and welcoming to family and friends, with her mother's signature *klaicha* (Iraqi cookies) always ready to offer guests. She has tried to recreate that atmosphere in her apartment on Zayed the First Street — a setting vastly different from the topiary-lined mansions of Baghdad's Jadirya neighbourhood, where she grew up. The centrepiece of her living room, an oil painting by her aunt, Widad Al Orfali, featuring a cityscape of domes, arches, and minarets, helps Reem keep the memories of home alive. Widad, an accomplished artist, sometimes referred to as the Iraqi Gertrude Stein, opened the first privately owned gallery in Baghdad, and her home was a salon for artists, writers, and musicians. One evening in 2004, I met Widad, who was visiting from Iraq. We were treated to an evening of artistic and culinary talents, with Widad alternating between the *oud* (string instrument) and piano, and Reem surprising us by accompanying her on the *dunbak* (a percussion instrument). I felt I had been transported to Widad's mid-twentieth-century salon in Baghdad, with a sumptuous spread of authentic Iraqi dishes.

The Baghdad of the mid-twentieth century was a cosmopolitan city, with diverse ethnic and religious communities. There was a thriving civic and social life including museums, universities, concert halls, restaurants, and sports clubs. In 1948, Iraq was the first Arab country to grant women the right to vote and appointed the first Arab woman cabinet member in 1959. Reem's university-educated mother, who had a long professional career, encouraged her to study chemical engineering, which she did. Reem had hoped to participate in the growth of her country's oil sector, but the series of wars that began in 1981 made that an impossible dream. With limited opportunities for women in engineering in the early 1980s in Abu Dhabi, which is a stark contrast to today, Reem ended up with a long and fulfilling career in higher education. 'I feel sorry for what has happened to my country, to my city, and to my home. Even though I cannot go back now, Iraq is in my blood and will remain so', Reem says, with a pang of homesickness.

What better way to cure homesickness than with food? I sit with Reem at her dining table as she flips through her handwritten notebook, its dog-eared pages full of recipes from her mother and those she has collected from friends over the past thirty years — it's a diary of her life since she left Iraq. Next to it is a ghee-stained copy of Naziha Adib's cookbook in Arabic, the first contemporary Iraqi cookbook, published in the 1960s. 'She is the Julia Child of Iraqi cooking. Every Iraqi newly-wed has a copy and we studied it in home economics', Reem explains.

As a traditionalist, Reem draws inspiration from Iraq's rich culinary history, which started in the Fertile Crescent, where agriculture began. In fact, the first collection of recipes was discovered in southern

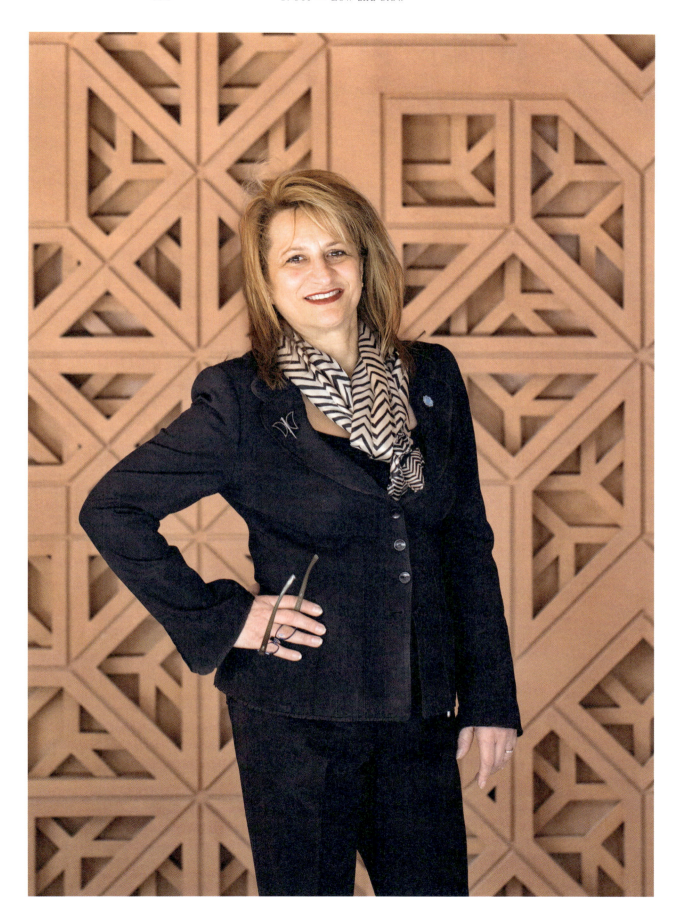

Mesopotamia on cuneiform tablets from around 1600 BC, making it the oldest known cookbook. The recipes included stews and cracked grains with herbs and spices and strong flavours, like many of Iraq's dishes today. Iraqis are veterans of wars. They have been conquered from east and west over the centuries while also expanding during the Abbasid Caliphate. 'The bright side of this history is that our cuisine has become a rich fusion of different culinary traditions', Reem remarks with irony. She shares the origins of the different foods that grace her table, a table that reflects Iraq's geographic location at the intersection of the Arabian Peninsula, Iran, the Levant, and Turkey: 'Our food tells the history of our country. We call stuffed vegetables *dolma* from the Turkish word for "to stuff", and we stuff everything, not just vine leaves! *Pardah pilau* is a spiced rice similar to Indian biryani, but sealed in filo, like a *pardah* (curtain). *Fesenjoon* (food of life) is a Persian dish with a pomegranate and walnut sauce. *Tashreeb*, bread soaked in meat broth, is an old desert food from the Arabian Peninsula that we enriched with Indian spices and *noomi Basra* (small dried limes). We drink from *glassat*, the Arabised plural of the English word "glass", picked up during the British rule'.

Though I've known Reem for over twenty years, she still chides me about our second encounter in 1994, when I visited her at home before our game of squash and walked in wearing my 'Free Kuwait' t-shirt. Though Reem was against Iraq's invasion of Kuwait, she was also against the ensuing war on her country. She nonetheless ignored the t-shirt and gave me the customary two kisses on the cheek. Having grown up in Kuwait, the Iraqi invasion of 1990 had devastated and changed the course of our lives. I had only recently left Kuwait, where the t-shirt was commonly worn, and had not considered the discomfort it could cause in another context. Reem and I ended up bonding over that incident and continued debating politics over many games of squash and elaborate Iraqi meals.

Standing in Reem's kitchen, I watch her meticulously knead and roll the klaicha dough, prepare the date filling, and steep the tea in a samovar, as many generations have done before. I realise that cooking is a refuge and extending hospitality to friends a salvation. 'Practising the social traditions I grew up with in Baghdad is an important way for me to stay connected to my culture and to pass it on to the next generation', Reem explains. Like the Sumerians who handed down their recipes 3,600 years ago, Reem will hand down her handwritten notebook to her son and daughter and with it, her many fond memories of home.

Iraqi cuisine is a rich fusion of different culinary traditions and tells the history of our country.

REEM

ISTIKAN CHAI
Iraqi Tea

Tea is near and dear to almost every culture in the world, and Iraq is no exception. Iraqi-style tea, also known as *istikan chai*, is found on the streets of Baghdad, in restaurants, cafés, villages, and homes worldwide. Iraqis love their tea year-round and sip it from *istikans*, small clear glasses that are cinched in at the waist. It is said that istikan is derived from the days when the British occupied Iraq and would ask for the 'East tea can', referring to a brand of tea imported from the East (India and Sri Lanka). Iraqi tea preparation is similar to that of Turkish and Persian tea, most probably influenced by the Russian Empire in that it uses a samovar.

REEM *We love our tea and we love our sugar! Our chai is brewed with patience and warmth. I remember my parents' home in Baghdad, where the samovar was always boiling with a strong brew of tea, ready for friends, neighbours, and family who might stop by at any time. Nowadays, we don't seem to have the luxury of time so we take a shortcut and brew our tea directly on the flame, but always with loose tea leaves. No tea bags!*

SERVES 6 TO 8

2 tbsp loose black tea leaves

4 cardamom pods, crushed

700 ml (3 c) water

Granulated sugar to taste

WITH A SAMOVAR

Bring a large metal teapot or samovar full of water to a boil. In a smaller metal teapot that can fit on top of the larger teapot, add the tea leaves, cardamom pods, and 700 millilitres (3 cups) of water. Place the small teapot over the large teapot/samovar (with lid removed) and let it brew, covered, for 45 to 60 minutes, while the water in the large teapot continues to boil.

To serve the tea, place a teaspoon of sugar in each istikan. Pour some of the concentrated tea from the small teapot into each glass and then top up with boiling water from the large teapot/samovar. Alternatively, offer sugar on the side.

WITHOUT A SAMOVAR

For a quicker version, place the tea leaves, cardamom pods, and 700 millilitres (3 cups) of cold water in a teapot over medium heat. Bring the water to a slow simmer, being careful not to let the water boil, as it will make a bitter tea. Simmer for 7 to 10 minutes and remove from the heat. Serve in istikans with a teaspoon of sugar in each or to taste.

Serve the tea with *klaicha*, Iraqi date cookies.

TATAR KULAGHI
Meat Dumplings with Yogurt Sauce

The ubiquitous dumpling may be considered the universal comfort food, satisfying the primordial desire for a bit of ground meat wrapped and cooked in a layer of dough. The road to the origins of the dumpling tends to lead to China, but dumplings can now be found in every corner of the globe. From Chinese *guo tie*, Japanese *giyoza*, Korean *mandu* to Indian *samosa*, Polish *pierogi*, Swedish *pitepalts*, Italian *ravioli*, and Turkish *manti*, dumplings come in a variety of shapes, sizes, fillings, and cooking methods.

Tatar kulaghi, meaning 'ear of the Tatar', is a variation on the Turkish manti. This dish may be the only favourable remnant from the Tatar's brutal siege and destruction of Baghdad in 1258, then the capital of the Abbasid Caliphate of Islam. Setting aside the political history of how these dumplings came across the Asian steppes, to this day they remain a staple in many Turkish, Armenian, Afghan, Kurdish, and Iraqi homes.

MAKES
35 TO 45

DOUGH

300 g (2 c) all-purpose flour

1 tsp salt

1 egg

FILLING

1 tbsp cooking oil

110 g (4 oz) onion, chopped

450 g (1 lb) finely minced beef

2 tsp seven spices

1 tsp salt

1 tsp black pepper

SAUCE

570 g (2 c) plain yogurt

1–2 cloves garlic, crushed

Salt and black pepper, to taste

GARNISH

1 tbsp sumac

1 tbsp dried mint

3 tbsp cooking oil

1 tsp red chili flakes, to taste

REEM *Tatar kulaghi is a popular dish in Baghdad, and very much a part of the Ottoman influence on our cuisine. These dumplings are delicious and best made at home. It is said that every mother's son has an opinion about who makes the best Tatar kulaghi and my son is no exception. The dough is easy to make, and rolling, cutting, filling, and shaping the dumplings is a labour of love I enjoy. The dumplings can be prepared ahead of time and frozen, so I make them in large batches. The yogurt sauce is quick and presents beautifully with the garnish for an impromptu meal.*

FOR THE DOUGH

Mix the flour, salt, and egg in a large bowl. Gradually mix in 120 millilitres (½ cup) of water or just enough for the dough to come together. Cover and set aside while making the filling.

FOR THE FILLING

Add the oil and chopped onions to a medium saucepan and sauté for 5 minutes, until the onions are translucent. Add the minced beef and stir while cooking to break the meat into small pebbles. Sprinkle in the seven spices, salt, and pepper and continue to stir for 15 to 20 minutes, until the meat is cooked.

Roll out the dough on a floured surface until it is very thin; cut into 4-centimetre (1½-inch) squares, or larger for bigger dumplings. Place a teaspoon of filling in each square and fold one corner over the filling to make a triangle, pressing the edges to seal. Twist the two tips of the triangle together to make an 'ear' shape. Repeat for the remaining dough. At this stage the dumplings can be frozen or refrigerated.

Bring a large pot of water and a pinch of salt to a boil. Carefully add the dumplings and cook for 5 to 8 minutes, until al dente. Drain well and place the dumplings on a serving plate.

Mix the yogurt with the garlic and season to taste; spoon over the dumplings. Sprinkle with sumac and dried mint. Heat the cooking oil with the red chili flakes and drizzle on top just before serving.

KLAICHAT TAMUR
Iraqi Date Cookies

Across the Arab world, people of all faiths prepare a version of these elegant pastries filled with dates or nuts. The aroma of freshly baked *kahk* in Egypt, *ma'amoul* in Syria, Lebanon or Palestine, and *klaicha* in Iraq signals a festive holiday. Most homes will have a freshly prepared batch of pastries to offer their guests with a strong cup of tea or coffee. Visiting is customary for religious holidays such as Easter and Eid, births, weddings, or recovery from an illness—all of which call for offering a variety of sweets, preferably homemade.

REEM *Klaicha are considered the national cookie of Iraq. They can be filled with dates or walnuts, mixed with cheese or simply plain. The plain klaicha are called* khufaifiya *and usually made with leftover cookie dough. The most popular klaicha are the ones filled with dates* (klaichat tamur), *from the rich palm groves of Iraq. Every Iraqi family makes their klaicha in different shapes and sizes. Following my mother's example, I prepare mine in a 'micro' version, which requires patience. My daughter, with her delicate touch, completes the cookies by dotting them with* habbat baraka *(nigella seeds), meaning seeds of blessings. Traditionally we make this klaicha for Eid, and refer to it as klaichat al Eid, but I make them year-round to share with family and friends.*

MAKES 5 TO 6 DOZEN

FILLING

- **450 g (1 lb)** dates, pitted
- **28 g (1 oz)** butter
- **½ tsp** cardamom
- **¼ tsp** cinnamon

DOUGH

- **450 g (3 c)** all-purpose flour or combination with whole wheat
- **225 g (8 oz)** butter or vegetable ghee
- **180 ml (¾ c)** low-fat milk, or more as needed
- **1 tbsp** baking powder
- **⅛ tsp** salt
- **1 tsp** nigella seeds

- **1 egg**, lightly beaten
- Sesame or nigella seeds

FOR THE FILLING

Place the pitted dates and butter in a skillet and sprinkle with the cardamom and cinnamon. Stir the mixture over medium heat until it comes together like a paste. Set it aside to cool.

Flatten a handful of date paste and then roll it to make a long cord-like shape that is about 0.5 centimetre (¼ inch) thick and approximately 20 centimetres (8 inches) long. Continue for all the date paste. The date cords do not need to be perfectly smooth, as the dough will be rolled around them.

FOR THE DOUGH

Preheat the oven to 180°C (350°F).

Mix the flour, baking powder, salt, and nigella seeds in a large bowl or food processor. Cut or pulse the butter or ghee into the flour until it resembles coarse crumbs. Gradually add the milk and knead until the dough is smooth and well combined. Cover and let rest for 30 minutes.

Working on a floured surface, roll one-third of the dough into a 0.5-centimetre (¼-inch) thick rectangle. Place a date cord along the long edge of the dough. Using a non-serrated knife, lift the dough over the date cord. Roll the dough around the cord one and a half times. Cut along the side of the dough/date roll to detach it from the rest of the dough. Using both hands, roll the dough/date roll on the work surface to firmly attach the filling to the dough. *[For a smaller cookie, continue to roll the dough/date roll by hand to double its length and make it thinner.]* Cut into 1-centimetre (½-inch) pieces and transfer to a greased and floured baking tray. Repeat for the remaining dough and date paste.

Brush the tops of the cookies with the egg. Sprinkle with nigella or sesame seeds. Bake for 10 minutes or until golden, being careful not to over-bake, as the cookies will harden. Let the cookies cool on the baking tray. They can be stored in an airtight container for up to ten days or frozen in plastic bags.

NADIA SEHWEIL AND MIRA NAAMAN

BODYTREE
◊
PALESTINE / US

NECTAR
◊
LEBANON / CANADA

When Nadia admits to me that she was not always a health nut, I find it difficult to imagine, because since meeting her in 2002, when she returned from college, she has always been health conscious. She grew up in Abu Dhabi in the 1980s, when a trip to the 'health club' meant, for most, lying by the pool. As a 'third culture kid', Nadia describes her memory of that period: 'I think I was a product of Abu Dhabi at the time. Life was initially hard but became easier over the years as my father built his business. I was raised in a comfortable and mostly sheltered environment thanks to my parents' sacrifice, but with a strong awareness of our roots and the realities of the world'.

Nadia's family moved to Abu Dhabi in the late 1970s, when her father came to work in the burgeoning oil industry. She went to college in Montreal and heeded her father's advice to major in business, although it was not her first love. Returning to Abu Dhabi after college was not her preference either. She wanted to explore the United States, but her mother's cancer diagnosis and treatment beckoned her home. 'It was a period when I was feeling a bit insecure and realising that my parents are not invincible. I decided to come home for one year, with no idea what I wanted to do.' She was, however, open to learning about the family business and joined the health and safety division of her father's company. She didn't find the oil industry fulfilling, but in the process discovered a discipline she was passionate about and established the environmental consultancy division at the company. After seeing that through, she felt she wanted to move onto something more personally fulfilling that would ultimately give something back to the community.

Inspired by her mother, who had embraced a holistic lifestyle after her cancer treatment, Nadia also started Pilates. Her mother had become a Pilates and yoga instructor and began to share the practice with family and friends. In 2007, they decided to move forward with their dream of having an integrated wellness studio. At that time, the real estate market was at its peak, so they rented a couple of small rooms in a villa to get started. Nadia's mother taught yoga and Pilates classes and Nadia worked the reception desk and managed the business, while training for her teaching certification. Their business grew organically as the city grew and people became increasingly concerned with incorporating fitness into their lives. In 2012, Bodytree moved to an unassuming villa in the Karama neighbourhood. The studio now includes Nectar, a juice bar run by Nadia's friend Mira, and has become a household name in the capital for anyone seeking a holistic lifestyle.

Mira, still in her yoga gear, meets me at Nectar and excitedly offers me her latest creation, a turmeric latte with organic coconut milk. The hint of black pepper accentuates the spices and 'enhances turmeric's health benefits exponentially', Mira explains. It tastes warm, slightly earthy, sweet, and savoury all at the same time. Next up is Nectars' double-chocolate sweet potato brownie: a moist, fudgy, chocolaty, grain-free vegan treat, made from dates and a surprising mix of sweet potato and nut flours to create an unbelievably tasty and guilt-free dessert. Her positivity is infectious, and while she juggles a young family with three children (including a set of twins) and the business, it's evident she loves what she does.

Mira's family emigrated to Canada in 1982 during the Lebanese civil war. She quickly assimilated and embraced her new home, adopting the Canadian philosophy of being environmentally friendly, socially aware, kind, and conscious, while staying connected to her Arab culture through her mother's cooking. The family then moved to southern France, where the French love of food ignited her appetite, not only for eating but also for cooking. She still considers France a large part of

her identity and an important layer of her food passion. At university in Boston, she recalls being the student with refined eating habits: 'I would go to the cafeteria and make myself a fantastic salad with a balsamic vinaigrette, which was not common at the time. I was lucky to have a kitchenette in my freshman dorm and enjoyed cooking for my friends. People who love to cook love to feed'.

With her international relations degree in hand, Mira moved to Washington, D.C., only to realise that while she loved learning about world relations and cultures, she didn't have the passion to work in that field. To her parents' surprise, she switched paths and went to culinary school, and this is where Mira found her calling. Ultimately becoming a pastry chef, she worked in Washington, D.C., London, and Paris with Michelin star chefs until her work permit expired, whereupon she returned to Abu Dhabi, where her parents still lived. While exploring the culinary scene in the city, she landed in the food and beverage unit of the FIFA Club World Cup local organising team, orchestrating the event's food concessions and VIP hospitality. As she recalls, 'It was a fascinating experience and still involved food, but it was removed from the creative part I so missed'.

So, that summer of 2012 when Nadia returned from Los Angeles, ready to open at the new premises of Bodytree, Mira

> We are excited to continue to grow and evolve with the city.
> NADIA

was the first person she called. Mira recalls, 'Nadia said, "This juice concept is blowing up in California and I want you to start one for us at Bodytree". I said, "Babe, I am a pastry chef! I have no concept of juicing"'. But Nadia wouldn't take no for an answer. Mira spent the next month experimenting with juice and smoothie creations until she found her signature style. She scoured the markets for the freshest produce, learned about the logistics of running a business, and built the juice bar concept from scratch. Once she had perfected her juice and smoothie recipes, she was ready to open Nectar. The juice bar gradually grew, more healthy snacks were added, and they made more of their own products, such as nut milk. Mira tells me, 'Nadia would go to California in the summer and come back with inspirations. I would play, play, play in the kitchen and send her samples to try. We'd go back and forth until we got it just right'.

The community space that Nadia and her mother nurtured has continued to grow, with Mira's nutritious creations an integral part. Nadia reflects, 'Abu Dhabi has changed by leaps and bounds, even in the past ten years. A healthy, mindful, and aware lifestyle is becoming more entrenched in the varied cultures that live in Abu Dhabi and we are excited to continue to grow and evolve with the city'.

> People who love to cook love to feed.
> MIRA

TRIO OF SMOOTHIES

NADIA — *Amongst the many healthy, fresh juices and smoothies that Mira concocts, one of my all-time favourites is the smoothie based on* chai karak, *the sugary sweet, Emirati cardamom milk tea. I love the delicious tea but can't indulge in all the refined sugar and dairy. I love Mira's version, which I can drink guilt free, sweetened with dates and spiced with cardamom and ginger. With so many juicers and blenders on the market, it's easy to make your own healthy juices and smoothies to be enjoyed at home or on the go.*

SERVES 4

---

240 ml (1 c) steeped black tea, chilled
240 ml (1 c) almond milk
4 dates, chopped
1 tsp ground cardamom
1 tsp ground ginger
1 tsp cinnamon
5–6 ice cubes

HEALTHY CHAI KARAK SMOOTHIE

MIRA — *Everyone loves a classic. Sometimes, favourite family recipes are heavy and unhealthy, and may be loaded with sugar. Don't give up on a favourite, reinvent it! This delicious frothy, spiced, chai karak smoothie embodies classic flavours with contemporary healthy living and eating.*

Combine all of the ingredients in a blender. Serve immediately in tall glasses.

---

1 kg (2¼ lb) Golden Delicious apples
110 g (4 oz) spinach
140 g (5 oz) pineapple
1 ripe avocado, peeled and pitted
1-2 tbsp spirulina (optional)
5–6 ice cubes

LEAN GREEN DETOXIFYING MACHINE

MIRA — *On some days, it's hard to eat a balanced diet. This detoxifying green juice is the perfect balance of fruit and vegetables and will ensure you get your daily greens. You can add spirulina, a natural algae powder high in protein and anti-oxidants.*

Process the apples, spinach, and pineapple in a juicer. Pour the juice into a blender, along with the avocado, spirulina, and ice cubes. Blend until smooth. Serve in tall glasses and garnish each with a slice of apple.

---

85 g (3 oz) blueberries
85 g (3 oz) blackberries
240 ml (1 c) orange juice
Zest of 1 orange
1 banana
240 g (1 c) organic yogurt
2 tsp maqui berry powder
5–6 ice cubes

MORNING MAQUI BERRY BLAST

MIRA — *You may have heard about superfoods and wondered what they are. 'Superfood' is a term used to describe many foods you are already familiar with, such as blueberries, broccoli, and kale, because they are nutritious and have many health benefits. This morning smoothie is the perfect way to incorporate tasty, healthy fruit into your diet. The tart, fruity flavour of maqui berry powder, also rich in anti-oxidants, will be a staple in your kitchen with this sumptuous smoothie.*

Combine all of the ingredients in a blender on high speed. Serve immediately in tall glasses.

TAHINI RAW POWERBITES

Tahini, made from sesame seeds, is used across the Arab world, eastern Mediterranean, and is even found in Chinese and Southeast Asian cuisine. As a good source of copper, manganese, and the amino acid methionine, tahini has great nutritional value. It is also a good source of omega-3 and omega-6 fatty acids, calcium, and protein, making it a popular element of vegetarian and vegan diets. Compared to peanut butter, it has more fibre and calcium and less sugar and saturated fats.

NADIA *When Mira first tested these tahini raw powerbites on me, I had an immediate association with halva, a traditional sweet in our region, known for its many nutritious benefits, especially for nursing mothers. Tahini, the main ingredient in halva and these powerbites, is used for sweet and savoury dishes, and is a comforting food element in the Arab world. This healthy, tasty snack incorporates a basic ingredient of our cuisine in a non-traditional way.*

MAKES 12 TO 14

50 g (½ c) ground almonds

50 g (½ c) gluten-free rolled oats

70 g (½ c) raw cashews

28 g (1 oz) dates, pitted

20 g (⅓ c) unsweetened shredded coconut

1 tsp vanilla

1 tsp cinnamon

Pinch of sea salt

60 ml (¼ c) tahini

2 tbsp raw honey

Mix the ground almonds, oats, cashews, and dates in a food processor on medium speed until crumbly, being careful not to over-blend. Add the coconut, vanilla, cinnamon, sea salt, tahini, and honey. Mix on medium speed until the dough forms into a ball. Add water 1 tablespoon at a time if needed to bind the dough.

Roll into 2.5-centimetre (1-inch) balls and store in the refrigerator in an airtight container. They can also be frozen.

GLUTEN-FREE NUT AND GOJI MAPLE GRANOLA

MIRA *Granola is so versatile and much more than just a breakfast food. It's an unprocessed and authentic snack. It can be made in handy clusters that are perfect for when hunger strikes! Keep some in your bag, on the kitchen counter, or at the office. Here are a few tips for turning out a perfect batch of granola: If you prefer clusters of granola, lightly press down on the mixture when spreading it on the baking tray and don't stir it frequently while baking or when it comes out of the oven. It is important to bake it at a low temperature so the nuts don't burn. The other great thing about granola is how easily adaptable it is to substitutions. If you want to replace the pistachios with pepitas or cranberries for goji berries, go for it, but keep your ratio of wet to dry ingredients roughly the same. If you try a different sweetener, like agave or honey, keep in mind that they might be sweeter so you may need less. Enjoy my granola goodness but have fun adapting it to your own tastes.*

—
SERVES
4 TO 6
—

- **110 g (4 oz)** organic grass-fed butter
- **80 ml (⅓ c)** maple syrup
- **1 tbsp** cinnamon
- **1 tsp** vanilla
- **200 g (2 c)** jumbo rolled oats
- **100 g (1 c)** walnuts, chopped
- **100 g (1 c)** almonds, slivered
- **100 g (1 c)** pistachios, chopped
- **½ tsp** salt
- **100 g (1 c)** goji berries

Preheat the oven to 180°C (350°F) and line a baking tray with parchment paper.

Melt the butter in a saucepan over low heat. Stir in the maple syrup, cinnamon, and vanilla until well combined. Remove from the heat and allow to cool slightly.

Toss the oats, walnuts, almonds, pistachios, and salt in a large bowl until well combined. Pour the melted butter mix over the oats and nuts and stir until the dry ingredients are well coated. Spread the granola on the baking tray in an even layer. Bake for 40 to 45 minutes until golden, stirring occasionally so it cooks evenly. Stir more frequently for a flakier texture. Turn off the oven and leave the granola inside for 20 minutes.

Remove from the oven and leave to cool and crisp on the tray. Stir in the goji berries. Store in an airtight container for up to three weeks.

Serve with almond milk, yogurt, or fresh berries.

SALMA AL RIYAMI AND AMIN KARIM

ORTHODONTIST ◊ UAE

DENTAL SURGEON ◊ UK

When I ask Salma and Amin what it was like growing up in Abu Dhabi in the 1980s, Salma laughs and says, 'Oh boy, are you ready for Amin's stories?' My interest piqued, I wait attentively as Amin settles into the red swivel chair. With boyish excitement, he begins to recount some of the shenanigans of his teenage years with a group of friends, who are still amongst his closest. 'I've known most of my friends since first grade. We hung out together after school and on weekends. I remember when we pooled our allowances to buy a dune buggy. We would take it into the desert and camp, sometimes as far as the Omani border. Eventually, we sold it, pooled more of our money, and bought a small fishing boat. The sea was our second home. We looked forward to the weekend; we would head to sea at sunrise and stay out well after dark. We didn't have radar or GPS, so we navigated by the moon and a few city lights. Sometimes huge sharks would pass under the boat!' After barbecuing their lunch on Saadiyat Island, but with plenty left in the coolers, Amin and his friends would return home and distribute the rest of the catch amongst their families and neighbours.

After completing his engineering studies in the United Kingdom, Amin's father arrived in Abu Dhabi in the late 1960s from Sudan to join his brother, who had a contracting business. Amin describes their neighbourhood: 'We lived in an area then known as the Maharba. The head of the Maharba tribe kept a few horses tied to the tree outside his home and we would take them for a bareback gallop around the neighbourhood. He also had a few salukis and a couple of camels. Coming back from school, there was always something going on with the animals and we would get right into the middle of it.'

There were also almost daily runs to Maharat Al Bahr in Bateen, a shop that specialised in fruit cocktail juices and sandwiches. Cocktail juices were the rage in Abu Dhabi then and can still be found on most street corners. They weren't just a simple mix of fruit juices, but rather elaborate concoctions. They came with chunks of fruit, crushed nuts, or whipped cream, and had names like 'Adnan Altilayani' (Adnan the Italian). Shawarma was king, along with other sandwiches: *kalawi ma' batata* (kidney with potatoes), hamburgers, hotdogs, and *keema* (minced beef). Another reason Amin and his friends frequented Maharat Al Bahr was the adjacent barber shop, Al Na'ama, and Nasser, its proprietor. Amin recounts, 'Nasser knew all the secrets in town. We would drive up after placing our juice order and ask him for the latest news. He always knew who was in town, who travelled to study, who was getting married, who was at the club, and would point out the cars with sheikhs also waiting for their juice order'. Satiated with information and food, the young men would set out to plan their next weekend's fishing trip.

I glance at Salma, who is grinning and enjoying her husband's stories as if hearing them for the first time. I ask her if growing up in Abu Dhabi was as adventuresome for her. 'Girls couldn't roam around as freely. We spent most of our free time with family. We loved to go to the old Central Market or eat out with our parents. Studying was a priority in our household, so that didn't leave us with much free time', Salma recalls. Salma's mother, originally from Oman, and her aunts were pioneering women in their fields and valued education. Her mother, a dentist, served in the United Arab Emirates Army and retired as a brigadier, the highest rank held by a woman. One aunt was the first Arab female ambassador to the United States, for the Sultanate of Oman, and her other aunt served as the Sultanate of Oman's representative to the United Nations, and is now posted in Germany. Following in their pioneering footsteps, Salma went to the United Kingdom in 1994 for her A levels and to pursue dentistry. She completed

her degrees at Bristol University and University College London, where she met Amin, who was finishing his degrees in dentistry and dental surgery.

Salma and Amin returned to Abu Dhabi in 2010 to start a family and pursue their careers. Their new home at Raha Beach, a Miami-style marina development, is now full of the sounds of their two young sons. Despite their frequent visits home while living in the United Kingdom, they have found significant changes. Gone are Maharat Al Bahr, the old Central Market, and the few restaurants they frequented. They now enjoy the diverse food offerings from restaurants serving Emirati food, gluten-free baked goods, vegan dishes, and many ethnic cuisines. Even the traditional family lunch at Amin's mother's home has become more diverse as cousins have married members of different nationalities. Alongside the traditional Sudanese *mullah* and *asida*, and the Ethiopian *zigni*, there are servings of Lebanese tabbouleh, Palestinian *fateh*, Thai noodles, ginger lemonade, and even the occasional roast turkey.

Amin and Salma are avid travellers and continue to bring home the cherished treats they came to love when they lived abroad. Rustling through the kitchen cupboard, Amin pulls out a bag of The Real McCoy's Ridge Cut Salt and Malt Vinegar crisps he brought back from a recent trip to the United Kingdom, where he maintains a dentistry practice. He insists I try them, so I can compare them to brands available locally. With their tangy flavour and crispy texture, I now understand the phrase, 'the real McCoy'. Next, he hands me a bottle of Thomas Henry Ginger Beer, another family favourite. Salma loves to stock up on artisanal chocolates when she travels and has a nice variety. She offers me one shaped like a cigar, something she brought back for Amin, a true cigar aficionado. As we sit around the kitchen counter, Amin introduces me to the world of cigar connoisseurship and his growing collection, and regales us with more stories from his youth. Hearing their stories, I realise that Amin's and Salma's memories of Abu Dhabi's earlier days exemplify the rapid changes that have taken place here, and the United Arab Emirates' increased interconnectedness with the world.

> The sea was our second home. We would head out at sunrise and return well after dark.
>
> AMIN

GINGER LEMONADE

As the saying goes, 'When life gives you lemons, make lemonade'. For many, lemonade symbolises an American childhood with the lemonade stand as an introduction to capitalism and entrepreneurship. However, lemonade is much older than America itself. It is believed to have originated in Egypt in the eleventh century as a lemon-based drink sweetened with sugar, known as *qatarmizat*. Lemons were indigenous to Asia but made their way to the Mediterranean coast. By the mid-1600s, the taste for lemonade spread to Europe, where it was sold on Parisian streets. It gained popularity in Victorian England during an alcohol abstinence movement. In the 1800s, lemonade arrived in America along with hundreds of thousands of European immigrants. The basic ingredients of lemonade — lemons, water, and sugar — remain the same, but some variations have developed, such as lemon soda, pink lemonade, and the addition of mint, lavender, or ginger.

SALMA *This lemonade recipe is my husband's favourite, and was given to me by his mother. The added kick of the ginger enhances the sweet and tart flavours of the lemonade. It's easy to make, refreshing in the Abu Dhabi heat, and a nice twist on traditional lemonade. You can also make this with lime juice or a combination of lemon and lime. Use the quantities as a guideline and adjust the sweetness to your taste.*

SERVES 4 TO 6

- **28 g (1 oz)** candied ginger
- **28 g (1 oz)** fresh ginger, grated
- **240 ml (1 c)** lemon juice
- **105 g (½ c)** granulated sugar, to taste
- **1 l (1 qt)** cold water
- **Handful** of ice cubes
- Fresh mint

Soak the candied ginger in a bowl with enough water to cover for 30 minutes; drain.

Place the candied ginger, fresh ginger, lemon juice, sugar, water, and ice in a blender and mix at high speed. Taste and add more sugar if desired. Strain and serve in tall glasses over ice with sprigs of mint.

A TRIO OF TARTINES

SALMA *I enjoy serving tartines (open-faced sandwiches) because they are versatile and attractive. Leftovers from a roast beef dinner are a wonderful base for other ingredients. Avocado are nutritious and on toast will even appeal to toddlers. Labneh, that staple of Levant cuisine, works perfectly with cucumber, mint, and other favourites from the area. Let your imagination run!*

—
SERVES 4 TO 6
—

ROAST BEEF

120 g (½ c) sour cream

2 tbsp prepared horseradish

Salt and black pepper

4 slices thick artisan bread

450 g (1 lb) roast beef, thinly sliced

Red onion, sliced in rounds

Cornichons, sliced

Watercress

AVOCADO TOAST

85 g (3 oz) soft goat cheese

3 ripe avocados

Salt and black pepper

½ tsp paprika

4 slices nut/seed bread

Olive oil

Pomegranate seeds

LABNEH

140 g (5 oz) labneh

1 tbsp dried mint

1 tbsp olive oil

Salt

4 slices rye bread

2 small cucumbers, thinly sliced

Za'atar

Fresh mint

Olives

ROAST BEEF WITH HORSERADISH AND WATERCRESS

Combine the sour cream and horseradish in a small bowl; season to taste with salt and pepper. Spread the sauce on each slice of bread. Place slices of beef on top and garnish with onions, cornichons, and watercress.

AVOCADO AND GOAT CHEESE TOAST

Mash the cheese and slice or mash the avocadoes; season with salt, pepper, and paprika. Lightly toast the bread. Spread the cheese on the bread and top with the avocado. Drizzle with some olive oil and garnish with pomegranate seeds.

LABNEH WITH MINT AND CUCUMBER

Combine the labneh, dried mint, olive oil, and salt in a small bowl. Spread the labneh on the bread and top with the cucumber rounds. Sprinkle with za'atar and garnish with fresh mint. Serve with a side of olives.

— 1990s —
LIFT THE LID

As Abu Dhabi enjoyed another up cycle in the economy at the end of the previous decade, regional political events inched even closer to home. On 2 August 1990, Saddam Hussein invaded Kuwait. This sent shock waves amongst the business and diplomatic communities, with some choosing to close and repatriate their employees and families. Oil prices spiked briefly at the onset of the invasion, then declined steadily until mid-decade. In 1991, the United Arab Emirates joined a thirty-four-nation armed coalition and sent troops to liberate Kuwait. It was a sombre time, with people fearfully huddling at home, gas masks and stockpiles of non-perishable food items by their sides.

When the Gulf War ended, neighbouring Dubai, with its port and duty-free zones at Jebel Ali and history of international trade, promoted itself as the logical place from which to direct the massive reconstruction efforts in Kuwait. The argument worked, and many companies established a presence in the duty-free zone, with Dubai reborn as a thriving hub for business, finance, and property development. Hotels, malls, golf clubs, museums, festivals, and international tournaments sprung up in the 1990s, providing business and leisure opportunities for Abu Dhabi residents. It was not uncommon to see a steady flow of cars on Wednesday evening heading to Dubai for the start of the weekend, and returning on Friday evening. The two-lane road connecting the two emirates had been upgraded to six lanes, brightly lit and with rest stops along the way, making for a relatively short two-hour drive on the new E-11 highway.

Oil prices picked up in the mid-1990s, as consumption increased due to the growth of the Asian tigers' and American economies. A portion of the revenues were channelled to expand the federal ministries and institutions. The country's provisional constitution was made permanent, with Abu Dhabi officially named the nation's capital. Government-led projects in Abu Dhabi continued, with emphasis on defence, which became a necessity after the Gulf War. Strategic programmes, such as the UAE Offset Program, created joint ventures in various sectors, bringing in more Western expatriates with expertise in areas such as defence, aviation, and the environment. Gradually, the lid was lifting on the country, as it forged deeper international connections. An American accent was becoming more common amongst English-speaking expatriates, as were American food products, cars, and celebrations. After it opened in Dubai in the late 1990s, a drive to Safeway became a regular trip to stock up on pecans, canned pumpkin and green chilies, and chewy caramel candy. This was the decade when Toys R Us, Hallmark, McDonald's, and Dunkin' Donuts also arrived in Abu Dhabi.

Abu Dhabi maintained its familiar, small-town feel as it continued to grow and welcome more newcomers. The community schools, the beach and sports clubs, ice rink, and business groups provided an opportunity for people from different cultures to mingle and learn about one another's customs and traditions. There were still no malls with multiplex cinemas and food courts—those would start opening in the 2000s. Entertaining at home or camping in the desert or on the beach were favourite pastimes. Government policies were generous. The workday ended in the early afternoon, providing a favourable work-life balance, with time to connect with family and friends. There wasn't much that wasn't available, so it was a comfortable life, to the point where many international companies ceased considering Abu Dhabi a hardship post.

RAMAN KHANNA

HOSPITALITY
◊
INDIA

It was the annual fundraising gala at Abu Dhabi's American Community School (ACS) and the ballroom buzzed with the five hundred parents, teachers, and their guests. Suddenly, the room fell silent as the auctioneer announced the most prized item on the list: a five-course gourmet dinner for fourteen, prepared at the winner's home by the executive chef at the Abu Dhabi Hilton and ACS parent, Raman Khanna. The bidding started at five thousand dirhams and tripled in a few seconds. This was a prize we aggressively bid for, as we all would have been proud to treat our friends to such an evening of gastronomy.

Cooking has been Raman's hobby for as long as he can remember. He had not considered becoming a professional chef until he was in college studying geography. 'As I learned about different countries, I realised that food is the key to understanding these cultures, so I decided to turn my hobby into a profession, and travel the world to cook', Raman recollects. After completing his studies in New Delhi, he enrolled in the Culinary Institute of America where he received his degree in culinary arts in 1989. This led to a fifteen-year career with Hilton International in New York, Toronto, and Abu Dhabi. As the executive chef at the Hilton Abu Dhabi, he was responsible for twelve outlets as well as catering for thousands at special events for the royal family and visiting heads of state. His calm and steady nature was ideally suited for such a demanding job. In 1999, Raman put Abu Dhabi on the culinary map when he won the trophy for the best culinary team at the Emirates Salon Culinaire, an honour previously held only by Dubai establishments.

Raman's extensive career has included a wide array of challenges. He has catered an international equestrian event for thousands of guests in the desert with just a week's notice, been part of the opening team for Abu Dhabi's seven-star Emirates Palace Hotel, led the development of five hotels in preparation for the Yas Marina Circuit Formula 1 inaugural race, and now oversees operations at the new presidential palace. Although his work now is more executive in nature, he admits he is happiest when he steps into the kitchen, dons his apron, and sharpens his knife. 'Cooking is my meditation', he admits. Raman's creations fuse ingredients, spices, and techniques to create unique dishes with complex flavours. He also likes to modify ethnic recipes to appeal to a cosmopolitan palate, while keeping their essence. The green prawn curry with fennel, a constant on the menu at Hemingway's in the Hilton Abu Dhabi, is one such recipe. When Raman introduced Vasco's, also at the Hilton, in 1999, it was the city's first fusion concept restaurant. Dishes with different influences, such as the Portuguese spiced hammour, were designed to appeal to the city's growing multicultural community.

Working together in my kitchen to prepare dal, we reflect on the changes in the city. I recall my first Thanksgiving in Abu Dhabi in 1993, when I attempted a pumpkin pie with fresh pumpkin, since canned was not available, only to end up with a runny filling and a soggy crust. Raman shares some of the challenges he had in the early days and what it was like to be part of a rapidly growing industry: 'Initially, the most important part of my job was planning. Many of the quality ingredients such as sushi-grade seafood, meat, and speciality vegetables were only delivered once a week from the wholesalers in Dubai. This meant that to vary the menu and satisfy the palates of different nationalities, I had to plan several weeks in advance.' Today, the local grocery stores and food markets carry products from around the world, reflecting the entire polyglot community. As a long-standing culinary force in Abu Dhabi's food culture, Raman continues to rethink the ordinary.

Food is
key to
understanding
cultures.

RAMAN

DUM KI DAL
Slow-Simmered Indian Lentils

In India, 'dal' refers to pulses, which include dry legumes that grow in a pod, such as beans, lentils, and peas. The term can also refer to a cooked dish that uses pulses. Indian pulses are available whole or split and with or without skin. Although *urad dal* is referred to as a lentil, it is actually a mung bean with a black skin and whitish interior. It is also known as black dal. It derives its strong, earthy flavour from the black skin and needs to be cooked for a long time.

RAMAN *Dum ki dal, a staple in every Punjabi home, became the favoured starter at Vasco's restaurant when we opened in 1999. At first, people were surprised that I included this humble dish as a starter in a gourmet restaurant in Abu Dhabi! While dal is usually an accompaniment or side dish, everyone loved to order a bowl with naan as soon as they were seated, instead of nibbling on the customary bread basket with olive oil and balsamic vinegar or butter. The key to this dish is the low and slow cooking of the black dal. At Vasco's, we would leave the dal overnight in a large pot on the embers of the tandoor. I have adapted the recipe below to be made at home, but it's important to use a heavy-bottomed pan. Let the dal simmer for a couple of hours, while keeping an eye on the liquid and adjusting the water as needed. There is nothing more satisfying for me, after a long day in the kitchen, than to sit down with my team and enjoy a bowl of dal and fresh naan.*

SERVES 6 TO 8

---

250 g (1¼ c) urad dal (black lentils)

1 bay leaf

1 cinnamon stick

2 black cardamom pods, crushed

4 green cardamom pods, crushed

6 black peppercorns

2 tsp salt, divided

110 g (4 oz) butter, divided

1 tsp cumin seeds

2 tsp ginger, crushed

2 tsp garlic, crushed

170 g (6 oz) tomato puree

1 tsp garam masala

2 tsp chili powder

1 tsp cumin

60 ml (¼ c) heavy cream

¼ tsp fenugreek powder

Cream

Fresh ginger

Pick clean, wash, and soak the black lentils overnight in enough water to cover.

Place the bay leaf, cinnamon stick, black and green cardamom pods, and black peppercorns on a square of cheesecloth and tie it up to form a pouch.

Drain the lentils and pour them into a heavy-bottomed skillet. Add 1.5 litres (1½ quarts) of water, 1 teaspoon of the salt, and the spice pouch. Bring to a boil, cover, lower the heat, and simmer until the lentils are overcooked and mushy, 2 to 4 hours. Add more water as needed. Avoid stirring while the lentils simmer. When cooked, whisk by hand until the lentils are roughly mashed.

Melt half of the butter in a heavy-bottomed skillet over low heat. Add the cumin seeds and stir until fragrant. Add the ginger and garlic and sauté for 2 to 3 minutes or until golden. Add the tomato puree and cook over medium heat for 15 minutes, until the oil starts to separate. Remove the skillet from the heat and add the garam masala, chili powder, cumin, and remaining salt. Stir for 2 minutes over low heat.

Stir the tomato spice mix into the lentils. Add the remaining butter and stir until incorporated. Cover and simmer for 1 to 2 hours, over low heat, until the dal is homogenised. Keep checking and add more water so the dal does not get too dry. It should be the consistency of a thick soup.

Before serving, stir in the cream until well blended. Simmer 2 to 3 more minutes and add the fenugreek powder. Serve hot, garnished with drops of fresh cream and julienned slices of fresh ginger with fresh naan on the side.

PORTUGUESE SPICED HAMMOUR

Hammour, from the Grouper family, is one of the most popular and prized fish in the Gulf. However, their population has been declining in the past few decades due to overfishing. Research into the Gulf's fish stocks is under way, as well as an effort to raise awareness amongst consumers and nudge them towards other non-endangered fish. The hammour, with its imposing size, is recognised as king of the fish. In colloquial dialect, the big businessman or boss at work is referred to as 'the big hammour'.

—
SERVES
4 TO 6
—

FISH

1 tsp chili powder

1 tsp turmeric

½ tbsp paprika

1½ tsp cumin

1½ tsp coriander powder

3 cloves garlic, minced

2 tbsp tamarind paste

3 tbsp fresh coriander, chopped

2 tbsp spring onion, chopped

3 tbsp olive oil

2 tbsp lemon juice

Salt and black pepper, to taste

4–6 hammour fillets, about 170 g (6 oz) each

Fresh coriander sprigs

BASIL BUTTER SAUCE

1 tbsp shallots, finely chopped

2 tbsp white grape vinegar

1 bay leaf

6–8 black peppercorns, crushed

60 ml (¼ c) fish or vegetable broth

170 g (6 oz) cold butter, cubed

1 tbsp heavy cream

3–4 tbsp basil pesto (ready-made)

Salt and black pepper, to taste

RAMAN *At Vasco's, I wanted to create a concept that fused the spices of the east with food from the west, imagining how the Portuguese would have used the pepper, turmeric, cumin, and coriander they exported from India in the fifteenth century. I marinate the hammour with the rich spices of India, pan sear it, and then serve it with a butter sauce, the Portuguese way. You can use any lean white fish that has large, meaty chunks.*

FOR THE FISH

Mix the chili powder, turmeric, paprika, cumin, and coriander powder in a bowl, then stir in the garlic, tamarind paste, fresh coriander, spring onions, olive oil, and lemon juice. Season with salt and pepper. Rub the hammour fillets with the spice mix, coating them thoroughly, and refrigerate for 2 to 3 hours.

Preheat the oven to 160°C (325°F). Heat a non-stick pan with a few drops of olive oil and sear the hammour fillets for 1 minute on each side. Transfer the fillets to a buttered glass baking dish large enough to hold the fillets in a single layer. Bake for 8 to 10 minutes, until just cooked.

FOR THE BASIL BUTTER SAUCE

Place the shallots, vinegar, bay leaf, and peppercorns in a small skillet and heat until the liquid is reduced to about a teaspoon. Don't walk away from it — it reduces very quickly. Strain through a small sieve into a small saucepan, using the back of a spoon to press down on the contents to extract as much liquid as possible. Add the broth to the shallot reduction and cook over medium heat, reducing it by two-thirds (to about 1 tablespoon). Remove from the heat and add the butter a little at a time, whisking until it is completely incorporated. Add the cream and pesto. Season with salt and pepper to taste. Keep warm until ready to use, whisking periodically so it does not separate.

Serve the hammour with sides of mashed potatoes and sautéed broccoli rabe or green beans. Drizzle with the butter sauce and garnish with fresh coriander sprigs.

GREEN PRAWN CURRY WITH FENNEL SHAVINGS

RAMAN *When I lived in New York in the late 1980s, I used to go to a restaurant off 5th Avenue that only served Thai curry and rice. This became my comfort food when I craved a spicy coconut curry. When I moved to Abu Dhabi in the early 1990s, these flavours remained with me. As I was developing the menu for the Jazz Bar at Hilton Abu Dhabi, I decided to add a green prawn curry with a twist of fennel, one of my favourite ingredients. It was a success from day one and stayed on the menu for many years.*

—
SERVES
4 TO 6
—

800 g (1¾ lb) king prawns

Salt and black pepper, to taste

60 ml (¼ c) olive oil, divided

½ tsp green chilies, chopped

110 g (4 oz) fennel

110 g (4 oz) tomatoes

1 tsp dill, chopped

Fresh coriander sprigs

GREEN COCONUT CURRY SAUCE

200 g (7 oz) coconut milk powder

85 g (3 oz) fresh coriander

2 tsp vegetable oil

1 tbsp garlic, chopped

1 tbsp ginger, chopped

1 stalk lemongrass, chopped

4 two-part kaffir lime leaves

2–3 tbsp Thai green curry paste, to taste

Salt and black pepper, to taste

Shell and devein the prawns, keeping the tails. Place in a medium bowl and season with salt and pepper. Add 2 tablespoons of the olive oil and the green chilies and toss to coat. Refrigerate for at least 1 hour.

Thinly shave the fennel with a mandoline and soak in ice water until ready to use. Peel, deseed, and dice the tomatoes.

Prepare the green curry sauce according to the recipe below; keep warm.

Heat a large skillet and sear the prawns until they are just done but not fully cooked.

Drain the fennel completely. Heat the remaining olive oil in a medium skillet and lightly sauté the fennel. Add the tomatoes and stir for 1 minute, making sure the fennel is not overcooked. Finish by stirring in the dill.

Return the skillet with the prawns to high heat to finish cooking. Add the curry sauce and heat for 1 to 2 minutes. Serve garnished with the fennel/tomato mix and coriander sprigs, with basmati rice passed separately.

FOR THE GREEN COCONUT CURRY SAUCE

Vigorously shake the coconut milk powder with 475 millilitres (2 cups) of hot water in a jar with a good seal. Combine the fresh coriander and 3 tablespoons of water in a blender to make a paste.

Heat the oil in a heavy-bottomed saucepan. Sauté the garlic and ginger over medium heat until fragrant and light golden. Add the lemongrass, lime leaves, and curry paste, along with a few tablespoons of water to prevent burning. Sauté for 1 minute and then add the reconstituted coconut milk. Simmer for 10 minutes over low heat. Strain the sauce and return it to the saucepan. Whisk in the coriander paste and mix well. Season with salt and pepper and thin the sauce with water if needed. Reheat when ready to serve. [*This sauce can be used as a base for chicken or vegetable curries.*]

BLUEBERRY RISOTTO

RAMAN *The menu at the Jazz Bar at Hilton Abu Dhabi changed frequently but mushroom risotto was one of the popular dishes that remained. A frequent guest suggested that we make a different risotto, so I experimented with various flavours and finally settled on blueberries, served with duck confit. The tangy, sweet taste was an unusual combination at the time, but a pleasant surprise to many of our guests. This is the Jazz Bar recipe from the late 1990s. Many people think risotto is difficult to make at home. The main trick is to stir the risotto as it cooks, without stopping. Enjoy this with a side of rocket salad or accompanied by duck confit, if you're feeling ambitious in the kitchen.*

—
SERVES
4 TO 6
—

2 tbsp olive oil

55 g (2 oz) unsalted butter, divided

28 g (1 oz) white onion, chopped

55 g (2 oz) celery, peeled, chopped

28 g (1 oz) leeks, white part only, chopped

Pinch of coarse salt

400 g (2 c) Arborio rice

60 ml (¼ c) white grape vinegar

225 g (8 oz) blueberries, divided

1 l (1 qt) vegetable broth

240 ml (1 c) heavy cream

25 g (¼ c) Parmesan cheese, grated

1 tsp chopped thyme

Salt and black pepper, to taste

Parmesan shavings

Fresh thyme sprigs

Swirl the olive oil and 28 grams (1 ounce) of the butter in a large saucepan or medium stockpot over medium heat until the butter melts. Add the onion, celery, leeks, and a pinch of salt and stir for 5 minutes, until the vegetables are translucent and soft. Add the rice and stir to ensure the rice is well coated. Pour in the vinegar, stirring until it has evaporated.

Sprinkle 55 grams (2 ounces) of the blueberries over the rice and stir gently. Add 700 millilitres (3 cups) of the broth, 120 millilitres (½ cup) at a time, while continuing to stir the rice. Once the broth starts to simmer, lower the heat and stir gently for 10 minutes. Add the remaining blueberries and more broth if needed, and keep stirring for another 5 to 10 minutes, until the rice is cooked. The rice is done when it is soft when squeezed, but, like pasta al dente, it shouldn't be mushy. The blueberries will get soft and the rice will turn a light purple colour.

Once all the broth is absorbed, add the cream and the remaining butter and continue to stir for a few minutes. Remove the pan from the heat and stir in the grated Parmesan cheese and the chopped thyme. Season to taste with salt and pepper.

Garnish each serving with Parmesan shavings and a sprig of fresh thyme.

REEM AND RAMZI GHANNOUM

HIGHER EDUCATION ◇ LEBANON / CANADA

CIVIL ENGINEER ◇ JORDAN / CANADA

It was a Friday morning and we were up early to pack the coolers for the much-anticipated family *dhow* (Arab sailing vessel) trip to Al Bahrani Island, off the coast of Abu Dhabi. Ramzi was always in charge of the food. He knew the best butcher in town and would pre-order the kafta, kebab, and lamb chops — perfectly marinated and ready for the grill. For the pre-lunch snack, he would pick up freshly baked za'atar and cheese *manakeesh,* a Levantine flatbread.

Born and raised in Amman, Jordan, Ramzi inherited his love for food and entertaining from his father, who opened the first *musakhan* restaurant in Amman in 1961, serving the traditional Palestinian roasted chicken, flavoured with onion and sumac. Ramzi grew up in the kitchen with him, at first watching, then chopping, grilling, and frying. He recalls, 'My dad was so loving and caring, and we could taste that with every bite of hummus or *foul* that he prepared'. Ramzi's appetite and taste for good food, cultivated at a young age, challenged him to stay fit as a teenager. Recognising the needed to exercise, he mapped a five-kilometre walking route starting from his home. A few hundred metres later, he stopped to refuel with a shawarma sandwich, and then as he turned downhill he came upon the best falafel shop. A falafel sandwich later, he headed towards the local bakery and indulged in a spinach *fatayer* (a stuffed pie). Having completed his cunning exercise plan, he returned home, fully satisfied. 'Basically, I devised a walking route that included my favourite food stops', Ramzi laughs.

Ramzi left Amman to study at Oklahoma State University, where he earned his civil engineering degree. He returned to work in Jordan and after unsuccessfully trying to eat his way out of military service by adopting a high-banana diet to increase his weight, he served the compulsory two years in the Jordanian army. Ramzi immigrated to Canada in the late 1980s, where he met and married Reem, who had moved there from Lebanon during the civil war in 1982.

To increase his earnings, Ramzi did what many engineering graduates were doing at the time: he took a hardship assignment with a large contractor developing the oil and gas infrastructure in the Middle East. His first assignment was in a remote location in Yemen, which was not suitable for families, so Reem stayed behind in Toronto. His next assignment was in 1994 to Habshan, a gas field about 160 kilometres west of Abu Dhabi. Apprehensive about leaving her life in Toronto, yet excited to join her husband, Reem took the leap and moved to Abu Dhabi, not realising that Ramzi would live five days a week in the camp in Habshan, and she would live in the city, alone. It was a shock at first, but she started working a few months later, which made it easier in some ways and more challenging in others, with two young boys. 'Rachel, our housekeeper for twenty years, has been a godsend. As Ramzi's sous-chef and learning from my mother when she visited, Rachel has been making all our favourite dishes', Reem says.

Now that they are empty nesters, Reem and Ramzi are finding new adventures, while continuing to share their love of food with friends in their new apartment on the outskirts of the city. Reem is pushing boundaries to expand her consciousness, deepen her yoga practice, and savour a balanced life. Ramzi has renewed his passion for motorbikes, riding weekly with different groups of bikers across the Emirates and Oman. Not surprisingly, Ramzi arranges the food stops for most of these rides. 'The wind in our faces, the sound of the machine, the camaraderie amongst the riders, the love for the outdoors, and good basic food — that's what bonds us', Ramzi tells me, with a big smile on his face.

The wind in our faces, the sound of the machine, the camaraderie amongst the riders, the love for the outdoors, and good basic food — that's what bonds us.

RAMZI

MUSAKHAN ROLLS
Sumac and Caramelised Onion Chicken Rolls

Musakhan, olive oil-basted bread topped with tender chicken, caramelised onions, and lemony sumac, is a traditional Palestinian dish originally prepared by farmers to celebrate their main product, olive oil. It is said that a high-grade olive oil won't cause heartburn, and since musakhan has a lot of oil, it is important to use the best quality you can. Sumac, another important ingredient, is a dried, ground berry from the plant genus *Rhus*. Its deep purple powder is sour and fruity.

RAMZI *For me, musakhan is a comfort food. My father served musakhan exclusively at his restaurant in Amman. He had a special oven to bake the taboon bread, a thick bread with dimples from the small round stones it is baked over. I have adopted a simplified musakhan roll variation, using Lebanese markook bread, which I like to serve as an appetizer while the grill is heating. Some call it the Palestinian version of taquitos or spring rolls. You can use flour tortillas if you can't find markook bread. And for the oil, I sometimes mix half olive oil and half vegetable oil for a lighter version. You have to try musakhan to see how a dish can be more than the sum of its parts.*

SERVES 6 TO 8

- 1.5 kg (3½ lb) chicken
- 1 carrot, cut into large pieces
- 1 onion, cut into quarters
- 2 tsp salt, divided
- 2 tsp black pepper, divided
- 5 cardamom pods, lightly crushed
- 1 cinnamon stick
- 1 bay leaf
- 120 ml (½ c) olive oil
- 1 kg (2¼ lb) yellow onions, chopped
- 45 g (⅓ c) sumac
- 35 g (¼ c) pine nuts
- 6 large markook bread sheets or flour tortillas

Cut the chicken into four pieces, removing the skin for a lighter version. Place the chicken, carrot, and onion in a pot and add hot water to cover. Add 1 teaspoon of the salt, 1 teaspoon of the pepper, cardamom pods, cinnamon stick, and bay leaf. Place the pot over medium heat and bring to a boil. Cover and allow the chicken to simmer for 40 minutes, or until it is tender. Remove the chicken and reserve the broth for later use in this recipe. When the chicken has cooled, shred it into small pieces.

Add the oil to a large skillet over medium heat. Add the onions and remaining salt and pepper. Turn the heat to low and cook, stirring continuously, until the onions are caramelised. Add the sumac, pine nuts, and 120 millilitres (½ cup) of the reserved chicken broth and continue to cook uncovered for another 10 minutes.

Preheat the oven to 200°C (400°F). Trim any tough edges from the markook bread. Cut the bread into squares, about 10 x 10 centimetres (4 x 4 inches).

For each roll, place 1 to 2 teaspoons of the chicken and onion mixture into the centre of a bread square and roll up, tucking in the edges as you go, to make rolls that are about 5 centimetres (2 inches) long and 2 centimetres (¾ inch) thick.

Place the rolls on a lightly greased baking tray. Baste generously with the oil reserved from cooking the chicken and onions. Sprinkle with sumac and bake for about 10 to 15 minutes, until crunchy.

ARAYES
Lamb-Stuffed Mini Pita Sandwiches

Arayes are pita bread sandwiches stuffed with minced beef or lamb, herbs and spices, and then grilled until crispy. *Arayes* is the plural of *arouseh*, Arabic for 'bride'. Traditional bridal wear included a cloth wrapped around the waist, so pita bread sandwiches got this name in the Levant because of the similarity to bridal wear. The term is now used to refer to all forms of sandwiches.

SERVES 6 TO 8

RAMZI

I frequently prepare arayes when we have friends over for a barbecue, serving them as an appetizer in mini pitas. They are usually gone minutes after I take them off the grill. Serve them with hummus on the side.

28 g (1 oz) spring onions, chopped

200 g (7 oz) tomato, chopped and drained

110 g (4 oz) green bell pepper, chopped

450 g (1 lb) finely minced lean lamb or beef

1 small red chili, to taste

1 tsp salt

1 tsp seven spices

1 tsp sumac

½ tsp black pepper

Small bunch of mint

Small bunch of parsley

60 ml (¼ c) pomegranate molasses

40 mini pitas or **6** full-size pitas

Olive oil

If baking, preheat the oven to 180°C (350°F).

Mix the spring onions, tomato, and green pepper in a food processor for 2 minutes. Add the meat, red chili, salt, seven spices, sumac, pepper, mint, and parsley, and mix again until well blended.

With the food processor on medium speed, add the pomegranate molasses in a thin stream and then set on high speed for one minute until a paste-like mixture forms. Transfer the mixture to a bowl.

Slice each pita halfway along the edge. Fill them with the meat mixture, being careful not to overfill. Drain any accumulated liquid from the meat mixture as you work.

Brush the tops of the pitas with olive oil. If grilling, place them on a wire rack and grill for 20 minutes or until the meat cooks and the pitas are crusty.

If baking, arrange the pitas on a cooking rack lightly coated with olive oil. Place the cooking rack over a large baking tray or roasting pan. Bake for 20 minutes or until the meat is cooked and the pitas are crusty.

SHEIKH AL MUKHSHI
Stuffed Eggplant with Pomegranate Molasses

Historically, the eggplant has been a favourite of the poor and ridiculed by the rich and famous. Early on, eggplants were round and white, resembling large eggs. Some say that its name in Arabic, *bad al jan*, which means 'the djinn (devil) has laid eggs', shows that it was even considered an evil vegetable. But not in this case! *Sheikh al mukhshi*, which translates to 'king of stuffed vegetables', is given this status because it is filled exlusively with meat, unlike other vegetables, which are normally stuffed with a combination of rice and meat. It is a favourite of the Levant.

REEM *This is one of my treasured recipes. It has been in my family for over a century, handed down to me from my mother, who learnt it from my Lebanese grandmother. It never fails to bring me back 'home' when I am feeling disconnected. It is amazing how the taste of some foods instantly brings back vivid memories of my mother's kitchen, and I experience the comfort of being transported to the simpler days of my childhood. Serve it hot with plain or vermicelli rice.*

SERVES 6 TO 8

3 tbsp olive oil, divided

35 g (¼ c) pine nuts

225 g (8 oz) yellow onion, chopped

500 g (1¼ lb) minced beef

Salt and black pepper, to taste

1 tsp seven spices

1 kg (2¼ lb) baby eggplant

240 ml (1 c) olive oil

2 tbsp tomato paste

1 tbsp lemon juice

1 tbsp pomegranate molasses

Preheat the oven to 180°C (350°F).

In a medium skillet, sauté the pine nuts with 1 tablespoon of olive oil until lightly browned. Immediately remove with a slotted spoon and drain on paper towels.

Add the remaining 2 tablespoons of olive oil to the skillet and sauté the onions until they become transparent. Add the minced beef and stir to combine over high heat.

Season with salt, pepper, and seven spices, reduce heat to low, and simmer for 15 minutes or until the beef is cooked. Remove from the heat.

Peel the eggplant lengthwise in alternating strips. Add the olive oil to a large, deep skillet over medium heat. Add the eggplant and fry until golden brown, working in batches if necessary.

Remove the eggplant from the oil and drain well; cool for 10 minutes. Slice each eggplant lengthwise along the side but not all the way through, to form a pocket.

Fill each eggplant with 2 to 3 tablespoons of the meat mixture (depending on the size of the eggplant) and arrange them side by side, with the opening facing up, in a 33 x 22-centimetre (13 x 9-inch) ovenproof dish. Sprinkle the remaining meat over the stuffed eggplant.

In a medium saucepan, combine the tomato paste and 240 millilitres (1 cup) of water; bring to a boil. Remove from the heat, add the lemon juice and pomegranate molasses, and mix well. Pour over the stuffed eggplant.

Bake for 20 to 25 minutes, until the tomato sauce bubbles. Remove from the oven and sprinkle the top with the reserved pine nuts.

BEEF SHAWARMA WITH TAHINI SAUCE

Shawarma is Arabic street food at its best. It is a sandwich-like wrap filled with shredded chicken, lamb, or beef cooked on a vertical grill. A variety of garnishes are included, such as pickles, tahini sauce, garlic, onions, and French fries. In Abu Dhabi, as the sun sets, the shawarma chefs don their white aprons, ready their knives, and turn on the fire of the towering grills. Until the early hours of the morning, cars line up in a steady stream as their drivers place their orders.

SERVES 4 TO 6

SHAWARMA

- 1 kg (2¼ lb) beef tenderloin or flank steak
- 1 tsp salt
- 1 tsp black pepper
- 1 tsp seven spices
- ¼ tsp cinnamon
- 1 tsp sumac
- 1 tsp ground cardamom
- 4 to 6 cardamom pods, lightly crushed
- Pinch of nutmeg
- 80 ml (⅓ c) olive oil
- 2 tbsp lemon juice
- 80 ml (⅓ c) red vinegar
- 1 onion, quartered
- 28 g (1 oz) butter
- 1 chicken bouillon cube (optional)

GARNISH

- 1 onion
- 1–2 tsp sumac
- Handful of parsley leaves
- Salt and black pepper
- Pickles
- 2 Roma tomatoes

TAHINI SAUCE

- 60 ml (¼ c) tahini
- 3–4 tbsp lemon juice
- Salt and black pepper
- ½ tsp cumin (optional)

RAMZI *The shawarmas you get on the street tend to be greasy because of the fat content of the meat that is used. I prefer to make mine at home from the best cut of meat and marinate it overnight with just the right mix of spices. I serve it on a plate for guests to make their own sandwiches with pita bread, garnishes, and tahini sauce on the side.*

FOR THE SHAWARMA

Thinly slice the meat into strips that are 1 centimetre (⅜ inch) wide and 5 to 7 centimetres (2 to 3 inches) long. Place in a large bowl. Combine the salt, pepper, seven spices, cinnamon, sumac, ground cardamom, cardamom pods, and nutmeg. Mix with the meat, coating it thoroughly. Combine the olive oil, lemon juice, and vinegar and mix well with the meat. Add the onion, cover the bowl with plastic wrap, and refrigerate overnight; stir occasionally.

When ready to cook, drain but retain the accumulated liquid from the meat. Melt the butter in a large hot skillet. Add the meat and bouillon cube (if using) and cook on medium heat, uncovered, stirring occasionally, for 30 minutes or until done. Add some of the retained marinade if necessary. Remove the cardamom pods before serving.

FOR THE GARNISH

Cut the onion in half and slice into long, thin strips. Sprinkle with sumac, parsley, salt, and pepper; toss. Cut the pickles into long strips and slice the tomato. Present the pickles, onions, and tomato on individual plates or on a common garnish plate, depending on how you are serving the shawarma.

FOR THE TAHINI SAUCE

Combine the tahini and lemon juice. Add water gradually, starting with 2 tablespoons, stirring continuously until the desired consistency is reached. Add salt and pepper to taste and add the cumin, if using. Drizzle the sauce over the meat before wrapping it or when serving on a plate.

SALAMA AL SHAMSI

CULTURAL MANAGER
◇
UAE

When I moved to the new offices of the Department of Culture and Tourism in Nation Towers, I noticed one corner where colleagues were always congregating. Salama had set up a round table by her office with a variety of snacks, which she generously replenished with homemade desserts and specialty treats brought back from her travels. According to Salama, 'Wherever there is food, there is happiness'.

We were a diverse group on the thirteenth floor working on the Saadiyat Cultural District museums — the Louvre Abu Dhabi, the Zayed National Museum, and the Guggenheim Abu Dhabi — and we enjoyed sharing our culinary creations and cultural traditions. We had *galette des rois* (king cake) to celebrate Epiphany, pecan pie on Thanksgiving, *pastiera napoletana* for Easter, and Syrian sweets, Emirati dates, and Omani halva for Eid. We were all pleasantly surprised by the levels of creativity and culinary prowess amongst our colleagues.

Salama tells me how a registrar's mistake in college led to her dream job in the arts. She learned she was three credits short of graduating, so she took a project-based architecture course and chose to study the work of Frank Gehry, who had recently been commissioned to design the Guggenheim Abu Dhabi. Her research led her to meetings with the local developer in charge of the project, where she learned about the plans for a cultural district on Saadiyat Island. Seven years later, Salama is proud to be leading the team developing the Sheikh Zayed National Museum, which will tell the story of the United Arab Emirates. 'Sheikh Zayed touches the deepest part of my heart. I was fortunate to have known him. He was very much part of the lives of my generation. What he gave his people and the world is so valuable and we need to share it with future generations, which is what we hope the museum will do', Salama articulates.

Sharing food and bringing people together comes naturally for Salama. She remarks, 'I think it is part of hospitality and what I learned from my mother and grandmother. We live in a world that is becoming more divided, so why not bring people together with something we can all enjoy'. Growing up in Abu Dhabi, Salama fondly remembers her family lunches. While their cook had been well trained by her mother and grandmother, Salama's discerning taste buds could always tell when her elders had done the cooking. I ask Salama to name her favourite dish and immediately she answers, '*Aish Ramadan* (Ramadan rice). It is unique to our family. My grandmother had eight children, so she had her hands full! One evening in Ramadan when they were young, there was only chicken, tomatoes and rice in the kitchen. She threw them into a pot with her spice mix to create a delicious and hearty meal. Today all the women in the family make it, each adding her own touch'.

Salama's love of food is as much a love of cultures and of sharing her own. When she travels she always seeks out the locals' favourite places to eat. She is also passionate about the emergence of Emirati cuisine and mentions the young entrepreneurs who are developing Emirati-inspired food ventures, including packaged mixes and spice blends. 'It's amazing and I am so proud of what they are doing to bring Emirati cuisine to the world. Contrary to what tourists might think, hummus and tabbouleh are not Emirati foods!' In an effort to do her part, Salama enthusiastically describes her work in progress: a restaurant that will serve her culinary favourites from around the world, as well as Emirati dishes infused with flavours and techniques of the different cultures in her hometown. 'Food is art,' she enthuses. 'It's something inside you that you want to express. I express it by baking a cake'. Salama looks forward to sharing her international creations, as well as aish Ramadan, when she opens her eponymously named restaurant.

Wherever there is food there is happiness.

SALAMA

TUNA TAHTA
Emirati Spiced Pilaf with Tuna

In the early days before air conditioning, refrigeration, and running water in the Emirates, the desert dwellers and seafarers found ways to preserve food and make it go a long way. Fish preserved in salt, known as *maleh* ('salty' in Arabic), could last for years. Cooking the maleh with spices and rice also meant that a frugal amount of fish could stretch to feed a large gathering. *Tahta* in Arabic means 'below', referring to the fish layer below the rice. It is a simple yet powerful dish that speaks to the resourcefulness of the people and the spice trade with India.

SERVES 6 TO 8

500 g (2½ c) basmati rice

4 cans of tuna (170 g / 6 oz), oil packed

2 tbsp cooking oil

28 g (1 oz) butter

285 g (10 oz) onions, chopped

1 tbsp ginger, crushed

1 tbsp garlic, crushed

2–3 small green chilies, diced

1½ tbsp Emirati bzar spice mix

1 tsp cumin

1 tsp turmeric

5 cardamom pods, crushed

1 tsp salt

½ tsp black pepper

3 lumi, pulp only

1 chicken bouillon cube

Handful of fresh coriander, chopped

340 g (12 oz) tomatoes, chopped

2 tbsp tomato paste

1 tsp saffron

1 sugar cube

60 ml (¼ c) rose water

2 tbsp ghee

SALAMA *This is a recipe my mother adapted from the traditional tahta maleh and has become a family favourite. It came about on one of our family summer trips abroad. My grandparents missed home-cooked food, so my mother made a version of this rice dish using canned tuna and the bzar (Emirati spice mixture) she had with her. It hit the spot! It's a quick and easy way to get a taste of home when on the road. When we travel now, I like to vary this dish using the spices and herbs of where we are, be it herbes de Provence or Southeast Asian spices. So, try your own combination.*

Rinse the rice and soak it in enough water to cover for 1 hour; drain. Drain the oil from 3 cans of the tuna and keep the oil of 1 can.

Heat the cooking oil and butter in a large non-stick saucepan over medium heat. Add the onions and sauté until golden. Add the ginger, garlic, and chilies and stir for 2 minutes. Stir in the tuna and oil. Sprinkle in the bzar, cumin, turmeric, cardamom, salt, and pepper. Add the lumi pulp, bouillon cube, and fresh coriander, and stir for 2 minutes. Stir in the chopped tomatoes, tomato paste, and 120 millilitres (½ cup) of water. Cover and cook over medium heat for 10 minutes.

Place the rice in a medium saucepan and add just enough hot water to cover. Parboil for 6 to 8 minutes until al dente, gently stirring once so the rice does not stick together. Drain the rice in a fine sieve and add to the tuna mixture. Pour 120 millilitres (½ cup) of water over the rice. Crush the saffron with the sugar cube and mix with the rose water. Sprinkle over the rice. For a hearty option, drizzle the ghee over the rice. Seal the pot with aluminium foil, cover, and place over very low heat, over a metal diffuser. Cook for 45 minutes, then remove from the heat and leave covered for 10 minutes.

Remove the foil, place a serving plate over the pot, and invert. Garnish the tuna tahta with fresh coriander and lemon wedges.

STICKY DATE PUDDING
with Cardamom Sauce

Date palms have a special significance in Arabian culture. The date palm is mentioned more than any other fruit-bearing tree in the Quran, and it is known that the Prophet broke his fast with two dates. Among many other benefits, dates were believed to be an antidote to poison, promote good health, and fight diseases whose causes were unknown at the time.

The date palm was first cultivated in Mesopotamia, and from early times all its elements have been incorporated into daily life; however, the fruit is the star of the show, enjoyed year-round, fresh or dried. There are hundreds of ways to cook with dates: stuffed in cookies, pastries, cakes, and puddings; braised in tagines and stews; distilled to a molasses; and the pits roasted, ground and brewed to make a coffee-like drink.

The palm groves in Al Ain and Liwa produce some of the finest quality dates. The palm-lined streets in Abu Dhabi are a testament to the importance of this fruit to the Emirati culture. It is said that Sheikh Zayed bin Sultan Al Nahyan directed that date palms planted in the city of Abu Dhabi not exceed a certain height, ensuring that pedestrians could help themselves to the fruit, thus sharing in the bounty of the land.

SERVES 6 TO 8

SALAMA *Dates are part of our everyday life, from the first bite before the morning coffee, to almond-filled and chocolate-covered treats and other delicious sweets and drinks. What better way to have them than in a pudding!*

SAUCE

475 ml (2 c) heavy cream

90 g (½ c) brown sugar

2½ tbsp golden syrup or molasses

½ tsp coarse salt

5-6 cardamom pods, crushed

PUDDING

180 g (6 oz) pitted dates, chopped

1 tsp baking soda

190 g (1¼ c) all-purpose flour

1 tsp baking powder

½ tsp salt

1 tsp cardamom

1 tsp cinnamon

½ tsp nutmeg

55 g (2 oz) butter, softened

150 g (¾ c) caster sugar

2 eggs

1 tsp vanilla

Preheat the oven to 180°C (350°F). Butter a 24-centimetre (9½-inch) soufflé dish or 8 individual ramekins.

FOR THE SAUCE

Combine the cream, sugar, golden syrup, salt, and cardamom in a medium saucepan. Bring to a boil over medium heat, stirring often to melt the sugar. Reduce the heat and simmer for 3 minutes, stirring constantly until the mixture is thick and coats the spoon. Remove the cardamom pods. Pour half the sauce into the soufflé dish, reserving the other half for serving. Place the soufflé dish in the freezer while preparing the pudding.

FOR THE PUDDING

Combine the dates and baking soda in a small bowl. Pour 240 millilitres (1 cup) of boiling water over them, stir well, and let soak for 15 to 20 minutes, until the dates soften. Do not drain.

Sift the flour, baking powder, salt, cardamom, cinnamon, and nutmeg in a medium mixing bowl. Cream the butter and sugar in a large bowl until light and fluffy. Gradually beat in the eggs, then the vanilla. Stir in half of the flour mixture. Blend in the date mixture, add the remaining flour, and mix until just combined. Do not overbeat the batter.

Remove the soufflé dish from the freezer and pour in the batter. Use a spatula to evenly spread the batter over the sauce. Bake for 45 minutes or until a toothpick inserted comes out with moist crumbs attached. Let cool slightly before serving.

Serve each portion with reserved sauce.

CAROLINA COLLAZOS AND LAURENT DEPOLLA

ART HISTORY ◊ COLOMBIA

STRATEGY ADVISOR ◊ FRANCE

The sign on the front door reads 'Gone Fishing' — Laurent's escape when he has free time. On a Friday afternoon, after a good catch, he detours by Mina Zayed, so the fishmonger can clean the fish. He then invites his friends to join them for his celebrated baked hammour. 'This is how I combine my love for fishing, cooking, and entertaining', he tells me. I watch him bathe the fish in white wine, drizzle on some olive oil, sprinkle it with fennel, coriander seeds, and red peppercorns, and finish with slices of lemon and fresh dill. He then bakes it to perfection with caramelised whole garlic heads and tomatoes and serves it with a lemon butter sauce. Meanwhile, Carolina has set the table Provençal-style with fresh flowers. The evening unfolds in a leisurely manner, with each course paired with the appropriate wine cépage. The meal is capped with Colombian coffee and homemade *alfahores* cookies.

Carolina and Laurent met in Cairo and shared a love for travel, good food, and wine. They were married in France in 2001, after which Carolina joined Laurent in Abu Dhabi, where he was working for a sovereign wealth fund. Now, with three children, their travels revolve around gastronomy and history, with Laurent conducting extensive research on the culinary options and Carolina planning visits to the local museums and historical sites. For Carolina, these trips also result in a replenishment of her pantry, with such items as *frijoles* (red kidney beans), *dulce de guyaba* (guava jam), *obleas* (extra-thin wafer cookies), Maizena (cornstarch), and coffee from Colombia; aged balsamic vinegar, dried porcini mushrooms, and risotto from Italy; olive oil and bottarga from Greece; and truffles and foie gras from France.

Carolina had not spent much time in the kitchen before getting married. After savouring her French mother-in-law's cooking, however, she realised she had some catching up to do. Carolina recalls, 'There wasn't much happening in Abu Dhabi when I first arrived, but I soon got busy with our young family and learning to cook'. Now, multicourse meals are common at the Depolla's home, even on weekdays with the family. Despite everyone's busy schedule, they manage to sit down for dinner, light the candles, and enjoy a three-course meal, allowing them to catch up on the day's events. However, making this happen is not an easy task. Carolina has the organisational skills of a master chef, with a blackboard in the kitchen listing the after-school activities for each child and the weekly meal plan catering to their diverse tastes.

Growing up in a multicultural family, with summers in Colombia, Europe, Florida, and Lebanon, the children have been exposed to many culinary traditions. 'Our eldest has a French/Italian palate and enjoys cooking when she has time. Our middle child loves hot dogs and ketchup, maybe because he was born in the US', she chuckles. 'Our youngest son is lean and prefers good quality meats and healthy food'. At the Depolla table, you can find a wide range of dishes, including *tostadas de platano con hagao* (fried green plantains with tomato salsa), *shish barak* (Lebanese meat-filled dumplings in yogurt sauce), and *lapin à la moutarde* (rabbit in white wine and mustard sauce), as well as French, Arabic, English, and Spanish spoken in the same sentence. Dinner at the Depolla's is guaranteed to be a culinary journey across continents, with interesting, lively, and fun-filled conversation.

Now that their children are older, Carolina has reconnected with her passion for the arts, and guides visitors through the Louvre Abu Dhabi, with its collection of objects and artwork spanning many civilizations and cultures. She remarks: 'Through food, language, and art we can best understand and appreciate the nuances of different cultures. Abu Dhabi has turned out to be an amazing place to bring up our children. We love it here'.

> Through food, language, and art we can best understand and appreciate the nuances of different cultures.
>
> CAROLINA

TOSTADAS DE PLATANO CON HOGAO
Fried Green Plantains with Tomato Salsa

Plantains, or cooking bananas, are a versatile superfood and a staple in many parts of Africa, Asia, the West Indies, and South America. They are a good source of carbohydrates, low in sugar and fat, and high in minerals and vitamins. Plantains are also a reliable food source because the plants bear fruit all year long and they can be prepared at any stage of ripeness. Botanically, plantains and bananas are considered different cultivars of the same plant, but for cooking and eating they are quite different. The banana is delicious, smooth, and sugary sweet and can be eaten raw at any stage of ripeness, as well as cooked. Plantains, on the other hand, are much less sweet, starchier, and rarely eaten raw. Cooking plantains brings out their subtle sweet flavours and crunchy texture. They can be fried, sautéed, boiled, baked, or roasted. *Tostadas de platano* are sliced fried green plantains, flattened and then refried.

CAROLINA *Tostadas are the French fries of Colombia. We have tostadas for lunch or as a dinner appetizer, served with* hagao, *a homemade tomato salsa. In Abu Dhabi, I use the plantains from India. The most important aspect of this recipe is that the plantains must be very, very green! Plantains ripen quickly so you must give them the first fry when they are still green and then you can freeze them for later use. Hagao is a staple in our kitchen. We use it for many Colombian dishes and spread it on arepas (a grilled cornmeal cake) and fried yuca (cassava), to name a few. Depending on how flavourful the tomatoes are, you can make the hagao with or without the bouillon cube and sugar. Enjoy the tostadas with a scoop of guacamole, hagao, or simply plain.*

SERVES 6 TO 8

HAGAO

- 3 tbsp olive oil
- 2 cloves garlic, chopped
- 55 g (2 oz) spring onions, chopped
- 140 g (5 oz) red onions, chopped
- 1 kg (2¼ lb) tomatoes, peeled and chopped
- 1 tsp cumin
- 1 tsp salt
- 1 vegetable bouillon cube (optional)
- ½ tsp granulated sugar (optional)

TOSTADAS

- 12 very green plantains
- Corn oil for frying

FOR THE HAGAO

Heat the oil in a skillet. Add the garlic, spring and red onions, and cook over medium heat until the onions are translucent. Add the tomatoes, cumin, salt, and the optional bouillon cube and sugar, and continue to cook, stirring occasionally for 15 to 20 minutes, until the sauce thickens. Remove from the heat and allow the hagao to cool.

FOR THE TOSTADAS

Use a sharp knife to cut off the ends of each plantain. Slice along the ridges, being careful not to cut any deeper than the peel. Use the knife to lift a corner of the peel along the cut edge and remove the peel by hand. Cut each plantain into 4-centimetre (1½-inch) chunks. Heat the oil in a heavy-bottomed skillet over medium-high heat. Fry the plantains in a single layer for about 4 minutes on each side, until golden. Carefully remove the plantains with tongs and drain them on paper towels. Let them rest for 15 minutes.

Working in batches, place some of the plantain sections in a resealable plastic bag. Using a culinary rock or any flat object, flatten the plantains as thinly as possible. *[At this point the plantains can be frozen for later cooking. Place a piece of wax paper between each flattened plantain so they don't stick together, and tightly pack them into a resealable plastic bag.]*

When ready to serve, reheat the oil and fry the plantains for 1 to 2 minutes, until golden brown. Remove with tongs and drain on paper towels. Sprinkle with salt and transfer to a serving platter with the hagao on the side.

SCALLOP CEVICHE WITH MANGO

Ceviche is an old world seafood dish from South America that has gained popularity in other parts of the world in the past few decades. It is prepared using a method of 'cooking' with acidic citrus juices instead of heat. When the fish is marinated in citrus juice, it eventually turns firm and opaque as the protein coagulates, as if it were cooked.

It is believed that the precursor to ceviche was prepared in Peru nearly 2,000 years ago, with the use of various fermented liquids to marinate fish. Meanwhile, Arab chefs in Moorish Spain had introduced citrus fruits. Spanish colonists planted citrus trees and the native people probably recognised the use of the acidic juice as another way to prepare their seafood.

CAROLINA *Ceviche is versatile, easy to make, and beautiful to present in individual glasses or a large bowl. You can play around with the ingredients: add red bell peppers for texture, substitute pineapple for the mango, and try different levels of heat from jalapeño to habanero. Most importantly, always use the best quality and freshest seafood and keep it chilled in the refrigerator over ice until ready to use. In Abu Dhabi, I also make ceviche with the local grouper, known as hammour, but you can use halibut, flounder, or swordfish. The length of 'marinating' depends on the cut of seafood, so watch for when it becomes opaque and firm to the touch. This is a perfect summertime dish—light, bright, and refreshing!*

SERVES 4 TO 6

450 g (1 lb) fresh sea scallops

110 g (4 oz) red onions, chopped

2 red chili peppers, chopped

1 tsp salt

240 ml (1 c) lime juice, divided

140 g (5 oz) mango, diced

1 tbsp fresh coriander

1 tbsp dill, chopped

2 tbsp olive oil

Black pepper, to taste

Rinse the scallops, pat dry, and cut into chunks. Place the scallops, onions, red chili peppers, and salt in a medium non-reactive bowl. Pour in just enough lime juice to completely cover the scallops. Cover and chill for up to 2 hours, until the scallops are opaque.

Drain the lime juice from the scallop mixture. Add the mangoes, coriander, and dill. Drizzle with the olive oil and the remaining lime juice. Toss gently and serve in a glass bowl; sprinkle with pepper.

PIE DE COCO
Colombian Coconut Pie

Coconut thrives in tropical climates, so it turns up in cuisines from the Polynesian islands to South Asia, as well as in parts of Latin America. It is abundant along the Colombian coasts, where it is used for sweet and savoury dishes. Street vendors sell it in different forms of candy and pastry, or simply shaved. This pie captures the purity of shaved coconut and the freshness of the sea breeze, with minimal ingredients.

CAROLINA *Pie de coco is an absolute favourite of our family and friends! I first tasted it in one of the fine dining restaurants in Cartagena, a historical Spanish colonial town and World Heritage Site on the Caribbean coast, referred to by some as the birthplace of Magical Realism, a literary style. I fell in love at first bite, so I went back to the kitchen to ask the chef for the recipe. He wasn't forthcoming with specifics, but he did tell me it had three main ingredients: fresh coconut, cream, and sugar. After a few trials on the family, I think my pie comes close to the one I had in Cartagena. With the magenta bougainvillea in our Abu Dhabi garden, freshly shaved coconut from the South Asian vendors at the Mina Zayed Market, and the salty sea breeze off the Arabian Gulf, I can close my eyes, savour a bite of pie de coco, and be transported thousands of miles away to my land of Magical Realism.*

SERVES 6 TO 8

CRUST

1 sweet shortcrust pastry for 30-cm (12-in) pie dish

FILLING

700 ml (3 c) whipping cream

105 g (½ c) granulated sugar

2 tbsp vanilla

450 g (1 lb) shredded fresh coconut

FOR THE CRUST

Preheat the oven to 180°C (350°F).

Roll out the dough on a lightly floured surface and transfer it to a 30-centimetre (12-inch) pie pan. Trim the edges about 2.5 centimetres (1 inch) above the rim of the pan, fold over in half, and flute the edges. This extra height is needed because the crust will shrink.

Prick the dough with a fork; place wax paper over the crust and top with pie weights to keep the crust flat while baking. Bake for 20 minutes, until light golden.

FOR THE FILLING

Whisk together the cream, sugar, and vanilla in a large bowl.

Place the coconut in a large skillet over medium heat. Stir constantly for 5 to 7 minutes, until the coconut starts to turn light golden and any liquid evaporates.

Pour the cream mixture into the pan with the coconut and stir over medium heat for 5 to 10 minutes, until the liquid evaporates.

Scrape the coconut mixture into the pre-baked crust and bake for 35 minutes. If the edge of the crust starts to get brown, cover it with aluminium foil. Serve warm with ice cream.

MONA ZAKI

TALENT MANAGEMENT
◊
EGYPT / US

It was a warm August evening in Kuwait in 1992. My husband Steve and I had finally dozed off around midnight, after being up late to nurse our newborn's fluctuating temperature. Suddenly, there was a loud knock on the door. Steve opened it to find a distraught woman he had never seen before. She said that her husband Adel, our next-door neighbour, was stuck in the elevator with their four-year-old daughter. They had just arrived from Cairo, and their oversized, heavy suitcases had caused it to stall. The temperature was soaring, and she was desperate to get them out. With all this commotion, I quickly followed, as the maintenance crew rescued the trapped neighbours. That is how I met Mona and her family, who have become lifelong friends. Working for a multinational construction company, our husbands' jobs took them from Kuwait to Abu Dhabi in 1993 and then to Iraq a decade later. For the most part, Mona and I maintained the family home bases in Abu Dhabi where the children went to school, while our husbands worked throughout the region.

Mona has pondered the notion of home for many years. On several occasions, we have debated if home is where you are born, where your family resides, or where your ancestors come from. Born in Cairo, Mona spent most of her childhood in Princeton, New Jersey. Regardless, her connections to Egypt remained strong through the food her mother prepared, the music they listened to, the holiday celebrations, and the annual summer trips back home. After finishing high school in the United States, Mona attended the American University of Cairo, but after marrying her Egyptian-American husband, she relocated to San Francisco. It was a difficult transition, and she didn't like being so far away from family. She yearned for the familiar. After five years in San Francisco, her husband's company relocated them to Kuwait, where we met that eventful evening.

Reminiscing about our early years in Abu Dhabi, Mona recalls how the city felt inclusive and welcoming when she first arrived: 'Besides you and Steve, I did not know anyone here. My children were young and as they made friends, so did I. There was an interest to meet people because they came from different parts of the world, and there wasn't much to do. Visiting others and learning about different cultures and traditions became the norm'. One of our favourite pastimes in those early days was cake decorating. As we planned our children's birthdays, we found that choices for ready-made cakes were few. We remembered a cake decorating session we had with a Vietnamese friend in Kuwait and decided to give it a try. We bought cake decorating equipment and pans over the summer while back in the States, and over many evenings, after putting the children to bed, perfected this art, with intricate borders, dainty flowers, and string and basket weaving techniques. Ruth, a friend of ours, also joined in, and the three of us bonded over this painstaking but fun way of celebrating family milestones. We became the go-to cake decorators for our friends' and colleagues' birthdays and anniversaries.

Despite having lived in global cities like Cairo, San Francisco, and Washington, D.C., Mona did not experience a true multicultural society until she lived in Abu Dhabi. Her first job was with a recruitment firm, where she got to know workers from India, Jordan, Lebanon, Philippines, Sri Lanka, and Syria, who gave her a window into their dreams and their aspirations. 'Everyone was here to contribute to the rapid development of the nation, not just the professionals but also the gas station attendant who filled your car in scorching temperatures, the fruit seller in the market, and the gardener who manicured the medians along the main city streets. The people were the richness of the place. It was a treat to meet new people and to learn about their culture over a plate of curry or noodles'.

There was a charm and familiarity to Abu Dhabi during this time, as Mona describes shopping with

her children at the open-air souks for fruit, vegetables, fish, or fabric. The neighbourhood grocery store, known as a *baqala*, worked on an IOU system. Mona explains, 'We would call down to the baqala to deliver anything from milk to diapers, and the shopkeeper would keep a running tab that we settled at the end of the month. One day our daughter took a taxi home from school and she didn't have enough money to pay the fare. So the shopkeeper paid the driver and added it to our tab'. There was also the Yemeni carpet salesman who packed Persian carpets worth thousands of dollars into a Nissan station wagon and sold them door-to-door. 'Boy, was he a good salesman', Mona laughs. 'He would leave the carpets at your home without any deposit, and they would grow on you. When you wanted to buy one, he made it easy by letting you pay in instalments. My carpets are some of the best purchases I have ever made. These carpets and my photographs make it home'.

Another aspect of the welcoming nature of the city was the collection of specialty food stores that imported different ethnic foods. Mona recalls the cheese and pickle shop that was dubbed the 'Egyptian Mecca', with its huge tubs of *torchi* (pickles), large wheels of *kashkaval* cheese, *mish* (a salty white cheese), and *feseekh* (dried fish), a specialty for the spring celebrations. For any Egyptian, a visit to the cheese and pickle shop would cure homesickness in a jiffy. There were similar shops for Indian, Filipino, and other ethnic cuisines. Mona truly believes that by catering to the different food cultures, Abu Dhabi was welcoming the expatriates to their new home. Similarly, the religious ceremonies, such as Sunday mass (delivered on Friday), were performed in multiple languages: Coptic, Latin,

> # I've come to realise that home is where you feel you belong, where you feel welcome, and where you feel safe.
>
> MONA

Amharic, Tigrinya, English, Arabic, and French, to reach the diverse population. The strength of the Coptic community in Abu Dhabi helped Mona's family stay connected to their faith.

Mona returned to the United States in 2004, not knowing if she would ever return to Abu Dhabi. However, twelve years later, her employer in Maryland asked if she would take a lead position on a project there. This would mean leaving her husband and children behind for a couple of years, as well as living alone for the first time. Her memories of the inclusive and welcoming place, in addition to the lifelong friendships she had formed, led her to accept the offer, despite the separation from her family. Mona shares: 'Landing in Abu Dhabi, I realised that it had become so much grander than I remembered. There were more bridges, buildings, suburbs, malls, and people. When I left, the Sheikh Zayed mosque was under construction, and now it crowns the skyline of the city'. She also noticed a shift in how people entertained. 'A big part of life in the 1990s was getting together at each other's homes. Now, many people are going to restaurants, which is easier for the hostess, but it isn't as intimate'. But for all the things that have changed in the new Abu Dhabi, Mona sees just as many that have remained the same. 'All those languages and dialects, the most delicious scents of multicultural cuisines along the city streets, and the legacy and love of Sheikh Zayed lives on'.

As the end of Mona's project approaches and she plans her return to the United States, she shares a thought: 'I've come to realise that home is where you feel you belong, where you feel welcome, and where you feel safe. Whoever said "you can't go home again" never lived in Abu Dhabi'.

MOLOKHIA
Jute Leaf Soup

Molokhia is considered a national symbol of Egypt, consumed by farmers and urbanites alike. The dish dates back to the days of the pharaohs, while there are some who believe it was first prepared by ancient Jews, which may account for its first translation, Jew's mallow soup. When chopped and added to chicken, rabbit, or duck broth, the leaves offer a mucilaginous quality. Egyptians maintain it has significant health benefits, as the leaves are rich in vitamins and minerals. Some believe it also has an aphrodisiac effect, which may account for why a siesta usually follows a molokhia lunch.

MONA *My teta (grandmother) used to make a huge pot on Sundays when we all gathered for lunch in Cairo. What I remember most was the gasp that she and Mom would make when they added the sautéed garlic (the* takliya*). That sound and smell meant lunch would be served momentarily. According to my teta, legend has it that by making this sound you guarantee the leaves don't settle below the broth, and that it keeps its mucilaginous texture.*

SERVES 6 TO 8

SOUP

1.5 kg (3½ lb) chicken, whole

1 onion, quartered

4–6 cardamom pods

2 bay leaves

1 whole nutmeg, cracked

Salt and black pepper

800 g (1¾ lb) frozen molokhia

TAKLIYA

2 tbsp butter, ghee or vegetable oil

6–10 cloves garlic, crushed

2 tbsp fresh coriander, chopped

GARNISH

1 red onion, finely chopped

120 ml (½ c) apple cider vinegar

2 pieces pita bread, toasted and broken in pieces

FOR THE SOUP

Prepare the chicken broth by placing the chicken, onion, cardamom, bay leaves, and nutmeg in a Dutch oven. Add water to cover; bring to a boil. Simmer, covered, for 1 hour or until the chicken is tender. *[Meanwhile, prepare the garnish, below.]*

Remove the chicken from the broth and set aside for later use. Strain the broth and return 700 millilitres (3 cups) to the Dutch oven. Season with salt and pepper. Bring to a boil and then let it simmer for 5 minutes. Drop the frozen molokhia into the simmering broth and let it thaw completely, stirring occasionally. Don't let it boil. Turn off the heat as soon as the molokhia has thawed. Don't cover the pot, as it will cause the leaves to sink to the bottom. If the soup is too thick, add some of the reserved broth, but not too much or the leaves will sink.

Cut the chicken it into quarters, rub with a bit of butter, and brown in a preheated oven, while preparing the takliya.

FOR THE TAKLIYA

Just before serving, bring the molokhia to a boil. Melt the butter or oil in a small skillet. Add the garlic and stir until it sizzles and turns golden; add the fresh coriander. Scrape everything into the molokhia, while gasping, and cook for 1 more minute, stirring gently.

FOR THE GARNISH

Soak the chopped onion in the vinegar for at least an hour.

Serve the molokhia in a large soup bowl, with the chicken, plain rice, toasted pita, and the onion/vinegar garnish on the side.

EGYPTIAN KONAFA
with Cream

If there were a queen of Arabic sweets, it would probably be *konafa*. There are variations across the region, in pronunciation and preparation, but all the different forms use threads of dough made from flour and water. Wherever it is made, this dessert is sinfully sweet, creamy, nutty, cheesy, and crunchy all at once. Konafa is prepared year-round but is especially popular during the month of Ramadan. It is said that Mu'awiya, the first Umeyyad caliph, on advice from his physician, ate konafa during Ramadan to satisfy his insatiable hunger.

MONA *My mother-in-law makes konafa that melts in your mouth and rivals any specialty pastry makers. The summer highlight for my kids was going to Teta's and diving into her homemade konafa with its creamy filling and crunchy crust. I have made this recipe with consistently delicious results.*

SERVES 8 TO 10

SYRUP

315 g (1½ c) granulated sugar

1 tbsp fresh lemon juice

1 tsp vanilla or **2 tsp** orange blossom water

FILLING

60 ml (¼ c) cold whole milk

40 g (¼ c) cornstarch

820 ml (3½ c) whipping cream

1 tsp vanilla or **2 tsp** orange blossom water

CRUST

340 g (12 oz) konafa dough, thawed

200 g (7 oz) butter, softened

Pistachios, shelled and coarsely chopped

FOR THE SYRUP

Mix the sugar and 180 millilitres (¾ cup) of water in a small saucepan over high heat, stirring frequently until the sugar dissolves. Add the lemon juice and boil for 2 minutes. Stir in the vanilla or orange blossom water. Remove from the heat and let it cool completely.

FOR THE FILLING

Combine the milk and cornstarch in a medium saucepan, whisking until the cornstarch is completely dissolved. Over low heat, slowly pour in 240 millilitres (1 cup) of the cream. Whisk until well combined. Add the second cup of cream, continuing to whisk. Do not let the mixture get so hot that it curdles or gets lumpy. As the mixture thickens, add the remaining cream, whisking continuously. The consistency should be like béchamel sauce. Remove from the heat, add the vanilla or orange blossom water, and stir until combined. Allow to cool completely.

FOR THE KONAFA

Shred the konafa dough into 3-centimetre (1-inch) pieces in a large bowl, keeping it covered while you work with it, so it doesn't dry out. Coat the bottom of a round 30-centimetre (12-inch) non-stick pan with a third of the butter. Cover the bottom of the pan with a thin layer of dough, about 1 centimetre (⅜ inch), patting it down firmly. Evenly spread the cream filling over the dough. Distribute the remaining dough over the filling to completely cover. Pat down the dough so all layers are connected.

Preheat the oven to 180°C (350°F). Melt the remaining butter and drizzle it evenly over the top of the konafa. Place the pan on the lower rack of the oven and bake for 30 minutes. The edges should be golden, and the top should be starting to turn golden. Move the pan to a rack in the middle of the oven and bake for an additional 15 minutes, or until the top is golden.

Working from the outside to the centre, drizzle about half of the cool syrup onto the konafa in a circular pattern. Flip the konafa onto a serving platter and drizzle with more of the syrup. Decorate with chopped pistachios. Serve it warm with the remaining syrup on the side.

LANA & HANI BARAMKI

LANA'S PARTIPERFECT
◊
PALESTINE / CANADA

MD SABER
◊
PALESTINE / CANADA

In April 2009, ahead of the International Venice Biennale, I co-hosted a luncheon for the commissioner of the United Arab Emirates' pavilion to celebrate the country's inaugural participation. The food was fresh and edgy and included Middle Eastern favourites with a twist. The eggplant *fatteh*, *koussa* gratin, mini *kibbeh* tartlets, *hindbeh* on *pommes paillasson*, mini grape-leaf skewers wrapped in lamb tenderloin, and the scrumptious pastries ignited as much enthusiasm as did this major art world event. That is how I met Lana, the founder of Lana's Partiperfect, a boutique catering company with food that is creative and as good as homemade.

Lana grew up in Abu Dhabi, where her parents, prominent members of the Palestinian and Lebanese communities, moved in the late 1960s from Beirut, having previously left their home in Palestine following the *Nakba* (displacement) of 1948. Lana's mother, a renowned hostess, was a great influence on her daughter. As a child, waking up to the clanking sounds of pots and pans and the delectable, comforting aromas of freshly baked *ka'ak* and *ma'amoul*, Lana was eager to help. Her mother's standard reply, however, was, 'You could help me by staying out of the kitchen'. With persistence, Lana eventually earned the position of resident chopper, peeler, and herb-picker and then graduated to table decorator. She muses, 'These childhood memories must have had a profound impact on me, because I ended up right where I started — in the kitchen'.

With a degree in mass communication from Boston University and experience in copy writing, the leap to catering wasn't obvious. Sitting in her cosy café cum cooking classroom, Lana recounts how moving to New York as a newly-wed led to her passion for food: 'Here I was, in our little studio in Midtown Manhattan, surrounded by some of the best restaurants in the world, and I was trying my hand at *kushari*, an Egyptian lentil and rice dish served with elbow pasta on the side and a spicy tomato sauce, while using a vintage General Electric stove from the 1950s. Unfortunately, the lentils were undercooked, the rice overcooked, the spicy tomato sauce was way too spicy, but the pasta was on point'. Sitting next to her, Hani laughs and reminds her that it wasn't the stove that was the issue that memorable day. Lana decided to immerse herself in New York City's rich food scene and enrolled at the Institute of Culinary Education (ICE), took a food writing course at Columbia University, and volunteered many hours at various upscale restaurants across the city.

Their move to Boston brought new opportunities and inspiration for Lana: 'It was my work at chef Mark Haley's Above and Beyond Catering, where endless hours of making thousands of hors d'oeuvres firmly rooted my desire to have a catering kitchen of my own someday. So, when we moved to Abu Dhabi in 2008, I started catering right out of the very kitchen I grew up in, with all its sounds and wonderful smells'. In 2010, now with two toddlers, Lana set up Lana's Partiperfect in a villa in the Marina area, with a dedicated catering kitchen, cooking classrooms, and a café. At a time when most catering in Abu Dhabi was done by hotels, this was a unique concept. When her mother visited, she was welcomed as quality control on some of the family heirloom recipes that Lana was adapting. According to Lana, 'Chefs are like artists — they are as good as their last creation, so it's important for them to keep innovating'. She is equally passionate about teaching the basics of cooking. The wide range of classes attract children, families, mothers, and corporate team building events, and can be tailored for any occasion. Lana confides, 'One bit of the philosophy at ICE that I absorbed, and still use as my secret weapon, is that you create good food from solid cooking techniques and not from recipes'.

Lana was able to perfect her own cooking techniques at Anissa in New York City, while trailing Chef Anita Lo, who encouraged her to allow her passion, culture, and background to seep into her style and approach to food.

Deeply rooted in their Palestinian culture, Lana, Hani, and their three children frequently travel to Palestine to visit Hani's parents and stay connected. Born and raised in Ramallah, Hani's earliest memories are tied to food: 'In the summer, my mother would make the famous *fatteh ghazawiye*, a combination of rice, lamb, and a specialty *shatta* (chili) sauce. She would assemble it in the morning in a tagine and give it to my brother and me to drop off at the baker's, who would cook it in his wood-fired oven while we went swimming on the beach in Gaza. Eventually feeling hungry, we were guaranteed not to forget it on our way back home for the family lunch'. With a smile, Hani says, 'My favourite is the Jerusalem ka'ak, which is baked in an oven traditionally fuelled by olive pits left over from the pressing process. They provide the perfect low, steady heat'. Palestinian food is a function of climate and geography. 'We eat what the land and sea provide each season, which is wonderful, and how I grew up. The grapes from Hebron are like candy. The onions in the spring are ripe for *musakhan*, the spinach fresh for a stew in the summer, and the cabbage heads are ready to be stuffed and rolled in the winter', Hani explains.

Hani honed his own cooking skills while at college in Boston. Calls home to his mother resulted in cryptic instructions for some of his favourite dishes, which always began with chopping and frying onions. He later developed his own dishes, including ginger butternut squash soup and pot roast with pearl onions and mushrooms. Lana and Hani enjoy planning highly elaborate menus for their families and have developed a well-choreographed way of working together in the kitchen. 'However', Lana says, 'out of all the cooking techniques we've experimented with, barbecuing is, hands down, our first love. I can blame my brother for that love affair. Early in our marriage, our apartment in Boston had a tiny hallway-like kitchen, so we'd pack our sweet Italian sausages and pre-cut filets of beef tenderloin and drive up to West Roxbury to fire up my brother's grill. One time, he and Hani set up a spit and grilled a whole lamb on an open fire, Arab style. It definitely smoked out the entire neighbourhood, which got everyone to gather around asking questions'.

Today, Hani and Lana's favourite way to celebrate the people they love is with a 'Yalla, come over. We'll have a barbecue!' They usually don't allow their guests to bring anything, unless a dessert is offered, because, as Lana puts it, 'Nobody says no to dessert'. Their new home in Khalifa A, with a custom-built barbecue station, swimming pool, and garden, is a far cry from the tiny studio in New York City, and their adventuresome recipes and array of items to grill are but a continuation of their passion for food, family and friendships.

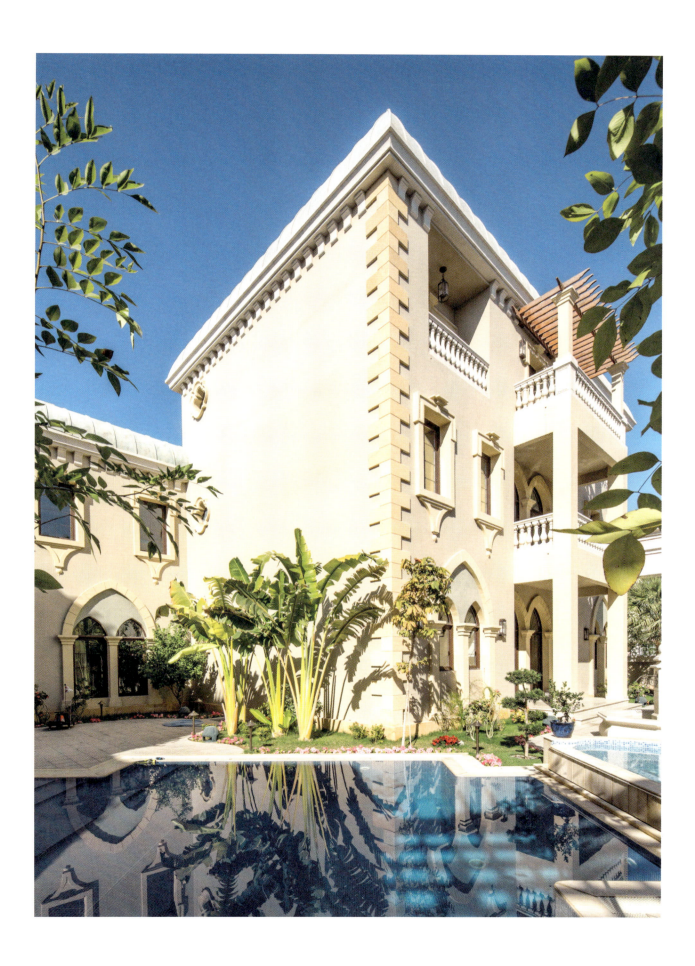

Yalla,
come over.
We'll have
a barbecue!

LANA & HANI

MARINATED BEEF TENDERLOIN

The most important part of grilling is managing the heat in the grill, both direct and indirect, and knowing when to use each. Beef tenderloin, also known as filet mignon, or chateaubriand for the centre cut, is the most expensive cut of beef, and should be grilled properly to take advantage of its buttery tenderness. It's important to choose prime or choice grade tenderloin from Angus or heritage breed steers, as it will have comparatively more marbled fat and flavour. The tenderloin does not have much fat on the outside, so it is easy to overcook it, resulting in dry meat. After searing, it is important to roast the beef slowly and evenly with indirect heat. Tenderloin is best cooked medium to medium-rare.

LANA *My all-time favourite barbecue memory was when we lived in Boston and I was too far into my pregnancy to fly internationally, so we couldn't spend New Year's Eve with our families in Abu Dhabi. It was snowing that night, but Hani decided it was the perfect time to have a barbecue dinner; I thought he was crazy. Curiously, I said, 'The porch is covered in snow! How are you going to get the grill on it?' and of course, Mr. Chill replied, 'I'll shovel a square just large enough for the grill to fit — you'll see!' And that I did. Hani put on his black puffer jacket that made him loowwk like the Michelin Man, a hat, and thick gloves, and grabbed an umbrella. After a bit of shovelling, he stood in the snow under his umbrella and barbecued away. Afterwards, we toasted our achievement with sparkling apple cider; they were the best damn steaks I've ever had. Our baby was born a week later.*

SERVES 6 TO 8

MARINADE

- **60 ml (¼ c)** molasses
- **2 tbsp** honey
- **2 tbsp** ketchup
- **1 tbsp** Dijon mustard
- **60 ml (¼ c)** V8 juice
- **2 tbsp** red vinegar
- **2 tsp** cayenne
- **10 g (½ c)** fresh thyme
- Salt and black pepper, to taste

- **1.75 kg (4 lb)** beef tenderloin
- **28 g (1 oz)** butter
- **2 tbsp** olive oil

Mix the marinade ingredients in a small bowl. Adjust the amounts to taste, keeping the consistency thick to coat the meat. Trim and tie the beef; rub with the marinade and set aside at room temperature for 1 hour.

Heat a large cast iron or heavy-bottomed skillet on the stove and add the butter and olive oil. Sear the tenderloin on all sides until caramelised, about 2 to 3 minutes on each side.

Set the grill to 230°C (450°F) or high heat. Place the beef in the centre of the grill rack. Lower the heat to medium. *[You can hold your hand 2.5 centimetres (1 inch) above the heat for 3 to 5 seconds.]* Cover the grill but turn the meat occasionally until a meat thermometer inserted into the centre registers 54°C (130°F) for medium rare and 60°C (140°F) for medium. Grilling time will vary depending on the thickness but can take 15 to 30 minutes. Remove the beef from the grill and tent loosely with foil. Let it rest for 15 minutes before slicing.

MINT AND PINE NUT-CRUSTED LAMB CHOPS
with Black Peppercorn Sauce

SERVES 6 TO 8

HANI *Grilling is probably one of the best ways to cook lamb chops, even for those who are not lamb lovers. The rib chops are our preferred cut but you can use loin chops as well. The smooth flavour and long rib bone, trimmed of fat, make for a nice presentation. For grilling, it's best to get chops that are thick — about 4 centimetres (1½ inches). We usually serve the chops with a mint sauce or black peppercorn sauce.*

LAMB CHOPS

30 g (1 c) mint, finely chopped

75 g (½ c) pine nuts, crushed

2 cloves garlic, finely chopped

60 ml (¼ c) olive oil

1 tsp salt

1 tsp black pepper

900 g (2 lb) lamb chops

BLACK PEPPERCORN SAUCE

2 tbsp olive oil

285 g (10 oz) lamb bones

1 carrot, cut in chunks

1 stalk celery, cut in chunks

140 g (5 oz) white onion

60 ml (¼ c) tomato paste

60 ml (¼ c) red vinegar

2 tbsp black peppercorns, crushed

28 g (1 oz) butter, melted

1 tbsp all-purpose flour

Salt and black pepper

FOR THE LAMB CHOPS

Mix the mint leaves, pine nuts, garlic, olive oil, salt, and pepper with a mortar and pestle or in a food processor to make a paste. Remove the excess fat from the lamb chops and place in a single layer in a large glass baking dish. Rub the mint mixture on all sides of the chops so they are evenly coated. Cover and refrigerate for 3 to 4 hours.

Set up the grill for medium-high heat. *[You can hold your hand 2.5 centimetres (1 inch) above the heat for no more than 3 seconds.]* Grill the chops for 4 minutes on each side for medium-rare and a couple of minutes more for medium-well. Close the grill lid so the chops will cook evenly. Transfer the chops to a platter and let them rest for 5 to 10 minutes before serving.

FOR THE BLACK PEPPERCORN SAUCE

Add the olive oil to a medium Dutch oven and sauté the lamb bones for 5 minutes, until browned. Add the carrots, celery, and onion and continue to sauté until they are lightly browned. Add the tomato paste and continue to sauté for another couple of minutes. Pour in the vinegar and 1 litre (1 quart) of water and bring to a boil. Simmer on low heat for 45 minutes, until the sauce reduces by half.

Strain the sauce and return it to the saucepan. Add the black peppercorns and continue to simmer for another 10 minutes. Combine the melted butter and flour in a small bowl and gradually add it to the sauce, stirring continuously until it thickens. Season with salt and pepper.

GRILLED HONEY AND MINT STRAWBERRIES
with Mascarpone

LANA *Vinegar and strawberries are not an expected combination, but when I served them at my last dinner party, they were a great hit! The sweet strawberries, the rich mascarpone and the tangy balsamic vinegar come together nicely. I prefer white balsamic to avoid colouring the berries. These grilled berries are also great over morning Greek yogurt, mixed with overnight oats, or sliced over a salad for lunch.*

SERVES 6 TO 8

- **60 ml (¼ c)** white balsamic vinegar
- **60 ml (¼ c)** honey
- **15 g (½ c)** mint, roughly chopped
- **700 g (1½ lb)** large strawberries
- **255 g (9 oz)** chilled mascarpone cheese
- **120 ml (½ c)** whipping cream
- **1 tsp** vanilla
- **2 tsp** granulated sugar

Combine the vinegar, honey, and mint in a bowl. Toss the strawberries in the mint syrup up to 2 hours before serving.

Whip the mascarpone, whipping cream, vanilla, and sugar in a medium bowl with a hand mixer until soft peaks form. Cover and refrigerate for up to 3 hours.

Set the grill for medium heat. *[You can hold your hand 2.5 centimetres (1 inch) above the heat for 3 to 5 seconds.]* Slide the strawberries onto skewers. Stainless steel skewers work best because the berries won't stick to them. If using wooden skewers, soak them in cold water before adding the strawberries. Grill the strawberries for 1 minute on each side, until lightly marked; transfer to a platter.

To serve, portion the mascarpone cream into glass goblets, remove the berries from the skewers, and place a few on top of each serving. Alternatively, serve the strawberries on the skewers and the mascarpone cream on the side.

NATHAN BROWN

FITNESS PROFESSIONAL ◊ NEW ZEALAND

When my husband and I decided to climb Mount Kilimanjaro in July 2001 with the first adventure challenge organised by Gulf for Good to raise money for Ambulances for Africa, I turned to Nathan for advice on acclimatisation. Not only did he give us a detailed training plan, but he also donated the proceeds from a full day of instruction at the Abu Dhabi Health and Fitness Club to our fundraising efforts. Nathan's perpetual smile, generous personality, and high energy were just what the newly opened club needed. He introduced the Les Mills fitness programme to the region and was their original master trainer. With his passion for fitness and an active lifestyle, a cult-like following rapidly developed around his classes, which always had waiting lists.

Fitness and a healthy lifestyle were integral parts of Nathan's upbringing. He grew up in the small town of Whakatane, on New Zealand's North Island, where his Polynesian ancestors had immigrated. The Māori are the indigenous people of New Zealand, known as *tangata whenua* (people of the land). Central to their beliefs are that land, water, and air are essential ingredients of life to be respected, cherished, and sustained. Nathan relates how he learned the Māori values: 'My grandmother lived to be 94 years old. She lived in a small cottage farmhouse in a beautiful little township called Manutuke, twenty kilometres north of Gisborne. The homestead was without electricity. She power walked everywhere. She ate everything fresh from the farm. She chopped her own firewood. She washed her clothes in the river with a piece of Palmolive soap. She had fourteen children and was the matriarch of the family. I was in awe of her healthy life and hard work'.

Both of Nathan's parents were involved in sports, providing a great example, but Nathan suffered from chronic asthma as a young boy, and sports that involved running were a struggle. His self-confidence was fading, so his father, a judo enthusiast, encouraged him to try martial arts. As a teenager, he joined the *whanau* (family) called Rangataua O Aotearoa (Warriors of New Zealand), which formed the foundation for his success in life. 'This club was founded by the late John Tahu Parae. It is based on our Māori cultural philosophies and our language. Known for its hard-core physical training methods, it set the standard for toughness. It has also helped to turn around the lives of many young Māori men, converting us to fitness junkies and building character', Nathan proudly tells me.

Having lived here for almost two decades, Nathan has seen the lifestyle changes and the explosive growth of the fitness industry. While there is an increased awareness of health and nutrition, the car culture still reigns supreme. Nathan imparts, 'If you think about today's society and how we live, people sit too much. Sitting is the new smoking'. He suggests being more active throughout the day—not relying simply on gym sessions and fitness equipment. Nathan explains the seven primal movements that underpin his training philosophy, 'These seven movements are used in day-to-day life. My grandmother would squat to milk the cow, lunge up the stairs, push the firewood trailer, pull the go cart, bend to wash the laundry, and walk everywhere. Nathan and his wife now run their own business in Dubai, where they specialise in functional well-being. He adds, 'We advocate the importance of these movement patterns in addition to eating clean and nutritious food. It's the "new millennium" direction towards holistic health'.

Looking across Saadiyat Beach, we eagerly await lunch, prepared by Chef Vladimiro at Saadiyat Beach Club. His warm lentil salad with garden vegetables and salt-encrusted sea bass with purple potatoes offer a healthy, delicious meal—just the right balance of protein and carbohydrates to energise Nathan for his afternoon training sessions.

> Sitting is the new smoking.
>
> NATHAN

WARM LENTIL SALAD
with Garden Vegetables and Poached Shrimp

SERVES 6 TO 8

DRESSING

- **60 ml (¼ c)** raw apple cider vinegar
- **2 tbsp** lemon juice
- **1 tbsp** Dijon mustard
- **1 tbsp** honey
- **1½ tsp** salt, to taste
- Black pepper
- **120 ml (½ c)** olive oil

SALAD

- **225 g (8 oz)** Le Puy green lentils
- **1** whole clove
- **1** small onion, peeled
- **1** medium carrot, cubed
- **1** celery stalk, chopped
- **1 clove** garlic, crushed
- **1** bay leaf
- **2 sprigs** thyme
- **700 ml (3 c)** vegetable broth or water
- **1 tsp** salt
- **110 g (4 oz)** fennel, thinly shaved
- **55 g (2 oz)** baby carrots, halved
- **55 g (2 oz)** asparagus tips
- **55 g (2 oz)** romanesco broccoli
- **55 g (2 oz)** broccolini florets
- **55 g (2 oz)** peas
- **12–16** shrimp, shelled
- **1** lemon, halved
- Olive oil
- Salt and black pepper

The French green lentils, *lentilles du Puy*, from the Auvergne region in France, are sometimes referred to as 'the caviar of lentils'. They are intensely flavoured and much less starchy than other lentils, so they hold their shape when cooked. They are easy to prepare and can be served warm or at room temperature. They make a great accompaniment to grilled fish, roasted root vegetables, or a leafy green salad. This lentil salad celebrates Mediterranean flavours with fresh vegetables and shrimp. Be sure not to overcook the lentils, and mix them with the vegetables and vinaigrette while they are still warm so they can better absorb the dressing.

FOR THE DRESSING

Whisk together the vinegar, lemon, mustard, honey, salt, and pepper. Slowly add the olive oil in a thin stream, whisking until well blended.

FOR THE SALAD

Put the lentils in a strainer, remove any small stones, and rinse with cold water. Press the clove into the onion and add the carrots, celery, garlic, bay leaf, and thyme to a medium saucepan. Add the lentils and pour in the broth or water to cover generously. Bring to a boil, add the salt, and simmer for 25 to 30 minutes, until the lentils are just tender. Add more water if needed but be sure not to overcook them. Drain the lentils. Remove the vegetables and herbs; discard.

While the lentils are cooking, shave the fennel paper thin, preferably with a mandoline, and soak in ice water so it remains crispy. Blanch the remaining vegetables, separately, then transfer them immediately to ice water. If desired, sauté the blanched vegetables in 1 tablespoon of olive oil to finish and set aside.

Poach the shrimp in boiling water with the lemon halves for 2 to 3 minutes, being careful not to overcook them; drain.

Toss the lentils with the cooked vegetables, shrimp, and dressing. Season with more salt and pepper to taste. Serve in a large bowl garnished with the crispy fennel.

BRANZINO AL SALE
Herb and Salt-Crusted Sea Bass with Porcini Mushrooms and Purple Potatoes

This is a classic Sicilian recipe introduced by Chef Vladimiro of the Saadiyat Beach Club's Safina Restaurant. Sicilian cuisine incorporates the many foreign influences of the conquerors of this Mediterranean hub, including the Greeks, Normans, Arabs, Spaniards, and Catalans. The origin of this dish is claimed by many, but cooking fish in salt is believed to have originated with the Phoenicians in Carthage, where they traded in salt. This technique produces a beautifully moist fish, as the salt crust seals in the juices. A variety of whole fish, such as hammour, sea bream, red snapper, or turbot can be baked this way. The chef likes to serve it with two of his favourite side dishes, samphire and purple potatoes. Samphire is a sea vegetable that grows on sea cliffs and rocks and has a crisp, salty taste. While it is known as 'the poor man's asparagus', it has many health benefits and is packed with vitamins. As for the purple potato, native to South America, what a great way to enjoy a nutritious starch that has the same anti-oxidant benefits as berries and pomegranates.

SERVES 4 TO 6

FISH

1 kg (2¼ lb) fresh sea bass, whole

2 lemons

6 tbsp thyme, chopped

6 tbsp rosemary, chopped

4 large egg whites

450 g (1 lb) rock salt

2 tbsp lemon zest

VEGETABLES

450 g (1 lb) tomatoes, vine-ripened

Rock salt

120 ml (½ c) olive oil, divided

1 kg (2¼ lb) purple potatoes, quartered

110 g (4 oz) butter, divided

Rosemary

Salt and black pepper

85 g (3 oz) porcini mushrooms, halved

Thyme

450 g (1 lb) samphire

Preheat the oven to 200°C (400°F). Arrange the racks to accommodate two baking trays.

Clean and gut the fish. Trim the fins, scale it, and remove the gills. Cut the lemons into slices and insert them into the cavity of the fish, along with half the thyme and rosemary. Whisk the egg whites until they form soft peaks and then fold in the rock salt, lemon zest, and remaining thyme and rosemary. Line a large baking tray with parchment paper. Spread one-third of the egg white mixture on the baking tray in the shape of the fish. Lay the fish on top and spoon the remaining mixture over the fish, covering it like a blanket. The head can stay exposed. Bake for 30 to 35 minutes or until crisp. To test, insert a knife through the crust at the thickest part of the fish. If it comes out hot to the touch, the fish is ready.

While the fish is baking, prepare the vegetables. Place the tomatoes on a baking tray, season them with rock salt, and drizzle with 3 tablespoons of olive oil. Bake them with the fish for 20 to 25 minutes or until soft. Parboil the potatoes in a saucepan with just enough water to cover. Drain and then sauté them in a skillet with half of the butter and 2 tablespoons of olive oil; sprinkle with rosemary. Season with salt and pepper, transfer to a bowl, and cover to keep warm. Sauté the mushrooms in the same skillet with the remaining butter and 2 tablespoons of olive oil; season them with thyme, salt, and pepper and set aside. Transfer to a bowl and cover to keep warm. Add 1 tablespoon of oil to the same pan and sauté the samphire until tender.

When the fish is done, break the crust and carefully remove it from the top of the fish (the skin will likely pull away). Serve the fish garnished with lemon wedges, a drizzle of olive oil, and the vegetables on the side.

2000s
A NEW COURSE

The United Arab Emirates ended 2004 in a sombre mood as it lay to rest Sheikh Zayed bin Sultan Al Nahyan, the founding father of the nation. He was immensely popular and had presided over a period of rapid development, peace and prosperity, in a region characterised by instability. At the beginning of the new millennium, the turbulent waters flowed close to home, with the events of 9/11 and the subsequent 2003 Gulf War.

During the last few years of Sheikh Zayed's rule, as his health declined, the pace of development had slowed. There was a feeling that Abu Dhabi had fallen behind. The next generation of leadership embarked on an accelerated vision, unveiled in 2008, to transform Abu Dhabi into a knowledge-based economy, with diversification and liberalisation programmes that would reduce its reliance on oil revenue in the coming decades. They sought to empower the private sector, encourage foreign investments, and forge international partnerships in industry, real estate, tourism, and education.

In 2005, a new law was passed allowing nationals to buy and sell property in the emirate, which was previously banned. A real estate market was born, seemingly overnight. With the meteoric increase in the price of oil and a new urban master plan, ambitious development projects in energy, industry, education, tourism, and culture were announced. Most notable was the Saadiyat Cultural District, future home to the Louvre Abu Dhabi, Guggenheim Abu Dhabi, and Sheikh Zayed National Museum. The vision to create a contemporary cultural locus was bold and unprecedented in the Arab world. Partnerships with New York University and Paris-Sorbonne University were also launched, to build degree-granting campuses in Abu Dhabi. World-class music performances, film festivals, and art exhibitions flourished, along with Formula One races, and international triathlons, tennis, and golf championships. The city's dynamism and energy were palpable at every level.

The announcements of these partnerships put Abu Dhabi firmly on the world map. Etihad was launched in 2003 as the national air carrier, establishing Abu Dhabi as a hub and destination for business travellers and tourists. The six-star Emirates Palace hotel, a modern-day Versailles, lured royalty and wealthy pleasure seekers from around the globe. Plans for more hotels and tourist attractions were on the drawing boards. Once again, the supply of housing, offices, and schools fell short of the demand, and the emirate experienced an unprecedented construction boom that only slowed at the end of the decade when the impact of the global economic crisis was felt.

A culinary highlight of the decade was the launch of Gourmet Abu Dhabi in 2009, bringing an all-star cast of Michelin chefs and international industry heavyweights. They were invited to the capital for a ten-day gastronomic extravaganza, which included cooking with locally based chefs, offering a range of masterclasses, and hosting special dinners. There was also the Gourmet Abu Dhabi Stars Awards, dubbed the Oscars of the local restaurant industry, aimed at recognising and encouraging local talent. Travellers and newcomers to the city during the second part of the decade sought finer dining experiences than what the handful of international hotels offered at the time. A burgeoning culinary and cultural scene was set in motion as the foundations for a cosmopolitan capital city were being built.

SHAIKHA AL KAABI

ENTREPRENEUR
◊
UAE

Shaikha Al Kaabi's passion for her local cuisine, which is not well known outside the country or amongst many residents, led her to create one of the first restaurants in Abu Dhabi serving home-style Emirati food. When she was twelve, her family moved to the United States, where her father was a fellow at the United States Army War College in Carlisle, Pennsylvania. Shaikha recalls, 'It was a closed community. The children at school would ask me if we had pencils and pens back home, and if my parents had a car or rode a camel'. For the school potluck lunch, usually graced by hamburgers and pizza, she asked her mother to make her favourite *machboos deyay*. The aromatic rice and chicken dish, flavoured with *lumi* (dried lime), and *bzar*, the magical Emirati spice blend, was a lesson in deliciousness, as well as in geography for her classmates. Thus began her ambassadorship for Emirati food and culture.

Years later, in her hometown of Abu Dhabi, she began to shape her dream of opening an Emirati restaurant that was authentic and contemporary. In 2011, during the 40th National Day celebrations in Zayed Sports Stadium, Shaikha was given the opportunity to test her idea. She had four kiosks, and with the help of her mother and grandmother, Shaikha developed the recipes for *fareed* (vegetable stew with flat bread), *batheetha* (date and cardamom crumble), *sagaw* (tapioca pudding infused with cardamom and saffron), and *rahesh* (sweetened tahini-based milkshake). To everyone's amazement, within thirty minutes of opening, the food at each of the kiosks was gone! Working quickly, the cooks diced, fried, rolled, and spread, while Shaikha organised delivery of more ingredients. Even Shaikha, who had always believed in the delights of Emirati cuisine, was taken by surprise.

Inspired by her inaugural and immediate success, Shaikha launched the Meylas food truck as the initial phase of establishing her restaurant. 'With the food truck, I could reach more people in Abu Dhabi and Liwa Oasis', Shaikha explained. The Meylas food truck made its debut at the 2014 Abu Dhabi Art Fair, and the star was *luqamaat,* (fried sweet dough with syrup). I found myself proclaiming to the international art-world visitors, who were queuing down the sidewalk, the unique flavour of these beignet-type sweets.

Ultimately, the Meylas restaurant opened in June 2015 with a full menu based on recipes from Emirati mothers and grandmothers. When I visited the restaurant as the finishing touches were being made, I felt a deep sense of nostalgia for the Abu Dhabi prior to the rapid pace of development, the large influx of people from all over the world, and the subsequent lifestyle changes to the city. The restaurant's interior is reminiscent of a time gone by, including the 1980s terrazzo-tile floors, the wooden school chairs, the naked lightbulbs, and the painted metal gates of the *shaabiyat* (sturdy modern housing).

Shaikha has great affection for her culture. The many days spent hunting for traditional doors, windows, and decorative motifs have paid off in the welcoming interior of Meylas. However, running a restaurant comes with its challenges. Shaikha recalls an interview with a South Asian cook who could not communicate in English or Arabic, but in the kitchen, he could produce a delicious machboos deyay. And just as that dish transcended language to communicate a shared respect through food and traditional flavours, Meylas's international staff communicates with each other and their customers through the savoury and sweet classic Emirati dishes.

As we sip *chai haleeb* in the corner window at Meylas, with the rhythms of Emirati music in the background and the sweeping curvilinear forms of the Yas Viceroy Hotel on the horizon, Shaikha and I acknowledge there is much to celebrate in Abu Dhabi: the city's cultural and technological tour de force, the delectable flavours of its food, and the many talents of the people who call this city home.

GAHWA ARABIA
Arabic Coffee

Westerners, whose only experience with Middle Eastern coffee may be the relatively thick Turkish variety served across the Levant and North Africa, are often surprised by how light Emirati coffee is. The coffee beans are lightly roasted, then coarsely ground with cardamom and cloves for fragrance. The grounds are boiled in a large *dalleh* (coffee pot) and left to brew before serving. The dalleh is considered a prized possession when inherited from family elders. There is an Emirati proverb that says, 'He who does not have a dalleh cannot be found'. The word for 'found' in Arabic sounds similar to 'dalleh'. So, he who does not have a coffee pot has not received guests, implying that no one would seek him.

Arabic coffee is entrenched in hospitality, tradition, and ceremony and is a symbol of generosity. Serving coffee has a deep cultural meaning that goes beyond a good brew or socialising with friends. It is a ceremonial act of extending hospitality and kindness, which both honours the guest and returns the honour to the host. The tradition of making Arabic coffee is now inscribed by UNESCO as an intangible heritage.

SHAIKHA *My grandma taught me the etiquette of serving coffee: start with the eldest family member or guest, make sure not to fill the tiny cup more than a third, hold the dalleh in the left hand and offer the cup with the right, and stand attentively for the traditional second and third refill or the quick jiggle, which means, 'No more'. We have adapted this tradition at Meyles by having guests order their own dalleh and then serve themselves after the waiter offers the first cup.*

SERVES 6 TO 8

1 l (1 qt) water

4 tbsp light to medium-roasted Arabica coffee, coarsely ground

2–3 tsp cardamom (ground or pods crushed)

2–3 whole cloves

Pinch of saffron

1 tsp rose water (optional)

Boil the water in a dalleh or medium-sized saucepan. Add the coffee and continue to boil, stirring as the foam rises so it does not overflow. Add the cardamom and cloves and continue to brew over medium heat for 10 to 15 minutes. Remove from the heat, cover, and let the grounds settle to the bottom. Meanwhile, preheat a thermal carafe with boiling water for a few minutes and discard the water. Sprinkle a pinch of saffron and the rose water into the carafe. Strain and pour the brewed coffee into the carafe and discard the grounds.

Allow the coffee to steep for 5 to 10 minutes before serving in *finjaans* (Arabic coffee cups). Serve with dates or other sweets.

LUQAMAAT
Fried Dumplings with Date Syrup

These decadent dumplings are a favourite across the region, made from a light yeasty batter, deep-fried and dipped in syrup, honey, or molasses, or sprinkled with sugar. In medieval Baghdad, these crispy golden orbs were known as *luqmat al qadi*, meaning 'judge's mouthful', and graced the caliph's table. With slight variations in texture and the type of sweetener used, they are now known by different names in different countries: *zalaabia* in Egypt; *aweimat*, meaning 'floaters' in Lebanon and Syria; *loukoumades* in Greece; *skarmati* in Somalia; and *luqamaat,* meaning 'little bites', in the Gulf.

SHAIKHA *These dumplings are addictive! They both tempt and motivate us during the fasting month of Ramadan. We prepare a fresh batch every day and anxiously await the first bite after the* iftar *meal, when a dose of sugar is much needed. We snack on them after iftar through to* suhoor, *the meal before going to bed. One bite is never enough!*

MAKES 20 TO 24

Pinch of saffron
1 tbsp rose water
2 tsp yeast
2 tbsp granulated sugar
375 g (2½ c) all-purpose flour
1 tbsp cornstarch
1 tsp cardamom
1 tbsp cooking oil
3 tbsp plain yogurt
Cooking oil, for frying
Date syrup or honey
Sesame seeds

Combine the saffron and rose water. Dissolve the yeast and sugar in 120 millilitres (½ cup) of warm water and let stand for 10 to 15 minutes, until it begins to froth.

In a large mixing bowl, combine the flour, cornstarch, cardamom, oil, and yogurt. Add the yeast mixture and saffron/rose water. Gradually pour in 120 millilitres (½ cup) of water and beat vigorously by hand in a circular motion for 5 minutes, until the batter is smooth and elastic with no lumps. Add more water as needed to get a thick, pancake-like batter and mix well. Cover with plastic wrap and let rise in a warm place for at least 1 hour. Beat the batter once more.

Make the luqamaat in batches in a deep pan that provides a large surface area. Heat the oil until it sizzles when a small piece of dough is added. Using an oiled teaspoon or by hand, drop in multiple 3-centimetre (1-inch) dough balls, but don't crowd them. Reduce the heat to medium and fry the balls for 10 minutes, stirring continuously with a slotted spoon until the balls are puffed, crisp and golden. They should be slightly crunchy on the outside and soft in the middle. The batter is light, so it may produce irregularly shaped balls. Remove the luqamaat to a strainer to drain for a few minutes. Raise the heat under the oil before cooking the next batch and repeat the process. Gently toss the luqamaat with date syrup or honey, coating completely. Sprinkle them with sesame seeds and serve immediately.

MACHBOOS DEYAY
Emirati Rice Pilaf with Chicken

Rice is a staple food in the Gulf countries. Its name in Arabic is *ruz*, but in the Khaleeji dialect it is *aish*, which means life. In Egyptian Arabic, aish refers to bread, signifying its centrality to the diet. It is unimaginable to have an Emirati meal without rice, and usually there are a few different types to choose from. *Machboos* is a cross between biryani and risotto, where the rice is cooked in the spiced broth of the meat or chicken, melding the spices and ingredients.

—
SERVES
4 TO 6
—

6 tbsp plain yogurt, divided

2 tbsp Emirati bzar spice mix

1.5 kg (3½ lb) chicken, cut into pieces

500 g (2½ c) basmati rice

80 ml (⅓ c) vegetable oil

5 cardamom pods, crushed

1 cinnamon stick

10 black peppercorns

2 whole lumi, cracked

450 g (1 lb) onions, chopped

1 tbsp ginger, crushed

1 tbsp garlic, crushed

4 small green chilies, halved

1 tsp turmeric

1 tsp cumin

1 tsp coriander powder

285 g (10 oz) canned tomatoes, chopped

1 tsp salt

Cooking oil

450 g (1 lb) potatoes, peeled and cubed

Handful of fresh coriander, chopped

GARNISH

3 tbsp cooking oil

2 onions, thinly sliced

85 g (½ c) raw cashews

55 g (¼ c) raisins

Fresh coriander, chopped

SHAIKHA *Machboos is a fixture at our Friday family lunch, made with chicken, lamb, fish, or shrimp. The secret to this dish and most of our food is the spice mix,* bzar, *the exact composition of which is a closely guarded secret in many families. You can serve machboos with* achaar *(mango or lime preserved in spicy oil),* daqoos *(a spicy tomato-based sauce), or yogurt with chopped cucumber and mint.*

Combine 4 tablespoons of the yogurt with 1 tablespoon of the bzar in a large bowl. Coat the chicken and marinade for 1 hour or longer. Rinse the rice and soak in enough water to cover for 1 hour; drain.

Heat the oil in a Dutch oven over medium heat. Add the cardamom pods, cinnamon stick, peppercorns, and lumi and stir for 2 minutes. Add the onions and sauté until golden. Add the ginger, garlic, and green chilies and stir for 2 minutes. Add the chicken and marinade and cook for a few minutes on each side. Sprinkle in the turmeric, remaining bzar, cumin, and coriander powder. Add the tomatoes, salt, and 475 millilitres (2 cups) of water; bring to a boil. Cover, lower the heat, and simmer for 30 to 45 minutes, until the chicken is done. Transfer the chicken to a roasting pan.

Remove the cinnamon stick and lumi from the broth and discard. Add the potatoes and fresh coriander and boil until the potatoes are just tender. Adjust the broth to get a one-to-one ratio with the rice. Stir in the remaining yogurt until dissolved and add the rice. Seal the Dutch oven with aluminium foil, cover, and cook over low heat for 30 minutes until the rice is done.

Turn on the oven broiler. Brush the chicken with some oil and broil until golden. Serve the rice on a platter with the chicken pieces on top. Garnish with sautéed onions, cashews, raisins, and fresh coriander.

FOR THE GARNISH

Place a large skillet over medium-high heat and add the oil and onions; sauté until they are dark brown, but not burnt. Remove the onions with a slotted spoon and drain on paper towels. Sauté the cashews in the same oil until golden brown; add the raisins during the last few minutes.

RANYA & SALIM NASSER

MUSEUM EDUCATOR ◊ **PALESTINE / US**

CIVIL ENGINEER ◊ **PALESTINE / US**

When the weather is lovely, one of my favourite walks on a Friday morning is to Ranya and Salim's house in Al Bateen. If I'm early, I'll find Ranya in the garden with a fresh pot of coffee, a book, and a couple of cats at her feet, enjoying the breeze and happy to welcome me into her solitude. If I'm late, and lucky, I'll find her in the kitchen baking something for the children and their neighbourhood friends, who endlessly buzz in and out of each other's homes. Sitting at the wooden refectory table in their kitchen, we've had some of our most memorable conversations about motherhood, marriage, aging, art, food, and friendship. It was at this table, many years ago, that they told me how the tragic events of September 11, 2001 in New York City, where Salim was living, expedited their wedding plans and landed them, newly married, in Abu Dhabi with just a couple of suitcases.

As with many expatriates who move to Abu Dhabi, the projected stay is short, with plans to return home after one or two years. Convinced they would only be here for just a few months, Ranya took a leave of absence from her job in arts education at the Kennedy Center for the Performing Arts in Washington, D.C. Little did she know that six months would turn into sixteen years and counting! Ranya smiles as she reminisces, 'It was during those early years in Abu Dhabi that I learned how to become a wife and mother. Cooking was the easy part; I had to learn how to dress a wound, change a diaper, and pack suitcases for three months!' Ranya remembers the feeling of being overwhelmingly happy, lost, and aimless at the same time: 'It was all so surreal, not being able to celebrate the joy of my new life with my family and old friends — it was like I was living someone else's life. It took me years to realise that we had built a new family and new circle of friends who became part of our story and witness to our life here'.

I've watched Ranya prepare countless meals, haphazardly pulling ingredients from the cupboards, and tossing them together to make something original each time. Ranya credits the lack of familiar ingredients in Abu Dhabi during those early years that made her the creative cook she is today. 'I was buying Martha Stewart magazines from Spinneys at 80 dirhams a pop to come up with new things for dinner and got frustrated when I couldn't find ingredients like poppy seeds or celery salt'. Instinctively, she learned how to adapt recipes and eventually started to reverse the process and buy ingredients first and figure out how to put them together later. She rarely prepares in advance, relying on having a well-stocked pantry and knowing she can send a child to a neighbour for an egg or some mint. This spur-of-the-moment approach lends some mystery to what she will bring to our Thanksgiving dinners, but her contribution is always delicious.

Her flurry and chaos in the kitchen can be nerve-wracking. She always laughs when I point this out and reminds me that she cooks instinctively and doesn't know how to follow a recipe, although she has a vast collection of beautiful cookbooks she reads like novels. She approaches the kitchen as an artist does a studio, feeling, smelling and tasting her way towards a meal. She rarely remembers how the food tastes but always remembers how she felt when she was making it. When things go right she regrets not having written down the steps and has spent countless hours trying to recreate favourites. Ranya is happiest when their table is full of friends who delight in her successful dishes and don't mind if they end up eating pizza if it all goes up in flames.

Embracing the creative spirit is what Ranya seeks to inspire in others, as well, through her professional role in arts education. After a ten-year hiatus, Ranya returned to working in arts and museum education. She adds, 'I got to know the community much better and the issues artists and art educators were facing. I could apply my knowledge to help. With that,

my personal self-worth became stronger. My identity became clearer. I am still a wife and mother first, but I am also a worker and contribute to society', she tells me with conviction.

This sense of rootedness in a community and forming lasting friendships with Emiratis has given Ranya a different perspective on the meaning of 'home'. She had always dreamed of a suburban American life in a peaceful neighbourhood, with a house, front lawn, and white picket fence, attracted by the sense of community. Recently, however, she confided, 'As we have made friends, as we've watched the kids and their friends grow together, as the city has evolved, and we've evolved, I realised Abu Dhabi *is* our home — this has become my white picket fence.

We have a vibrant, massive pink bougainvillea instead of an oak tree outside our door, but this is as close as a community can possibly get'. Ranya remembers a walk she took with Salim down the Corniche towards Marina Mall several years ago. She got emotional as they looked towards the evening skyline and realised this was their city together — it wasn't Washington, New York, or Athens, it was Abu Dhabi, for better or for worse. She says she remembers her family milestones in connection to the buildings that went up or stores that opened or shut down.

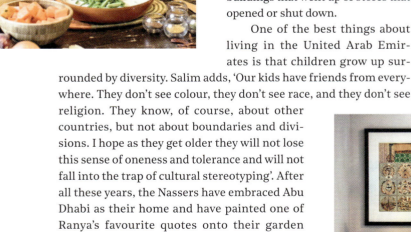

One of the best things about living in the United Arab Emirates is that children grow up surrounded by diversity. Salim adds, 'Our kids have friends from everywhere. They don't see colour, they don't see race, and they don't see religion. They know, of course, about other countries, but not about boundaries and divisions. I hope as they get older they will not lose this sense of oneness and tolerance and will not fall into the trap of cultural stereotyping'. After all these years, the Nassers have embraced Abu Dhabi as their home and have painted one of Ranya's favourite quotes onto their garden wall: 'Bloom where you are planted'.

> As we have made friends, as we've watched the kids grow, as the city has evolved, I realised Abu Dhabi is our home — this is my white picket fence.
>
> RANYA

CRAB CAKES WITH MANGO AVOCADO SALSA

RANYA *There is nothing more delicious than the ugly crab. If you're like me and love everything about the spiny creature, then you'll appreciate the purity of this recipe. I've cut out all the traditional fillers you'd find in a typical crab cake so that the lumpiness and texture of the crab can be fully enjoyed. Maryland crabs are really the only food I truly miss here in Abu Dhabi. Only recently have we been able to find shelled crab meat in the grocery stores, so making these when we first moved here was impossible. I tried once to get enough crab meat from the skinny local crabs but it resulted in an epic fail—small cuts to my fingers, hungry kids, and homesickness like you wouldn't believe. If you can't find Old Bay Seasoning, use any ready-made seafood seasoning. Serve with mango avocado salsa or lemon wedges if you are a purist.*

SERVES 8

CRAB CAKES

- **1** egg
- **½ tsp** Worcestershire sauce
- **3 tbsp** mayonnaise
- **1 tsp** whole grain mustard
- **1 tbsp** Old Bay Seasoning
- **½ tsp** celery salt
- **½ tsp** coarse salt
- **½ tsp** white pepper
- **1 tbsp** parsley, chopped
- **3 tbsp** panko breadcrumbs
- **450 g (1 lb)** lump crab meat
- Lemon wedges (optional)

MANGO AVOCADO SALSA

- **750 g (1½ lb)** mangoes
- **55 g (2 oz)** sweet onion
- **2** avocados
- **1** small green chili
- **2 tbsp** fresh coriander, chopped
- **60 ml (¼ c)** lime juice
- **½ tsp** brown sugar
- **1 tsp** coarse salt

FOR THE CRAB CAKES

Whisk the egg in a large bowl until fluffy. Stir in the Worcestershire sauce, mayonnaise, mustard, Old Bay Seasoning, celery salt, coarse salt, white pepper, parsley, and panko. Gently fold in the crabmeat, keeping most as lumps.

Grease a baking tray. Form each patty by placing a round egg or pastry mould, about 8 centimetres (3 inches) diameter, on the baking tray and gently pressing the crab mixture into the mould. Be sure to lift the mould straight up to retain the round shape. Cover with plastic wrap and chill for 1 to 2 hours.

Preheat the oven to 200°C (400°F). Bake the crab cakes for 10 minutes on each side until lightly brown. Be careful when flipping them over so they don't fall apart. Serve with the mango avocado salsa or lemon wedges.

FOR THE MANGO AVOCADO SALSA

Peel the mangoes and dice into medium-size cubes. Cut the onions into thin slices. Peel and chop the avocados, but don't mash them. Chop the chili; include the seeds and pith for a spicy kick or discard them for a milder version. Combine all the ingredients and refrigerate for at least 1 hour.

GEMISTA ME FETA
Greek Stuffed Tomatoes with Quinoa, Capers, and Olives

Mediterranean cuisine has included a plethora of stuffed items, from the ancient Greeks, to Romans, Byzantines, medieval Arabs, and the Ottomans. The elaborate stuffing of fish, lamb, and goat was a demonstration of culinary skills, power, and wealth. Travel anywhere in the Mediterranean region today and you will find stuffed meat and vegetables. Greeks and Turks may debate the origin of stuffed dishes, though it is generally believed that the highly elaborate stuffing of vegetables such as vine leaves, zucchini, onions, bell peppers, and eggplant originated with the Ottoman cuisine and spread across the region during the four hundred years of their rule. In Greece, stuffed grape leaves are called *dolmades*, derived from the Turkish word *dolma*, which means 'filled' or 'stuffed'. In Lebanon and Syria, the meatless stuffed grape leaves are called *yalantzi*, which in Turkish means 'fake', that is, they don't contain meat.

RANYA *Imagine yourself in a bathing suit on a Greek island. You have just come out of the sea, the saltwater still in your hair. You step into the beachside taverna and order* gemista me feta. *You take the first bite with a big dollop of Greek yogurt, a drizzle of olive oil, and a fresh chili pepper on the side. This is the quintessential summer lunchtime meal, ideally followed by a lovely siesta. I replace the traditional rice stuffing with quinoa for a lighter variation.*

SERVES 8

---

120 g (⅔ c) quinoa, uncooked

Salt, to taste

8 large, firm tomatoes

80 g (½ c) pine nuts

120 ml (½ c) olive oil, divided

115 g (½ c) sun-dried tomatoes, chopped

40 g (¼ c) capers

80 g (½ c) green olives, sliced

175 g (1 c) feta cheese, cubed

4 g (¼ c) fresh dill

½ tsp black pepper

1 tsp brown sugar

55 g (2 oz) butter

Preheat the oven to 180°C (350°F).

Rinse and drain the quinoa. Add it to 320 millilitres (1⅓ cups) of lightly salted water in a medium saucepan and bring to a boil. Reduce the heat to low, cover, and simmer until tender and the liquid has been absorbed, 15 to 20 minutes. Remove from the heat, fluff it with a fork and transfer it to a large bowl.

Meanwhile, for each tomato, slice off the top and set it aside — it will be used to cap the stuffed tomato. Remove the core with a small knife, being careful not to slice through the bottom of the tomato. Gently remove the remaining juice and pulp by hand. Mix the juice and pulp in a blender and set aside for later use in this recipe. Salt the inside of the tomato shells and place them upside down on a tray to drain while preparing the stuffing.

Lightly sauté the pine nuts in 1 tablespoon of olive oil. Add the pine nuts, sun-dried tomatoes, capers, olives, feta, dill, pepper, and 60 millilitres (¼ cup) of the olive oil to the quinoa and stir well to combine. Use some of the reserved tomato pulp to achieve a moist stuffing.

Coat a baking dish just large enough to accommodate all the tomatoes with 3 tablespoons of the olive oil. Place the tomatoes in the baking dish and spoon the quinoa stuffing into each one, almost to the rim. Drizzle some olive oil over the stuffing and brush some on the rims of the tomatoes. Add a sprinkle of the sugar on the rims and then a dab of butter to the top of each tomato. Cap the tomatoes with their tops, or bake uncapped for a slightly toasted stuffing.

Bake for 30 minutes, until the tomatoes soften but do not collapse.

CARAMELISED ONION AND FIG TART
with Manouri Cheese

SERVES 6 TO 8

RANYA *Manouri is a semi-soft, creamy Greek goat cheese. It is milder than feta and holds up well to grilling. Pair it with caramelised anything and it's delicious. I love this tart with figs and rosemary—it's autumnal and heady. If figs are not in season, you can substitute plums or pears. It's one of our favourites for Friday brunch.*

SHORTCRUST PASTRY

- **300 g (2 c)** all-purpose flour
- **200 g (7 oz)** unsalted butter, cubed
- **½ tsp** salt

FILLING

- **28 g (1 oz)** unsalted butter
- **2 tbsp** olive oil
- **750 g (1¾ lb)** sweet onion, thinly sliced
- **1 tbsp** fresh rosemary
- **1 tbsp** brown sugar
- **1 tbsp** fig balsamic vinegar
- **120 ml (½ c)** whole milk
- **2** eggs
- **450 g (1 lb)** figs
- **200 g (7 oz)** manouri cheese
- **80 g (½ c)** pine nuts, toasted
- **6–8 sprigs** fresh rosemary
- **2 tbsp** honey

FOR THE PASTRY

Place the flour, butter, and salt in a food processor. Mix on low speed until crumbs form and then start to come together. Add ice water 1 tablespoon at a time until the dough holds together. *[Alternatively, you can combine the flour and salt in a mixing bowl and then cut in the butter with a pastry blender or two knives until crumbly. Add the water a tablespoon at a time, using your fingers or a fork to bring the dough together.]* Turn out the dough and shape it into a flat circle, about 5 centimetres (2 inches) thick; wrap it in plastic wrap and chill it for 2 to 4 hours.

Preheat the oven to 200°C (400°F). Line a large baking tray with parchment paper. On a floured surface, roll out the shortcrust pastry to form a 23 x 28-centimetre (9 x 11-inch) rectangle, about 2.5 centimetres (1 inch) thick. Transfer the pastry to the baking tray by rolling it around the rolling pin. Refrigerate it while preparing the filling.

FOR THE FILLING

Melt the butter and oil in a large skillet. Add the onions, rosemary, and sugar and sauté until the onions are golden brown, about 30 minutes. Stir in the vinegar, being sure to scrape up all the bits that may be on the bottom of the skillet. Cut the figs into 2-centimetre (¾-inch) thick slices. Cut the cheese into 1-centimetre (½-inch) thick slices.

In a medium bowl, whisk together the milk and egg and fold in the onion mix. Scoop onto the pastry using a slotted spoon, keeping the excess egg in the bowl. Evenly spread the onion mix over the pastry, leaving a 2.5-centimetre (1-inch) border. Layer the cheese and fig slices over the onions. Sprinkle with the pine nuts and evenly distribute the fresh rosemary sprigs.

Brush the edges of the tart with the leftover egg mixture and fold in half. Brush the newly formed edge with more egg. Bake for 30 to 35 minutes, until the pastry is puffy and golden. Serve warm with a drizzle of honey.

MANGO AND BLACKBERRY COCONUT BUCKLE

Buckle, crumble, grunt, slump, crisp — are these exercises, yoga positions, or do they describe the way you feel afterwards? As a matter of fact, they are traditional American desserts that involve fruit, sugar, butter, and flour in some way or another. A crumble has fresh fruit with a flour and/or oat-based topping and a cobbler is like a crumble but has a biscuit topping resembling a cobblestone road. Grunts and slumps are like cobblers, but are cooked on the stove. As the fruit cooks, it bubbles and 'grunts' around the biscuits or some say it slumps onto the plate. A buckle has the fruit on top of the cakey layer, and as it bakes, the fruit sinks, buckles, and the batter rises around it.

SERVES 6 TO 8

TOPPING

80 g (½ c) all-purpose flour

90 g (½ c) light brown sugar

¼ tsp coarse salt

½ tsp cinnamon

55 g (2 oz) unsalted butter, cubed

3 tbsp desiccated coconut

CAKE

190 g (1¼ c) all-purpose flour

160 g (¾ c) granulated sugar

2 tsp baking powder

½ tsp salt

1 egg

240 ml (1 c) coconut milk

80 g (⅓ c) Greek yogurt

1 tsp vanilla

450 g (1 lb) mangoes, cubed

225 g (8 oz) fresh blackberries

120 ml (½ c) coconut cream

65 g (¾ c) desiccated coconut

28 g (1 oz) unsalted butter

RANYA *I've always felt that cooking can be like painting. This dessert is my version of a Jackson Pollock — total chaos inspires me to create it, it's a mess to make, and, in all honesty, even if you're the type of baker who weighs and measures with precision, it can come out differently every time. Try making it my way the first time and then channel your own inner artist. Change the fruit, add some nuts, sprinkle in something that you love — cinnamon or chocolate — and make it yours. It's a recipe that is very forgiving, so experiment! A friend once told me it was so sweet it tasted like cough medicine. He was right in that it is totally healing — all you need is a big spoon, a cup of tea, and a friend by your side and all your troubles will magically disappear.*

I used to make this recipe with peaches, but one day I went to the supermarket and was greeted by a promotion for a mango festival. There were zillions of varieties on sale! I had no idea that mangoes came in so many shapes, sizes, and varying shades of yellow. In my quest to find the perfect variety, I've asked my family to endure some pretty funny 'creations', but this one is our favourite.

FOR THE TOPPING

Combine the flour, brown sugar, salt, and cinnamon; cut in the butter until small crumbs are formed. Add the coconut and toss to combine.

FOR THE CAKE

Preheat the oven to 180°C (350°F).

Combine the flour, sugar, baking powder, and salt in a large bowl. Add the egg, coconut milk, yogurt, and vanilla. Mix just long enough for everything to be well combined.

In a separate bowl, gently toss the mango and blackberries with the coconut cream and the coconut.

Melt 28 grams (1 ounce) of butter over medium heat in a 30-centimetre (12-inch) skillet or tarte tatin pan suitable for the oven. Immediately pour in the cake batter and let it bubble on the stove for 1 minute. Remove from the heat and evenly distribute the fruit mix over the batter. Sprinkle with the topping to completely cover the fruit.

Bake for 40 to 45 minutes, until the cake and topping are puffy and golden.

MARJON AJAMI

RESTAURATEUR
◊
AFGHANISTAN / US

Marjon's restless energy was palpable when she joined our exercise group one morning in September 2006. Starting early to beat the heat, we would begin with a brisk walk at Ras Al Akhdar, followed by a few sprints and then a series of resistance exercises at the demanding pace of our trainer. Coming from a robust Afghan bloodline, Marjon did not seem to run out of breath even as she grumbled about life in between squats. After marrying her Lebanese husband, for whom Abu Dhabi was home, she moved from her hometown of San Francisco in 2004. Those of us who met Marjon in those early days — a new mother uneasy about leaving friends and family — could never have predicted the transformation.

During our morning walks, Marjon would share with me her frustration at moving from the Golden Gate City, home to hippies, techies, and foodies with its cool summers, landmark architecture, rolling hills, and fog. 'I came from San Francisco, which is progressive and has a unique and healthy food culture, to a city that felt twenty-five years behind!' Food and hospitality are central to Marjon's life. Her parents emigrated from Kabul to San Francisco in the late 1970s, and her mother opened an Afghan restaurant in their new hometown. Marjon was raised in her mother's kitchen with the delectable flavours of *qabili pallow* (lamb shanks with Afghan brown rice), *mantoo* (beef dumplings in a yogurt tomato sauce), and *borani kadoo* (squash with apricots and yogurt sauce), along with the fresh and healthy cuisine of Northern California. 'For me, a city is made and defined by its food offerings and that was my initial struggle living in Abu Dhabi', Marjon adds.

As she came to terms with her new surroundings, her California positivity kicked in and Marjon decided to investigate what she could do to enhance the city's food offerings. Abu Dhabi was experiencing a real estate boom at the time, with new developments that targeted mainly international franchises. 'To me, many of those restaurants lacked soul. I wanted to do something different — to contribute to the city and have the freedom to create dishes that responded to what people living here wanted to eat. It was a struggle, but today I am so proud to see what is available compared to a decade back', Marjon recalls.

Nolu's Café opened its first location in Al Bandar at Raha Beach in 2012, offering California-style cuisine with an Afghan twist. The cooking reflects simple, health-conscious food with complex flavours introduced in a wholesome way. The ambiance is laid-back with large tables to welcome the neighbourhood families and convivial groups, as well as stools at a window-side counter to welcome solo diners. The open kitchen, pop music, generous portions, and child-friendly atmosphere bring soul to Nolu's; two other outlets have since opened in the city. The blending of options at Nolu's, named after the combination of Marjon's children's names, is much like Abu Dhabi: a mix of different cultures and cuisines, both traditional and contemporary. Marjon adds, 'I grab people with traditional cuisine and then introduce variations'.

Nolu's has also benefited from a high-profile patronage. Marjon explains, 'I have been blessed with the support of HH Sheikh Mohammed bin Zayed, who made me feel anything is possible in Abu Dhabi. I have fed many of his international guests and some of the most powerful leaders in the world, at times with just an hour's notice'. Marjon credits her success to a great team who are more like her family, and to the importance of knowing what drives you in life. As a restaurateur, leader, mother, wife, and friend, she is always there to help in any way she can. Marjon muses: 'I have realised that no matter where life takes me, I will always have one foot in the UAE for the rest of my life. I hope the country continues to accept me as I have grown to accept it', Marjon affirms.

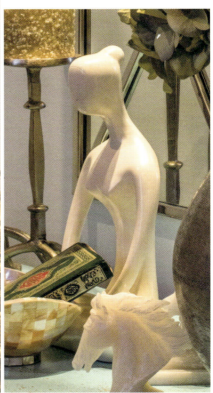

I grab people with traditional cuisine and then introduce variations.

MARJON

BORANI BANJAN
Eggplant with Tomato and Mint Yogurt Sauce

MARJON

This Afghan eggplant dish, with creamy yogurt and spicy tomato sauce, is delicious and simple to make. It is one of the favourites at Nolu's and has been on the menu since we opened. Traditionally, the eggplant is fried but you can also bake it. I serve this as a side dish or starter, warm, with Afghan naan or pita bread. As Afghans say, ischtia khoob (Bon appetit)!

SERVES 6 TO 8

1 kg (2¼ lb) eggplant
430 g (1½ c) plain yogurt
4 cloves garlic, divided
Salt, to taste
120 ml (½ c) cooking oil
200 g (7 oz) canned tomatoes
55 g (2 oz) red bell pepper, diced
1 tbsp jalapeño pepper, chopped
60 ml (¼ c) olive oil
1 chicken bouillon cube
2 tsp coriander powder
½ tsp turmeric
4 Roma tomatoes
1 tbsp dried mint

Peel the eggplant in alternating strips and cut into 2-centimetre (¾-inch) slices. Place the slices in a colander and sprinkle generously with salt. Let it rest for an hour. Rinse and pat dry with a paper towel.

Combine the yogurt and 2 cloves of crushed garlic and season with salt. Bring to room temperature before assembling the dish.

Preheat the oven to 190°C (375°F).

Heat the cooking oil in a large skillet and fry the eggplant slices for 2 to 3 minutes on each side, until lightly browned. Arrange them in a single layer in a glass baking dish.

Whirl the tomatoes, red bell pepper, and jalapeños in a blender to make a smooth sauce. Heat the olive oil in a large skillet over high heat and add 2 cloves of chopped garlic, stirring until golden. Add the tomato/bell pepper sauce, bouillon cube, coriander powder, and turmeric, and bring to a boil. Lower the heat and cook for 10 to 15 minutes, until the oil separates.

Cut the Roma tomatoes into 2-centimetre (¾-inch) slices. Place one slice on top of each slice of eggplant. Top with a generous amount of the sauce, making sure the eggplant slices are evenly covered. Cover with aluminium foil and bake for 30 to 40 minutes. The eggplant is done if it is soft when pierced with a fork and the sauce is bubbling.

Spread the yogurt in a thick layer on a serving platter and carefully arrange the eggplant slices on top, leaving space between each one. Sprinkle with dried mint.

BORANI KADOO
Sautéed Butternut Squash with Saffron and Yogurt

SERVES 6 TO 8

MARJON — *This is a flavourful Afghan side dish that brings the homey squash out of its shell. With a hint of sweetness, it is infused with saffron, cardamom, and a touch of heat, smoothed by the creamy garlic yogurt. It was a favourite at my mother's restaurant in San Francisco and now at Nolu's in Abu Dhabi. It can be served warm or at room temperature with Afghan naan or pita bread.*

430 g (1½ c) plain yogurt

1 clove garlic, crushed

Salt, to taste

Pinch of saffron

60 ml (¼ c) vegetable oil

140 g (5 oz) yellow onion, chopped

2 chicken bouillon cubes

1–2 tbsp granulated sugar, to taste

1 tsp red chili flakes

1 kg (2¼ lb) butternut squash

1 tsp ground cardamom

110 g (4 oz) pitted dried apricots, halved

1 tbsp dried mint

Combine the yogurt and garlic and season with salt. Bring to room temperature before assembling the dish.

Grind the saffron in a mortar and add 2 tablespoons of boiling water to release the colour and fragrance.

Heat the oil in a Dutch oven until hot. Add the chopped onions; cook over low heat while stirring, caramelising until light golden. Add a little water to stop the caramelising process. Crumble in the bouillon cubes and carefully pour in 120 millilitres (½ cup) of hot water, stirring to make a sauce. Add the saffron liquid, sugar, and chili flakes. Bring to a boil and then lower the heat.

Peel, slice, deseed, and chop the squash into 4-centimetre (1½-inch) squares. Add them to the Dutch oven and toss to combine all the ingredients. Sprinkle in the cardamom and apricots and add 120 millilitres (½ cup) of water. Bring the mixture to a boil and then lower the heat and simmer, covered, for 15 minutes. Stir occasionally, until the squash is cooked al dente and the liquid has evaporated. Do not overcook the squash. Adjust the seasoning to taste to balance the sweet, salty, and spicy flavours.

Spread the garlic yogurt on a serving platter and arrange the squash on top. Sprinkle with dried mint.

CAULIFLOWER AND ROASTED BEETROOT SALAD
with Tahini Dressing

MARJON

This is a vibrant, hearty salad for all seasons. I much prefer roasting the beetroots to boiling, as the flavours are richer. The tahini dressing and feta cheese beautifully compliment the vegetables.

SERVES 4 TO 6

1 kg (2¼ lb) cauliflower
60 ml (¼ c) olive oil
Salt, to taste
450 g (1 lb) beetroots
70 g (½ c) shelled almonds, whole
15 g (½ c) mint
15 g (½ c) parsley
55 g (2 oz) feta cheese, crumbled
75 g (½ c) pomegranate seeds

DRESSING

60 ml (¼ c) tahini
60 ml (¼ c) lemon juice
60 ml (¼ c) olive oil
1 tsp salt
1 tbsp pomegranate molasses

Preheat the oven to 180°C (350°F).

Break the cauliflower into bite-size florets, toss with the olive oil, and sprinkle with salt. Place on a baking tray with sides and roast for 20 to 25 minutes, until they can be easily pierced with a fork. Shake the tray occasionally so the florets brown evenly. Set aside on the tray to cool.

Wrap each beetroot separately with aluminium foil and bake for 45 to 60 minutes or until they are soft when pierced. *[These can bake in the oven at the same time as the cauliflower.]*

While the vegetables are roasting, soak the almonds in lukewarm water for an hour to soften. Drain off the water when ready to use.

Combine the dressing ingredients in a blender at medium speed. Add water a tablespoon at a time to thin the dressing as needed, but not so much that the taste is diluted.

When the beetroots are cooked, unwrap them and let them cool enough to be handled. Peel them and cut into medium-sized cubes. Since the beetroots bleed quite a bit when tossed, combine them with the cauliflower in a large work bowl. Toss with most of the dressing, keeping the rest to serve on the side. Transfer the vegetables to a serving bowl and top with the mint, parsley, and almonds. Sprinkle with the crumbled feta and pomegranate seeds.

KALE CAESAR SALAD WITH YOGURT DRESSING
and Za'atar Croutons

Kale is one of the 'superfoods' that has shot into the limelight in the past few years, making one wonder about the 'tale of kale'. It is from the same plant family as cabbage, cauliflower, and broccoli. It is quite easy to grow in a planter or garden as long as the temperature is below 26°C (79°F). It is high in fibre, protein and omega-3 fatty acids, so suitable for those with nut allergies and non-seafood eaters. Kale was popular in the United States, United Kingdom, Canada, and Australia during the food shortages of World War II because it was easy to grow and full of nutrients. After the war it was not consumed, as people associated it with war, deprivation and poverty.

SERVES 4 TO 6

MARJON *I use kale in this salad in place of the traditional Romaine lettuce. To break kale's squeaky cellulose structure, you will need to massage it by hand. It's best to salt the kale, drizzle with some oil and lemon, and then give it a few minutes of love. The yogurt dressing and za'atar croutons adapt the traditional Caesar salad to favoured flavours here in Abu Dhabi. Make the dressing several hours ahead, if you can. It will allow it to thicken and help the flavours meld.*

CROUTONS

1 pita or flatbread
2 tbsp olive oil
2 tbsp za'atar
Coarse salt

DRESSING

140 g (½ c) Greek yogurt
1 clove garlic, chopped
Zest of half a lemon
60 ml (¼ c) lemon juice
2 tsp Worcestershire sauce
2 tsp Dijon mustard
1 tsp honey
60 ml (¼ c) olive oil
28 g (1 oz) Reggiano cheese, grated
Salt and pepper, to taste

SALAD

1 bunch kale
2 tbsp olive oil
Coarse salt
10–15 cherry tomatoes, halved
1–2 avocados, cut in chunks
Freshly shaved Parmesan

FOR THE CROUTONS

Preheat the oven to 200°C (400°F). Cut the bread into 1-centimetre (½-inch) pieces. Toss them with the olive oil and za'atar, coating them thoroughly. Spread them evenly on a baking sheet lined with parchment paper and bake for 10 to 15 minutes, until the bread is crispy and golden. Sprinkle with salt.

FOR THE DRESSING

Place all the ingredients in a blender or food processor and blend until creamy. Transfer the dressing to a covered container.

FOR THE SALAD

De-stem and chop the kale and place it in a salad bowl. Add the olive oil and some coarse salt and massage with your hands to soften the kale. Add the cherry tomatoes. Drizzle with the dressing and toss gently until it is well distributed. Garnish with the croutons, avocado pieces, and shaved Parmesan just before serving.

ROULANA AND MUHANNAD QUBBAJ

VOLUNTEER
◊
PALESTINE / LEBANON / CANADA

INVESTMENT
◊
PALESTINE / JORDAN / UK

It was during the long school board meetings in 2007 that I got to know Roulana, then the president of the PTA. Her positive attitude, sociable nature, and drive for excellence helped transform the PTA and strengthen its role in school governance. We worked together on several committees and passionately advocated for strengthening the Arabic curriculum, a cause dear to both our families. Muhannad's mother, their family's matriarch, taught Arabic for over fifty years in various countries. Though she is not pleased that her grandchildren are not fluent in their mother tongue, she does recognise the global shift to English as the lingua franca of their generation.

Born in Toronto and raised in Jeddah, Saudi Arabia; London; and Abu Dhabi, the Quabbaj's children are true third-culture kids; they are flexible, globally aware, and able to move between worlds. The diverse yet familiar surroundings of Abu Dhabi have helped them embrace their multicultural background. When I ask the two eldest children where they are from, they answer, 'We are Arabs and proud of that. We love that we are citizens of the world. We have become unique by taking from different cultures and choosing what our combined new heritage will look like'. Muhannad thinks about the dilemma of multiple nationalities he has presented to them: 'The struggle lies in how to create a balance between the luxury of choice and the pride in origin'.

Food and culture help Roulana and Muhannad anchor their children to their Arab origins as they traverse the globe. Muhannad recounts when Roulana first moved to Jeddah from Toronto in the late 1990s. He had to endure endless cheese sandwiches and takeouts the first few weeks, until something magical happened. 'A month into our marriage there was an exponential elevation in Roulana's culinary skills, which baffled but delighted me immensely. No complaints. Then the phone bill arrived!' Muhannad, ever the investment banker, came to realise that he had been eating some very expensive meals. 'Every dish was the result of a step-by-step instruction process with either my mother in Amman or hers in Toronto over the phone!' Muhannad laughs at that memory but would not have had it any other way.

Roulana was building a solid foundation, though, carefully documenting the families' recipes and then adapting them to her life style. She enjoyed cooking and sharing her newfound talent with friends at home. For Roulana and Muhannad it was all about developing friendships whenever they settled in a new city. Muhannad explains, 'The concept of going out to restaurants for lunch or dinner allows you to enjoy certain afternoons or evenings here and there, but the connection remains at a superficial level. However, bringing people into your home and enjoying a casual meal or a festive one creates a special bond, and in due time, it accentuates the relationship to become almost family-like'. This sense of connection around food and shared circumstances was compounded when they moved to Abu Dhabi with the familiar sounds, aromas, and foods of the Arab world.

Steve and I always look forward to a meal at the Qubbaj's home, be it with a few close friends, the annual Club Q dance party, or the Eid lunch. Eid, after all, is about celebrating your blessings with family. Yet in the expatriate life, it is rare to have more than one or two family members living in the same city, so friendships take on another meaning during holidays and religious feasts. Roulana adds, 'We want our children to enjoy the sense of celebration and excitement that we had for Eid growing up, in terms of religious pride and from a cultural perspective'. Roulana and Muhannad developed strong friendships that have, in many cases, turned into the base for a family away from home: weekend trips, lunches and dinners together, and generations bonding continuously.

Bringing people into your home …

… and enjoying a meal creates a special bond.

MUHANNAD

BRUSSELS SPROUTS WITH MINT YOGURT SAUCE

Brussels sprouts are no longer relegated to once-a-year Christmas dinner. They have gone through a culinary renaissance of late, celebrated as something of a superfood. The increase in demand outside of the Christmas season has led to farmers growing different varieties, breeding them specifically for flavour, thus sweeter than what was on offer a few decades ago. Their popularity has inspired a range of sprout concoctions at trendy restaurants and health juice bars. They are a rich source of vitamins and rivalled only by kale as the 'come-back veggie'.

ROULANA *Muhannad and I first tasted these crispy caramelised Brussels sprouts at one of our favourite restaurants in New York City, Ilili. This dish reminded me of one my mom makes with cauliflower and yogurt. Upon returning home to Abu Dhabi, I recreated Ilili's Brussels sprouts with my own variation using dates instead of figs. This salad has been a great hit amongst family and friends, and it has helped redeem the not so favourable reputation of Brussels sprouts amongst some. The combination of sweet dates, creamy salty yogurt, crunchy bitter sprouts, and toasted nuts is perfectly balanced. It also comes together easily for impromptu gatherings.*

SERVES 4 TO 6

SALAD

450 g (1 lb) Brussels sprouts

60 ml (¼ c) olive oil

Salt and black pepper

2 tbsp red vinegar

110 g (4 oz) red grapes, halved

MINT YOGURT

285 g (1 c) plain yogurt

3 tbsp mint, chopped

1 clove garlic, crushed

GARNISH

60 ml (¼ c) date molasses

110 g (¾ c) pomegranate seeds

50 g (½ c) walnut halves, toasted

FOR THE BRUSSELS SPROUTS

Preheat the oven to 260°C (500°F). Line a baking tray with parchment paper.

Remove any yellow or brown leaves from the Brussels sprouts and trim the woody bases, being careful not to cut so high that you sever the part that holds the sprout together. Cut the sprouts in half.

Toss the sprouts with the olive oil and salt and pepper to taste. Evenly distribute on the lined baking tray. Roast in the oven until softened and brown, about 15 to 20 minutes, shaking the pan a couple of times during the roasting process so the sprouts cook evenly. The sprouts are done when they are brown and crispy on the outside, but the inner leaves are green and the centre is tender but not mushy. Remove to a bowl and drizzle with the vinegar.

FOR THE MINT YOGURT

Combine the yogurt, mint, and garlic in a small bowl. Stir in salt to taste.

TO ASSEMBLE

Smear the mint yogurt on a serving platter. Mound the Brussels sprouts and grapes over the yogurt and drizzle with the date molasses. Sprinkle with the pomegranate seeds and walnuts.

AISH AL SARAYA
Lebanese Bread Pudding

Aish al saraya, which translates to 'bread of the royal palace', is a luscious sweet of Ottoman origin, fit for a sultan, but surprisingly easy to make. It is popular in the Levant, Egypt, and Turkey and served in speciality sweet shops and cafés. It is essentially a bread pudding, traditionally made with *aishta*, the thick cream that rises to the top when milk is boiled, and garnished with pistachio slivers and a sprinkle of preserved safflower blossoms.

ROULANA *This is one of my favourite Arabic sweets, not only because it's delicious, but because it's simple and adaptable. I can make it anywhere we live, as the ingredients are readily available: bread, cream, and sugar! You can use clotted cream or canned cream, such as Nestlé or Puck, which is very common in the Gulf, or mascarpone cheese. The key is to caramelise the sugar to a rich brown hue. It is easiest to make in one large dish, but you can also make it in ramekins for individual servings.*

SERVES 8 TO 10

---

730 g (3½ c) granulated sugar, divided

3 tbsp orange blossom water

1 tbsp strong coffee

1 tbsp honey

12–15 slices bread

340 g (12 oz) canned or clotted cream

105 g (¾ c) pistachios, ground

Preserved safflower blossoms or pomegranate seeds

Place 520 grams (2½ cups) of the sugar and 700 ml (3 cups) of water in a medium saucepan. Bring to a boil and then turn the heat to low and simmer, stirring until the sugar dissolves. In another saucepan, over medium heat, add the remaining sugar. Swirl the pan until the sugar dissolves and turns golden brown. Remove from the heat before the sugar crystallises and gradually pour it into the sugar syrup. Stir vigorously until all the sugar dissolves. Remove the saucepan from the heat and stir in the orange blossom water, coffee, and honey.

Remove the crust and shred the bread slices into a large bowl. Pour in the syrup and stir until the bread is mashed. Cover and leave at room temperature for 1 to 2 hours to allow the bread to absorb the syrup. *[This can be made several hours ahead of time, with the remaining steps done just before serving.]*

Using a slotted spoon to avoid excess syrup, transfer the bread to a circular or rectangular serving dish that is at least 5 centimetres (2 inches) deep, and level with the back of the spoon. Evenly spread the cream over the top to cover the bread. Garnish with the pistachios. Refrigerate for at least 1 hour before serving. Sprinkle with the preserved safflower blossoms or pomegranate seeds.

FATTET AL HUMMUS
Chickpeas with Pita and Tahini Yogurt

Fatteh is a traditional Levantine dish consisting of fried or toasted Arabic bread layered with grain, meat, or vegetables and topped with yogurt. There isn't a direct translation in English for fatteh, which is derived from the Arabic verb *fatta,* meaning 'to crumble bread'. There are many variations of the creamy-nutty *fattet al hummus* in Lebanese, Palestinian, Jordanian, and Syrian kitchens despite the few basic ingredients that make up this dish. Fattet al hummus is a typical weekend breakfast dish for family gatherings.

ROULANA *I like to add some hummus bi tahini to the yogurt topping of my fatteh, for a creamier taste. This hummus bi tahini recipe was passed down to me from my father. His dedication to making the perfect hummus translated into many batches that were either too thick, too pasty, or too lemony. Finally, with a chemist's precision, he weighed and measured the simple ingredients of this dish to bring it to perfection. As the traditionalist, my father starts with dried chickpeas and soaks and boils them. I take the shortcut and use canned chickpeas with similar results.*

SERVES 6 TO 8

HUMMUS BI TAHINI

340 g (12 oz) cooked chickpeas

240 ml (1 c) tahini

160 ml (⅔ c) lemon juice, divided

1–2 tsp salt

½ tbsp garlic powder

FATTEH

2 pitas

120 ml (½ c) olive oil

55 g (½ c) pine nuts

450 g (2 c) plain yogurt

1–2 cloves garlic, crushed

Salt and black pepper, to taste

120 ml (½ c) hummus bi tahini

400 g (14 oz) cooked chickpeas

Parsley, chopped

Paprika

FOR THE HUMMUS BI TAHINI

Boil the canned or soaked and cooked chickpeas in their liquid for 10 to 15 minutes or until soft. Drain them and rub by hand to remove the outer skin, which will make a smoother hummus.

Place the chickpeas, tahini, 120 millilitres (½ cup) of the lemon juice, salt, garlic powder, and a couple of ice cubes in a food processor; blend until creamy. Taste and add the remaining lemon juice if desired. Drizzle in a few tablespoons of ice water as needed to create the desired consistency. Adjust seasoning to taste.

FOR THE FATTEH

Cut the pita bread into 2-centimetre (¾-inch) squares. Heat the olive oil in a small saucepan. Fry the pita bread pieces for 1 to 2 minutes, until golden brown. Remove with a slotted spoon and drain on paper towels. *[Alternatively, open the pita bread and toast it in the oven and then crush into pieces.]* Sauté the pine nuts in the same oil. Drain on paper towels but retain the oil.

Mix the yogurt with the garlic, salt, and pepper. Stir in 120 millilitres (½ cup) of the hummus bi tahini, reserving the rest to enjoy as mezze.

Boil the canned or soaked and cooked chickpeas in a saucepan with their liquid for 10 to 15 minutes, until they soften, adding more water as needed to yield 240 millilitres (1 cup) of liquid. Reserve some of the chickpeas for garnish.

When ready to serve, place the pita pieces in a deep serving dish. Pour the chickpeas and some of their cooking liquid over the bread, soaking it generously. Smear the yogurt mixture over the chickpeas so they are completely covered. Garnish with pine nuts, parsley, and the reserved chickpeas. Drizzle with some of the remaining olive oil and sprinkle with paprika for colour. Serve at once while the chickpeas are warm and before the bread becomes soggy.

YUNIB SIDDIQUI

ENTREPRENEUR
◇
UK

Living in New York City in the early 1990s, I became obsessed with the recently opened Dean & DeLuca flagship store in SoHo. On Saturday mornings, I would bundle up my infant daughter and take the M5 bus from the Upper West Side to the corner of Prince and Broadway for my weekend gastronomic pilgrimage. Walking into the large marketplace with massive exposed columns, Carrara marble floors, and white tile walls with metal shelving full of gourmet products and housewares, I was in heaven! The classical music soothed my daughter and samples of smoked brie, poppy seed rugelach, and artisan kettle corn satiated my appetite as I browsed through cookbooks and cookware. I chatted with the fishmonger, trying to decide between the rainbow trout or the branzino for dinner, and he would offer suggestions on how to prepare it. Dean & DeLuca was a culinary trendsetter that turned food into a celebration. I missed my weekly pilgrimage when we moved to Abu Dhabi and had to settle for an annual one instead, when we travelled to New York for the summer holidays.

Some sixteen years later, when Jones the Grocer, the Australian gourmet food emporium, opened in Abu Dhabi in 2009, I thought, 'Finally, we have our own version of Dean & DeLuca!' Jones the Grocer spawned a culinary revolution in the region: a destination café not located in a mall or hotel, offering gourmet food products. With an open kitchen and demonstration area, a walk-in cheese room, a European-style deli, freshly baked pastries, artisanal groceries, and housewares, it was a totally new experience and my favourite meeting place. I was eager to meet the person behind this store. It turned out to be easier than I thought because Yunib was omnipresent at the café, tending to customers, serving the food, and clearing tables — unusual for the proprietor of a business in this region.

Over a Japanese slow-drip, cold brew coffee, Yunib recounts the story of how he ended up back in Abu Dhabi some twenty-five years after he left. Born in Karachi, he moved to Abu Dhabi with his parents in 1978, where he stayed for three years before going to boarding school in Devon. He went on to complete his economics degree and started a business sourcing handmade products from different countries and distributing them to retail giants such as Liberty, Harrods, and Galeries Lafayette. In 2008, while returning from a business trip to Vietnam, Yunib was flipping through *Wallpaper* magazine and came across an advertisement for Jones the Grocer's recently opened store in Singapore. 'The concept appealed to all my senses and I thought it was a great idea to pursue. I have always been a foodie, cooking at home and watching food shows on TV as a teenager, and it was time for a change', he recalls. Without any background in hospitality and acting strictly on instinct, Yunib immediately contacted the company when he landed in London. A week later, he travelled to meet with them in Singapore and left with an agreement to bring Jones the Grocer to the United Arab Emirates. 'I would stop in the UAE to visit my parents in my business travels, and I always struggled to find somewhere casual to eat. I thought this concept would fit an uncharted niche', Yunib adds.

At the time, the economy was booming and real estate prices were skyrocketing. While Dubai would have been the natural location for a new venture like Jones the Grocer, Yunib once again trusted his instinct and chose a new commercial development in Abu Dhabi, in a non-residential neighbourhood. According to Yunib, this location proved to be his best business decision. I ask him for more details, and he tells me, 'The site I picked had been rejected by other, more prominent brands. I realised it was a risk, as it was not in a mall, not fully occupied, and not completely built. So, the only way to manage this risk was to get to know the place'. Yunib spent a week just watching cars come into the building car park in the morning

having lunch with the country's Prime Minister, or where the Crown Prince of Abu Dhabi is enjoying a quiet meal with his guests.

Yunib strives to maintain quality and innovate while addressing the challenges of growing the business in an oversupplied food and beverage market. When I ask him about his strategy, he says, 'We do our best to listen to our customers. We survey them at every store and incorporate comments. We look at global trends and find inspiration in the café scene in Melbourne and Sydney. Other than some core items, the menu changes quarterly and we're always running something seasonal or promotional'. With thirteen outlets opened in the first few years in the Gulf region, I wonder if Yunib has any spare time, and if so, how he spends it. He tells me he enjoys writing, squash,

and leave at the end of the work day. He relates, 'I discovered that more than eighty percent of the cars were top-line models. I also stumbled across a small office for a travel agent that handled only the tenants of the building. After talking with the staff, I discovered they were issuing mainly first and business class tickets. I crossed off two key risks: low footfall and low average spend'.

Yunib's instincts and hard work were well rewarded when Jones the Grocer opened its doors on the ground floor of the Al Mamoura building, a powerhouse of the Abu Dhabi government. 'We were overwhelmed', Yunib recalls. 'From the beginning, we had people waiting outside the door to get in; it was totally crazy'. I remember how friends from Dubai made the ninety-minute drive to Abu Dhabi to try this new café and stock up on a few gourmet items. Finally, we had a culinary experience to rival Dubai! The café, with its long communal table, has a mix of Emirati professionals in national dress, mothers with strollers, business men in suits, and government officials. Given its location, it is not uncommon to find yourself sitting across from a table where members of the United Arab Emirates Cabinet are

yoga, and walking along the beach near his home. There will be no relaxing for the business, though. Yunib says, 'We bought the brand globally and our objective now is to grow it beyond this region, with franchising partners in Europe and Asia. We want a more global footprint'. With its birth in Australia, Jones the Grocer is back out in the world with additional DNA from Abu Dhabi.

ROASTED PUMPKIN AND FETA CHEESE SALAD
with Yuzu Dressing

What is the difference between pumpkin and squash? So, all pumpkins are squash but not all squash are pumpkins. All are members of the Cucurbitaceae family and the same genus. They are all fruits that grow on a vine, with the stem of the pumpkin being more stiff and spikey than some other types of squash. The seeds of the pumpkin are edible and make a healthy snack when roasted. Squash comes in many varieties throughout the world. There are also summer and winter varieties, based on when they are harvested. The word 'pumpkin' is a confusing reference, though. In Australia, it can refer to any winter squash, regardless of appearance, but in North America and the United Kingdom, it refers to something large, orange, and associated with pies and Halloween. There is also an Indian pumpkin that is readily available in Abu Dhabi, but because of its moisture content, it cannot be used for the same purposes. This is something that the expatriate cook will eventually learn after some confusion.

YUNIB *This roasted pumpkin and feta cheese salad, topped with sun-dried tomatoes and a lemon/yuzu dressing, has been on the menu at Jones since we opened. It is a favourite of our guests year-round. Whenever we have tried to remove it from the menu, we have had to bring it back by popular demand. It's healthy and simple to recreate at home. You can also use butternut squash to make it.*

SERVES 6 TO 8

---

1 kg (2¼ lb) pumpkin

60 ml (¼ c) cooking oil

3 cloves garlic, crushed

3 sprigs thyme, leaves only

1 tsp salt

1 tsp black pepper

225 g (8 oz) rocket

55 g (2 oz) sun-dried tomatoes, cut in strips

110 g (4 oz) feta cheese

DRESSING

80 ml (⅓ c) olive oil

2 cloves garlic, crushed

2 tbsp lemon juice

1 tsp salt

1 tsp black pepper

3 tbsp yuzu juice or lime juice

Preheat the oven to 200°C (400°F) and line a baking tray with parchment paper.

Peel and cut the pumpkin into 2-centimetre (¾-inch) cubes. Whisk the oil, garlic, thyme, salt, and pepper in a bowl until well mixed. Toss the pumpkin cubes in the mixture. Spread them evenly on the lined baking tray and roast for 20 minutes until soft and slightly coloured. Allow to cool to room temperature.

Prepare the dressing by whisking together all the ingredients until thoroughly combined. Be sure to mix again before dressing the salad.

Place the rocket, sun-dried tomatoes, feta, and roasted pumpkin cubes in a bowl and toss with the dressing until all elements are coated. Serve at room temperature in a large bowl, rearranging the ingredients so they are evenly presented.

WAGYU BURGER
with Bois Boudran Sauce

SERVES 6

PATTIES

- **5** cornichons, chopped
- **30 g (1 c)** parsley, chopped
- **55 g (2 oz)** white onion, chopped
- **2 cloves** garlic, minced
- **1 tsp** Tabasco sauce
- **3 tbsp** ketchup
- **2 tbsp** Worcestershire sauce
- **1 tbsp** Dijon mustard
- **2 tsp** salt
- **1 tsp** white pepper
- **35 g (¼ c)** breadcrumbs
- **1 kg (2¼ lb)** minced Wagyu beef

BOIS BOUDRAN SAUCE

- **120 ml (½ c)** olive oil
- **1½ tbsp** red vinegar
- **1 tsp** salt
- **½ tsp** black pepper
- **120 ml (½ c)** ketchup
- **2 tbsp** whole grain mustard
- **2 tbsp** Worcestershire sauce
- **1 tsp** Tabasco sauce, to taste
- **55 g (2 oz)** shallot, chopped
- **1 tbsp** tarragon, chopped
- **1 tbsp** chives, chopped
- **1 tbsp** parsley, chopped

- **6 rashers** veal bacon
- **6 slices** cheddar cheese
- **6** brioche buns
- Mixed lettuce leaves

I always say eat clean to stay fit; have a burger to stay sane. –GIGI HADID

The evolution of the hamburger, hailed as America's favourite food, is a tale of globalisation. While the hamburger did not originate in Hamburg, Germany, a common misconception, it does owe its name to that city. In the nineteenth century, Hamburg was known for its quality beef. It was commonly ground, seasoned, and formed into patties to make the Hamburg steak. When Germans started immigrating to America, many opened restaurants in the large cities and served a popular version of the Hamburg steak: minced beef mixed with chopped onions, garlic, salt, and pepper, and grilled or fried. Fast-forward a few years and the hamburger as we know it today was created. Many Americans were working in industrial factory jobs in the mid-1800s, with little time to sit down and eat a large lunch. Food carts serving coffee and cold sandwiches to the factory workers added gas grills, and someone had the culinary genius to serve the workers a Hamburg steak inside a bun. By the turn of the twentieth century, the hamburger was considered an American classic and can now be found in every corner of the globe.

YUNIB *This thick patty is moist and tender, layered with veal bacon, cheese, lettuce, and our Bois Boudran sauce, sandwiched between two halves of a milky, slightly sweet brioche bun. It's indulgent but worth it. To take it to another level, you could add foie gras, truffle mayonnaise, or even melted truffle Brie. The Bois Boudran sauce is also an excellent accompaniment to grilled steak, roast chicken, or poached salmon. It is a light, fresh sauce that is easy to prepare and can be made ahead of time.*

FOR THE PATTIES

Mix all the ingredients except the beef in a large bowl. Add the beef and mix by hand until all the ingredients are evenly incorporated. Divide and shape into 6 patties, approximately 190 grams (7 ounces) each. Cover and refrigerate until ready to cook.

FOR THE BOIS BOUDRAN SAUCE

Whisk together the oil, vinegar, salt, and pepper in a small bowl. Add the ketchup, mustard, Worcestershire sauce, Tabasco sauce, shallots, and herbs. Stir until well combined. Taste and adjust the seasoning. Serve the sauce at room temperature, but it can be refrigerated in an airtight container for up to three days.

TO FINISH

Fry the bacon and drain it on paper towels. Cook the patties in a heavy-bottomed skillet or on a grill to the desired doneness. When the patty is a couple of minutes from being ready, top with a slice of cheese so that it melts. Break each piece of bacon in half and arrange two halves on top of the cheese.

Cut the buns in half and toast them until golden. Dress each bun with condiments as desired. Place some mixed lettuce leaves on each bottom half, add a patty, and close the burger. Serve with French fries and Bois Boudran sauce on the side.

NADA AKKARI

DESIGNER
◊
LEBANON

Nada's understated elegance is a hallmark of her style, whether it is in her home, fashion, or work. A love for her culture and nostalgia for Beirut, the city where she was born but left at the start of the civil war in 1974, continue to inspire her design and culinary tastes. After college, she co-founded the London-based DN Designs Collection, an interior design practice. Twenty years later, at the end of the civil war, home was calling, so Nada returned to Lebanon. With her interest in traditional craft, the company expanded to include its own line of contemporary furniture and home accessories, all handmade by Lebanese and Syrian craftsmen.

In 2009, when her husband was offered the opportunity to set up the Abu Dhabi office for BLOM, one of the leading banks in Lebanon, they decided to relocate for a twelve-to-eighteen-month stay. Nada maintained her business in London and worked remotely, travelling frequently to Beirut to oversee the craftsmen. She recalls, 'I was very pleasantly surprised by what I found in Abu Dhabi in terms of arts, culture, and social life'. Abu Dhabi was enjoying a cultural renaissance with an international offering of music, theatre, film, art, and design exhibitions. An established community of Lebanese expatriates also welcomed Nada and her family, making for an almost seamless transition to her new home. Like many of us, the stay in Abu Dhabi extended to many years, and the temporality of her new home began to shift.

Sitting in Nada's nineteenth floor apartment overlooking Abu Dhabi's corniche, I ask about the metal sculpture of the city skyline mounted on the blue wall: 'I bought this piece by the artist Abdallah Hatoum before leaving Beirut. It is a profile of Beirut's corniche, a special place for me. That stretch of waterfront is the only constant in our war-torn city accessible to everyone. I remember going for walks there with my grandparents when I was a child, then jogging with my father as a teenager, and later taking my children as toddlers to ride their bicycles. We would stop to buy candy floss or freshly grilled corn and watch the fishermen'.

As it turns out, Nada's choice of residence in Abu Dhabi was not coincidental. Longing to remain connected to the waterfront, she chose an apartment with expansive views of Abu Dhabi's corniche, although it is very different than the one in Beirut. The immaculate tree-lined waterfront, with biking and jogging paths, as well as beaches, offers a space of respite along the capital's main artery, in contrast to Beirut's chaotic, vibrant, and contested waterfront. Nada says, 'I enjoy my serene morning walks along Abu Dhabi's corniche in the cool early morning hours'.

Nada's personal aesthetic has responded to the environment of this city. While her home in Beirut is large, spacious, warm, decorated with dark and rich hues, and layered with antiques, her apartment in Abu Dhabi is simple, minimal, light, and painted in cool colours. Similarly, her culinary choices have been affected. Nada explains: 'In Beirut, I love to cook traditional Lebanese dishes, which are complex and rich in flavour, infused with my Iraqi and Iranian grandmothers' twists. When I moved here, I really missed the fresh produce. Most of the fruits and vegetables in Abu Dhabi are imported, and while we have everything we may need all year round, they don't have the seasonal freshness I am used to. So, I started incorporating more Asian flavours like soya and ginger'. She avoids cooking aromatic dishes, since opening windows in the hot weather to ventilate is difficult.

Nada frequently travels back home to work with the craftsmen as she reimagines her designs, which have also been influenced by the local aesthetics and her experiences in Abu Dhabi. On return trips from Beirut, she invariably will pack some candy floss, liquorice pasties, and *arameesh* (candied pistachios) to satiate her sweet tooth and to remind her of the flavours of home.

I enjoy my serene morning walks along Abu Dhabi's corniche in the cool early morning hours.

NADA

QUINOA HERB SALAD

Quinoa, once a sacred crop of the Andean culture, is now one of the most popular health foods globally. Its highly nutritious quality led NASA to include it in the astronauts' diet on space missions. In its countries of origin, Peru and Bolivia, the grain thrives in the high-altitude arid regions, in some of the most hostile conditions: nightly frosts, daytime temperatures exceeding 40°C (104°F), scarce oxygen and water, and saline soil. Quinoa is sometimes compared to other grains as beluga is to caviar. Its recent recognition as one of the most nutritious foodstuffs on the planet is also making it more expensive and less accessible to those who grow it in its native land.

SERVES 6 TO 8

NADA *This is a light and healthy salad, rich in anti-oxidants. You can make your own variation with seasonal herbs and vary the quantities, as well. In Abu Dhabi, we have fresh herbs from all around the world, all year round!*

DRESSING

- 120 ml (½ c) olive oil
- 80 ml (⅓ c) lemon juice
- Rind of half a preserved lemon, chopped
- Salt and black pepper, to taste

SALAD

- 300 g (1¾ c) quinoa, uncooked
- 285 g (10 oz) French green beans, trimmed
- 200 g (7 oz) peas, podded
- 60 g (2 c) flat parsley, chopped
- 15 g (1 c) dill, chopped
- 15 g (½ c) mint, chopped
- 15 g (½ c) chervil, chopped
- 5 g (¼ c) tarragon, chopped
- Salt and black pepper, to taste
- 50 g (1 c) pea tendrils
- 30 g (1 c) baby spinach

FOR THE DRESSING

Mix the olive oil, lemon juice, and preserved lemon. Add salt and pepper to taste.

FOR THE SALAD

Cook the quinoa using a 2:1 ratio of water to uncooked quinoa. Rinse and drain the quinoa. In a medium saucepan, combine the quinoa and water and bring to a boil. Reduce the heat to low, cover, and simmer until tender and the liquid has been absorbed, about 15 minutes. Fluff with a fork and spread the quinoa on a large tray to cool, about 30 minutes.

Blanch the beans for 2 to 3 minutes; drain and rinse with cold water. Blanch the peas for 2 to 3 minutes; drain and rinse with cold water.

Combine the beans, peas, herbs, and quinoa in a large salad bowl. Season to taste with salt and pepper. Add the dressing and toss to combine. Refrigerate until required.

Before serving, add the pea tendrils and spinach and toss to combine.

ROASTED EGGPLANT
with Avocado, Thyme, and Green Olives

The eggplant has proven to be the most transcultural vegetable (actually, it's a fruit) in this collection of recipes. It comes in a variety of shapes and colours: long and slender or short and round, purple or white or yellow or green. It is grilled, fried, braised, boiled, or sautéed, and either salty or with sugar, from kitchens of the Near to the Far East.

NADA *This eggplant dish, which I got from my aunt in Lebanon, is now a favourite amongst friends in Abu Dhabi. When fresh thyme (za'atar) is in season, my aunt uses it at most every meal. Olives are a staple of the Lebanese home, of course. I serve this as an appetizer and it goes beautifully with grilled fish.*

SERVES 6 TO 8

900 g (2 lb) eggplant

Cooking oil

1–2 tsp olive oil

35 g (¼ c) pine nuts

35 g (¼ c) pistachios, shelled

2 avocados, sliced and cut in wedges

Handful of fresh thyme

80 g (½ c) sliced green olives

80 g (½ c) pomegranate seeds

DRESSING

1 tbsp pomegranate molasses

1 tbsp lemon juice

1 tbsp balsamic vinegar

60 ml (¼ c) olive oil

Salt and black pepper, to taste

Preheat the oven to 220°C (425°F).

Peel the eggplant in alternating strips and cut into 2-centimetre (¾-inch) thick slices. Brush both sides of the eggplant slices with cooking oil. Line a baking tray with parchment paper and arrange the eggplant slices in a single layer; bake for 10 to 15 minutes, until they start to turn golden. Midway through the baking process, turn the eggplant slices over until evenly golden on both sides.

While the eggplant bakes, sauté the pine nuts in 1 to 2 teaspoons of olive oil in a small skillet. Be careful not to overcook, as they brown quickly. Remove from the skillet with a slotted spoon, leaving as much oil behind as possible. Add the pistachios to the pan and sauté lightly.

Combine the pomegranate molasses, lemon juice, balsamic vinegar, olive oil, salt, and pepper; whisk together.

To serve, plate the roasted eggplant, topping each slice with an avocado wedge, a sprinkle of fresh thyme, sautéed pine and pistachio nuts, green olives, and pomegranate seeds. Drizzle the dressing over the top.

ASIAN GLAZED SALMON

Baked, grilled, or smoked, the rich flesh of the salmon does not need elaborate preparation to be flavourful. Baked with butter and garlic, grilled on a cedar plank, or smoked and added to a cream sauce over pasta — the list goes on. Although there is one species native to the Atlantic Ocean, most are found in the Pacific Ocean, ranging from the central California coast to the Canadian Arctic and in the western Pacific along the coasts of Japan, Korea, and Russia. Salmon is farmed or caught wild, but wild-caught, especially king or chinook, is prized for its superior taste and is a good source of omega-3s. For the indigenous people of the Pacific Northwest coast of North America, salmon is an important part of the diet and culture, with archaeological evidence dating to 5,000 years ago. Salmon fishing in the Pacific Northwest is a popular activity but has become regulated to prevent overfishing and to ensure availability for the coastal tribes.

NADA *I have shared this recipe with so many of my friends around the globe! It is surely one of my most popular dishes. It is easy, quick, and perfect for last-minute entertaining, especially when there is little time to spend in the kitchen. The sharp flavour of the ginger balances perfectly with the rich taste of the salmon. Serve with jasmine or brown basmati rice.*

SERVES 4 TO 6

Olive oil

1 kg (2¼ lb) salmon fillet, skin on

140 g (5 oz) ginger, grated

200 g (7 oz) spring onions, thinly sliced

120 ml (½ c) teriyaki sauce

2 tbsp light soya sauce

Preheat the oven to 220°C (425°F).

Line a baking pan with foil. Rub some olive oil on the foil to prevent the salmon from sticking. Lightly score the salmon and lay it on the foil, skin down. Sprinkle the grated ginger and sliced spring onions over the salmon. Combine the teriyaki and soya sauces and pour over the salmon. Let it sit at room temperature for 30 minutes. Bake for 20 to 25 minutes or to taste.

Transfer the salmon to a large platter and serve immediately.

GUAVA AND POMEGRANATE SALAD

Guava is said to have originated in Mexico and Central America and has since become a staple in many Asian countries. Early Spanish explorers began cultivating guava in the West Indies, from where it spread to the Bahamas and Bermuda. Because the fruit was too delicate to last on ocean voyages and Europe did not have the subtropical/tropical climate to grow guava trees, the fruit remained relatively unknown in Europe. The Spanish and Portuguese explorers carried the seeds to India and further to Southeast Asia, where the guava tree thrived. It was later adapted in Egypt and onwards to Palestine. It is rich in vitamins and minerals and the whole fruit is edible, including the skin. In Asia, guavas are used in pies, desserts, drinks, salads, and vegetable dishes.

NADA *This is a delicately flavoured and refreshing fruit salad that I immediately adopted when we moved to Abu Dhabi, after tasting it at an Emirati friend's home. The key to this salad is having ripe guava. Like avocados, you may need to let the guavas ripen before using them. I prefer the Egyptian longneck guava, which ripens faster and is more aromatic. Soaking the pine nuts and pistachios overnight not only enhances the flavour but also helps with digestion. The proportion of guava to pomegranate can be adjusted to your taste. This salad is particularly attractive when served in a clear glass bowl.*

SERVES 6 TO 8

700 g (1½ lb) pomegranates

70 g (½ c) pine nuts

35 g (¼ c) pistachios, shelled

800 g (1¾ lb) ripe guavas

400 ml (1⅔ c) guava nectar

Remove the seeds from the pomegranate and refrigerate. Soak the pine nuts and pistachios in separate bowls of water and refrigerate overnight.

Peel the guavas and discard the skin. Cut them in half and scoop out the seeds with some of the pulp and reserve. Cut the skinned and deseeded guavas into 1-centimetre (½-inch) cubes and place in a large glass serving bowl.

Mix the guava nectar and reserved guava seeds and pulp in a blender. Pass the mixture through a medium-size sieve to remove the seeds. Add the guava pulp mixture to the cubed guava.

When ready to serve, add the pomegranate seeds and gently toss to combine. Drain the pine nuts and pistachios and sprinkle over the top.

BUTHAINA AL MAZRUI & NOOR BANI HASHIM

ENTREPRENEURS
◊
UAE

When I received a much-coveted invitation to The Dinner Club by No. 57 shortly after it was launched in November 2012, I was intrigued by this new culinary dimension of the capital. The personalised invitation included the date and time but no location. Directions arrived a day before the event and were more like a treasure hunt, with no street address. While navigating the map across town, I realised I was approaching the Abu Dhabi Mall. This time, though, I accessed it through a service delivery corridor leading to a furniture store that had been transformed for the dinner. After Buthaina and Noor, our hostesses, greeted us, we were seated at one long, elaborately decorated table and treated to a three-hour epicurean feast that tantalised the senses.

Dinner clubs have been trending in cities across the world, initially as a reaction to expensive and impersonal fine dining restaurants. Hosted in private homes as an alternative dining experience, they offer good food, a warm welcome, and a cosy atmosphere. Their predecessors, such as the Prohibition-era speakeasies and Cuban *paladares* (private in-home restaurants), started as acts of rebellion. Fashionable dinner clubs now offer an intimate and posh pop-up dining experience with a dollop of mystery and mouth-watering food. Buthaina and Noor's dinners are held in clandestine locations, the guests don't know each other, and the menu and theme are varied. The hostesses describe the evening as a 'surprise underground party for your senses. But better'.

Initially, Buthaina and Noor thought the dinner club would be a good promotion for their café once it opened, but it quickly took on a life of its own. High-end luxury brands started approaching them to host dinners for clients, and a new business model was born. Buthaina recalls, 'Four dinners in, we got a call from Christian Louboutin's team asking if we would co-host a dinner with them'. Excited to meet the man who has come to define glamorous footwear, Buthaina and Noor jumped on the opportunity. To create a truly unique experience, they transformed a Dubai plant nursery into an enchanted forest. Since then, Buthaina and Noor have hosted numerous dinners for leading brands in unexpected locations, such as an empty swimming pool, a school bus, and a concrete plant. The elaborate tablescapes always include the whimsical touch of their signature animal figurines — a takeaway from the evening and evidence that the guest has been inducted into their dinner club.

Their long-time friendship developed into a partnership when Buthaina returned from her studies in London in 2007 and found the dining options in the city uninspiring. She approached Noor about creating a café that fused elements of their life abroad with their own traditions. Regulatory obstacles delayed the opening but proved to be a blessing in disguise since the result was the dinner club. Noor says: 'We realised that supper clubs were done all over the world, but normally hosted in homes, which wouldn't work for us culturally. So, we added a unique element: hosting the dinners in crazy locations where you would never expect to dine'.

Noor and Buthaina are hands-on with every aspect of the dinners and their café (which finally opened in 2014). They have found the perfect division of labour, with Noor orchestrating the decor and Buthaina handling everything edible. Noor's instincts for urban space allow her to create a setting that is sometimes an antidote to the surroundings. Buthaina responds with a menu that is seasonal, transportable, and rarely repeated. One exception, though, is their signature dessert, the heavenly *ermahgerd*, a mini-marshmallow-topped confection named for the sound a mouth full of it makes when saying 'oh my God'. Buthaina and Noor are among the Emirati millennial entrepreneurs deliciously transforming the culinary culture of the city.

Our dinner club is a like a surprise underground party for your senses.
But better.

BUTHAINA

SPICY TUNA ON CRISPY RICE

Spicy tuna with crispy rice is ubiquitous at trendy Japanese restaurants like Katsuya, Koi, and Zuma. The genius of the dish is the crispy sushi rice, which is crunchy on the outside and soft and chewy on the inside. These little morsels of crispy rice and spicy tuna drizzled with some soya sauce result in an irresistible combination of flavours and textures.

BUTHAINA *I first tasted spicy tuna on crispy rice in Los Angeles and it was love at first bite. I created a healthier version without frying the rice, although it loses the crunch. It is important to use only sushi-grade tuna. It's better to make the spicy mayo with Japanese Kewpie Mayonnaise if you can find it, as it is made with rice vinegar. I top the spicy tuna with an Asian slaw, but you can try other variations with jalapeño peppers or eel sauce.*

SERVES 6 TO 8

450 g (1 lb) sushi-grade tuna

SPICY MAYONNAISE

110 g (½ c) mayonnaise

1–2 tbsp sriracha sauce, to taste

2 tsp lime juice

½ tsp salt

SUSHI RICE

300 g (1½ c) sushi rice

Black sesame seeds

SLAW

110 g (4 oz) Chinese cabbage

110 g (4 oz) red cabbage

60 ml (¼ c) rice vinegar

3 tbsp dark soya sauce

1 tbsp brown sugar

80 ml (⅓ c) sesame oil

1 tbsp red chili flakes

Slice the tuna against the grain, chop into small cubes and place in a bowl. Combine the mayonnaise, sriracha sauce, lime juice, and salt. Add enough of it to coat the tuna, mix well, and refrigerate the tuna and the excess spicy mayonnaise until ready to use.

FOR THE SUSHI RICE

Prepare the sushi rice according to the method in the recipe on page 314. Flatten the cooked rice on a baking tray so it is 2.5 centimetres (1 inch) thick; refrigerate. It is important that the rice is cold so it will not fall apart while frying. Cut the rice with a 5-centimetre (2-inch) round cookie cutter or rectangular sushi mould and place on another tray. Each rice cake should be packed as tightly as possible so it will hold its shape when frying. Sprinkle the rice cakes with the sesame seeds and press them into the cakes. Coat the bottom of a non-stick skillet with vegetable oil and place over high heat. When the oil is hot enough to sizzle, fry each rice cake for about 1 minute on each side, or until golden brown.

FOR THE SLAW

Chop the cabbage into thin slivers and place in a medium bowl. Whisk the rice vinegar, dark soya sauce, brown sugar, sesame oil, and red chili flakes in a small bowl. Add the desired amount of dressing to the cabbage mix and toss.

TO ASSEMBLE

Place the rice cakes on a platter. Top each with a rounded spoonful of the tuna/mayonnaise mix. Gently mound some of the coleslaw on top of each and drizzle with the dressing to taste. Serve the additional slaw and spicy mayonnaise on the side.

BISCOFF CHEESECAKE
with Salted Caramel Sauce

Salted caramel can easily be considered the flavour of the century, having spread rapidly from rarefied Parisian pastry shops and top New York restaurants, down through the layers of popular desserts and coffee drinks. The original salted caramels are a traditional treat in Brittany, invented in the 1970s by chocolatier Henri Le Roux, who was searching for something unusual to make his candy stand out and decided to use salted butter. Brittany, which has always been famous for its salted butter, was one of the few provinces in France exempted from the fifteenth century gabelle, the widely impopular tax imposed on salt, and one of the causes of the French Revolution. Today, salted caramel cookies, brownies, cupcakes, and lattes are ubiquitous at trendy eateries across the Gulf.

NOOR *For this cheesecake, we use Lotus Biscoff cookies (a brand of speculoos, a crisp spice cookie from Belgium), instead of digestives or graham crackers. The delectable caramelised flavour of the Biscoff crust pairs well with the salted caramel sauce. We also prefer a lighter cheesecake, mixing mascarpone with the cream cheese.*

SERVES 6 TO 8

CRUST

285 g (10 oz) speculoos cookies, such as Biscoff

50 g (¼ c) brown sugar

110 g (4 oz) butter, melted

FILLING

450 g (1 lb) cream cheese

450 g (1 lb) mascarpone

210 g (1 c) brown sugar

4 eggs

1 tsp vanilla

SALTED CARAMEL SAUCE

210 g (1 c) granulated sugar

85 g (3 oz) butter, cubed

120 ml (½ c) heavy cream

1 tsp fleur de sel or coarse salt

FOR THE CRUST

Heat oven to 180°C (350°F). Grease a 23-centimetre (9-inch) springform pan and wrap the bottom and half-way up the sides with heavy-duty aluminium foil. Crush the cookies into a medium bowl until fine and mix them with the brown sugar and melted butter until well combined. Press the mix into the bottom and slightly up the sides of the pan. Bake for 10 minutes. Lower the oven temperature to 160°C (325°F).

FOR THE FILLING

Beat the cream cheese, mascarpone, and sugar with an electric mixer on medium speed until smooth. Beat in the eggs, one at a time, and the vanilla, until blended. Pour the filling into the crust and spread it evenly with a spatula. Place the springform pan into a larger baking pan and add hot water to reach half the height of the springform pan. This will prevent the cheesecake from cracking as it cooks.

Bake for 60 minutes or until the edge of the cheesecake is set but the centre still jiggles slightly. Turn off the oven, open the door part way, and leave the cheesecake in the oven for another 30 minutes. Remove the springform pan from the water bath and let the cheesecake cool for 30 minutes. Run a knife around the edge to loosen the sides. Refrigerate at least 6 hours or preferably overnight.

FOR THE CARAMEL SAUCE

Heat the sugar in a medium saucepan over medium heat, swirling the pan until the sugar melts and becomes honey-coloured. Immediately add the butter and whisk vigorously until it melts. Remove the pan from the heat and slowly drizzle in the cream, stirring continuously until thoroughly blended. Stir in the salt and allow the sauce to cool for 15 minutes prior to serving or pouring it into a glass jar to cool completely. *[This sauce can be made ahead of time and refrigerated in a tightly covered container for up to two weeks. Warm the sauce before using.]*

Transfer the cheesecake with the springform base to a serving platter. Slice and drizzle each slice with the salted caramel sauce.

Table Tales

PEGGI AND ALFRED BLOOM

INSTRUCTOR
NYUAD
◊
US

VICE
CHANCELLOR
NYUAD
◊
US

With the end of World War II, the expansion of international trade, a strong dollar, and advances in transportation, an unprecedented number of Americans began to travel abroad. This new wave of American globetrotters brought back from their adventures miles of undeveloped film, pounds of souvenirs, and hours of mouth-watering descriptions of the unexpectedly wonderful food they had eaten at the street stalls, restaurants, and the homes of hospitable citizens overseas. Al and Peggi Bloom grew up in New York and Boston, respectively, listening to such stories from family and friends who had taken part in post-war reconstruction in Europe and Asia, and travelled abroad for education, business, or pleasure. They heard great stories about people with other customs and histories who led satisfying lives, laughed at much the same jokes, and shared fundamental aspirations for themselves, their communities, and the future, and they couldn't wait to take their own pictures and collect their own stories. As Peggi remembers, 'We studied geography, read and re-read issues of *National Geographic*, collected stamps, travel books and posters, went to Saturday movie matinees set in the Kalahari, the Arctic, the Amazon, and the Outback, and watched Lowell Thomas' adventure travelogues on TV'.

Peggi made her first journey abroad after college—a month in Europe on $5 a day (exclusive of airfare and Euro pass). The same year, Al and his college roommate took the long way to Taiwan, via Beirut, Kabul, and Katmandu, to study Chinese. By the time they met in graduate school, the Blooms' independent travels had not only whetted their appetites for faraway places but for faraway cuisines, as well. And, in 1971, anticipating geographic adventures spiced with culinary delight, they set out for their first taste of the world together aboard Air Afrique to Dakar for *ceebu jen* (Senegalese fish and rice), then on to Bamako for *tigadèguèna* (meat in peanut sauce), Strasbourg for *choucroute garnie*, and Paris for *caneton à la presse*. A year later, unable to resist the appeal of crossing, twice in one month, the International Date Line, the Equator, the Tropics of Cancer and Capricorn, and twelve time zones, they took advantage of Pan Am's twenty-eight-day round-the-Pacific fare from New York to Perth. They made fifteen stops en route and sampled a staggering number of exotic dishes from the Pacific Rim. Peggi lists the memorable ones: '*Hai zhe pi* in Hong Kong, chili crab in Singapore, durian in Jakarta, *gado-gado* in Denpasar, carpetbagger steak in Melbourne, *yolla* in Sydney, lamingtons in Wellington, *poi* in Suva, *terrine de foie gras à la vanille Tahitienne* in Papaeete, and *mole poblano* in Mexico City'.

Beyond great meals and photogenic temples, that trip introduced them to cities undergoing cultural and economic transformation, to wombats, kiwi birds, and cassowaries. Peggi recalls that 'somewhere along that route it became obvious that Al's Ph.D. research couldn't be responsibly pursued without a round-the-world ticket, allowing further adventurous dining'.

For the first thirteen years of their marriage, Al's academic interests (linguistics and psychology) took them annually to East Asia and the rich cuisines of China. Many of their favourite dishes were difficult, if not impossible, to find in restaurants outside of Hong Kong and Taiwan at the time, so they learned from Chinese friends, a few chefs, and some reliably authentic cookbooks how to make many of them themselves. 'One Chinese New Year, we prepared a seventeen-course dinner for seventy-five guests, with homemade fortune cookies — each with a different message, in verse — written by a faculty friend. After that, Lunar New Year parties became an annual tradition', Peggi tells me.

In 2009, I joined New York University Abu Dhabi's (NYUAD) start-up team to build a campus to support the university's ambitious vision to develop a global undergraduate and graduate educational

institution, ready to open its doors in 2010. Al was the first vice chancellor of the newly established campus. His eighteen years as president of Swarthmore College, twelve years of teaching linguistics and psychology, and his international travels and language studies, were a fitting blend of experiences for the leader of the new global institution that now has a student body representing more than 115 countries. His guiding belief is that 'the world is now a place to which the members of every society and nation bring their intellectual resources and contributions. Unless you have an educational context in which no culture is dominant, you cannot educate as effectively for a global world'. Peggi is an instructor in NYUAD's academic enrichment programme, which helps first-year students master the writing and critical thinking skills required to navigate the global education that the university is developing.

By the time Al and Peggi arrived in Abu Dhabi, they had retired twelve passports, lived in five countries, and travelled in another 155. Their home has yards of bookshelves filled with slides from their travels, masks, calligraphy, textiles, baskets, pottery, foreign cookbooks, and restaurant menus. Peggi tells me that gathering the ingredients to make favourite Chinese dishes is not without its challenges in Abu Dhabi. While she continues to search the markets here for the 'correct' bean sauce for Chinese eggplant, she is developing a taste for local dates at every stage of maturation.

A tradition of building a community through sharing meals with faculty, students, and administrators is one Al and Peggi had embraced at Swarthmore and have continued at NYUAD. Their travels have allowed them to share enough local delicacies and laughter with local gourmands to support their conviction that 'across all human communities, offering and accepting food—gestures that invariably warm bodies, relax tension, and release pleasure—can also open hearts, establish trust, and remind us that what all human beings have in common far outweighs whatever distinguishes them. One's own social and cultural value set does not necessarily represent the only natural or right way to respond to the world'.

> What all human beings have in common far outweighs whatever distinguishes them.
>
> PEGGI

BONG BONG GEE
Bong Bong Chicken

SERVES 4

The name *Bong Bong Gee* originates from the process used to separate the chicken into pieces once it has been cooked: the chicken is struck with a wooden rolling pin, which produces a sound like 'bong bong'. The poaching method for the chicken produces silky, smooth meat perfect for salads or soups.

PEGGI *Chinese food is all about preparation. While this dish may seem daunting at first, make it once and you'll be surprised at how simple it actually is. Texture is as important a criterion for Chinese gourmets as taste, so, while you could slice rather than shred the chicken, the contrast between the slippery noodles, uneven pieces of silky chicken, crunchy cucumber, and a slightly rough sauce guarantees the cook high marks. Serve this salad at room temperature (or a little warmer) but not cold.*

CHICKEN

700 g (1½ lb) chicken breast

1 tbsp fresh ginger, crushed

4 spring onions, chopped

4 cloves garlic

2 tsp salt

SAUCE

4 cloves garlic, minced

15 g (¼ c) fresh coriander, chopped

3 tbsp Chinese sesame paste

2 tbsp Chinese sesame oil

80 ml (⅓ c) soya sauce

1 tbsp dark soya sauce

2 tbsp honey

1 tsp hoisin sauce

2 tsp hot chili oil

2 tbsp rice vinegar

½ tsp Szechwan pepper-salt (recipe follows)

OTHER

340 g (12 oz) small cucumbers

310 g (11 oz) mung bean noodles

GARNISH

Fresh coriander

Red or green chilies

Spring onions, green parts, thinly sliced

Sesame seeds

FOR THE CHICKEN

Fill a medium saucepan with 1.5 litres (1½ quarts) of water. Add the ginger, spring onions, garlic, and salt, and bring to a boil over high heat. Add the chicken, making sure there is enough water to cover it by about 5 centimetres (2 inches). Lower the heat to medium, cover the pan, and simmer for 10 minutes. Turn off the heat and leave the chicken in the broth until you can lift it out by hand.

Skin the chicken and remove the meat from the bones. Discard any membranes or tendons. Pound the meat with a rolling pin or meat mallet to separate the fibres. Tear the meat by hand into 0.5-centimetre (¼-inch) wide shreds. *[Reserve the broth for any other use.]*

FOR THE SAUCE

Combine the sauce ingredients in a small bowl and mix well. Add just enough water to make the sauce pourable, but not so much that the flavour is diluted. Adjust for sweetness and piquantness. It should be a little spicy and fierce right off the spoon. *[This can be made a day ahead and refrigerated.]*

ASSEMBLING THE SALAD

Peel the cucumbers, halve them lengthwise, and remove the seeds. Slice into strips thinner than the chicken shreds.

Prepare the noodles according to the package instructions; drain. Spread them on a large serving platter, layer on the cucumbers, and top with the chicken. Just before serving, lace thin streams of some of the sauce over the chicken. Garnish with fresh coriander, chilies, spring onions, and sesame seeds. Serve the remaining sauce on the side.

SZECHWAN PEPPER-SALT

Combine 2 tablespoons Szechwan peppercorns and 4 tablespoons coarse salt in a heavy skillet. Stir over medium heat until wisps of smoke appear and the mixture is fragrant, 8 to 10 minutes. Let the mixture cool and then grind or crush until fine. Store in an airtight container away from light, heat, and moisture.

CHINESE 'STRANGE FLAVOUR' EGGPLANT

In China, 'strange flavour' food means an extraordinary combination of spicy, tangy, sweet, tart, and subtle tastes all at the same time. Traditionally, 'strange flavour' sauces have sesame paste from the Szechwan region, which results in a thicker sauce. This 'strange flavour' sauce is thinner, permeating the eggplant. Typically, the Chinese cooking method is based on stir-frying, as it consumes less fuel for home cooks and is faster for professional chefs working with high heat.

PEGGI *This dish is quite versatile. It can be served hot or cold, shredded as a salad or pureed as a dip with crackers, and it can be made ahead of time. You'll need to use Chinese or Japanese eggplant, as the skin is thin and tastes sweet. I prefer to bake the eggplant: it is less oily, easier to prepare (no salting and draining), and just as delicious. Chinese food is cooked fast, so be sure you've got everything cut, mixed, and prepared before the cooking starts. You can use the time while the eggplant is baking to prepare and measure the remaining ingredients.*

SERVES 4

450 g (1 lb) eggplant, Chinese or Japanese
1½ tbsp light brown sugar
2½ tbsp soya sauce
1 tbsp rice vinegar
28 g (1 oz) spring onions
2 tbsp vegetable oil
2 cloves garlic, minced
1 tbsp ginger, minced
½ tsp red chili flakes
1 tsp sesame oil

GARNISH

Spring onions, thinly sliced
Sesame seeds
Fresh coriander

Preheat the oven to 250°C (475°F).

Clean, dry and pierce the eggplants so they won't explode when baking. Bake for 30 to 40 minutes, turning them once, until each gives easily when pressed. Remove them from the oven when they're done and let them cool to the touch. If using Chinese or Japanese eggplant, leave them unpeeled and retain the liquid. For any other type of eggplant, remove the skin and pour off the liquid. Shred the eggplant by hand into pencil-thin strips.

Combine the brown sugar, soya sauce, rice vinegar, and 1 tablespoon of hot water in a small bowl and stir until dissolved. Chop the spring onions in 2-centimetre (1-inch) lengths.

Heat a light-weight skillet or wok over high heat. Swirl in the vegetable oil and lower the heat to medium when the oil is hot enough to sizzle a bit of garlic. Stir-fry but don't brown the garlic, ginger, and spring onions. Add the red chili flakes. When the fragrance is pronounced, stir in the soya sauce mix. When the liquid boils around the edges, add the eggplant 'pencils' and liquid (if you are using Chinese or Japanese eggplant). Taste and adjust for sugar, as it brings up the spiciness, but it shouldn't be too sweet.

Remove from the heat, stir in the sesame oil, and transfer to a serving platter. Garnish with spring onion slices, sesame seeds, and fresh coriander.

TAMU AND AMIR AL ISLAM

DIVERSITY PROFESSIONAL NYUAD
◊
US

FACULTY MEMBER ZAYED UNIVERSITY
◊
US

Amir still marvels at how one phone call from John Sexton, then president of New York University, and an invitation to visit Abu Dhabi, changed his life. Tamu was part of the early start-up team that had travelled to Abu Dhabi to help establish the new campus. She was excited by the opportunity to contribute to this new venture. However, convincing her husband to move halfway around the world was slightly more difficult. Amir was well entrenched in his community in New York as an active leader on the national African American Islamic scene and in the international multifaith community. It was a lot to leave behind, but ultimately, Tamu moved to Abu Dhabi in February 2009, and Amir followed nine months later. After spending just a week in Abu Dhabi, though, Amir felt the opportunity was a blessing from Allah.

One Friday, Tamu accompanied me to the Sheikha Maryam bint Sultan mosque in Bateen to hear the *khutba* (sermon) in English. At the end of the noon prayer, we lingered to chat with some fellow worshippers. Tamu heard someone say, 'That sounds like an American voice'. She turned around and said, 'Yes, it is'. That is how Tamu met Bayyinah, her first African American friend in the United Arab Emirates. Bayyinah and her husband, Jamal, introduced Tamu and Amir to the United Arab Emirates' growing African American community, some of whom Amir knew from New York and Chicago when they had worked together on issues of race, social justice, and community development. Amir found that gatherings with African Americans across the United Arab Emirates were nurturing spaces, which allowed him to continue to contribute to the Black community.

Over time, Tamu and Amir's move to Abu Dhabi has given them a whole new world. 'There are many expats who come here and don't engage with Emiratis', Amir said. 'But, the greatest experience I have had is the privilege of working closely with them'. As a professor of history, philosophy, and culture at Zayed University, Amir teaches both Emirati men and women at separate campuses. As he gains a deeper understanding of the local culture and history, and of the great work of the country's first president, Sheikh Zayed bin Sultan Al Nahyan, Amir feels a sense of purpose, including contributing to the future leadership of a young country, which brings immense gratification. 'I have been to most of the Muslim world, and there is something unique about this place. I don't know how to articulate it specifically, but there is something special about the Emirati people, their sense of tolerance and their sense of themselves', Amir reflected.

For Tamu, taxi rides in Abu Dhabi continue to be an adventure in history and anthropology. On her first taxi ride to the office, a Pakistani driver asked: 'Where are you from?' Tamu replied: 'I am American'. The driver insisted: 'No, but where are you originally from?' Tamu repeated: 'I am from America, from New York City'. The driver: 'Oh, but where are your parents from?' Tamu: 'They are from America, too'. Taxi driver: 'But I mean where were you born?' Tamu calmly repeated: 'I was born in Arkansas in America'. It was clear that there was something either about the way Tamu was dressed, with a colourful turban wrapped high on her head and the West African bone bangles, or the colour of her skin, that did not match the driver's idea of an American. Reflecting on these encounters, which Tamu feels stem from a genuine curiosity, she says, 'I find myself having to fight to claim my "Americanness", which is not something I ever thought I would have to do'.

From their new perspective as residents of the United Arab Emirates, Tamu and Amir often reflect on their previous experience of living in the United

> There is something very special about the Emirati people, their sense of tolerance and their sense of themselves.
>
> AMIR

States as African Americans. As Amir put it, 'It's hard to live in America as a Black person and not be scarred by the notion and consciousness of how others are looking at you. The great intellectual Frantz Fanon spoke of this "gaze". Black people can see when others look at them with this particular gaze, what we call "othering", or a way that gives you the sense that you are somehow inferior. I get that in most places I have been. But I rarely get it from Emiratis. We truly feel like citizens of the world here, interacting with different people and different cultures'.

The life that Tamu and Amir have built in Abu Dhabi is purposeful and consistent with their philosophy and outlook on life. Their deep commitment to African American culture is reflected in their home but shared with the Arab-aesthetic influences they have more recently embraced. The focal point is the African American wall: a series of framed original black and white photographs hanging along the staircase. The portraits of the scholars, artists, and activists culminate at the top of the stairway with a portrait of President Barack Obama. Tamu calls them 'our he-roes and she-roes'. She recalls a proverb from the African American community: We stand on the shoulders of others. She says, 'These photos reflect the intergenerational inspiration that helped us get to where we are'.

Since moving to Abu Dhabi and travelling in the region, Tamu has been drawn to the crafts and flavours of the Arab world and other parts of Asia she had not previously explored. Today, her cooking incorporates a diverse range of spices, such as nigella seeds, *za'atar*, and sumac.

When the day comes that Tamu and Amir return home to the United States, their perspective will have shifted after the years in Abu Dhabi. They view the United Arab Emirates as a model for the region, demonstrating how people from different parts of the world can live together in a society, practise their religion and culture, and enjoy a multicultural environment. 'There is a lot that we will miss when we return home: our friends, the diversity of people, the perennial fruits and vegetables in the markets, *fattoush*, lemonade with mint, and *za'atar*', Tamu and Amir foresee. For now, their wall of photographs helps ground them in the world they came from, even as they live the life of their dreams.

COUSCOUS WITH A TRIO OF FLAVOURS

SERVES 4 TO 6

LEEKS

1 tbsp olive oil

450 g (1 lb) leeks, sliced

1 tsp cumin

2 tbsp za'atar

Salt and pepper, to taste

15 g (½ oz) butter

255 g (9 oz) mushrooms, sliced

SPINACH

1 tsp olive oil

450 g (1 lb) baby spinach leaves

2 tbsp basil pesto, ready-made

Salt and pepper, to taste

2 tsp toasted sesame seeds

OLIVE MIX

1 tbsp olive oil

3 cloves garlic, sliced

255 g (9 oz) assorted whole olives

50 g (⅓ c) capers, drained

1 tbsp rosemary

340 g (12 oz) cherry tomatoes

Pinch of coarse salt

Lemon zest

COUSCOUS

450 g (1 lb) couscous

Pinch of coarse salt

Pinch of paprika

Pinch of cumin

55 g (2 oz) spring onion, chopped

1 tbsp fresh coriander, chopped

TAMU *This unusual platter melds flavours from across several different cuisines — Asian, Mediterranean, and Arabic — in a way that is symbolic of the wide variety of cultures I have experienced in Abu Dhabi. It is best served with a protein of your choice. Any leftover vegetables make a good base for a frittata or quiche, and add some mozzarella to the olive mix and you have a delicious Caprese salad.*

LEEKS AND MUSHROOMS WITH ZA'ATAR

Heat the olive oil in a large skillet; add the leeks and sauté over medium-low heat. Sprinkle in the cumin, za'atar, salt, and pepper. Cook for 5 minutes, tossing periodically, until the leeks begin to soften. Remove from the heat and scrape them into a medium bowl.

Heat the butter in the skillet and sauté the mushrooms over medium-high heat, tossing as needed until lightly golden. Remove with a slotted spoon to the bowl with the leeks. Toss to combine and add more za'atar, if desired. Cover and keep warm until ready to serve.

PESTO SPINACH

Heat the olive oil in a large saucepan. Sauté a portion of the spinach, stirring constantly as it wilts. Keep adding more as space allows, until all of it is wilted and warmed in the oil. Halfway through, add the pesto a tablespoon at a time, stirring well after each addition. Add the salt and pepper. Drain any excess liquid, cover and keep warm until ready to serve. Sprinkle with toasted sesame seeds to serve.

CHUNKY TOMATOES, OLIVES, AND CAPERS

Heat the olive oil in a saucepan over medium heat. Sauté the garlic until it begins to soften. Quickly toss in the olives and capers; stir for 1 minute. Add the rosemary and simmer for another minute. Add the tomatoes and cook for 1 minute until just heated through. Sprinkle in the salt and toss. Transfer the mixture to a bowl and garnish with lemon zest.

COUSCOUS

Prepare the couscous according to the instructions on the package. Add salt, paprika, cumin, spring onion, and coriander. Mix and fluff with a fork.

PUTTING IT ALL TOGETHER

Spoon the vegetable mixtures in separate mounds around the edge of a large circular serving platter. Pile the hot couscous in the middle and garnish with more za'atar and chopped fresh coriander.

NAZZY BEGLARI AND PETER SCARLET

DESIGNER / JOURNALIST
◊
IRAN / US

FILM FESTIVAL DIRECTOR
◊
US

The scene: The awards ceremony for the 2009 edition of Abu Dhabi's international film festival at the opulent Emirates Palace Hotel. The festival's new artistic director, Peter Scarlet, is the host of the star-studded evening. After the award ceremony he introduces the final screening, *Men Who Stare at Goats*, and explains to the audience, 'Unfortunately, none of the film's stars — George Clooney, Kevin Spacey, Jeff Bridges, or Ewan McGregor — was able to be here tonight. So, since the men who stare at goats are not here, please welcome onstage some of the goats who undoubtedly stared right back at them'. At this point, four smiling goatherds led their charges onstage, to the audience's surprised hilarity. Perhaps no film festival had featured such a spontaneous and unexpected climax; it was a good example of Peter's talent for sharing his passion for film with a community by always keeping the door open for the whimsical, the quirky, the fanciful, the serious, and the unexpected.

Peter has long been interested in movies from the Middle East and North Africa and was one of the few American film festival directors who actively pursued movies from this region. When he was approached in 2009 to head the film festival in Abu Dhabi, Peter felt it was a natural progression to deepen his connection with the region. He talked things over with his wife, Nazzy, who at the time was a senior international correspondent for Voice of America. She had frequently travelled to the region to cover stories, but never to Abu Dhabi. Nazzy was eager to move closer to her birthplace, Iran, which she had left in 1978 to study abroad. So, together they embarked on an adventure!

For Peter, film festivals foster a sense of community, which is an integral part of appreciating film and the broader culture of a place. As he recalls, 'After we were married in 2001, whenever I was involved with a film festival, it benefited from Nazzy's indefatigable passion for food and entertaining'. At Tribeca, Nazzy would entertain a hundred people at home, and with less space in Abu Dhabi, their gatherings became more intimate. My husband and I look forward to Friday film nights at the Scarlets. Peter selects a film from his extraordinary collection, and a small group of friends assemble in the comfortable home cinema that he adapted in a spare bedroom, complete with reclining armchairs. 'Like flying business class with no danger of jet lag', Peter adds. He then unveils the name of the film at the last moment, while Nazzy prepares the food that is perfectly timed to be served when the film ends. The table, an art installation unto itself, is already set, awaiting the sumptuous Persian feast and lively film critique.

Nazzy incorporates fruit into many of her savoury dishes, a hallmark of Azeri cuisine she learned from her grandmother. Tart cherry rice and pomegranate soup are among Nazzy's signature dishes. Over several afternoons, Nazzy has patiently taught me the art of rice making and the delicate balance of opposing impulses in Persian food, such as savoury with sweet and hot with cold. Here, the idea of hot with cold food is not based on spiciness or temperature but on the notion of whether the food creates energy or a cooling effect on the body. Nazzy achieves this balance beautifully in all aspects of her creativity, either the tart and sweet duck *fesenjan*, or the contrasting patterns and colours of her kaftan designs.

After dinner, we sip orange blossom tea under the jasmine tree in the courtyard. Our conversation wanders to the idea of 'home', and where we might be at this time next year. For Nazzy, who describes herself as a global nomad, her home is her country, and she recreates it wherever she goes, with food at its heart. Nazzy fondly shares, 'My grandmother taught me that a house without an active kitchen is not a home'.

My home
is my
country.

NAZZY

SUP-E PESTEH
Pistachio Soup

Pistachio trees have been cultivated for thousands of years in the deserts of West Asia. The high desert in Iran, with its abundant sunshine, is ideal for growing what is sometimes referred to as 'green gold'. The origins of the name pistachio, *pesteh*, comes from Persia. Pistachios have pride of place in Iranian homes, set in large bowls on the coffee table and offered to guests. They are eaten fresh, roasted, on their own, ground in sweetmeats, cooked in soups and stews, caramelised, and mixed into puddings.

NAZZY *This pistachio soup, with its combination of fruit and nuts, is from a favourite recipe handed down from my grandmother. It can be served either hot or at room temperature. When I serve it in the summer, I mix in some yogurt to make it cooler, and in the winter I spice it up with more chili powder. I only use coarse or Himalayan salt and love to garnish the soup with dried rose petals. As with many soups, this one is better the next day.*

SERVES 6 TO 8

SOUP

- **80 ml (⅓ c)** olive oil
- **1½ tbsp** ginger, chopped
- **½ tsp** chili powder
- **½ tsp** turmeric
- **1 tbsp** coriander seeds, ground
- **450 g (1 lb)** leeks, chopped
- **450 g (1 lb)** unsalted shelled pistachios
- **30 g (1 c)** parsley or basil, chopped
- **2 tsp** coarse or Himalayan salt
- **½ tsp** black pepper
- **120 ml (½ c)** orange juice
- **60 ml (¼ c)** lemon juice

GARNISH

- **1 tsp** saffron
- **1** sugar cube
- Greek yogurt
- Shelled pistachios, julienned
- Pomegranate seeds, barberries or rose petals

Heat the oil in a large stockpot and add the ginger, chili powder, turmeric, and coriander seeds; sauté for 2 minutes. Add the leeks and sauté on medium heat for 10 minutes, until golden.

Grind the pistachios in a food processor until fine. Add 240 millilitres (1 cup) of water to make a thick paste. Scoop the paste into the stockpot and add 1.25 litres (1¼ quarts) of water. Bring to a boil, cover, and simmer for an hour.

Add the parsley or basil and cook for another 5 minutes. Working in batches, puree the soup in a blender and return it to the stockpot. Season with salt and pepper. Pour in the orange juice and simmer for 40 minutes. Add more water for the desired consistency. Remove from the heat and add the lemon juice.

Crush the saffron threads with the sugar and add 2 tablespoons of hot water to release the colour. Serve the soup in individual bowls, garnishing each with a dollop of yogurt, a drizzle of the saffron liquid, some of the julienned pistachios, and a few pomegranate seeds, barberries, or rose petals.

KASHK-E BADEMJAN
Eggplant and Yogurt Dip

Kashk-e bademjan is the quintessential Persian appetizer. It features *bademjan* (eggplant), known as the 'potato of Iran', and *kashk*, a firm, strained buttermilk, like whey, either compressed into balls or powdered. Before adding kashk to a dish it is mixed with water to create a tahini-like paste. It has a distinctive depth of flavour, which gives the rich eggplant a special edge. The flavours of the sautéed garlic, eggplant, and mint fuse together deliciously.

NAZZY *I prefer to use thick Greek yogurt, which has a milder taste than kashk. I enjoy the presentation of this dish as much as I do the taste. The brownish eggplant mash is a perfect canvas on which to drizzle the yellow saffron, blot the white yogurt, sprinkle with the crimson pomegranate, and splash with the green mint. So, let your inner artist flow and use your imagination when garnishing. This dish can be served warm or at room temperature as a dip with lavash or pita bread.*

—
SERVES
4 TO 6
—

EGGPLANT BASE

- **1.5 kg (3½ lb)** eggplant
- **120 ml (½ c)** olive oil
- **1 tsp** black pepper
- **2 tbsp** dried mint, divided
- Salt, to taste
- **60 g (¼ c)** Greek yogurt or kashk

GARNISH

- **2 tbsp** garlic, diced
- **1 tbsp** olive oil
- **½ tsp** turmeric
- **1 tbsp** dried mint
- **1 tsp** saffron
- **Pinch** of granulated sugar
- Greek yogurt or kashk
- Pomegranate seeds

FOR THE EGGPLANT BASE

Peel and slice the eggplant into 2-centimetre (¾-inch) thick slices. Sprinkle the slices with salt and leave them in a strainer for 30 minutes; pat dry. Heat the oil in a large skillet over medium heat and fry the eggplant slices in batches until they are golden brown, turning once. *[The eggplants can also be brushed with olive oil, sprinkled with pepper, dried mint, and salt, and baked at 200°C (400°F) for 25 minutes or until softened and golden brown.]*

Place the eggplant slices in a medium saucepan and add 120 millilitres (½ cup) of water; bring to a boil. Lower the heat and simmer for 10 minutes, until the eggplant is very tender. Mash the eggplant with a fork, leaving some lumps. Sprinkle in the pepper, mint, and salt to taste. Continue to simmer over low heat until the water has evaporated; remove from the heat. *[This dish can be prepared through this stage a day ahead of time and refrigerated.]* When the eggplant mash has cooled, stir in 60 grams (¼ cup) of the Greek yogurt or kashk, mix well, and adjust the seasoning to taste.

FOR THE GARNISH

Sauté the garlic in the olive oil for 2 minutes. Add the turmeric and stir until the garlic is golden. Remove the garlic from the pan and drain on a paper towel. Remove the pan from the heat and stir the mint into the remaining oil. Using a mortar and pestle, crush the saffron with the sugar. Stir in 2 tablespoons of hot water and set aside for the colour to diffuse.

Serve garnished with dollops of yogurt or kashk and the sautéed garlic and mint. Drizzle with the saffron liquid and sprinkle with some pomegranate seeds.

ALBALOO POLOW
Sour Cherry Rice

Persian cuisine sets itself apart with the cultivation and preparation of rice, which is considered an art form. The addition of dried fruit, nuts, herbs, and spices produces a rich array of dishes. The Caspian region in northern Iran is the main rice growing area, where people eat rice for every meal, including breakfast.

NAZZY *Rice is the star of my table, not a side dish, and preparing it is a ritual. The most coveted part of this dish is the crunchy crust we call* tadig. *The tadig can be made from a yogurt/rice mix, potatoes, lavash (flat bread), or even carrots. In this sour cherry rice, the tadig burns a little because of the sugar from the cherries. The secrets to successful rice are: a commitment to the process (no shortcuts), a non-stick pot, very low heat, and lots of patience! This is one dish that shouldn't be rushed, so proper timing when serving your dinner guests is important. As rice is traditionally a tribal food, I usually make it in large quantities, and leftovers are equally good.*

SERVES 6 TO 8

SOUR CHERRIES

250 g (9 oz) dried sour cherries

1 tbsp granulated sugar

RICE

500 g (2½ c) basmati rice

3 tbsp coarse salt

80 ml (⅓ c) + 1 tbsp olive oil, divided

2 potatoes, peeled and sliced 2 cm (¾ in) thick

28 g (1 oz) butter, melted

SAFFRON LIQUID

1 tsp saffron

1 sugar cube

Rinse the rice well and soak in lukewarm water with the salt. Let it stand for an hour; drain but don't rinse it.

Rinse the sour cherries with cold water, drain, and place them in a medium saucepan. Add 3 tablespoons of water and the sugar and cook over low heat until the cherries soften. Drain the liquid if any remains.

Boil 1.5 litres (1½ quarts) of water in a large non-stick saucepan. Add the rice and parboil for 6 to 8 minutes until al dente, gently stirring once so the rice doesn't stick together. To test, lightly squeeze a grain of rice; it should be soft on the outside but firm on the inside. The size of the grain will almost double in size. Drain the rice in a fine sieve and rinse with hot water; set it aside without stirring it.

Pour 80 millilitres (⅓ cup) of the olive oil into the same saucepan. Arrange the potato slices to cover the bottom. Using a slotted spoon, layer the parboiled rice and sour cherries over the potatoes in a pyramid shape, being careful not to move the potato slices; end with a rice layer. Poke holes in the rice mixture with the end of a wooden spoon to allow the steam to escape. Cover the saucepan and place it over medium heat for 10 minutes, until the steam builds up and starts to condense on the underside of the lid. It will make a sizzling sound.

Combine the melted butter, remaining 1 tablespoon olive oil, and 120 millilitres (½ cup) of boiling water and drizzle it over the rice. Wrap the lid with a cotton kitchen towel and cover the pot, making sure the fabric is wrapped around the handle so it doesn't catch fire. Reduce the heat to its lowest setting and let the rice cook for 50 to 60 minutes without uncovering.

While the rice is cooking, crush the saffron with the sugar cube using a mortar and pestle. Add 2 tablespoons boiling water, and set aside to infuse. When the rice is ready, drizzle it with the saffron liquid and stir the top layer to colour the rice. Level the rice with the back of a wooden spoon, cover, remove from the heat, and allow to rest for 5 minutes. When ready to serve, flip the rice onto a serving platter so the potato tadig is on top. It should be golden and crunchy.

FESENJAN BA ORDAK
Duck with Walnut and Pomegranate Sauce

Fesenjan, meaning the 'food of life', originated from the Caspian Sea region, where ducks are plentiful and walnuts rich in flavour. It is a hearty dish that best captures the philosophy and principles of harmony in Persian food, with elements that cool the body, pomegranates, and those that lend energy, walnuts. There are as many variations of fesenjan recipes as there are Persian kitchens.

NAZZY *I learned to make duck fesenjan from my Azerbaijani grandmother and Georgian great aunt. You can also make it with chicken or lamb, or eggplant for a vegetarian version. Balancing the sour flavours of the pomegranate molasses and the sweetness of the honey is a personal taste, so you might want to start with less honey than called for in the recipe and adjust to your preference. I serve fesenjan with saffron-flavoured basmati rice.*

—
SERVES
6 TO 8
—

- 2 kg (4½ lb) whole duck
- Salt and black pepper
- 255 g (9 oz) walnuts
- ½ tsp chili powder
- 240 ml (1 c) pomegranate molasses
- 120 ml (½ c) honey, to taste
- 475 ml (2 c) pomegranate juice
- 2 tbsp tomato paste
- 1 orange
- 1 orange, juiced
- 1 pomegranate, halved

Drain any juices from the duck and pat dry. Remove the extra skin around the neck and rub with salt and pepper. Place the duck, breast side down, in a preheated cast iron Dutch oven. Cover and cook over low heat for 30 minutes, turning after 15 minutes so both sides brown. It will fry in its own fat. Remove the duck from the pot; drain and dispose of the fat.

Meanwhile, finely grind the walnuts in a food processor. Place the ground nuts in a large saucepan and dry roast them for 5 minutes to release the flavour. Add the chili powder and continue to stir over low heat for another 2 minutes. Remove from the heat.

Combine the pomegranate molasses and honey in a small bowl. Taste and adjust the sweetness and sourness as desired. Pour it over the nut mix and return to the heat. Add half the pomegranate juice and the tomato paste; stir well and cover. Simmer over very low heat for 40 minutes, adding the remaining pomegranate juice halfway through. Stir periodically, until the mixture bubbles and has a slightly caramelised consistency. Adjust for desired balance of sweet and sour. Remove from heat.

Cut the orange into 1-centimetre (½-inch) slices and arrange evenly in the bottom of the Dutch oven. Place the duck on top of the oranges, breast down. Pour the orange juice and 350 millilitres (1½ cups) of water over the duck; place it over high heat and cover. Bring the liquid to a boil and then simmer for 1½ to 2 hours or until the meat falls off the bone.

Transfer the duck to a cutting board to cool. Discard the skin. Remove the meat from the bones and cut it into medium pieces. Add the meat to the saucepan with the pomegranate/nut sauce and heat through. Transfer to a serving tureen and garnish with the pomegranate halves.

2000s — A New Course

— 2010s —
WHAT'S BREWING

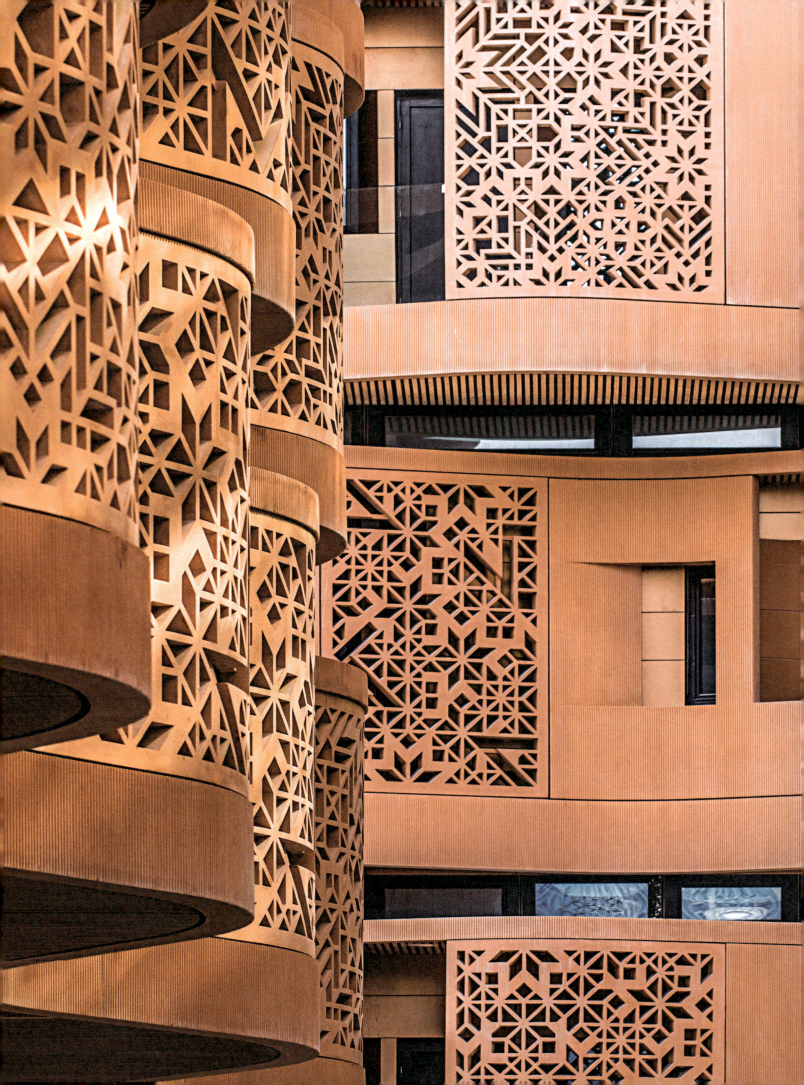

Political unrest across the Middle East and North Africa, the global economic crisis, and collapsing oil prices — this decade ushered in significant change across the region. The government undertook a review of the capital projects to prioritise resources. A more measured approach was adopted based on the blueprint for the economic vision that had been unveiled in 2008. Abu Dhabi's international reputation continued to grow as it became a key partner of many of the world's largest economies, and increasingly to Asia.

The government projects to diversify the economy and develop the social infrastructure literally changed the landscape of the emirate in a few short years, as earth was moved to shape buildable land. The newly built Cleveland Clinic Abu Dhabi, New York University Abu Dhabi, Yas Mall, Abu Dhabi Global Markets, and Louvre Abu Dhabi, transformed the capital from an island city to a city of islands. The opening of the global headquarters of the International Renewable Energy Agency (IRENA) in 2015 came six years after Abu Dhabi won the bid to host the international body. This was the first international organisation to be headquartered in the Middle East, recognising Abu Dhabi as an international player.

At the federal level, new ministries were founded for tolerance, happiness, youth, food security, and artificial intelligence, embracing innovation and empowering more women and the youth. The government also encouraged the private sector by supporting small and medium-sized enterprises, nurturing local business, and promoting entrepreneurship among young Emiratis. These initiatives attracted a new and diverse breed of global workers, while also opening up new employment sectors for nationals.

The number of international visitors coming to the emirate increased as it became a destination for cruise ships and cultural, sports, and business events. New hotels and retail and dining outlets opened across the city's new urban centres. As Abu Dhabi became an increasingly cosmopolitan society, there was a sense of urgency to preserve local traditions and the emirate's distinct cultural heritage. Efforts to protect and promote Emirati culture and history accelerated during this period, with initiatives for digitising historical records, recording oral histories, and registering sites and traditions as UNESCO tangible and intangible heritage. The Qasr Al Hosn Festival was launched to commemorate the symbolic birthplace of Abu Dhabi at the site of the first permanent structure built in the emirate and former home to the ruling family.

With the shift in the urban centres and the increase in visitors, many new and creative food concepts were launched. Previously, most restaurants were associated with hotels, but the 2010s brought stand-alone cafés, bars, and restaurants with the new real estate developments, often modelled after Western coastal cities. More homegrown food concepts started popping up as Emirati entrepreneurs launched cafés, food trucks, dinner clubs, and catering services. Choices for vegans, vegetarians, and the health-conscious grew, responding to the diverse population. Awareness and appreciation of local customs and traditions became more accessible to expatriates and visitors.

In this highly connected social media society and in a time when food is the new fashion, the city continues to adapt and grow, accommodating the many competing influences. Today, 200 different nationalities call the United Arab Emirates home.

MAISA AL QASSIMI

CURATOR
◊
UAE

The tissue box is a ubiquitous part of an Emirati living room, alongside the Arabic *dallet gahwa* (coffee pot) and date platter. When I first walked into Maisa's home in Abu Dhabi, my eyes were drawn to a different kind of tissue box. Sitting on a table, surrounded by photographs, paintings, and sculptures by contemporary artists from Tunisia to Korea, are a pair of wooden tissue boxes covered with sections of film posters from the golden age of Egyptian cinema. The boxes were created by the Palestinian/Saudi Arabian artist Ayman Yossri Daydban.

'I loved Daydban's *Maharem* [handkerchiefs or tissues] series from the first time I saw it in 2010, because it reminded me of my childhood in Sharjah, watching Egyptian films with my family on Friday afternoons and listening to Umm Kulthum on the radio', explains Maisa. Umm Kulthum, the internationally acclaimed Egyptian singer, stunned the Arab world with her voice for over fifty years. Entire families would gather around the TV to watch her almost sacred broadcasts, as she faced the microphone in a diamond-studded gown, twisting and wringing her *mahrama* (handkerchief) in her hands.

In Maisa's spacious villa in Bloom Gardens, where she now lives with her husband, Tareq, friends always seem to be at the threshold, either passing by or visiting from out of town, and always anticipating a home-cooked meal. Bibi, a Cavalier King Charles spaniel, and Ruby, a longhaired Chihuahua born in Al Dhaid, Sharjah, from the Al Qassimi family's breed bloodline, are usually waiting at the garden gate to greet the guests.

Having grown up in Sharjah, the eldest of six siblings, Maisa naturally became the sous-chef in her mother's kitchen as soon as she could reach the counter. Her mother, an avid cook and traveller, would bring home cookbooks from each trip, amassing an eclectic collection. Maisa loved to flip through these cookbooks while other kids her age were flipping through comic books.

Nonetheless, it wasn't until Maisa moved to London to pursue her master's that she came into her own in the kitchen. Her international group of friends wanted to taste Emirati food, so Maisa called her mother on Skype and asked for help with *salonat lahem* (meat stew with vegetables). 'While my mother was happy to hear from me, she didn't really have three hours to hang out with me in the kitchen. So she gave me a few pointers and said, "You are on your own. Trust in what you know". This lesson extended to other parts of my life', Maisa recounts.

Maisa's salonat lahem, flavoured with her grandmother's *bzar* (Emirati spice mix), is renowned among her friends. I first tasted Maisa's dish at a Ramadan *iftar* gathering, and I was surprised to see it again on her Thanksgiving table. Though she was only two years old when she left the United States, where her parents had been studying, Maisa loves to celebrate the American holiday. The Thanksgiving message of gratitude and community resonates deeply with Maisa's family, and every November, Maisa serves this quintessentially Emirati stew alongside a delicious turkey, *findal* (Emirati sweet potatoes), and cranberry sauce to the international gathering at her table. She fondly remembers her Thanksgiving gatherings in London: 'Those dinners were so much fun, with everyone bringing a dish from their home country to share. We had grilled moose steaks from Norway, sweet potato pie from Texas, *perogi* (dumplings) from Poland, dried ostrich from South Africa, my salonat lahem, and turkey. We were grateful for our friendships and learned about each other's cultures around the table'.

When Maisa and Tareq visit her family's farm in Sharjah, they stock up on fresh fruit and vegetables. Maisa loves to shop at the outdoor fruit and vegetable market in Abu Dhabi, but the farm-fresh produce results in juicier, more flavourful dishes. Maisa adds, 'I look forward to sharing my love for food and fresh produce when I open Food Shed, a 'farm to table' dining concept, in Abu Dhabi'.

> We were grateful for our friendships and learned about each other's cultures around the table.
>
> MAISA

MARBLED CHEESECAKE BROWNIES

MAISA

These brownies are a family favourite. My mom and aunts used to get the Australian Women's Weekly magazine in the 1980s and they loved to try different recipes. These brownies were the speciality of my Aunt Aisha. She always made them for the weekend lunch at my grandmother's and they were the highlight! Recently, this recipe won the award for best comfort food at our office competition.

MAKES 16 TO 20

BROWNIE BATTER

- **170 g (6 oz)** unsalted butter
- **175 g (1 c)** dark chocolate (70% cocoa)
- **20 g (¼ c)** unsweetened cocoa powder
- **210 g (1 c)** granulated sugar
- **2** eggs
- **150 g (1 c)** all-purpose flour
- **¼ tsp** baking soda
- **1 tsp** vanilla

CHEESECAKE BATTER

- **225 g (8 oz)** cream cheese
- **80 ml (⅓ c)** sour cream
- **55 g (¼ c)** granulated sugar
- **1 tbsp** all-purpose flour

Preheat the oven to 180°C (350°F). Grease a 28 x 18-centimetre (11 x 7-inch) pan.

FOR THE BROWNIE BATTER

Break the chocolate into pieces. Combine the butter, chocolate, and cocoa powder in a double boiler over medium-low heat. Stir until the chocolate melts and the mixture is smooth. Remove from the heat and set aside to cool. Beat the sugar and eggs in a large bowl with a hand mixer until pale in colour. Whisk in the cooled chocolate mixture and the vanilla.

Sift the flour and baking soda over the chocolate mixture and mix well.

FOR THE CHEESECAKE BATTER

Beat the cream cheese, sour cream, and sugar in a medium bowl with an electric mixer until smooth and creamy. Add the flour and mix until well combined.

Alternately place large spoonfuls of the chocolate and cheese mixtures into the prepared pan. Using a round-bladed knife, gently swirl the mixture to create a marbled affect.

Bake for 40 to 45 minutes. Cool in the pan before cutting to serve.

SALONAT LAHEM
Braised Goat and Root Vegetable Stew

This is the quintessential Emirati stew, bursting with the flavours of seasonal vegetables and meat, along with the aroma of the local spice mix, *bzar*. The bzar alchemy is at the heart of most Emirati dishes. Not to be forgotten is the incomparable *lumi*, or black lime, which adds a pungent, fruity flavour. This sun-dried lime is used abundantly in the Gulf and gives the food a unique flavour. *Salona*, which originates from the Urdu *salan*, is adapted from South Asian curries. The stew is intentionally brothy so it can be soaked up with rice.

MAISA *Traditionally, my family makes salona with goat meat, but you can easily make it with lamb, mutton or chicken. Root vegetables, such as potatoes and carrots, are key, and I add beans, okra, squash, or any seasonal vegetable at hand. You can adjust the seasoning and spiciness to your taste, as well. I serve it in a large tagine, with plain basmati rice and* achaar *(pickled mango or lime) on the side.*

—
SERVES 6 TO 8
—

- **3 tbsp** Emirati bzar spice mix
- **1 tsp** cinnamon
- **½ tsp** coriander powder
- **¼ tsp** cloves
- **½ tsp** black pepper
- **½ tsp** chili powder, to taste
- **2 kg (4½ lb)** bone-in goat meat, medium pieces
- **2 tbsp** cooking oil
- **450 g (1 lb)** onion, chopped
- **2 cloves** garlic, crushed
- **10** cardamom pods, crushed
- **2** cinnamon sticks
- **2** bay leaves
- **2** dried lumi, cracked in half
- **1–2** green chilies, halved
- Salt and black pepper, to taste
- **1.5 l (1½ qt)** chicken broth or water
- **225 g (8 oz)** canned tomatoes, chopped
- **2 tbsp** tomato paste
- **2** tomatoes, cut in half
- **340 g (12 oz)** potatoes, peeled and cubed
- **225 g (8 oz)** carrots, peeled, and cut in chunks
- **225 g (8 oz)** green beans or okra, halved
- **25 g (½ c)** fresh coriander, chopped

Mix the bzar, cinnamon, coriander powder, cloves, pepper, and chili powder in a small bowl. Rub the meat with *half* of the spice mixture. Set aside for 30 minutes.

Swirl the oil in a large Dutch oven over high heat. Add the onions and sauté for 5 minutes until golden. Add the crushed garlic and continue to sauté for 2 minutes. Working in batches, sear the meat on high heat in the Dutch oven, browning on all sides; remove all when finished and keep warm. Add the cardamom, cinnamon, bay leaves, lumi, and fresh green chili and stir for 1 minute. Stir in the remaining powdered spices, salt, and pepper. Return the meat and pour in the chicken broth or water. Bring to a boil and then simmer, covered, for 1½ to 2 hours, until the meat is almost tender.

Stir in the canned tomatoes, tomato paste, and halved tomatoes and simmer for 20 minutes. Add the potatoes and carrots and let them cook for 10 minutes before adding the beans and any softer vegetables. Bury the meat in the stew; add more broth if needed and simmer for another 30 minutes, until the meat is tender but still clings to the bone. Adjust the salt and pepper to taste. Sprinkle in the fresh coriander, cover, and cook for another 5 minutes. Serve in a large bowl, family style.

RICKIE NAITO AND MANAMI TOMINAGA

COOKING INSTRUCTORS ◊ JAPAN

Rickie clasps a vinegared rice ball and swiftly pastes the fresh wasabi on a thin slice of raw *akami* (lean tuna). She places the rice ball on the akami, turns it over and presses it tightly into shape with her palm and fingers. The entire process takes under 30 seconds. In a few minutes, her kitchen counter is laden with a dazzling array of *nigirizushi* (hand-pressed sushi). Meanwhile, her sister, Manami, rubs the mint-green fresh wasabi root that she brought from Tokyo against a sharkskin grater. I try to balance a piece of sushi with my chopsticks to avoid testing its integrity. I am unsuccessful, but Rickie encourages me to pick it up with my fingers, which is perfectly acceptable, if they are clean. I then learn that dousing the nigirizushi in soya sauce compromises the techniques that most sushi masters take years to perfect, and that pickled ginger is intended to cleanse the palate between sushi pieces and not as a topping for them.

When Rickie, her Greek/American husband, and their daughter arrived in Abu Dhabi in 2007, she didn't find many restaurants that served authentic Japanese sushi. In Tokyo, sushi is always eaten out, at one of the many sushi bars in the upscale Ginza neighbourhood, but Rickie realised that her overseas life would demand otherwise. So, the following summer, she enrolled in the Tokyo Sushi Academy and completed the year-long course in two months. Rickie is respectful of the concept of *shokunin*, an artisan singularly dedicated to his or her craft, which is at the core of her culture. While she may not compare to the famous Jiro Ono, immortalised in the documentary, *Jiro Dreams of Sushi*, she strives to perfect her craft and enjoys teaching it to her diverse group of friends in Abu Dhabi.

Rickie tells us about the key elements of nigirizushi: *shari*, the seasoned rice that forms the base, and *neta*, the slice of fish on top. 'What most people don't realise is that sushi is as much about the rice as it is about the fish', she adds, as she demonstrates the careful thought that goes into preparing the rice, including washing out the excess starch through successive changes of water, figuring out the perfect ratio of water to rice, fanning it, balancing the acidity, and seasoning it with precise diagonal slashes using a *shamoji* (rice paddle). She then unveils another secret by using an angled knife stroke to relax the tight muscle fibres in the fish. The santoku knife she uses is among the most coveted in the culinary world and made in Sakai, a town south of Osaka that was once home to Japan's finest sword makers. The blade angle dictates the use. There are knives for everything from fish to root vegetables to meat. Clearly, Japanese cooking is not only about the end — it's also about the means.

Rickie has struggled to prepare Japanese food in Abu Dhabi. Kobe beef and sushi-grade fish, which must be sourced from wholesalers in Dubai, come at a premium price. But, according to her, it is mostly about the seasons: 'The most important part of Japanese cuisine is a strong sense of the seasons. We use a little bit of something at the beginning of each season to signal its arrival. For spring, we might use bamboo shoots. It's subtle. You can't replicate that outside of Japan. We aim to enhance the flavours of the seasonal ingredients rather than overwhelm them with spices and sauces'. Manami, who visits frequently from Tokyo, brings a suitcase full of seasonal supplies. Manami is equally passionate about their food and curious to learn about different cuisines.

Growing up in Tokyo, Manami and Rickie were exposed to a variety of cuisines at a young age. Their father, a renowned scholar of Russian literature, who was hosted by a Russian family when he was studying in northern Manchuria, influenced their eating habits. Breakfast might have included toast with butter and *natto* (Japanese fermented soya beans that usually go with rice), English tea, rose petal jam from Bulgaria, and kosher cucumber pickles. 'Very fusion and weird', remarks Rickie. Their mother was a good cook, and of the twenty-one meals she prepared each week, nothing was

> The most important part of Japanese cuisine is a strong sense of the seasons.
>
> RICKIE

> When we are young, drinking broth of different flavours, like seaweed and fish flakes, develops our taste buds.
>
> MANAMI

repeated except rice, which is eaten with every meal in Japan. In fact, the word for rice in Japanese, *gohan*, also means 'meal'. Manami explains that, 'When we are young, drinking broth of different flavours, like seaweed and fish flakes, develops our taste buds. In fact, we have more taste buds than Americans and Europeans, and that is reflected in the seasonal variety of our food'. Manami was the fastidious child who could sniff out the day-old miso soup and refuse to eat it.

Neither of the sisters learned to cook until they went overseas to study and then married. Manami's first foray into cooking came when, as a student, she lived in Pennsylvania with an Amish family, who prepared all their food at home. They loved the *nikujaga* she cooked for them — a simple beef and potato dish. While completing her MBA in Boston, her roommate, from an affluent Indian family, did not know how to cook. Manami took on the challenge of expanding her culinary skills, while her roommate washed the dishes. She recalls, 'Cooking was therapeutic, as we were studying ridiculously hard'.

When Manami quit her job with Bloomberg in Tokyo to take care of their ailing father, she began to cook more regularly. She catered her friends' office parties and soon she began teaching classes. One of her favourite cuisines is Indian, which she learned to cook while visiting her college roommate in Bangalore, where she still travels. Manami found a niche in Tokyo to teach Japanese students non-Japanese dishes. 'My signature dish is chicken biryani. I make the best version in Tokyo, not too starchy or greasy'. While she may not have the pedigree, ethnic or otherwise, as an authority on Indian cooking, she does have a precise palate, cultivated at a young age, that can tease out individual flavours. Manami shows me the notebook that includes her intricate illustrations of the step-by-step process for making the perfect biryani, as well as beautiful illustrations of other dishes she has been learning.

Manami now spends several months a year visiting Rickie in Abu Dhabi, seeing friends and collecting recipes such as Turkish *dolma*, Egyptian *molokhiya*, and Emirati *luqamaat*. Her students in Tokyo are thrilled to learn how to prepare a Levantine breakfast of *labneh*, *foul medames*, hummus, *za'atar*, and Arabic bread. She continues to expand her collection of handwritten, illustrated recipes as she eats her way through Abu Dhabi's multicultural cuisines. Using a *chasen*, a bamboo tea whisk, Rickie whips hot water and matcha powder into a frothy cup of emerald tea. I sip the thick vegetal tea as we discuss the seven spices in Levant cuisine. With the same dedication to a craft for which Japanese culture is known, the sisters pursue their passion for teaching the culinary alchemy of sushi and expanding their knowledge of world cuisines and cultures.

NASU TAMA MISO
Eggplant Miso

Miso, a fermented soybean and grain paste, holds a special place in Japanese culture. It originated in China and was introduced in Japan by Buddhist priests. At the time, it was considered a delicacy because it was made from soya beans, which were a luxury available only to nobility. After hundreds of years of carefully crafting miso, it is now thoroughly incorporated into Japanese cuisine, beyond the miso soup. The health benefits are numerous, and it is packed with protein. Choosing a glossy miso with vivid colour and a good aroma is important. The texture should be smooth and melt easily on the tongue, with no coarseness or stickiness.

RICKIE *This is an irresistible combination of creamy eggplant and aromatic miso. There are different types of miso with varying sodium content. For this recipe, you should use* saikyo *miso, a delicacy of Kyoto, with only five percent sodium. If the miso has more sodium, increase the sugar to balance the sweet and salty flavours.* Tama *is the abbreviation of* tamago, *meaning 'egg' in Japanese, so this recipe uses saikyo miso combined with egg yolk to make a creamy custard. You can try different miso combinations and create your own blend, with or without the egg, for a vegan option. You can also use this miso paste over cooked daikon, grilled tofu, or grilled cod.*

SERVES 4 TO 6

TAMA MISO

110 g (4 oz) saikyo miso

70–105 g (⅓–½ c) granulated sugar

20 ml (4 tsp) mirin

2 egg yolks

EGGPLANT

450 g (1 lb) long Japanese eggplant

Vegetable oil for frying

White sesame seeds

FOR THE TAMA MISO

Place the miso, sugar, mirin, and 20 millilitres (4 teaspoons) of water in a saucepan and mix well. Stir in the egg yolks. Place over low heat and stir for 10 minutes, until the mixture becomes thick, the consistency of custard. Do not boil — the egg yolk should not cook.

FOR THE EGGPLANT

Preheat the oven to 200°C (400°F).

Cut the unpeeled eggplant into 4-centimetre (1½-inch) thick rounds. Deep-fry the eggplant rounds in hot oil until lightly browned. Remove and drain on paper towel. When ready to serve, arrange the eggplant rounds on a baking tray and spread some tama miso on top of each one. Sprinkle with white sesame seeds and then broil in the oven for 3 to 5 minutes, until the tama miso is bubbly and golden.

KYURI TO WAKAME NO SUNOMONO
Marinated Cucumber and Seaweed with Sweet Vinegar Dressing

Wakame is a greenish sea vegetable used in many Japanese, Korean, and Chinese dishes. It is an important component in the Japanese-influenced macrobiotic diet and loved for its cool, sweet, and slightly salty flavour. As a 'superfood', it is packed with powerful anti-oxidants and essential nutrients. It makes a great addition to soups, salads, stews, and smoothies.

RICKIE *This cucumber and seaweed salad is fresh and easy to prepare ahead of time. The sweet vinegar dressing brings out the tastes and textures of the simple ingredients. The key is to use small cucumbers, preferably organic, and slice them very thin. It is also important to drain the cucumbers and seaweed well so the tanginess of the dressing is not diluted. This dish is a perfect palate cleanser to follow any meat dish.*

SERVES 4 TO 6

450 g (1 lb) small cucumbers
1 tbsp coarse salt
3 tbsp dried seaweed

DRESSING

120 ml (½ c) rice vinegar
2½ tbsp granulated sugar
¼ tsp coarse salt
Sesame seeds

Slice the cucumbers paper-thin. Sprinkle them generously with the salt and mix by hand, rubbing them so the salt is absorbed. Set aside for 15 minutes. Drain in a colander, pressing on them to remove as much liquid as possible. Refrigerate until ready to use.

Soak the dried seaweed in cold water for 10 to 15 minutes until soft. Drain and squeeze out as much water as possible. Cut it into bite-size pieces, if not already cut. Refrigerate until ready to use.

Combine the rice vinegar, sugar, and ¼ teaspoon of salt in a small bowl and whisk until the sugar and salt are dissolved. Cover and refrigerate until ready to use.

To assemble the salad, drain any excess liquid from the cucumbers and seaweed. Combine in a medium bowl and toss with the dressing. Serve on individual plates with a sprinkle of sesame seeds.

GYU-NIKU NO TATAKI
Seared Beef with Microgreens

Tataki is the Japanese method of cooking meat or fish by quickly searing over high heat, leaving the centre rare. It is then thinly sliced and served with a citrus-infused soya sauce. The best beef comes from the Tajima-gyu breed of the Kobe region. These cattle were introduced as work animals for rice cultivation many centuries ago and became isolated from other breeds, resulting in their unique taste. Kobe beef is only grain-fed, which makes the fat evenly marbled. Some stories depict the cows lounging to classical music and enjoying massages with sake and diets that include beer. Whatever truth to these stories, Kobe beef is prized for its flavour, marbling, and buttery smooth texture.

MANAMI *Historically, we didn't eat meat in Japan until the end of the Edo period, some 150 years ago, when modernisation began. For religious reasons, people were only allowed to eat vegetables and fish. When meat was introduced it was only eaten in thin slices, as it was expensive, and also in keeping with cultural traditions of food being prepared in single bites, to eat with chopsticks. It was also thought to be healthier for digestion. Western-style steak cuts are relatively new additions to Japanese cuisine. This is a simple dish to prepare and is a crowd pleaser for carnivores. The type and cut of beef is very important. In Japan, we use the sirloin cut of Kobe beef because it is well-marbled with fat, an important feature. Here in Abu Dhabi, when we can't find Kobe beef, we use Australian Wagyu beef.*

SERVES 6 TO 8

PONZU SAUCE

60 ml (¼ c) aged soya sauce

120 ml (½ c) rice vinegar

2 tbsp lemon juice

3 cm (1 in) square piece of kombu

2 tbsp fresh ginger, grated

BEEF

900 g (2 lb) sirloin, preferably Kobe

Salt

Black pepper

1 tbsp sesame oil

2 tbsp vegetable oil

Handful of microgreens

GARNISH

Daikon, finely grated

Chili powder, to taste

½ tsp wasabi paste

1 clove garlic, finely chopped

Make the ponzu sauce the night before serving. Combine the soya sauce, rice vinegar, lemon juice, kombu, and ginger in a bowl. Refrigerate; strain before using.

With the beef at room temperature, trim any excess fat on the outside. Season it with salt, pepper, and sesame oil on all sides. In a heavy-bottomed skillet, heat the vegetable oil for a few minutes. Sear the beef over high heat, turning it so all sides are browned, making sure to keep the centre rare, about 3 to 4 minutes per side. Cover the pan and turn the heat to low for another 5 to 6 minutes for medium rare. Transfer the beef to a cutting board and let it rest for 20 to 30 minutes, preferably in the refrigerator, so that it's easier to slice.

With a sharp knife, slice the beef as thinly as possible. Place a small bunch of microgreens on each beef slice and roll up; place the rolled beef on a platter or individual plates in such a way that they don't unroll. Combine the grated daikon and chili powder. Dab the beef rolls with a bit of wasabi, sprinkle with the chopped garlic and daikon, and serve with ponzu sauce on the side.

CHIRASHI ZUSHI
Garnished Sushi

RICKIE — *Chirashi zushi is one of the dishes we prepare to celebrate Hina-Matsuri or Girl's Festival in the spring. It is our 'home sushi' and comfort food. Presentation of chirashi zushi is very important. We always have five colours in the dish — for instance, white rice, red shrimp, green peas, golden eggs, and black nori, but you can try your own combinations. Chirashi zushi is perfect for entertaining a large number of guests and can be prepared ahead of time and served at room temperature.*

SERVES 4 TO 6

SUSHI RICE

- **300 g (1½ c)** Japanese short grain rice
- **60 ml (¼ c)** rice vinegar
- **2 tbsp** granulated sugar
- **1 tsp** coarse salt

KINSHI TAMAGO

- **4** eggs
- **1 tbsp** granulated sugar
- **½ tsp** coarse salt
- Vegetable oil

SEAFOOD

- **8** large prawns, with shells
- **1 tsp** coarse salt
- **110 g (4 oz)** fresh salmon, cubed
- **2 tsp** rice vinegar
- **1 tsp** granulated sugar
- **2 tbsp** white sesame seeds
- **225 g (8 oz)** frozen edamame beans, boiled
- Kizami nori (shredded seaweed)

FOR SUSHI RICE

Fill a bowl with cold water and add the rice. Stir it by hand and discard the water. Pour more water over the rice and rub the grains; soak for 20 minutes. Drain and rinse the rice until the water is almost clear. With the rice in a sieve, make a cavity in the middle, and let it rest for 30 minutes. Meanwhile, combine the vinegar, sugar, and salt in a small saucepan. Stir over low heat until the sugar dissolves.

Determine the amount of soaked rice; place in a medium saucepan and add an equal amount of water. Partially cover and bring to a boil. Reduce the heat to low, cover tightly, and simmer for 15 minutes. Turn off the heat and leave covered for 15 minutes. Do not open the lid.

Spread the rice evenly in a *hangiri* (flat-bottomed wooden bowl) and sprinkle evenly with the vinegar mix. With a wooden rice paddle or flat wooden spoon, slice the rice with diagonal cutting strokes while cooling it with a fan. Cover the rice with a damp towel until ready to use.

FOR KINSHI TAMAGO (GOLDEN THREAD EGGS)

Beat the eggs, sugar, and salt in a medium bowl. Pass through a fine sieve. Thinly coat a non-stick skillet with oil and place it over medium heat. Before the skillet gets too hot, pour in a small amount of the egg mixture and quickly swirl it around, tilting in all directions to spread it as thinly as possible. Gently flip the omelette over and cook over low heat for 1 minute. Transfer to a work surface. Repeat this process for all of the egg mixture, re-oiling after each omelette. If burnt spots build up in the pan, wipe them clean. When the omelettes are cool, roll them tightly and cut into thin strips.

FOR THE SEAFOOD

Rinse the prawns and place them in a medium saucepan. Add just enough water to cover and the salt. Bring to a boil and then simmer until the water evaporates. When cool, shell and devein the prawns and cut into thirds or half, depending on the size. Combine the prawns and salmon in a medium bowl. Combine the vinegar and sugar and dissolve over low heat. Pour the vinegar mix over the seafood and cover until ready to assemble the dish.

To assemble, sprinkle the sesame seeds over the rice and stir gently. Transfer vthe rice to a large bowl and pack down as the base layer. Scatter the egg threads over the rice. Arrange the shrimp and salmon over the eggs. Evenly distribute the edamame and sprinkle the shredded nori on top.

ALIA AND ADNAN AMIN

INVESTMENT BANKER
◊
AFGHANISTAN / US

DIRECTOR GENERAL IRENA
◊
KENYA

The seventeenth-century Pashtun poet Khushal Khattak said: 'It goes to waste if you feed yourself alone. It gives satisfaction to have your meal with company'. In Alia's Pashtun culture, *melmestia*, extending hospitality, is so important that they have a special word for the spread of food offered to the guests — *dasterkhwan*. Pashtun hospitality standards are very high; the dasterkhwan needs to be both a feast for the eyes and tantalising to the taste buds. An array of no less than a dozen dishes would be considered modest for Alia. When she welcomes us for dinner, the table is filled with an assortment of platters, with the prized *narinj palau* (rice with orange peel) at the centre. Alia takes much pride in entertaining her guests and sharing her culture and traditions. Her culinary prowess also extends to other cuisines, reflecting the international life she has led with her husband, Adnan. Alia explains, 'For those of us who have experienced many different cultures and perspectives and, in a way, belonged to different culinary traditions, food becomes an important marker of our identity'.

Adnan, born and raised in Kenya, is deeply connected to his homeland. His ancestors immigrated to Kenya from Pakistan and established themselves among the political elite in Nairobi. Wistfully, he recalls, 'We lived in a home on the outskirts of the city, surrounded by open fields. I had the most wonderful childhood, surrounded by lush vegetation, fresh air, and the freedom to explore'. His love for nature provided the foundation for a long career in international development at the United Nations (UN).

Curious, I ask Adnan how he came to head up the International Renewable Energy Agency (IRENA), headquartered in Abu Dhabi, one of the world's largest oil exporters. With his refined and measured voice, he tells me the story of a chance encounter at a dinner in Copenhagen in December 2009 and how it led him to become the world's ambassador for renewable energy. 'I was at the UN Climate Summit, working closely with the secretary general. We had invested a lot in the Copenhagen conference and this was where the deal on climate change was supposed to be made. After intense diplomacy and private meetings among heads of state amidst a contentious atmosphere, the whole thing collapsed. It was a depressing time', he recounted.

At a private dinner at the end of the Copenhagen conference, Adnan was seated by an Emirati gentleman he had not met before. The conversation led to a fledgling renewable energy organisation being set up in Abu Dhabi, and the need for expertise in establishing it. One thing led to another and Adnan was soon on a plane to Abu Dhabi in January 2010 to attend the Future Energy Summit as a guest of the Emirati gentleman, HE Sultan Al Jaber, Minister of State and Chairman of Masdar. The pleasant weather and welcoming hospitality at Abu Dhabi National Exhibition Centre was a stark contrast to the freezing temperatures at the desolate Bella Center on the outskirts of Copenhagen, where they had last met. Adnan recalls, 'I was very impressed by what I saw here. It was a vibrant summit with many interesting people. There was a lot happening at the intersection of public and private sectors'. Ultimately, Adnan took a leave of absence from the UN and moved to Abu Dhabi in November 2010. Following several months of intense work, IRENA became a full-fledged organisation and Adnan was voted its first director general. He is currently serving a second term, having led IRENA to become a global authority on renewable energy with near-universal membership.

Alia joined her husband later that year with their high-school-aged daughter, leaving behind a career in investment banking on Wall Street. Setting up a home, while Adnan continued to travel the globe, was not an easy task at first. Missing her older boys and life in New York, she set about discovering the city, its diverse cultural offerings, and making new friends. She became an

active member of the Diplomatic Club, supporting communities affected by natural disasters worldwide and volunteering locally to help people with disabilities. As a member of the diplomatic community, Alia was also obliged to entertain frequently, preparing some of her signature Thai, Moroccan, and Afghan dishes. Hosting alfresco dinners in the garden with a diverse mix of friends and an array of home-cooked Afghan food became her hallmark.

I ask Adnan and Alia about the role food has played in their lives and work as diplomats. With mock seriousness, Adnan says, 'I am sure the food offered at the Copenhagen and Paris climate conferences contributed to their respective outcomes. The Copenhagen venue was unwelcoming, and it was bitter cold. Delegates from Africa who had never experienced such weather had to queue outdoors for forty-five minutes without winter coats to get through security. The food was overpriced and quite inedible — cold slices of chicken or ham sandwiched between two pieces of mushy white bread'. The contrast to the Paris conference in 2015 could not have been greater. As Adnan remembers, 'The setting for the conference at Le Bourget was accessible, with plenty of places for delegates to congregate. The French officials paid attention to the food, offering a wide array of regional dishes. We experienced French cuisine at its best'. The fortnight of talks resulted in the successful signing of the Paris Agreement.

Undoubtedly, food and hospitality play an important role in these large international convenings, which for Abu Dhabi is but a continuation of traditional Arabian hospitality. 'During our meetings here, the ministers and government officials are shown generous hospitality, including a constant flow of food for breakfast, snacks, and lunch, with dinner in one of the many elegant restaurants in the city. So, as long as we do that, we cannot fail', Adnan chuckles. Having lived here for a few years, he cautions: 'Hospitality is so ubiquitous that if you are not careful you will keep eating, either not to offend your host or because it is so delicious'.

While Alia and Adnan experience hospitality at many official events, it is the intimate gatherings around the dinner table with their family that they treasure most. 'We always have at least one meal a day together as a family', says Alia, 'and we hope our children will continue that tradition. Food plays an important role in keeping families together'.

> For those of us who have experienced many different cultures, food becomes an important marker of our identity.
>
> ALIA

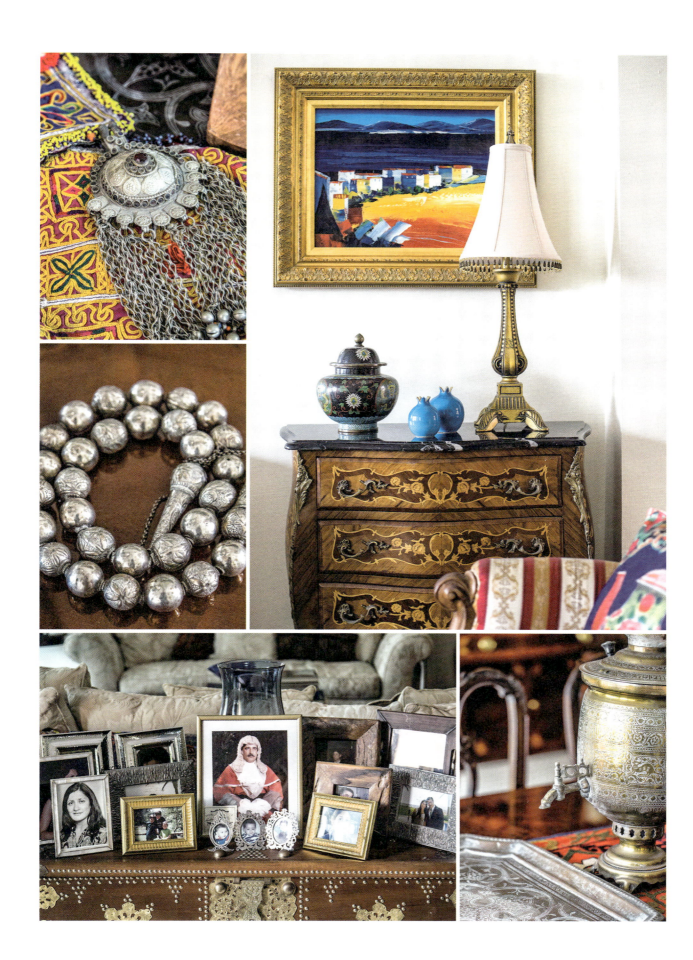

AFGHAN AUSH
Afghan Noodle Soup with Swiss Chard

Afghan *aush* is the perfect soup for a winter's day, making a wholesome meal all in one dish. Aush can be made with minced beef or chicken, or it can be vegetarian. It is basically a bean and noodle soup with the magic seasoning of cumin, red chilies, dill, mint, and parsley. The contrast of the hot and tangy soup with the creaminess of the *chakkah* (seasoned yogurt) creates a rich and delicious flavour. Some say it is Afghanistan's equivalent to Italian minestrone or American chili.

SERVES 6 TO 8

1–3 tbsp olive oil

285 g (10 oz) onions, chopped

450 g (1 lb) minced beef or chicken (optional)

2 cloves garlic, minced

½ tsp red chili flakes

1 tsp cumin

400 g (14 oz) canned chopped tomatoes

200 g (7 oz) potatoes, peeled and diced

285 g (10 oz) carrots, peeled and diced

400 g (14 oz) canned chickpeas

400 g (14 oz) canned red kidney beans

400 g (14 oz) canned black beans

1 tsp dried mint

1 tsp dried dill

450 g (1 lb) Swiss chard, de-stemmed and chopped

55 g (½ c) parsley, chopped

40 g (½ c) vermicelli pasta, uncooked

120 ml (½ c) lemon juice

Salt and black pepper, to taste

Fresh dill

CHAKKAH

285 g (1 c) Greek yogurt, labneh or sour cream

1 clove garlic, crushed

60 ml (¼ c) lemon juice

ALIA *My mother made this soup for us in the winter and especially during Ramadan. I add Swiss chard and lemon for a tangier flavour. I serve the soup with a thick dollop of chakkah and garnish with fresh dill and dried mint. The chakkah lightens the dish, so don't skip it. The list of ingredients may look daunting, but it is a simple soup to prepare because it is made in one pot. I prefer to use dried beans, soaked overnight, but sometimes use canned beans to save time. It is a family favourite whether we are in New York, Nairobi, or Abu Dhabi.*

If using beef or chicken: Sauté the onions and garlic in 1 tablespoon olive oil in a large Dutch oven over medium heat until lightly golden. Add the meat and cook until browned. Add the cumin and chili flakes and cook for 1 to 2 minutes.

For the vegetarian version: In a large Dutch oven, sauté the chopped onion in 3 tablespoons of olive oil until light golden. Stir in the garlic, chili flakes, and cumin. Cook for 1 to 2 minutes.

For both versions: Add the tomatoes, potatoes, and carrots; cook for 5 minutes. Add the chickpeas, kidney beans, and black beans, including their liquid, and then the dried mint and dill. Pour in 1.5 litres (1½ quarts) of water. Bring to a boil, lower the heat, and simmer the soup for 30 to 45 minutes, until the vegetables and beans are just tender. In the meantime, prepare the chakkah as described below.

To finish the soup, fold in the Swiss chard and stir well. Sprinkle in the parsley and continue to cook for 10 minutes. Toss in the vermicelli and lemon juice and simmer for another 10 minutes. Swiss chard is delicate so cook just until done. Add more water to thin the soup, if needed. Season with salt and pepper to taste. To serve, ladle each serving into soup bowls and top with a dollop of chakkah; sprinkle with fresh dill and dried mint.

FOR THE CHAKKAH

Combine the Greek yogurt, labneh, or sour cream with the garlic and lemon juice in a small bowl. Cover and refrigerate until you are ready to serve the soup.

CHAPLI KEBAB
Afghan Beef Patties

The practice of cooking meat on a skewer dates to prehistoric times, when humans began cooking with fire. Excavations in Santorini, Greece, unearthed stone barbecue sets with skewers from the seventeenth century BC. In more recent history, the kebab is considered to have originated in Turkey, where soldiers used to grill chunks of freshly hunted meat on swords over open fires. The word 'kebab' is derived from Farsi, meaning to 'fry', and is synonymous with burning or roasting. The variety of kebab from Asia is endless, including shish kebab, doner kebab, kakori kebab, and chelow kebab, to name a few. However, not all kebabs are cooked on a skewer, like this chapli kebab popular in Afghanistan and Northern Pakistan. It is a patty whose name probably derives from its flat shape, like the flat, open-toed *chapli* (sandals) worn in that region. Kebab is now a popular street food across the world and a satisfying snack after a fun night out.

ALIA *While kebabs are traditional in many parts of the world, the minced beef chapli kebab is uniquely Pashtun. The dried pomegranate and coriander seeds give it a unique taste and texture and the addition of flour produces a light and moist kebab. To make it spicier, simply add more green chilies. Traditionally, chapli kebab is a large thin patty, but I like to make mine small and round, like a hamburger patty. It's important that the meat is not too lean, so it binds together more easily. I serve the kebabs with sides of yogurt mint sauce and Afghan naan.*

SERVES 6 TO 8

KEBABS

1 kg (2¼ lb) minced beef (20% fat)

340 g (12 oz) tomatoes, finely chopped

285 g (10 oz) red onions, finely chopped

110 g (4 oz) spring onions, finely chopped

2 cloves garlic, crushed

55 g (2 oz) fresh coriander, chopped

2 tsp coriander seeds, ground

1 tsp salt

1 tsp garam masala

1 green chili, finely chopped

3 tbsp dried pomegranate seeds

2 tbsp flour

Cooking oil for frying

YOGURT MINT SAUCE

285 g (1 c) plain yogurt

Small bunch of mint, chopped

Small bunch of fresh coriander, chopped

Salt, to taste

Green chilies, chopped (optional)

FOR THE KEBABS

Place the minced beef in a large bowl with the tomatoes, red onions, spring onions, garlic, and fresh coriander; mix well. Sprinkle in the coriander seeds, salt, garam masala, green chili, pomegranate seeds, and flour and mix thoroughly until everything holds together. Shape the meat into hamburger-sized patties, flatten, and place on a baking tray that has been greased or lined with wax paper. Refrigerate for at least an hour. Prepare the yogurt mint sauce as described below.

When ready to cook, heat some oil in a large skillet and shallow fry the patties until cooked, turning midway through.

FOR THE YOGURT MINT SAUCE

Combine all the ingredients in a small bowl and mix well. Refrigerate until ready to serve.

FONDANT AU CHOCOLAT
Molten Chocolate Cake

Here is a throwback to the 1990s when molten chocolate cakes were all the rage and served at many upscale restaurants from New York City to Los Angeles. They say that Chef Jean-Georges Vongerichten was the first to revamp the French low-flour chocolate cake into one of America's hottest desserts, serving it at his restaurant, Jo Jo, in Manhattan. One day, by accident, he pulled a chocolate sponge cake (his mother's recipe) from the oven too soon. But when he tasted it, the gooey undone centre was absolutely delicious. The cake thus became one of the delicacies on the menu, known as the Valrhona Chocolate Cake. Since then, molten chocolate cakes have made it to amusement parks and supermarkets, and are always associated with decadence, sinfulness, romance, and elegance.

ALIA *I first made these rich, moist, intensely chocolate-flavoured cakes when I lived in New York in the 1990s. We used to entertain a lot at home and even though my Afghan dishes were popular with our guests, I enjoyed making new and challenging recipes. My friends and I were always trying to see who could master the fanciest of desserts. To make these molten cakes more alluring I add cardamom. This is an ideal dessert for large parties, as the batter can be prepared well ahead, refrigerated, and then baked just before serving the delightful individual treats. The trick is to not overbake or you will have brownies rather than a lava-like centre; if underbaked, the cakes will not properly unmould. They are great with whipped cream or ice cream and fresh berries on the side.*

SERVES 8

Butter to grease the ramekins

Cocoa powder to dust the ramekins

170 g (6 oz) unsalted butter

170 g (6 oz) dark chocolate (70% cocoa)

3 whole eggs and **3** egg yolks

180 g (1 c) caster sugar

1 tsp vanilla

80 g (½ c) all-purpose flour

½ tsp ground cardamom

Preheat the oven to 180°C (350°F). Butter the insides of eight ramekins that are 7 centimetres (2¾ inches) in diameter and dust with cocoa powder.

Place the butter and chocolate in a double boiler or in a heatproof bowl that can sit atop a similarly sized saucepan of boiling water. Stir over medium heat until melted. Remove from the heat and let the mixture cool slightly.

In another bowl, beat the whole eggs, yolks, sugar, and vanilla with an electric mixer until pale and fluffy. Gently fold in the melted chocolate. Sprinkle in the flour and cardamom and stir until combined.

Spoon the batter into each ramekin to just below the rim. *[At this stage, the ramekins can be covered and refrigerated for several hours until needed, or they can be frozen for up to a month. Bring to room temperature before baking.]*

Place the ramekins on a baking tray with sides and bake on the middle oven rack for 10 to 15 minutes or until the tops are set and the cakes come away from the sides of the ramekins. Let them rest for 1 minute. Serve in the ramekins or turn them upside down onto plates.

VARIATIONS

Once you've mastered a basic chocolate fondant, the world is your oyster in terms of flavour combinations. For a salted caramel version, place eight 1-teaspoon portions of dulce de leche sprinkled with a little sea salt on a parchment-lined plate or tray and freeze for 3 or 4 hours. Drop each portion tinto the centre of the uncooked batter. For a caramel-nut version, add crushed hazelnuts or peanuts. And for a fruity twist, nestle some raspberries, cherries, or blackberries into the centre of each ramekin.

MANUELA MIRKOS AND JOHN DEFTERIOS

MEDIA ◊ GREECE / ITALY

MEDIA ◊ GREECE / US

As you set out for Ithaka/ hope the voyage is a long one/full of adventure, full of discovery (...)/May there be many a summer morning when,/with what pleasure, what joy,/you come into harbours seen for the first time;(...)/Keep Ithaka always in your mind./Arriving there is what you are destined for./But do not hurry the journey at all./Better if it lasts for years,/so you are old by the time you reach the island,/wealthy with all you have gained on the way,/not expecting Ithaka to make you rich.
– Konstantinos Kavafis, a Greek son of the cosmopolitan city of Alexandria, Egypt.

It is with this spirit of discovery, curiosity, and adventure that John, Manuela, and their two daughters arrived in Abu Dhabi, 'the crossroads of East and West', as John likes to say. It was the summer of 2011 and CNN had offered him a full-time position as emerging markets editor and anchor in the country's capital, thus recognising the geographical shift of economic power to the east and south of the world. 'For us, the beauty of adventure also consists of challenges and surprises, of which we have had a few. Like many expatriates, we oscillate between an excitement for the new and a longing for the familiar: home, family, and roots', Manuela expresses.

This is where the passion for homemade food, enjoyed together around a table, comes into play for John and Manuela. When family and friends are far away, and familiar habits are mostly relegated to the past, rebuilding a sense of togetherness and 'breaking bread' with people of different backgrounds yet with similar life circumstances becomes central to the transition to a new home. Manuela and John both inherited their passion for cooking from their grandmothers: Manuela's from the central Italian region of Umbria, and John's from the Greek community in Istanbul. 'I learned the traditional recipes influenced by Turkish flavours, some of them revisited to reflect the new American world that welcomed my grandparents after World War I. This lifelong passion for food was the inspiring force behind my first on-air experience, when I launched a cooking show on a California cable TV channel while still in university', recounts John.

Their love of all things Mediterranean has prompted them to launch a supper club that includes members of countries along the Mediterranean coast and the Arabian Gulf, an expansion of the Best of the Med Supper Club John had started in Washington, D.C. Manuela remarks, 'We have been fortunate to meet so many diverse people here with whom we share not only a passion for food and fresh ingredients, but also family values and an appreciation for life's adventures. And like our friends, we discovered that food and cuisine, with the rich flavours and fragrances and the memories attached to them, are powerful connections to our identities as well as strong bridges towards the unknown'.

At home in Abu Dhabi, London, or Rome, Manuela and John have merged their culinary backgrounds to include their common Greek heritage, Middle Eastern and Italian regional influences, and Asian touches acquired in Abu Dhabi. While experimenting with new spices and ingredients, they have learned how to give fresh life to old recipes. On their kitchen counter, lemons, olive oil, and oregano coexist with ginger, cardamom, and lemongrass. 'While it may be difficult to wean our daughters off their favourite pasta dishes, today their top ten food preferences include hummus, falafel, and Asian stir-fry', Manuela laughs.

John and Manuela reflect, 'Abu Dhabi may be a temporary stop for many of us, but what we will miss when we leave will be the depth of human relations acquired here and the peaceful coexistence we experienced at a time when it was such a challenging goal for the region and for that matter the world at large to achieve'.

GARIDES ME FETA
Shrimp with Feta Cheese

The commonly held notion of not mixing seafood with cheese goes by the wayside with this traditional Greek dish. Feta, a crumbly white cheese, has varying textures and flavours depending on the origin. Greek feta tends to be salty and crumbly while Bulgarian feta is creamy. The feta, when melted, blankets the shrimp and the salty flavour balances the tanginess of the tomatoes.

JOHN *This is an old favourite and inspired from grandparents on both sides of my family hailing from opposite sides of Greece — the island of Marmara south of what is now Istanbul, and Kefalonia in the Ionian Sea. The vine-ripened tomatoes in Greece are a highlight of the summer so when I can't get them I use cherry tomatoes for a sweet taste. The dish is full of flavour and can be prepared in half an hour.*

SERVES 4 TO 6

2 tbsp olive oil

1–2 cloves garlic, chopped

110 g (4 oz) spring onions, chopped

15 g (½ c) parsley, chopped

1 small red chili, chopped, or a few dashes of Tabasco sauce

700 g (1½ lb) large shrimp, peeled and deveined

1 tsp oregano

200 g (7 oz) canned tomatoes, chopped

450 g (1 lb) cherry tomatoes, cut in half

3 tbsp lemon juice

Salt and black pepper, to taste

400 g (2 c) hot cooked white rice

140 g (5 oz) feta cheese, crumbled

Parsley, chopped

Preheat the oven to 200°C (400°F).

Heat the olive oil in a large skillet and sauté the garlic and the spring onions until the edges start to colour. Add the parsley and red chili and continue to sauté for a few minutes. Add the shrimp and oregano and sauté for 2 minutes, just until the shrimp start to turn pink, being careful not to overcook them. Remove the shrimp from the skillet with a slotted spoon. Add the canned tomatoes, cherry tomatoes, lemon juice, salt, and pepper; simmer for 10 minutes, until the sauce bubbles. Remove from the heat, add the shrimp, and stir well.

Spread the cooked rice in a 20 x 20-centimetre (8 x 8-inch) baking dish. The rice layer should be no more than 1 centimetre (½ inch) deep to prevent the rice from absorbing all the sauce. Spread the shrimp and sauce evenly over the rice; crumble the feta on top. Bake for 10 minutes or just until the feta softens. Garnish with parsley and serve.

UMBRIAN FARRO AND PEARL BARLEY SALAD

The farro grain boasts an ancient pedigree, originating in the Fertile Crescent. It was also found in the tombs of Egyptian kings and fed the Roman Legions. While farro tends to be referred to as one grain, it is actually three: farro *piccolo* (einkorn), farro *medio* (emmer), and farro *grande* (spelt). As a whole grain, it is rich in fibre and full of minerals and complex carbohydrates, which keep energy levels stable. With the renewed interest in whole grains, farro has gained popularity internationally with home cooks, as well as in restaurants.

MANUELA *This is a delicious, simple salad with lots of flavour and a satisfying bite. The recipe uses farro, of which the region of Umbria is a great producer, especially the organic variety. We Italians have dined on farro for centuries, using it in salads and soups. You can vary this salad by adding other vegetables such as asparagus or lima beans.*

SERVES 4 TO 6

- 150 g (¾ c) pearl barley
- 150 g (1 c) semi-pearled farro
- 30 g (1 c) wild rocket
- 140 g (5 oz) cherry tomatoes
- 140 g (5 oz) cherry-size mozzarella
- 50 g (½ c) green olives, pitted
- 80 ml (⅓ c) olive oil
- 80 ml (⅓ c) white grape vinegar
- Salt and black pepper

Cook the farro and barley separately in salted water, according to the package instructions, just until al dente. Depending on the type of grain, it may take between 20 and 40 minutes. Rinse with cold water to stop the cooking; drain well. Transfer both cooked grains to a large bowl and mix well.

In the meantime, chop the rocket, tomatoes, mozzarella, and olives. When the grain mixture has cooled, add these prepared ingredients to the bowl. Combine the olive oil and vinegar. Drizzle about two-thirds of the dressing over the salad. Toss to combine. Add salt and pepper to taste, as well as more dressing if desired.

CARDAMOM SPICED ORANGE CAKE

Cardamom, the queen of spices, with its distinct and complex flavour, is versatile and delicious in everything from desserts to main courses. Its citrus qualities open up the palate and the floral nature adds sweetness. Originating in India and spreading across the spice routes, cardamom is used in curries, rice, lentil and meat dishes, milky sweets, tea, coffee, Arabic pastries, and even traditional Swedish cookies, despite Sweden not being on the spice routes. The Vikings became fond of cardamom on one of their expeditions to Europe via Constantinople, a major spice route stop, and took it back home, where it has been a mainstay ever since. The Scandinavian countries have the third largest consumption rate of cardamom after the south and west Asian countries.

SERVES 8 TO 10

SYRUP

- 160 ml (⅔ c) orange juice
- 80 ml (⅓ c) lemon juice
- 1 tbsp water
- 140 g (⅔ c) brown sugar
- 2 tbsp honey
- 2 tbsp orange zest
- 5 star anise
- 5 cardamom pods, crushed
- 2 cinnamon sticks, halved

CAKE

- 170 g (6 oz) butter
- 210 g (1 c) granulated sugar
- 2 tbsp orange zest
- 2 eggs
- 1 tsp vanilla
- 2 tbsp orange juice
- 225 g (1½ c) all-purpose flour
- 2 tsp baking powder
- ½ tsp baking soda
- ¼ tsp salt
- 1 tsp ground cardamom
- 285 g (1 c) Greek yogurt
- 40 g (½ c) desiccated coconut
- 5–6 star anise
- 1 orange rind, julienned

MANUELA *This is a recipe that I discovered when I moved to Abu Dhabi. I love it and it is easy to make! The Greek yogurt produces a moist cake and the syrup strengthens the citrus flavour. I infuse the syrup with cardamom, cinnamon, and star anise, all spices I have grown accustomed to using in Abu Dhabi and mixing with Mediterranean ingredients. If possible, make the syrup the day before so the flavours can intensify.*

FOR THE SYRUP

Place all the ingredients in a medium saucepan and bring to a boil over medium heat, stirring occasionally to dissolve the sugar. Reduce the heat and let it simmer for another 10 minutes. Remove from the heat and set aside to cool. *[The syrup can be made a day ahead and refrigerated in a covered container.]*

FOR THE CAKE

Preheat the oven to 180°C (350°F) and grease and flour a 25-centimetre (10-inch) Bundt cake pan. If the syrup has been refrigerated, bring it to room temperature.

In a large mixing bowl, cream together the butter, sugar, and orange zest until pale and fluffy. Add the eggs, one at a time, beating well after each addition. Pour in the vanilla and orange juice; beat for 1 to 2 minutes until fluffy.

In another large bowl, whisk together the flour, baking powder, baking soda, salt, and cardamom. Add a third of the flour mixture to the wet ingredients and mix using a hand mixer's low speed until just combined. Scoop in half of the yogurt and mix until just combined. Repeat this process with the remaining flour and yogurt. Add the coconut and beat on low speed until there are no lumps in the batter, but don't over-mix.

Pour the batter into the prepared pan and level. Place on the centre rack of the oven and bake for 35 to 45 minutes. The cake is done when a toothpick inserted in the centre comes out clean. Remove from the oven and allow it to cool for 20 minutes.

While it is still in the pan, poke a few holes in the cake using a chopstick. Strain the syrup and drizzle half of it over the cake, allowing the syrup to seep in. Flip the cake onto a serving platter and decorate with star anise and julienned orange rind. Serve with the remaining syrup on the side.

MARIA EDUARDA GRILLO AND JAIME VAN ZELLER LEITÃO

INTERIOR DECORATOR ◊ PORTUGAL

AMBASSADOR ◊ PORTUGAL

Some five hundred years after the voyage of Vasco de Gama around the Cape of Good Hope, which opened a sea route to India and allowed Portugal to dominate the spice trade across the Arabian Gulf, the country sent Jaime van Zeller Leitão to be its first resident ambassador to the United Arab Emirates. Jaime and his wife, Maria, arrived in Abu Dhabi in January 2011, 'with no house, no office, and no staff — only a strong will to start building an enduring relationship between our two countries', Jaime recalls.

Maria, a talented interior decorator with a knack for finding diamonds in the rough, set out to discover the city, and furnish the official residence for the Portuguese embassy. I plan to try her counterintuitive approach to shopping: 'I walk into shops when I see things in the windows I don't like. Those are the highest selling and most expensive items. That means there will be a few gems inside that you can get for a bargain'. After exploring most of the shops in the country, Maria had a good sense of what was available and soon began to help her fellow diplomats settle in, advising them on where to find everything from chairs to shoes. Laughingly, she adds, 'I was known as the yellow pages of Portugal, and now I'm known as the yellow pages of the UAE'.

Jaime and Maria's hospitality is an extension of their diplomacy. Jaime reveals: 'I prefer not to host large receptions. We like to sit around the table with our guests and get to know them'. Maria's elaborate table settings and menus are inviting and creative. Though the food is varied, there is a cohesiveness that she strives to maintain. Combining her artistic talent and national pride, the courses include the colours of the Portuguese flag: green asparagus flan, red beetroot soup, and yellow egg custard cups, for instance. Portugal has a rich tradition, both religious and caloric, when it comes to desserts, especially those with eggs. Maria explains: 'Everyone had chickens, so eggs were offered as tithes to the convents. The nuns used the whites to starch their wimples, and the yolks were used for baking'.

Maria and Jaime happily regale me with stories of the culinary souvenirs left by early Portuguese explorers: a Brazilian version of *caldeirada* (fish stew) and *feijoada* (a bean dish); Goa's vindaloos; Japan's *kasutera* (sponge cake), thanks to the introduction of sugar by the Portuguese; and tea, made fashionable in Britain after King Charles II married the Portuguese princess, Catherine de Braganza, who brought it to the royal court, along with *mermalada* (quince jam, later marmalade). Jaime exclaims, 'The codfish, the basis for our traditional *bacalao*, is not native to Portugal. We are the only nation where the primary ingredient of our national dish cannot be found in our country!' The Portuguese have been obsessed with codfish since the early sixteenth century, when the fishing boats reached Newfoundland.

As with the voyagers of old, trade is at the heart of modern Portugal's mission in the United Arab Emirates, which is a regional hub for Portuguese exports. Maria is quick to add that when she goes on a tour of the Sheikh Zayed Grand Mosque, she often corrects guides who say the marble is Italian, because it is Portuguese. In the same vein, she says, 'We have the finest olive oil, but Italian or French oils are more prominent. Perhaps we did a better marketing job in the sixteenth century!' Jaime laughs and says, 'Today we travel to Portugal on Emirates Airlines. It is Emirates that is connecting the world now!'

As they prepare to depart for their next post, Jaime says, unequivocally, 'This has been the best post in my life! I will miss my colleagues and our friends. I admire the tolerance and respect for the various creeds and beliefs that coexist here. In fact, I feel that diversity and understanding is indeed the greatest wealth the UAE has to offer'.

I feel that diversity and understanding is indeed the greatest wealth the UAE has to offer.

JAIME

CHILLED BEETROOT SOUP WITH YOGURT

This cold beetroot soup is a Polish classic, referred to as *chłodnik*, meaning chilled. It is one of the most appetising and gratifying soups, especially in the warm summer months when the beets are tender and sweet. The Poles also enjoy cold spinach, cucumber, and fruit soups. A sort of alchemy occurs between the beetroot and dill once chilled and the added yogurt creates a sweet and sour balance.

MARIA *Beetroot soup is not only a fabulous colour but delicious, too! It can be made well ahead of time, so it's perfect for sit-down dinners. You can add an ice cube or two before serving if there isn't enough time for it to chill. Garnish with chopped dill, mint, or simply a swirl of yogurt.*

SERVES 4

700 g (1½ lb) beetroots
1 tbsp olive oil
Coarse salt
Black pepper
55 g (2 oz) butter
140 g (5 oz) onions, finely chopped
475 ml (2 c) vegetable broth or water
3 tbsp lemon juice
Salt and black pepper, to taste
285 g (1 c) plain yogurt
Fresh dill or mint, chopped

Preheat the oven to 200°C (400°F).

Trim the stems and place the beetroots on a large baking tray covered with a double layer of aluminium foil. Drizzle with the olive oil, sprinkle with salt and pepper, and then tightly wrap them in the foil. Roast for 1 to 1½ hours, until the beetroots are tender when pierced with a knife. Unwrap and transfer them to a plate to cool. When cool enough to handle, peel the beetroots and cut them into chunks.

Melt the butter in a large saucepan over medium heat. Add the onions and sauté, stirring occasionally until translucent, about 7 minutes. Add the beetroot and broth or water and bring to a boil. Lower the heat and simmer for 15 minutes. Working in batches, puree the soup in a blender until smooth, thinning with additional broth or water as needed. Add the lemon juice and season with salt and pepper to taste.

Refrigerate the soup for at least 2 hours. Before serving, stir in the yogurt for a creamy consistency while maintaining the vibrant colour. Serve with a swirl of yogurt and garnish with dill or mint.

CHICKEN SATAY WITH PEANUT SAUCE

Indonesian, Malaysian or Thai—which is the authentic satay? Satay is one of those dishes that many Southeast Asian countries claim as their own. Its origins can be traced to Java, where the Indian kebab was brought over by Muslim merchants and later infused with Southeast Asian flavours. Traders from Siam, Cambodia, and Malaysia took the recipe back home and adapted it to their tastes. The marinades and sauces for the basic grilled meat now vary widely in ingredients and complexity.

MARIA *This chicken satay recipe uses peanut butter as the base for the sauce, which makes it quick and easy to prepare. I developed a shortcut for dinner parties, where I cook the chicken and then skewer it, which makes for an elegant presentation without the awkwardness of removing the chicken from the skewers when it has been cooked on them. You can use smooth or chunky peanut butter, but buy a brand that only contains peanuts and salt —no sugar or shortening.*

—
SERVES
4 TO 6
—

CHICKEN

120 ml (½ c) coconut milk

1 tbsp brown sugar

1 tbsp curry paste or powder

1 tbsp garlic, crushed

1 tbsp ginger, crushed

1 tbsp soya sauce

1 tsp salt

½ tsp black pepper

2 tbsp cooking oil

800 g (1¾ lb) skinless, boneless chicken breast

PEANUT SAUCE

240 ml (1 c) coconut milk

1–2 tbsp curry paste or powder

130 g (½ c) peanut butter

2 tbsp brown sugar

60 ml (¼ c) lime juice

1 tbsp dark soya sauce

Salt and black pepper

FOR THE CHICKEN

Combine the coconut milk, brown sugar, curry powder, garlic, ginger, soya sauce, salt, and pepper in a large bowl. Cut the chicken into cubes and toss with the marinade, being sure the chicken is well coated. Cover and refrigerate for 1 to 12 hours.

FOR THE PEANUT SAUCE

In a medium saucepan, whisk the coconut milk, curry powder, peanut butter, and brown sugar over medium heat. Simmer for 5 minutes, stirring constantly until smooth and thickened. Remove from the heat and stir in the lime juice and soya sauce. Season to taste with salt and pepper. If the sauce is too thick, thin it with water or chicken broth.

Drain the marinade from the chicken pieces and discard. Heat the cooking oil in a large skillet and sauté the chicken pieces over medium heat for 10 to 15 minutes, until cooked. Thread the chicken onto 15-centimetre (6-inch) bamboo skewers. Drizzle with some of the peanut sauce and serve the rest on the side. Serve with brown rice and steamed vegetables.

BUTHAINA KAZIM AND MISHAAL AL GERGAWI

CINEMA AKIL
◊
UAE

DELMA INSTITUTE
◊
UAE

Mishaal and Buthaina moved to Abu Dhabi in 2014 as newly-weds. Both natives of Dubai, and accustomed to the almost frantic pace of the bustling metropolis, the first year in Abu Dhabi, the calm capital city, allowed them a slower pace. They did a lot of quiet things: they took walks, focused on their health, and learned to cook together. While they were only an hour and a half away from their families, they initially felt like they were in a diaspora, learning to navigate a new place, not knowing many people and being somewhat anonymous. They took refuge in one of the interests that had first brought them together. Cocooned in their high-rise apartment in Zayed Sports City, they watched and discussed many movies, and amidst this period of intense movie critique, the idea of creating Cinema Akil, an independent art house cinema, was hatched.

Mishaal left a career in investment banking in 2007, which was not an easy decision. He had returned from France with a master's degree in finance and an expanded appetite for intellectual engagement. In his search for more critical conversations, he stumbled upon the nascent art scene in Dubai, where he met the owners of the Third Line and Traffic galleries. Mishaal saw what each was doing in visual arts and design and wondered what he could do. 'Fundamentally, I am a story teller, and film is a way to tell these stories, so I decided to open an independent cinema house', he says. At the time, Buthaina had a successful career in radio and television and wanted to set up an art channel. They were introduced by a mutual friend and met to talk about ways they could work together. Mishaal says, 'We met at Caribou Coffee. She thought she'd hold events in my space for free. I thought she'd buy ad slots before my shows. We were both wrong'.

With the economic crisis of 2008, they both ended up shelving their plans. Buthaina moved to New York as a Fulbright scholar in media, culture and communication at New York University and returned to Dubai in 2013. Meanwhile, Mishaal pursued his writing and set up the Delma Institute in Abu Dhabi, a think tank studying change and its political, social, economic, and security impacts, primarily focusing on West Asia and North Africa. They reconnected over work and realised that the professional was secondary, and the personal was primary; they were married in December 2013.

With the institute taking up all of Mishaal's time, he happily turned over the concept of Cinema Akil to his wife to develop. 'Buthaina has taken Cinema Akil to a place I wouldn't have dreamt of going', Mishaal says proudly. With difficulties in setting up a permanent space and a limited budget, Buthaina turned the obstacles into an opportunity and created a pioneering concept of a cinema that travelled — a pop up, something new to this region. The nomadic Cinema Akil has since traversed the Emirates, bringing art-house independent films from around the globe, along with aromas of fresh popcorn, to unusual venues such as basketball courts in the Dubai Design District, a courtyard in a historical neighbourhood in Sharjah, and a warehouse in Abu Dhabi's Mina Zayed. Buthaina likens her cinema to other community-based public initiatives, such as organic food markets. She says, 'Cinema is about shared experiences. People have a real hunger to come together. At any Cinema Akil screening you find people lingering, reflecting on what they have seen, and getting to know each other'.

At home, Mishaal and Buthaina translate these sentiments by bringing diverse people together. Buthaina remarks, 'Our first year in Abu Dhabi actually pushed us to entertain at home. Unlike Dubai, where most people go out to eat, here we were invited to friends' homes, so wanted to reciprocate'. Their gatherings now include intimate dinners and large all-night parties with a diverse crowd, but my favourites are the

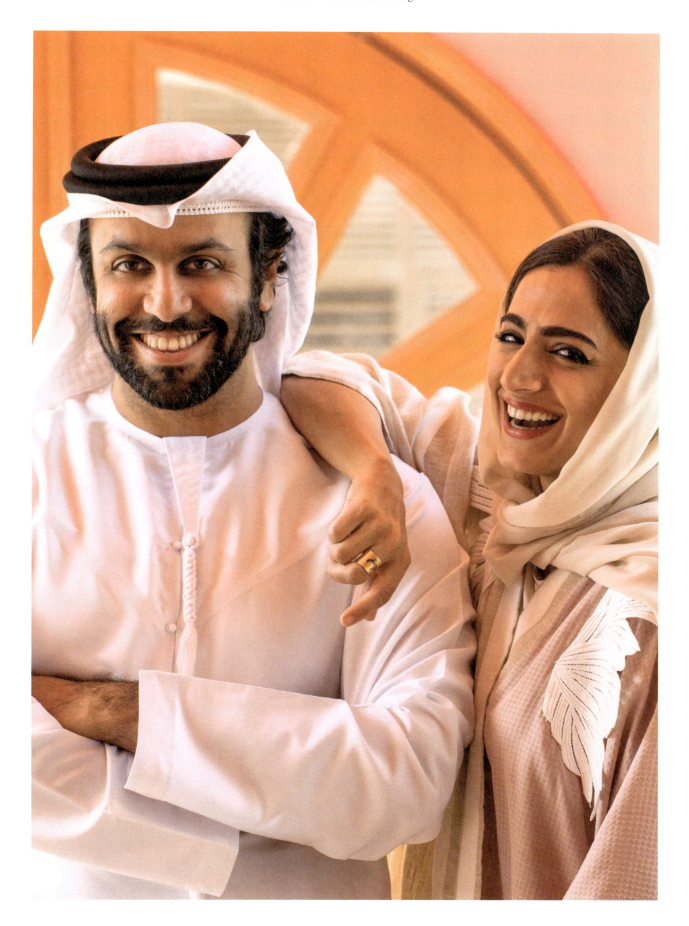

Mad Hatter-like breakfasts. They offer a range of oriental and occidental dishes with an elaborate spread of cheeses and breads, a variety of egg dishes, including *shakshuka* (poached eggs in a tomato-based sauce), a selection of honey, and a range of sausages such as *sujuk* and *makanek* (although there are less now that Mishaal and Buthaina have embraced a vegetarian diet). Mishaal's love for cheese expanded with his stay in France. He chuckles and adds, 'France was the most influential experience for my palate. I went there drinking still water and came back drinking sparkling. I used ketchup and came back using mustard. I used to eat my steak medium well but came back eating it medium rare'.

When we visit Mishaal and Buthaina, the conversations are always spirited, engaging, and thought-provoking. Mishaal's storytelling manner is layered with metaphors and analogies demanding our full attention. He doesn't shy away from tackling difficult topics or expressing unpopular opinions. Buthaina's interjections will also challenge and often serve as a reminder that they not take themselves too seriously. Be it through film, writing, or media, Buthaina and Mishaal's endeavours to understand our complex, ambiguous, and multifaceted world are an infectious, authentic expression of their curiosity and passion for life.

> Cinema is about shared experiences. People have a real hunger to come together.
>
> BUTHAINA

CHILI CON CARNE WITH DAQOOS

Chili is known as a frontier dish of the American West. Its origins are shrouded in mystery and part of the lore of Native Americans in the Southwest. Spanish priests referred to the potent chili stew as 'soup of the Devil' and warned against overindulging, which only fuelled the fire and made it more popular amongst the cowboys and outlaws. The ingredients of dried meat, fat, and spices were easy to transport and reconstitute on an open fire at the campsite. Chili became popular after the Civil War and spread across the country. Americans are passionate about their chili, and those who cook probably have a recipe they swear by. Chili cook-offs are favourite events across the country, from office parties to summer community gatherings. Regional rivalries abound, and the big debate is: beans or no beans. Chili con carne was dubbed Texas' state food in 1977. The Texas Red is made only with meat, spices, and the hottest of chilies. The addition of beans is a Midwestern variation.

BUTHAINA *If there were such a thing as being genetically predisposed to certain foods or flavours, then it would be chili con carne for me. Growing up in Dubai, my favourite family outing was to a nearby Mexican restaurant, where I had my first chili bowl. (Only later did I realise that Mexicans indignantly deny any association with this dish.) My father passed on his love for spicy Tex-Mex food, acquired when he studied in the United States. Whenever we travelled as a family, we would hunt for the best chili in town, like many do for burgers. Recently I have been making my own and adding the daqoos hot sauce, a staple of Emirati cuisine. They say chili is a frontier food and you just need to 'shoot from the hip', so use this recipe as a guide and adjust to your taste. Frankly, my chili varies each time I make it, depending on what I have at hand, how spicy I want it, and who our guests are. Cooking with patience, on low and slow, is one of the cardinal rules of chili, and it's best made a day ahead.*

SERVES 6 TO 8

---

200 g (7 oz) white onion, chopped

4 cloves garlic, chopped

3 tbsp olive oil

1 kg (2¼ lb) lean minced beef

1 tbsp cumin

1 tbsp dried oregano

1 tbsp chipotle chili powder, to taste

1 tbsp hot sauce (daqoos or Louisiana style)

35 g (1¼ oz) package chili con carne spice mix

Coarse salt and black pepper, to taste

800 g (28 oz) canned crushed tomatoes

475 ml (2 c) beef or chicken broth

1 tbsp honey

1 tbsp apple cider vinegar

400 g (15 oz) canned black beans, drained

400 g (15 oz) canned red kidney beans, drained

GARNISH

Sour cream

Spring onions, chopped

Sharp cheddar cheese, grated

Tortilla chips

Sauté the onion and garlic in olive oil in a Dutch oven over medium-high heat for 2 minutes. Add the minced beef and cook until the meat starts to brown; drain off excess fat and discard. Add the cumin, oregano, chipotle chili powder, hot sauce, chili con carne spice mix, salt, and pepper, and mix well over medium heat. Pour in the tomatoes, broth, honey, and vinegar and stir well. Bring to a boil and then reduce the heat to low; simmer, covered, for 2 to 3 hours, stirring occasionally. Add the black and red kidney beans an hour into cooking. Continue to add more broth or water for the desired consistency, stirring occasionally.

Serve in individual bowls and garnish with sour cream, spring onions, and sharp cheddar cheese, with tortilla chips on the side.

TOASTED PUMPKIN SEED GUACAMOLE

The avocado, originally known as *ahuacate*, was a staple food among the Aztecs. In the sixteenth century, the Spanish conquistadors fell in love with it and introduced it as a New World food. At that time, the locals of South and Central America were making a sauce called *ahuaca-mulli*, meaning 'avocado sauce'. Ahuacate in Aztec meant 'testicle', and the name was given to the fruit for its shape and reputation as an aphrodisiac. California farmers later changed the name to avocado, as it was easier to pronounce. Like most fruit, the avocado grows on a tree, but its flesh is unlike that of any other fruit: smooth but not sweet, nutty in flavour, firm enough to slice but also mashable.

BUTHAINA *Guacamole is one of my favourite go-to dishes when friends come over. Avocados are back in as a healthy fat and there is no better way to enjoy them than mashed with onions, chili, fresh coriander, and lime. Pumpkin seeds are a casual snack in our region and a healthy source of anti-oxidants, so try some with your next batch of guacamole.*

SERVES 4 TO 6

- **4** ripe avocados
- **2 tbsp** lemon juice
- **3 tbsp** lime juice, to taste
- **2** spring onions, finely chopped
- **1 clove** garlic, minced
- **1 tbsp** fresh coriander, chopped
- **1 tsp** coarse salt
- **½ tsp** cayenne pepper or 1 fresh serrano chili, seeded and finely chopped
- **1 tsp** black pepper
- **2** Roma tomatoes, seeded and diced
- **110 g (4 oz)** shelled, toasted, salted pumpkin seeds, divided
- **1 tbsp** olive oil

Cut the avocados in half and remove the pits. Scoop out the flesh into a medium bowl and roughly mash it with a fork. Add the lemon and lime juices, onions, garlic, coriander, salt, cayenne pepper, and black pepper and mix to desired chunkiness. Stir in the tomatoes and season to taste.

Pulse 90 grams (3 ounces) of the pumpkin seeds in a food processor until finely chopped. Pour in the olive oil and pulse again until the mixture becomes a thick paste. Add the pumpkin seed paste to the avocado mixture and blend well. Level the guacamole and lay a piece of plastic wrap directly over the surface, leaving no gaps. Tightly cover the bowl with another piece of plastic wrap and refrigerate.

Sprinkle with the remaining pumpkin seeds and serve with pita or tortilla chips.

LAILA AFRIDI

LAWYER
◊
PAKISTAN / UK

For Laila, the United Arab Emirates was not a foreign place when she left her job as a corporate lawyer in London to move to Abu Dhabi in 2012. She grew up in Dubai, where her father had moved the family from Pakistan in the 1970s to establish a legal practice. Working twenty-hour days and seeking a better work/life balance, but with no intention of leaving London, she nevertheless considered a recruiter's call about a position in Abu Dhabi. The job sounded interesting and the enticing blue waters of the Gulf beckoned — she was ready for a new adventure.

Initially, Laila could not find her bearings in the new city. 'In Dubai, I could locate places via landmarks, but in Abu Dhabi I didn't know any. Why were there two Airport Roads and how come one of them didn't seem to go to the airport? Why was there an area called Tourist Club — one of the few places where I didn't see any tourists?' Such questions baffled Laila as she realised she had a lot to learn about her new home. Within a few short months, though, she had settled into her new life. In other cities where she had lived, tracking down South Asian shops to find fresh spices had taken some effort, but in Abu Dhabi, the freshest ingredients were everywhere, and she could ask for them in Urdu!

Laila grew up in a home where meals were the main event. Her mother, Gillo, was known as the 'Queen of Dubai' because of her gracious hospitality. Their home was a hub for people of all ages, nationalities, and backgrounds with most every Pakistani and Indian newcomer and long-time resident visiting. 'There was a constant flow of food, from breakfast to coffee to big lunch spreads to delicious teatime snacks to lavish dinner parties', Laila recalls. 'But, I opted for more continental cuisine such as fish and chips and roast chicken, taking for granted my mother's rich and flavourful cooking, which people flocked to our house for'.

It was not until Laila went to university in the United Kingdom that she reconnected with the cuisine of her homeland. After a week dining on bland food, Laila went to the nearest pay phone and pleaded with her mother to tell her how to cook even the simplest of her dishes. On the next trip home, she asked her mother if she could jot down some of her recipes. Gillo's recipe book, which Laila had watched expand to bulging over the years, contained handwritten recipes she had collected from *her* elders and friends over the years. Laila remembers the moment with amusement: 'I started copying the *allo gosht* (potato and meat stew) recipe: heat the oil, add onion, ginger, garlic, turmeric, green chili. Add the meat then potatoes and put on dum. WHAT? How much ginger and garlic? Grated, whole or sliced? How long to stir and what is DUM?' Pumping her mother for specifics proved futile, as every answer was an approximation. Even the instruction for *dum*, a shorthand way of saying 'low heat', didn't have a specific cooking time. Laila realised the only way to begin to replicate her mother's cooking was to spend time in the kitchen, absorbing one of the most defining features of Pakistani cuisine: *andaza*, cooking by watching, tasting, smelling, and touching.

While in her profession, specific details and accuracy are essential, Laila came to appreciate that in the kitchen, she need not be burdened by counting teaspoons. 'It was a steep learning curve. But once I learned to trust my senses while being generous with quantities and patient with stirring, confidence just found its way', Laila shares with me over a hearty meal of *keema* (spiced minced meat). Clearly, her mother's passion for Pakistan's culinary heritage has fuelled Laila's. 'Although I was born in London and grew up in Dubai, I am at heart a true Pakistani because of my love for our food and flavours', she says proudly.

Although I was born in London and grew up in Dubai, I am at heart a true Pakistani because of my love for our food and flavours.

LAILA

MIRCH MACHLI
Red Snapper with Green and Red Chilies

Pakistan's geography, dramatic landscapes, history of migrations and invasions, and ethnically diverse provinces have shaped its culinary heritage and flavours. In Karachi, cuisines of Sindhis, Hindus, Indian Muslims, Arabs, and other ethnic communities combine in an eclectic way to create unique dishes that tend to be heady and spicy. The North-West Frontier Province, the tribal area, has a more rustic cuisine based on grains and meat (goat, mutton, and beef) either slow-cooked or grilled, with mild aromatic spices. In Pakistani cuisine, spices are generally used to enhance rather than hide the taste. They bring flavour to a dish without burning the palate.

—
SERVES
4 TO 6
—

LAILA *This is one of my mother's easy-to-make dishes that is satisfying, flavourful and colourful. It's originally from the Karachi coastal area where seafood is abundant. I love the spiciness of the fresh chilies and tanginess of the mustard seeds. It's quite a versatile dish and you can make it with almost any type of fish that can be filleted, as well as prawns. The onion/chili masala is the base, so feel free to try your own masala/spice variations. You can break some of the chilies in half for a spicier version. I serve this dish with plain basmati rice.*

MARINADE

1 tsp turmeric

1 tsp chili powder

1 tsp Madras curry powder

½ tsp salt

2 tbsp lemon juice

2 tbsp mustard oil

800 g (1¾ lb) red snapper fillets or other flaky white fish

3 tbsp mustard oil

2 tsp mustard seeds

8–10 curry leaves, divided

285 g (10 oz) white onion, sliced

1 tbsp garlic paste

1 tbsp ginger paste

6 green bird's eye chilies

6 red bird's eye chilies

½ tsp turmeric

½ tsp chili powder

½ tsp Madras curry powder

285 g (10 oz) cherry tomatoes, halved

½ tsp salt

Cooking oil

120 ml (½ c) lemon juice

Fresh coriander, chopped

Combine the marinade ingredients and mix well. Coat the fish with the marinade and set aside for 15 to 20 minutes.

Pour the mustard oil into a heavy-bottomed skillet over high heat. Add the mustard seeds and stir until they start popping. Add 6 curry leaves and the onions and sauté over high heat for 2 to 3 minutes, until the onions start to turn golden. Add the garlic and ginger pastes, toss in the red and green chilies, and continue to sauté over high heat for another 2 to 3 minutes.

Remove the skillet from the heat and add the turmeric, chili powder, and curry powder. Return the skillet to medium heat and stir for another couple of minutes until the onion/chili masala is well mixed.

Add the cherry tomatoes to the pan and cook over high heat, adding the salt to taste. Keep stirring for 2 to 3 minutes over high heat until the tomatoes start to soften. Remove from the heat.

Add a few drops of oil to another skillet and sear the marinated fish for 2 to 3 minutes on each side until almost done. Add the onion/tomato/chili masala to the fish skillet, along with the remaining curry leaves and lemon juice and cook for 2 to 3 minutes until the juices are well combined, swirling the pan so as not to break up the fish. The fish is done when it flakes easily. Cover and let it sit on the lowest heat for about 5 minutes. Garnish with fresh coriander.

KEEMA MATAR AND RAITA
Minced Meat with Peas and Cucumber Yogurt Sauce

Keema is a versatile dish that is popular in southwest Asia, and can be eaten as a starter, main course, or snack. Its name is derived from the Turkish word *kiyma*, for minced meat, but its origins probably go back to Persia. Keema can be made with minced lamb, goat, or beef combined with fried onions, chilies, and the special garam masala, which translates to 'hot spice mix'. It is said that the garam masala spices warm not only the body, but the mind and soul. They bring flavours to a dish without excessive heat. They can be used whole to infuse the aromatics into the oil before cooking the meat, ground and added during the cooking, or as garnish to enhance the flavours of the main ingredients in the dish.

SERVES 4 TO 6

YOGURT MASALA

- 60 ml (¼ c) plain yogurt
- 1½ tsp turmeric
- 1½ tsp coriander powder
- 1 tsp chili powder, to taste
- 1 tsp salt
- 1 tbsp garlic paste
- 1 tbsp ginger paste

- 2 tbsp ghee
- 200 g (7 oz) onion, chopped
- 110 g (4 oz) crushed tomatoes
- 800 g (1¾ lb) lean minced beef
- 170 g (6 oz) green peas
- 28 g (1 oz) ginger, julienned
- 2 bird's eye chilies, halved

- 1 tsp cumin seeds, toasted
- 25 g (½ c) fresh coriander, chopped

RAITA

- 1 large cucumber
- 3 tbsp onion, chopped
- 570 g (2 c) plain yogurt
- ½ tsp cumin
- ⅛ tsp chili powder
- Salt
- Fresh coriander, chopped

LAILA *This is one of the first dishes I learned to make when I was at university in the United Kingdom and yearning for Pakistani food, but not just any Pakistani food, which was abundant but laden with chili-hot spices that overwhelmed the palate. I wanted my mother's Pakistani food: fresh and subtle and with the whole rainbow of flavours that titillated the senses. This keema is a basic recipe and a canvas for vegetables. You can add any seasonal vegetables or legumes for a hearty stew over rice, or use it to stuff samosas or spread on naan, or with raita. I invite you to try your own combination of these spices and let the aroma guide you as you cook.*

Combine all the ingredients of the yogurt masala in a small bowl and mix well.

Place a large, heavy-bottomed skillet over high heat and melt the ghee. Add the onions and fry until golden. Pour in the yogurt masala and stir over medium heat for 2 minutes, until it browns. Add the tomatoes and continue to stir until the fat starts to separate. It should have a paste-like consistency. If it is too dry, add a tablespoon of water.

Increase the heat to high and add the meat, breaking it up with a potato masher so it becomes finely crumbled. Continue to stir for another 10 to 15 minutes, until the meat is cooked. Stir in the peas or other vegetables, ginger, and green chilies. Turn the heat to low, cover the skillet, and cook for another 10 to 15 minutes. Just before serving, stir in the toasted cumin seeds and fresh coriander and adjust the seasoning to taste.

Serve hot with naan and raita.

FOR THE RAITA

Peel, seed, and coarsely grate the cucumber. Combine it with the onion and yogurt in a small bowl. Add the cumin, chili powder, salt to taste, and fresh coriander. Cover and refrigerate until ready to use.

FATIMA AND ALYAZYAH AL SHAMSI

FOUNDERS OF JAF INK
◊
UAE

I first met Fatima, the globetrotting Emirati foodie, film buff, and football fanatic on the pages of *The National*, Abu Dhabi's English language daily. Her weekly column, 'My Life', offered witty and candid views on a wide range of topics from a young Emirati who had grown up and studied abroad. Fatima, with her big hair and quirky style, has a knack for storytelling tinged with sarcasm and playfulness. When I met her sister, Alyazyah, demure and introspective, I learned that she also shared a talent for the written word and creative endeavours, as well as a passion for cooking.

Fatima and Alyazyah are among a new breed of Emirati creatives who are shaping contemporary culture with collective initiatives. Outside of their government jobs, they developed JAF Ink, an online environment for literary endeavours. Fatima tells me: 'We are passionate about cultivating a creative community that is caring, respectful, and tolerant. We live in a time when it is so easy to be fuelled by hate and bigotry, and fear of what is different'.

Born in Geneva to diplomat parents, their childhood was spent in Brasilia, Paris, New York, Madrid, and Rome. Despite spending most of their lives away from home as the daughters of two ambassadors, their upbringing was rooted in Emirati traditions and values, of which sharing food and extending hospitality were cornerstones. Fatima recalls, 'Food became a way to learn about and become part of where we lived. It was also the way you got to know people. You shared your stories over some spiced *kofta* and listened to theirs over some *chai haleeb*. Opening your home and sharing something delicious made it easier to connect and see past the constructs of ethnicity, religion, or nationality'.

It was their father's love of cooking that lured them into the kitchen at a young age. Alyazyah is fascinated by the mixture of science, art, and math that comes together in cooking, with the special prize — something good to eat — at the end. She would spend hours perched on the kitchen counter, observing her father as he flitted from pan to cutting board to refrigerator, ingredients appearing and disappearing, and humming along to some old Arabic music. Alyazyah watched quietly, fearful of interrupting the seamless flow, but her father would narrate what he was doing as if he were speaking out loud to himself. Eventually, Alyazyah realised he was inviting her to ask questions — a slight nudge to appease her curiosity about the magic in the kitchen. 'My questions evolved to being useful; I'd ask and stir as he checked the dish in the oven. I'd chop and taste as he adjusted the seasoning. I still love to watch him cook, with the music from his iPad and no invitation needed to ask questions anymore', Alyazyah adds.

Similarly, one of the first dishes Fatima learned to cook was a simple *baith wu tomat* (scrambled eggs with tomato). With a smile, she explains, 'The reason this dish is so close to my heart, even though any breakfast egg dish is generally a win in my book, is because my father taught me how to make it when I was eight years old'. Fatima, an independent and precocious child, insisted that she learn how to make a basic egg dish as a matter of survival and has been making it ever since. In addition to memories of family gatherings, food has become tied to a variety of celebrations for the sisters, especially Thanksgiving. Alyazyah explains, 'I honestly think our love for Thanksgiving is just an excuse to make turkey and all the trimmings. The pleasure is not just in making the food but in having others eat and enjoy your labour of love'. Fatima sums it up by saying: 'Trying different cuisines can open our minds to accepting different cultures. And when you share food, suddenly, everyone becomes human, with the same desire for health, happiness, and a satisfied belly'.

When you share food, suddenly, everyone becomes human, with the same desire for health, happiness, and a satisfied belly.

FATIMA

CHICKEN MAC AND CHEESE

The idea of mixing pasta and cheese has been around since the thirteenth century in Italy. A more recent source of the dish was Thomas Jefferson, who introduced it when he returned to Virginia from Europe in the 1790s. It has become increasingly popular and has found its way onto many upscale restaurant menus, taking it from a childhood standby to something sophisticated and complex. Although easy-to-use box mixes are available, the base of pasta and cheese sauce can be embellished in many interesting ways, so the discerning cook will enjoy making it from scratch and adding everything from jalapeños to lobster and experimenting with different types of cheese.

ALYAZYAH *If you had told me twelve years ago that I would, one day, excitedly be making mac and cheese for friends and family, I would have laughed. Despite spending almost half my life in New York, I never understood the appeal of mac and cheese, as blasphemous as that might sound to most North Americans. My first experience with mac and cheese was the processed type that you make from a box mix. The synthetically orange cheese compelled me to avoid the dish almost instinctively. Somewhere along the line, between learning how to thicken cream-based dishes and deciding protein should be the guest of honour in everything made with pasta, I realised that great mac and cheese could be made from scratch, so I developed my own version. It has become my go-to recipe when I'm unable to decide what to make for dinner. Mac and cheese is the ultimate comfort food. It invokes a feeling of warmth, starting at your belly and spreading to your fingertips.*

SERVES 10 TO 12

---

450 g (1 lb) penne or other tube pasta

700 g (1½ lb) chicken breast, boneless, skinless, and cut into bite-size pieces

3 tsp salt, divided

½ tsp black pepper

1 tbsp paprika

2 tbsp olive oil

3 cloves garlic, crushed

55 g (2 oz) butter

1 chicken bouillon cube (optional)

40 g (¼ c) flour

475 ml (2 c) milk

475 ml (2 c) whipping cream

½ tsp white pepper

1½ tbsp ground mustard

450 g (1 lb) cheese, coarsely grated (mix of cheddar, Parmesan, provolone, jack, or Pecorino)

60 g (1 c) panko breadcrumbs

Cook the pasta in boiling salted water until al dente. Drain the pasta and set aside.

Season the chicken pieces with 1 teaspoon of the salt, the black pepper, and paprika. Heat the oil in a skillet; add the garlic and sauté for 1 minute. Add the chicken and sauté until cooked. Set aside to cool, reserving the garlic and cooking juices.

Preheat the oven to 190°C (375°F). Make sure the oven rack is in the middle of the oven. Butter a 33 x 23-centimetre/13 x 9-inch baking dish.

In a large saucepan over medium heat, melt the butter and crush the bouillon cube, if using. Sprinkle in the flour and whisk with the butter to make a roux. Cook, stirring constantly with a wooden spoon for about 3 minutes, until the roux is light golden. Combine the milk and cream and gradually pour into the roux, whisking constantly to avoid any lumps, to make a béchamel sauce. Bring the sauce to a boil while whisking continuously and then reduce the heat; stir occasionally for another 5 minutes, until it is thick and coats a wooden spoon. Stir in the remaining 2 teaspoons of salt, the white pepper, and ground mustard. Add the cheese a little at a time, stirring after each addition until the cheese is melted. Remove from the heat.

Fold the pasta, chicken, garlic, and their cooking juices into the cheese sauce and stir well to coat. Transfer the macaroni/chicken mixture to the baking dish and sprinkle with the panko. Bake for 25 to 30 minutes, until golden and bubbly.

PECAN PIE

While their history stretches back to the ancient Egyptians, pies have woven their way into American food culture, becoming a symbol of home, tradition, and patriotism. The saying 'as American as apple pie' reflects the national status of this treat. The early American settlers adapted their pie traditions from Europe, incorporating the bounty of the American land to create an array of fillings, including fruit, nuts, vegetables, and game. And as the settlers migrated, their pies reflected regional influences. Pumpkin pies sweetened with maple syrup were savoured in the Northeast. Blueberries were plentiful in Maine and often found their way into pies, which became the official dessert of that state. Florida's abundance of citrus fruit turned limes into key lime pie. The Midwest, famous for its dairy farms, favoured cream and cheese pies. French immigrants to New Orleans created the pecan pie. As the ultimate home-baked dessert, the smell of freshly baked pie is etched in many Americans' memories. Pies are part of the lore of many families, with heirloom recipes handed down through the generations, but also with rivalries over who makes the best crust. It's a dessert that never goes out of style.

ALYAZYAH *Of all the pies that are traditionally served at Thanksgiving, this is my favourite. It is easy to make, sweet and delicious, and I don't really like pumpkin. There's a sense of immense satisfaction when making pie, from rolling out that handmade crust to the contrast between the crunch of the filling's top, to the smooth slide of its centre as you cut out a slice. Pecan pie will satisfy anyone's sweet tooth and pairs perfectly with a scoop of vanilla ice cream. You can bake the pie a day ahead, chill it, and then bring it to room temperature before serving.*

SERVES 8 TO 10

CRUST

190 g (1¼ c) all-purpose flour

1½ tbsp granulated sugar

¼ tsp salt

¼ tsp cinnamon

110 g (4 oz) butter, chilled, cubed

1 egg yolk

FILLING

55 g (2 oz) butter, melted

150 g (¾ c) light brown sugar, packed

180 ml (¾ c) light corn syrup

2 tbsp honey

½ tsp salt

2 tsp vanilla

3 eggs, lightly beaten

200 g (7 oz) pecans, chopped

FOR THE CRUST

Combine the flour, sugar, salt, and cinnamon in a medium bowl. Blend the butter with the dry ingredients using a pastry blender or two knives, just until it resembles coarse crumbs. Add the egg yolk and drizzle in 2 to 3 tablespoons of ice water a tablespoon at a time. Blend the dough until all the ingredients are well incorporated, but do not overwork it or it will be tough. Turn the dough onto a lightly floured surface and knead for 1 or 2 minutes to distribute the butter. Shape it into a disk, wrap in plastic, and refrigerate for at least 30 minutes.

Roll out the dough on a floured surface into a 30-centimetre (12-inch) circle and transfer to a 23-centimetre (9-inch) pie plate. Trim the edge, leaving a 2-centimetre (1-inch) overhang. Fold over in half and crimp the edges. Prick the crust with a fork in random locations. Chill for another 30 minutes before baking.

FOR THE FILLING

Preheat the oven to 180°C (350°F).

Mix the melted butter, brown sugar, corn syrup, honey, salt, and vanilla until smooth. Whisk in the eggs. Fold in the pecans and combine thoroughly.

Pour the filling into the pie shell and bake for 50 to 60 minutes. Cover the edges of the pie crust with aluminium foil if they start to brown too much.

SNICKERDOODLE COOKIES

FATIMA *I am not usually big on dessert or anything too sugary. I was the daemon child who wiped the 'excess' icing off my cupcake. This is why I fondly remember the first time I ate a snickerdoodle. It was early spring and I had to roam beyond my usual Lower Manhattan haunts for an appointment. On my way to catch the subway back down, I stopped to pick up a cup of coffee from Blue Bottle and was offered a snickerdoodle by the overly chipper cashier. At first, I was going to simply brush it off, but with a name like snickerdoodle, how could I not give it a try? It was a truly magical experience. The cinnamon sugar cookie had the perfect balance between sweet and tart with a lovely firm exterior and a chewy, almost fluffy, interior. This recipe is simple and delicious. I stand by it as a tried and trusted method for garnering some lifelong friends, even those who are lactose intolerant. Snickerdoodles have become a Christmas staple at our home.*

—
MAKES 40 TO 45
—

COOKIES

225 g (8 oz) butter, softened

315 g (1½ c) granulated sugar

2 large eggs

1 tsp vanilla

410 g (2¾ c) all-purpose flour

2 tsp cream of tartar

1 tsp baking soda

½ tsp coarse salt

COATING

3 tbsp granulated sugar

1 tbsp cinnamon

Preheat the oven to 190°C (375°F). Line two cookie sheets with parchment paper.

Cream the butter and sugar in a large bowl with a hand mixer until light and fluffy. Add the eggs and vanilla and mix thoroughly. Combine the flour, cream of tartar, baking soda, and salt in another bowl. Gradually blend the dry ingredients into the butter mixture, scraping the sides as needed. Cover the dough with plastic wrap and chill for 15 to 30 minutes.

Meanwhile, prepare the coating by mixing the sugar and cinnamon in a small bowl.

Shape the dough into 2.5-centimetre (1-inch) balls and roll them in the coating. Place them 5 centimetres (2 inches) apart on the cookie sheets and bake for 10 to 12 minutes, until lightly browned. Let them cool on the cookie sheet for 5 minutes before transferring them to a wire rack to cool completely. The cookies will remain soft and fresh for 3 to 5 days if stored in an airtight container at room temperature.

PASCALE AND ALAIN SABRI

DESIGNER ◊ LEBANON / FRANCE

PHYSICIAN ◊ LEBANON / FRANCE

Criss-crossing the Atlantic and Mediterranean became a way of life for Pascale and Alain, who, like many of our compatriots, were uprooted at a young age by the Lebanese civil war. Whenever the fighting intensified Pascale's father would send the family to Lorraine, France, where her mother is from. Despite the troubles in Lebanon, she was always keen to return home. Some of her fondest memories are of growing up in Zahle—the city of mezze, poets and wine—and spending time in the family's centuries old vineyard.

Ironically, Pascale learned to make all the delectable Lebanese *mezze* while studying in France, away from her family. In Bordeaux, while at medical school, she got to know a woman from Zahle who taught her about Lebanese cuisine. 'Those two years were more cooking school than medical school', Pascale laughs, because she knew all along that she was not cut out for medicine. She returned to Beirut and completed her studies there. She adds, 'Throughout my childhood, the family would say I would be a doctor like my dad and I would say no. Then I married one!'

Alain escaped the war in 1982 with his father, arriving in Reston, Virginia, where his uncle lived. He attended high school there and played varsity tennis (which he still plays). Home beckoned and he returned to complete medical school at the American University of Beirut but bounced back to the United States to specialise at the hospitals of Georgetown, Cleveland, and Vanderbilt universities. He practised, taught, and did research at the Mayo Clinic. With the end of the civil war, he returned to work in Beirut, where he and Pascale met.

In 2013, Alain received an offer to join the new Cleveland Clinic Abu Dhabi, and with the situation in Lebanon taking another turn for the worse with the Syrian civil war, he accepted the offer. Alain and Pascale enthusiastically embraced their new home in Abu Dhabi. In fact, I marvelled at how quickly they settled in. The customary six-month transition period was more like six weeks. All the years of being uprooted during the war and maintaining the attitude of 'plant yourself where you land', have made them resilient and efficient. With a can-do spirit and hard work, Alain spent the next year establishing the clinic's Department of Otolaryngology Head and Neck Surgery and Pascale set up their home and managed her bespoke lighting studio from afar.

Pascale loves to create with her hands, be it in the workshop or the kitchen. She fearlessly reimagines traditional recipes and recreates dishes by taste. Cooking with their diverse circle of friends became a favourite pastime in Abu Dhabi. With the variety of cultures, cuisines, and ingredients in the city, Pascale extended her culinary forays further east, with butter chicken becoming their daughter's favourite and homemade sushi a Thursday evening tradition. Alain remarks, 'We have made some amazing friends here and met many diverse people. We also met friends of friends from Lebanon, like you and Steve'. As with most Lebanese, there is only one degree of separation. He continues, 'Now, I have an opportunity to go back home to be the assistant dean, professor, and chairman of the ENT department at the Lebanese American University of Medicine, so I will be teaching a new generation and practising medicine and surgery in my home country'.

I ask Pascale and Alain what they will miss most about the city. Though their stay was relatively short compared to that of some expatriates, what they accomplished professionally and the friendships they forged will be long lasting. Alain reflects, 'Besides the friendships, I am going to miss the calmness, organisation, and structure in our life here; every day you know what to expect. In Beirut, you wake up each day and have no idea what is going to happen. That is exciting, but also tiring'. Pascal assures me, 'I will miss the friends we made and the family time we had, but Alain plans on returning each year to watch the Mubadala Tennis tournament, so we will be back'.

PAIN PERDU
French Toast with Salted Caramel Sauce

Early references to the idea of reviving stale, hard bread by soaking it came from the Roman Empire of the fifth century. Not wanting to let anything go to waste, families made what the French call *pain perdu* or 'lost bread' by softening stale bread with milk and eggs and then frying it. By the fifteenth century, pain perdu was all the culinary rage in Europe. Today, variations can be found around the world, served as sweet or savoury and at various times of the day. Although it probably didn't originate in France, maybe it is also referred to as French toast because the recipe works well with French bread.

PASCALE *Whenever I have leftover baguettes, pain perdu is my go-to treat for brunch or as a dessert. This oven-baked pain perdu is fast and easy to make. It allows you to make enough for everyone at once without having to fry each piece individually, plus you can make it a day in advance, which can be very practical when you are throwing a big dinner. Just remember to put it in the oven half an hour before it is dessert time! It is also lighter than fried pain perdu and if you ask me, much more refined, too. Serve with salted caramel sauce and a scoop of ice cream, if you like.*

SERVES 6 TO 8

225 g (8 oz) baguette, day old

3 eggs

350 ml (1½ c) whipping cream

350 ml (1½ c) milk

2 tbsp icing sugar

1 vanilla bean

SALTED CARAMEL SAUCE

210 g (1 c) granulated sugar

85 g (3 oz) salted butter

120 ml (½ c) heavy cream

1 tsp coarse salt

FOR THE PAIN PERDU

Cut the baguette in half lengthwise and then slice it into 5-centimetre (2-inch) thick pieces. Arrange the pieces of bread in a single layer in a 28 x 18-centimetre (11 x 7-inch) baking dish. It is important for the bread pieces to be snug in the baking dish. Individual ramekins can be used and the bread cut into smaller pieces.

In a large bowl, mix the eggs, cream, milk, sugar, and vanilla bean with a fork for 30 seconds. Pour it evenly over the bread and refrigerate, ideally for at least 4 hours. Occasionally relocate the vanilla bean and turn the slices of bread to allow the egg mixture to be evenly absorbed. Make sure the crusts are at the bottom before baking.

Preheat the oven to 200°C (400°F). Remove the vanilla bean. Bake the pain perdu for 30 minutes, until the top is golden and puffy and the custard has set. Serve immediately with warm salted caramel sauce on the side.

FOR THE SALTED CARAMEL SAUCE

Heat the sugar in a medium saucepan over medium heat, stirring constantly until the sugar melts and becomes honey coloured. Immediately add the butter and stir for 3 minutes until melted. Slowly drizzle in the heavy cream, stirring continuously until thoroughly blended. Remove from the heat and stir in the salt. Allow the sauce to cool before using. *[This sauce can be made ahead of time and refrigerated in a tightly covered container for up to two weeks. Warm the sauce before using.]*

TABBOULEH
Parsley and Bulgur Salad

Tabbouleh is a Lebanese staple salad originating in the mountain region of Zahle, located in one of the most fertile valleys, the Bekaa. Zahle is known for its temperate climate, fresh air, rich agricultural produce, and the Berdawni River flowing from Jebel Sanine. It is famed as the homeland of *mezze* culture. *Mezze*, a selection of small dishes served to whet the appetite, is an accompaniment to the anise-flavoured grape liquor that is another speciality of Zahle. In the 1920s, the locals of the region started gathering along the Berdawni River to share their dishes and specialities. In the 1950s, restaurants started lining the riverbank, welcoming Lebanese and tourists alike, especially on weekends when *mezze* is served for a leisurely Sunday lunch. The *mezze* offerings have grown more elaborate, but tabbouleh remains its jewel.

PASCALE *Tabbouleh varies widely in homes and restaurants, so what makes a good tabbouleh? The key is to start with the freshest ingredients and make sure all your vegetables are chilled. Good juicy tomatoes are the main secret to a good tabbouleh, so choose them carefully and don't hesitate to use cherry tomatoes, which might seem like a lot of work to chop, but well worth the effort. Another secret is not to add too much lemon. A sprinkling of sumac will give it an extra fruity acidity, as will the pomegranate molasses. I prefer my tabbouleh without any bulgur, but if you do add some, just use a couple of tablespoons. If the tabbouleh is not cold enough when serving, add a couple of crushed ice cubes.*

SERVES 6 TO 8

- **450 g (1 lb)** parsley
- **400 g (14 oz)** cherry tomatoes
- **20 g (½ c)** mint
- **85 g (3 oz)** spring onions
- **2 tbsp** fine white bulgur (optional)
- Romaine lettuce hearts or cabbage leaves

DRESSING

- **1 tsp** salt, to taste
- **½ tsp** black pepper, to taste
- **½ tsp** red bell pepper powder or paprika
- **1 tbsp** sumac
- **1 tbsp** lemon zest
- **60 ml (¼ c)** lemon juice
- **1 tbsp** pomegranate molasses
- **120 ml (½ c)** olive oil

Refrigerate all the fresh produce before starting to prepare the salad. It is best to prepare the tabbouleh just before serving it. If preparing it ahead of time, keep all the chopped ingredients separate in the refrigerator and assemble and dress when ready to serve.

Wash the parsley, discarding the thicker stems and retaining the leaves and upper stems. Dry thoroughly and set aside. If including bulgur, soak it in cold water and set aside.

Dice the tomatoes, preserving all the juice, and place in a large bowl. If the tomatoes do not have much juice, add 2 crushed ice cubes. Chop the parsley very finely by hand. Do not use a food processor, as that will liquefy it. Place the parsley in the bowl over the tomatoes. Finely chop the mint and tuck it under the parsley so it doesn't turn black. Finely chop the spring onions and layer over the parsley.

Just before serving, sprinkle with the salt, black pepper, red bell pepper powder, sumac, and lemon zest. Add the bulgur if using it. Drizzle with the lemon juice, pomegranate molasses, and olive oil, and toss. Taste and adjust the seasoning. If the tabbouleh seems a bit dry, add a couple of tablespoons of ice water.

Serve immediately with romaine lettuce hearts or cabbage leaves on the side.

TOM YUM GOONG
Spicy and Sour Shrimp Soup

A hot bowl of *tom yum goong* reflects the essence of Thai cuisine: bold flavours, fragrant aromas, fearsome chili heat, and appealing presentation. Thai food is a fusion of foreign influences and techniques. This recipe highlights the distinctive characteristic of using fresh products, such as lemongrass, kaffir lime leaves, galangal, and ginger, to create lemony and peppery flavours. Ingredients such as fish sauce and shrimp paste add a salty taste, chilies some heat, and coconut brings sweetness. These flavours are not subtle, but Thai cuisine, like this soup, carefully blends them so that no one taste overpowers the other.

—

SERVES
8 TO 10

3 tbsp olive oil

4 cloves garlic, chopped

110 g (4 oz) shallot, chopped

55 g (2 oz) ginger, chopped

110 g (4 oz) lemongrass, chopped

2 red chilies, to taste, finely chopped

55 g (2 oz) galangal, chopped

200 g (7 oz) cherry tomatoes, cut in half

2 l (2 qt) fish broth

Salt and black pepper, to taste

8 two-part kaffir lime leaves

25 g (½ c) fresh coriander, chopped

400 ml (1⅔ c) coconut milk

1 kg (2¼ lb) shrimp, cleaned, to yield 500 g (about 1 lb)

285 g (10 oz) oyster mushrooms, quartered

110 g (4 oz) spring onions, chopped

2 tbsp fish sauce

80 ml (⅓ c) lime juice

Chili oil (optional)

PASCALE *When I was a teenager, an old Portuguese lady told me the famous saying: 'The way to a man's heart is via his stomach'. This soup may have made her point. My husband and I first tasted this soup at a Thai restaurant in Beirut when we were dating. The restaurant eventually closed and I was left to my own devices to try and recreate the soup. Not knowing much about Thai food and with limited products in Beirut at the time, I started to experiment, and ended up surprising my husband-to-be with a version that he absolutely loved. A dear friend of ours also loved this soup and ended up drinking it out of a mug one evening so other guests wouldn't notice how many servings he had. I've now enhanced it with some of the authentic Thai flavours of kaffir lime, galangal, and lemongrass that are readily available in Abu Dhabi.*

Heat the oil in a large stockpot. Sauté the garlic over medium heat for 1 minute, then add the shallots and sauté for 1 minute, until translucent. Add the ginger and lemongrass and sauté for 2 minutes and then add the red chilies and galangal; stir for another minute.

Dump in the cherry tomatoes and sauté for 1 minute. Pour the fish broth into the pot and bring to a boil. Season with salt and pepper and reduce the heat to simmer. Lightly crush the kaffir lime leaves by hand and drop them into the pot with the coriander. Pour in the coconut milk and stir continuously, being careful not to let the soup boil.

Add the shrimp, mushrooms, and spring onions and stir over medium heat for 3 minutes, until the shrimp turn pink. Pour in the fish sauce and lime juice and season to taste. Let the soup simmer for another 3 minutes. Serve it immediately in individual bowls. Serve the chili oil on the side for those who want a bit of a kick.

THANK YOU

While the words are mine, this book would not exist without the stories and recipes of the contributors who have joined me on this culinary adventure. To each of you, thank you for opening your home and sharing your memories and meals, to help me capture the essence of a city we all call home. Thank you, readers, for taking an interest in the vibrant and delicious culture of Abu Dhabi. Whether or not you are a global nomad, may these stories resonate with you. I wish you *sa7a wa hana* (health and bliss) with each recipe you make.

Shukran (thank you) to my family near and far. My daughter, Tala, an artist, inspired and encouraged me to take on a creative project. My son, Badr, was a continual source of positivity. My sister, Hazami, and her family welcomed me into their Philadelphia kitchen and let me overfeed them. My brother, Hazem, helped with tech support whenever I needed it. My sister, Haneen, tested some of the recipes. The Worrell clan enthusiastically sampled my cooking during shared beach holidays. Above all, I am thankful to my husband, Steve, for his endless support and devotion. When I was overwhelmed with recipes, drafts, and work, he was there to help, whether it was by grocery shopping or reminding me of anecdotes of the past twenty-five years. To my mother, who marvelled that I would be writing about food, not having raised us in the kitchen, I hope you will enjoy this book. There is nothing I would have wanted more than for my father to hold this book in his hands. It isn't the PhD thesis he had hoped I would complete, but it sure feels like one!

Standardising over a hundred recipes from multiple sources and diverse cuisines was a daunting task. Friend and chef Raman Khanna provided invaluable advice on cooking techniques. Delving into the kitchen to try all the recipes would not have been possible without the skills of chef Michael Reyes. I enjoyed his sunny disposition on the many Fridays we spent perfecting a global collection of dishes. Thank you to our housekeepers, Salam and Mimi, for their support in the kitchen.

A big thank you to the photographers: Martin Kunz and Heike Fademrecht immersed themselves in this project and saw the city through my eyes, but with their lenses. Their passion and professionalism captured the best of this global nomad cuisine while also having fun. My friend, Mohamad Somji, was an invaluable resource on all things photographic. Rasha Amer, with her boundless enthusiasm, generously stepped in to complete the photo shoots when needed.

For the past three years, my dear friend and editor Ruth Fowler has been an alter ego separated by thousands of miles. She has meticulously edited each recipe, tried most of them, and given me feedback beyond the editorial. Her knowledge of Abu Dhabi made for a rich review and many Skype conversations. Thank you, Ruth, for being my fiercest critic and avid supporter. Another dear friend, writer and filmmaker, Faiza Ambah, encouraged me to write and to be honest with my readers. Thank you, Faiza, for your insight and critiques, and for showing me what it means to perfect a craft. Many thanks to Shahnaz Habib, whose coaching helped me frame the initial narrative, and to Elizabeth Franzen for her thoughtful comments on the mock up.

Thank you to friends and partners around the globe: Mariët Westermann for generously sharing her perceptive observations of our community; Ambassador Barbara Leaf and her belief in culinary diplomacy; Hala Achkar and her voluminous cookbook library; and to Etihad Airways, Cinema Akil, and Warehouse 421 for their support. To Noor Al Suwaidi, Lale Ansingh, Yasmeen Bardan, John and Tanya Habib, Monika Krauss, Khadija Qudsi, and too many more friends to name here, I greatly appreciate your support. My sincere gratitude goes to my colleagues at Abu Dhabi Department of Culture and Tourism, the British Museum, the Guggenheim Foundation, Louvre Abu Dhabi, and Agence France-Muséums, for sharing your culinary traditions and sampling my creations with gusto.

I previously thought of writing as an individual endeavour, but I now know that it 'takes a village' to publish a book. Thank you, Ben Wittner, Sascha Thoma, and Marco Kratzer at Eps51 for your thoughtful and creative layouts and for making the journey a fun one! Wissam Shawkat, I am honoured to have your beautiful Arabic calligraphy adorn the cover of this book. Many thanks to Francesco Baragiola for believing in this project, and to Marco Ausenda, Cecilia Curti, Sara Saettone, Sylvia Notini, and Elena Rocco at Rizzoli for making the book the best that it can be.

Finally, a special thank you to HE Noura Al Kaabi for her support and belief in the power of storytelling and shared experiences over a home-cooked meal. In this Year of Zayed, a special thank you to the legacy of the founding father of the United Arab Emirates, who welcomed us to this city a quarter of a century ago.

THE AUTHOR

Hanan Sayed Worrell is an international recipe hunter. As a Lebanese-Egyptian-American, she grew up in Kuwait and was educated in the United States, earning bachelor's and master's degrees in engineering at Stanford University. A global nomad herself, Hanan has lived on four continents and travelled extensively, allowing her to move adeptly between cultures and cuisines. As a careful and affectionate observer of Abu Dhabi for a quarter of a century, she is uniquely qualified to guide the reader on a culinary pilgrimage by way of its streets, homes, and flavours. Through her professional career, Hanan has worked on many diverse initiatives in the realms of aviation, energy, wildlife, environment, education, culture, and the arts. She has a deep appreciation for the role of culture and architecture and how they shape a city. The connections she has made professionally and in her personal life form the rich tapestry of friendships presented in *Table Tales: The Global Nomad Cuisine of Abu Dhabi*.

INDEX

A

ACHAAR, 32, 67
- channa bhatura (spiced chickpea curry with fried bread), 85
- machboos deyay (Emirati rice pilaf with chicken), 218
- tahta lahem (Emirati lamb pilaf), 67

ALMONDS
- apfeltorte ohne deckel (apple tart without a lid), 51
- cauliflower and roasted beetroot salad with tahini dressing, 238
- gluten-free nut and goji maple granola, 144
- tahini raw powerbites, 143

ALMOND MILK
- trio of smoothies, 142

APPLES
- apfeltorte ohne deckel (apple tart without a lid), 51
- trio of smoothies, 142

APRICOTS, DRIED
- borani kadoo (sautéed butternut squash with saffron and yogurt), 237

ARUGULA
(see rocket)

ASPARAGUS
- warm lentil salad with garden vegetables and poached shrimp, 205

AUBERGINES
(see eggplant)

AVOCADO, 345
- crab cakes with mango avocado salsa, 225
- kale Caesar salad with yogurt dressing, 240
- roasted eggplant with avocado, thyme, and green olives, 261
- toasted pumpkin seed guacamole, 345
- trio of smoothies, 142
- a trio of tartines, 150

B

BANANAS, 182
- banana bread with crystallised ginger and walnuts, 21
- tostadas de platano con hogao (fried green plantains with tomato salsa), 182
- trio of smoothies, 142

BARLEY
- Umbrian farro and pearl barley salad, 330

BASIL
- polpette con salsa di pomodoro (Italian meatballs and tomato sauce), 93
- Portuguese spiced hammour, 160
- sup-e pesteh (pistachio soup), 289

BEANS, BLACK
- Afghan aush (Afghan noodle soup with Swiss chard), 321
- chili con carne with daqoos, 344

BEANS, BROAD
- paella de marisco (seafood paella), 102

BEANS, EDAMAME
- chirashi zushi (garnished sushi), 314

BEANS, GREEN
- quinoa herb salad, 260
- salonat lahem (braised goat and root vegetable stew), 304

BEANS, KIDNEY
- Afghan aush (Afghan noodle soup with Swiss chard), 321
- chili con carne with daqoos, 344

BEEF
- Afghan aush (Afghan noodle soup with Swiss chard), 321
- arayes (lamb-stuffed mini pita sandwiches), 168
- beef shawarma with tahini sauce, 170
- chapli kebab (Afghan beef patties), 322
- chili con carne with daqoos, 344
- gyu-niku no tataki (seared beef with microgreens), 313
- harira (Moroccan tomato lentil soup), 109
- keema matar and raita (minced meat with peas and cucumber yogurt sauce), 351
- marinated beef tenderloin, 199
- polpette con salsa di pomodoro (Italian meatballs and tomato sauce), 93
- sheikh al mukhshi (stuffed eggplant with pomegranate molasses), 169
- tahta lahem (Emirati lamb pilaf), 67
- Tatar kulaghi (meat dumplings with yogurt sauce), 135
- a trio of tartines, 150
- Wagyu burger with Bois Boudran sauce, 254

BEETROOT
- cauliflower and roasted beetroot salad with tahini dressing, 238
- chilled beetroot soup with yogurt, 338
- fennel, beetroot, and orange salad, 126

BEVERAGES
- chai karak (cardamom milk tea), 119
- gahwa Arabia (Arabic coffee), 215
- ginger lemonade, 149
- istikan chai (Iraqi tea), 134
- lassie – spicy or fruity, 83
- trio of smoothies, 142
- za'atar chai (thyme tea), 43

BLACKBERRIES
- mango and blackberry coconut buckle, 230
- trio of smoothies, 142

BLUEBERRIES
- blueberry risotto, 162
- trio of smoothies, 142

BREAD
- aish al saraya (Lebanese bread pudding), 247
- arayes (lamb-stuffed mini pita sandwiches), 168
- banana bread with crystallised ginger and walnuts, 21
- beef shawarma with tahini sauce, 170
- channa bhatura (spiced chickpea curry with fried bread), 85
- fattet al hummus (chickpeas with pita and tahini yogurt), 248
- fattoush (bread and purslane salad), 99
- gazpacho (chilled tomato soup), 101
- grilled cheese sandwich with Marmite, 57
- kale Caesar salad with yogurt dressing, 240
- kashk-e bademjan (eggplant and yogurt dip), 290
- pain perdu (French toast with salted caramel sauce), 363
- a trio of tartines, 150

BROCCOLI AND BROCCOLINI
- warm lentil salad with garden vegetables and poached shrimp, 205

BROTH
- chicken broth Arabic style: molokhia (jute leaf soup), 191
- chicken broth Asian style: bong bong gee (bong bong chicken), 276

BRUSSELS SPROUTS
- Brussels sprouts with mint yogurt sauce, 246

BULGUR
- tabbouleh (parsley and bulgur salad), 364

BUTTERNUT SQUASH
- borani kadoo (sautéed butternut squash with saffron and yogurt), 237
- roasted pumpkin and feta cheese salad, 253

BZAR (EMIRATI SPICE MIX), 32, 304
- machboos deyay (Emirati rice pilaf with chicken), 218
- salonat lahem (braised goat and root vegetable stew), 304
- tahta lahem (Emirati lamb pilaf), 67
- tuna tahta (Emirati spiced pilaf with tuna), 175

C

CABBAGE
- spicy tuna on crispy rice, 270
- tabbouleh (parsley and bulgur salad), 364

CAKE
- cardamom spiced orange cake, 332
- fondant au chocolat (molten chocolate cake), 324
- mango and blackberry coconut buckle, 230
- pastiera napoletana (Italian Easter cake), 94
- sticky date pudding with cardamom sauce, 176

CALAMARI
- paella de marisco (seafood paella), 102

CANDIED FRUIT
- pastiera napoletana (Italian Easter cake), 94

CANDIED GINGER
- ginger lemonade, 149

CAPERS
- couscous with a trio of flavours, 282
- gemista me feta (Greek stuffed tomatoes with quinoa, capers, and olives), 226

CARAMEL, 271
- Biscoff cheesecake with salted caramel sauce, 271
- pain perdu (French toast with salted caramel sauce), 363

CARDAMOM
- cardamom spiced orange cake, 332
- chai karak (cardamom milk tea), 119
- chbaab (Emirati pancakes), 118
- gahwa Arabia (Arabic coffee), 215
- istikan chai (Iraqi tea), 134
- sticky date pudding with cardamom sauce, 176
- trio of smoothies, 142

CARROTS
- Afghan aush (Afghan noodle soup with Swiss chard), 321
- mint and pine nut-crusted lamb chops, 200
- salonat lahem (braised goat and root vegetable stew), 304
- warm lentil salad with garden vegetables and poached shrimp, 205

CAULIFLOWER
- cauliflower and roasted beetroot salad with tahini dressing, 238

CHAI
- chai karak (cardamom milk tea), 119
- istikan chai (Iraqi tea), 134
- trio of smoothies, 142
- za'atar chai (thyme tea), 43

CHEESE
- Biscoff cheesecake with salted caramel sauce, 271
- blueberry risotto, 162
- caramelised onion and fig tart with manouri cheese, 229
- cauliflower and roasted beetroot salad with tahini dressing, 238
- chicken mac and cheese, 356
- garides me feta (shrimp with feta cheese), 329
- gemista me feta (Greek stuffed tomatoes with quinoa, capers, and olives), 226

- grilled cheese sandwich with Marmite, 57
- grilled honey and mint strawberries with mascarpone, 201
- kale Caesar salad with yogurt dressing, 240
- ma'amoul bil jibn (cheese-filled shortbread pastries), 78
- marbled cheesecake brownies, 303
- pastiera napoletana (Italian Easter cake), 94
- polpette con salsa di pomodoro (Italian meatballs and tomato sauce), 93
- roasted pumpkin and feta cheese salad, 253
- a trio of tartines, 150
- Wagyu burger with Bois Boudran sauce, 254

CHERRIES, SOUR
- albaloo polow (sour cherry rice), 293

CHERVIL
- quinoa herb salad, 260

CHICKEN
- Afghan aush (Afghan noodle soup with Swiss chard), 321
- bong bong gee (bong bong chicken), 276
- braised chicken with lemons and olives, 108
- chicken mac and cheese, 356
- chicken satay with peanut sauce, 339
- Circassian chicken (Syrian poached chicken with walnut sauce), 74
- fesenjan ba ordak (duck with walnut and pomegranate sauce), 294
- harira (Moroccan tomato lentil soup), 109
- machboos deyay (Emirati rice pilaf with chicken), 218
- molokhia (jute leaf soup), 191
- musakhan rolls (sumac and caramelised onion chicken rolls), 167
- salonat lahem (braised goat and root vegetable stew), 304

CHICKPEAS, 85
- Afghan aush (Afghan noodle soup with Swiss chard), 32
- channa bhatura (spiced chickpea curry with fried bread), 85
- fattet al hummus (chickpeas with pita and tahini yogurt), 248
- harira (Moroccan tomato lentil soup), 109

CHOCOLATE
- fondant au chocolat (molten chocolate cake), 324
- marbled cheesecake brownies, 303

CLAMS
- paella de marisco (seafood paella), 102

COCONUT OR COCONUT MILK, 184
- cardamom spiced orange cake, 332
- chicken satay with peanut sauce, 339
- green prawn curry with fennel shavings, 161
- lobster maharaja with green rice, 86
- pie de coco (Colombian coconut pie), 184
- mango and blackberry coconut buckle, 230
- sambal udang (prawn sambal), 77
- tahini raw powerbites, 143

- tom yum goong (spicy and sour shrimp soup), 366

COFFEE
- aish al saraya (Lebanese bread pudding), 247
- gahwa Arabia (Arabic coffee), 215

COOKIES
- klaichat tamur (Iraqi date cookies), 136
- snickerdoodle cookies, 358

CORIANDER, FRESH (CILANTRO)
- bong bong gee (bong bong chicken), 276
- channa bhatura (spiced chickpea curry with fried bread), 85
- chapli kebab (Afghan beef patties), 322
- crab cakes with mango avocado salsa, 225
- green prawn curry with fennel shavings, 161
- hamam mahshi bil freek (freekeh-stuffed squab), 68
- harira (Moroccan tomato lentil soup), 109
- keema matar and raita (minced meat with peas and cucumber yogurt sauce), 351
- lobster maharaja with green rice, 86
- molokhia (jute leaf soup), 191
- salonat lahem (braised goat and root vegetable stew), 304
- sambal udang (prawn sambal), 77
- scallop ceviche with mango, 183
- tahta lahem (Emirati lamb pilaf), 67
- toasted pumpkin seed guacamole, 345
- tom yum goong (spicy and sour shrimp soup), 366
- tuna tahta (Emirati spiced pilaf with tuna), 175

CORNICHONS
- a trio of tartines, 150
- Wagyu burger with Bois Boudran sauce, 254

CORNISH GAME HEN
- hamam mahshi bil freek (freekeh-stuffed squab), 68

COUSCOUS
- couscous with a trio of flavours, 282

CRAB
- crab cakes with mango avocado salsa, 225

CRANBERRIES, DRIED
- fennel, beetroot, and orange salad, 126

CREAM
- aish al saraya (Lebanese bread pudding), 247
- blueberry risotto, 162
- chicken mac and cheese, 356
- Egyptian konafa with cream, 192
- grilled honey and mint strawberries with mascarpone, 201
- pain perdu (French toast with salted caramel sauce), 363
- pie de coco (Colombian coconut pie), 184
- sticky date pudding with cardamom sauce, 176

CRÈME FRAÎCHE
(see sour cream)

CROUTONS
- fattoush (bread and purslane salad), 99
- gazpacho (chilled tomato soup), 101
- kale Caesar salad with yogurt dressing, 240

CUCUMBER
- bong bong gee (bong bong chicken), 276
- fattoush (bread and purslane salad), 99
- gazpacho (chilled tomato soup), 101
- keema matar and raita (minced meat with peas and cucumber yogurt sauce), 351
- kyuri to wakame no sunomono (marinated cucumber and seaweed with sweet vinegar dressing), 312
- a trio of tartines, 150

CURRY
- channa bhatura (spiced chickpea curry with fried bread), 85
- green prawn curry with fennel shavings, 161
- mirch machli (red snapper with green and red chilies), 350

D

DATE SYRUP OR MOLASSES
- chbaab (Emirati pancakes), 118
- luqamaat (fried dumplings with date syrup), 216

DATES, 176
- klaichat tamur (Iraqi date cookies), 136
- sticky date pudding with cardamom sauce, 176
- tahini raw powerbites, 143
- trio of smoothies, 142

DESSERTS
- aish al saraya (Lebanese bread pudding), 247
- apfeltorte ohne deckel (apple tart without a lid), 51
- banana bread with crystallised ginger and walnuts, 21
- Biscoff cheesecake with salted caramel sauce, 271
- cardamom spiced orange cake, 332
- Egyptian konafa with cream, 192
- fondant au chocolat (molten chocolate cake), 324
- grilled honey and mint strawberries with mascarpone, 201
- klaichat tamur (Iraqi date cookies), 136
- luqamaat (fried dumplings with date syrup), 216
- ma'amoul bil jibn (cheese-filled shortbread pastries), 78
- mango and blackberry coconut buckle, 230
- marbled cheesecake brownies, 303
- pastiera napoletana (Italian Easter cake), 94
- pecan pie, 357
- pie de coco (Colombian coconut pie), 184
- snickerdoodle cookies, 358
- sticky date pudding with cardamom sauce, 176

DILL
- gemista me feta (Greek stuffed tomatoes with quinoa, capers, and olives), 226
- quinoa herb salad, 260

DIPS
- Chinese 'strange flavour' eggplant, 277
- hummus bi tahini, 248
- kashk-e bademjan (eggplant and yogurt dip), 290
- muhammara (walnut and red pepper dip with flax seed), 73
- toasted pumpkin seed guacamole, 345

DUCK
- fesenjan ba ordak (duck with walnut and pomegranate sauce), 294

DUMPLINGS, 135
- luqamaat (fried dumplings with date syrup), 216
- Tatar kulaghi (meat dumplings with yogurt sauce), 135

E

EGGPLANT, 169
- borani banjan (eggplant with tomato and mint yogurt sauce), 236
- Chinese 'strange flavour' eggplant, 277
- fesenjan ba ordak (duck with walnut and pomegranate sauce), 294
- kashk-e bademjan (eggplant and yogurt dip), 290
- nasu tama miso (eggplant miso), 311
- roasted eggplant with avocado, thyme, and green olives, 261
- sheikh al mukhshi (stuffed eggplant with pomegranate molasses), 169

EGGS
- tortilla Española de patatas (Spanish omelette with potatoes), 100

F

FARRO
(see barley)

FENNEL
- fennel, beetroot, and orange salad, 126
- green prawn curry with fennel shavings, 161
- warm lentil salad with garden vegetables and poached shrimp, 205

FIGS
- caramelised onion and fig tart with manouri cheese, 229

FISH
(see hammour, lobster, monkfish, mussels, prawns, red snapper, salmon, scallops, sea bass, shrimp, sushi rice, tuna)

FREEKEH
- hamam mahshi bil freek (freekeh-stuffed squab), 68

FRENCH TOAST
- pain perdu (French toast with salted caramel sauce), 363

FRUIT
(see specific fruit)

G

GINGER
- banana bread with crystallised ginger and walnuts, 21
- ginger lemonade, 149

GOAT
- keema matar and raita (minced meat with peas and cucumber yogurt sauce), 351
- salonat lahem (braised goat and root vegetable stew), 304
- tahta lahem (Emirati lamb pilaf), 67

GOJI BERRIES
- gluten-free nut and goji maple granola, 144

GRAPES
- Brussels sprouts with mint yogurt sauce, 246

GUAVA
- guava and pomegranate salad, 264

H

HAMMOUR, 160
- branzino al sale (herb and salt-crusted sea bass), 206
- Portuguese spiced hammour, 160
- scallop ceviche with mango, 183

HONEY
- chbaab (Emirati pancakes), 118
- fesenjan ba ordak (duck with walnut and pomegranate sauce), 294
- grilled honey and mint strawberries with mascarpone, 201
- honey-basted turkey with chestnut stuffing, 128
- luqmaat (fried dumplings with date syrup), 216

HUMMUS
- fattet al hummus (chickpeas with pita and tahini yogurt), 248
- hummus bi tahini, 248

J

JUTE MALLOW
(see molokhia)

K

KALE
- kale Caesar salad with yogurt dressing, 240

KONAFA
- Egyptian konafa with cream, 192

L

LABNEH
- Afghan aush (Afghan noodle soup with Swiss chard), 321
- a trio of tartines, 150

LAMB
- arayes (lamb-stuffed mini pita sandwiches), 168
- beef shawarma with tahini sauce, 170
- fesenjan ba ordak (duck with walnut and pomegranate sauce), 294
- harira (Moroccan tomato lentil soup), 109
- keema matar and raita (minced meat with peas and cucumber yogurt sauce), 351
- machboos deyay (Emirati rice pilaf with chicken), 218

- mint and pine nut-crusted lamb chops, 200
- salonat lahem (braised goat and root vegetable stew), 304
- tahta lahem (Emirati lamb pilaf), 67

LEEKS
- blueberry risotto, 162
- couscous with a trio of flavours, 282
- sup-e pesteh (pistachio soup), 289

LEMONGRASS
- green prawn curry with fennel shavings, 161
- tom yum goong (spicy and sour shrimp soup), 366

LEMONS, PRESERVED
- braised chicken with lemons and olives, 108
- quinoa herb salad, 260

LENTILS
- dum ki dal (slow-simmered Indian lentils), 159
- harira (Moroccan tomato lentil soup), 109
- warm lentil salad with garden vegetables and poached shrimp, 205

LETTUCE
- fattoush (bread and purslane salad), 99
- tabbouleh (parsley and bulgur salad), 364

LIMES, PRESERVED (LUMI), 304
- machboos deyay (Emirati rice pilaf with chicken), 218
- salonat lahem (braised goat and root vegetable stew), 304
- tahta lahem (Emirati lamb pilaf), 67
- tuna tahta (Emirati spiced pilaf with tuna), 175

LOBSTER
- lobster maharaja with green rice, 86
- paella de marisco (seafood paella), 102

M

MANGO
- crab cakes with mango avocado salsa, 225
- lassie – spicy or fruity, 83
- mango and blackberry coconut buckle, 230
- scallop ceviche with mango, 183

MAQUI BERRY POWDER
- trio of smoothies, 142

MARMITE
- grilled cheese sandwich with Marmite, 57

MARSHMALLOWS
- spiced sweet potatoes with marshmallows, 127

MEAT
(see beef, goat, lamb)

MILK
(see also almond milk, coconut milk)
- chai karak (cardamom milk tea), 119

MINT
- arayes (lamb-stuffed mini pita sandwiches), 168

- borani banjan (eggplant with tomato and mint yogurt sauce), 236
- borani kadoo (sautéed butternut squash with saffron and yogurt), 237
- braised chicken with lemons and olives, 108
- Brussels sprouts with mint yogurt sauce, 246
- cauliflower and roasted beetroot salad with tahini dressing, 238
- chapli kebab (Afghan beef patties), 322
- fattoush (bread and purslane salad), 99
- grilled honey and mint strawberries with mascarpone, 201
- kashk-e bademjan (eggplant and yogurt dip), 290
- lassie – spicy or fruity, 83
- mint and pine nut-crusted lamb chops, 200
- quinoa herb salad, 260
- tabbouleh (parsley and bulgur salad), 364
- Tatar kulaghi (meat dumplings with yogurt sauce), 135
- a trio of tartines, 150

MISO
- nasu tama miso (eggplant miso), 311

MOLOKHIA
- molokhia (jute leaf soup), 191

MONKFISH
- paella de marisco (seafood paella), 102

MUSHROOMS
- branzino al sale (herb and salt-crusted sea bass), 206
- couscous with a trio of flavours, 282
- harira (Moroccan tomato lentil soup), 109
- tom yum goong (spicy and sour shrimp soup), 366

MUSSELS
- paella de marisco (seafood paella), 102

N

NIGELLA SEEDS
- klaichat tamur (Iraqi date cookies), 136

NUTS
(see also almonds, pine nuts and pistachios)
- aish al saraya (Lebanese bread pudding), 247
- apfeltorte ohne deckel (apple tart without a lid), 51
- banana bread with crystallised ginger and walnuts, 21
- Brussels sprouts with mint yogurt sauce, 246
- caramelised onion and fig tart with manouri cheese, 229
- cauliflower and roasted beetroot salad with tahini dressing, 238
- Circassian chicken (Syrian poached chicken with walnut sauce), 74
- Egyptian konafa with cream, 192
- fattet al hummus (chickpeas with pita and tahini yogurt), 248
- fennel, beetroot, and orange salad, 126
- fesenjan ba ordak (duck with walnut and pomegranate sauce), 294
- gemista me feta (Greek stuffed tomatoes with quinoa, capers, and olives), 226
- gluten-free nut and goji maple granola, 144

- guava and pomegranate salad, 264
- hamam mahshi bil freek (freekeh-stuffed squab), 68
- honey-basted turkey with chestnut stuffing, 128
- klaichat tamur (Iraqi date cookies), 136
- lobster maharaja with green rice, 86
- mint and pine nut-crusted lamb chops, 200
- muhammara (walnut and red pepper dip with flax seed), 73
- musakhan rolls (sumac and caramelised onion chicken rolls), 167
- pecan pie, 357
- roasted eggplant with avocado, thyme, and green olives, 261
- sambal udang (prawn sambal), 77
- sheikh al mukhshi (stuffed eggplant with pomegranate molasses), 169
- sup-e pesteh (pistachio soup), 289
- tahini raw powerbites, 143

O

OATS
- gluten-free nut and goji maple granola, 144
- tahini raw powerbites, 143

OLIVES
- braised chicken with lemons and olives, 108
- couscous with a trio of flavours, 282
- gemista me feta (Greek stuffed tomatoes with quinoa, capers, and olives), 226
- roasted eggplant with avocado, thyme, and green olives, 261
- Umbrian farro and pearl barley salad, 330

ONIONS
- Asian glazed salmon, 263
- caramelised onion and fig tart with manouri cheese, 229
- musakhan rolls (sumac and caramelised onion chicken rolls), 167
- tabbouleh (parsley and bulgur salad), 364
- tortilla Española de patatas (Spanish omelette with potatoes), 100
- tostadas de platano con hogao (fried green plantains with tomato salsa), 182
- a trio of tartines, 150
- tuna tahta (Emirati spiced pilaf with tuna), 175
- Wagyu burger with Bois Boudran sauce, 254
- warm lentil salad with garden vegetables and poached shrimp, 205

ORANGE BLOSSOM WATER
- aish al saraya (Lebanese bread pudding), 247
- Egyptian konafa with cream, 192
- pastiera napoletana (Italian Easter cake), 94

ORANGES
- cardamom spiced orange cake, 332
- fennel, beetroot, and orange salad, 126
- fesenjan ba ordak (duck with walnut and pomegranate sauce), 294
- trio of smoothies, 142

P

PANCAKES
- chbaab (Emirati pancakes), 118

PARSLEY
- cauliflower and roasted beetroot salad with tahini dressing, 238
- fattoush (bread and purslane salad), 99
- quinoa herb salad, 260
- tabbouleh (parsley and bulgur salad), 364

PASTA AND NOODLES
- Afghan aush (Afghan noodle soup with Swiss chard), 321
- bong bong gee (bong bong chicken), 276
- chicken mac and cheese, 356
- polpette con salsa di pomodoro (Italian meatballs and tomato sauce), 93

PEANUT BUTTER
- chicken satay with peanut sauce, 339

PEAS
- keema matar and raita (minced meat with peas and cucumber yogurt sauce), 351
- paella de marisco (seafood paella), 102
- quinoa herb salad, 260
- warm lentil salad with garden vegetables and poached shrimp, 205

PEPPERS, BELL
- gazpacho (chilled tomato soup), 101
- paella de marisco (seafood paella), 102

PEPPERS, JALAPENO
- borani banjan (eggplant with tomato and mint yogurt sauce), 236

PESTO
- couscous with a trio of flavours, 282
- Portuguese spiced hammour, 160

PIES, 357
- apfeltorte ohne deckel (apple tart without a lid), 51
- Biscoff cheesecake with salted caramel sauce, 271
- pecan pie, 357

PILAF
- machboos deyay (Emirati rice pilaf with chicken), 218
- tahta lahem (Emirati lamb pilaf), 67
- tuna tahta (Emirati spiced pilaf with tuna), 175

PINEAPPLE
- trio of smoothies, 142

PINE NUTS
- caramelised onion and fig tart with manouri cheese, 229
- fattet al hummus (chickpeas with pita and tahini yogurt), 248
- gemista me feta (Greek stuffed tomatoes with quinoa, capers, and olives), 226
- guava and pomegranate salad, 264
- hamam mahshi bil freek (freekeh-stuffed squab), 68
- mint and pine nut-crusted lamb chops, 200
- musakhan rolls (sumac and caramelised onion chicken rolls), 167
- roasted eggplant with avocado, thyme, and green olives, 261
- sheikh al mukhshi (stuffed eggplant with pomegranate molasses), 169

PISTACHIOS
- aish al saraya (Lebanese bread pudding), 247
- Egyptian konafa with cream, 192
- guava and pomegranate salad, 264
- gluten-free nut and goji maple granola, 144
- roasted eggplant with avocado, thyme, and green olives, 261
- sup-e pesteh (pistachio soup), 289

PLANTAINS
- tostadas de platano con hogao (fried green plantains with tomato salsa), 182

POMEGRANATE MOLASSES
- arayes (lamb-stuffed mini pita sandwiches), 168
- fattoush (bread and purslane salad), 99
- fesenjan ba ordak (duck with walnut and pomegranate sauce), 294
- muhammara (walnut and red pepper dip with flax seed), 73
- sheikh al mukhshi (stuffed eggplant with pomegranate molasses), 169

POMEGRANATES
- Brussels sprouts with mint yogurt sauce, 246
- cauliflower and roasted beetroot salad with tahini dressing, 238
- chapli kebab (Afghan beef patties), 322
- fesenjan ba ordak (duck with walnut and pomegranate sauce), 294
- guava and pomegranate salad, 264
- kashk-e bademjan (eggplant and yogurt dip), 290
- a trio of tartines, 150

POTATOES
- Afghan aush (Afghan noodle soup with Swiss chard), 321
- albaloo polow (sour cherry rice), 293
- branzino al sale (herb and salt-crusted sea bass), 206
- honey-basted turkey with chestnut stuffing, 128
- machboos deyay (Emirati rice pilaf with chicken), 218
- salonat lahem (braised goat and root vegetable stew), 304
- tortilla Española de patatas (Spanish omelette with potatoes), 100

POULTRY
(see chicken, Cornish game hen, duck, turkey, squab)

PRAWNS AND SHRIMP
- chirashi zushi (garnished sushi), 314
- garides me feta (shrimp with feta cheese), 329
- green prawn curry with fennel shavings, 161
- lobster maharaja with green rice, 86
- machboos deyay (Emirati rice pilaf with chicken), 218
- mirch machli (red snapper with green and red chilies), 350
- paella de marisco (seafood paella), 102
- sambal udang (prawn sambal), 77
- tom yum goong (spicy and sour shrimp soup), 366
- warm lentil salad with garden vegetables and poached shrimp, 205

PUMPKIN, 253
- roasted pumpkin and feta cheese salad, 253
- toasted pumpkin seed guacamole, 345

PURSLANE
- fattoush (bread and purslane salad), 99

Q

QUINOA, 260
- gemista me feta (Greek stuffed tomatoes with quinoa, capers, and olives), 226
- quinoa herb salad, 260

R

RADISHES
- fattoush (bread and purslane salad), 99

RAISINS
- hamam mahshi bil freek (freekeh-stuffed squab), 68
- machboos deyay (Emirati rice pilaf with chicken), 218

RED PEPPER PASTE, 32
- Circassian chicken (Syrian poached chicken with walnut sauce), 74
- muhammara (walnut and red pepper dip with flax seed), 73

RED SNAPPER
- branzino al sale (herb and salt-crusted sea bass), 206
- mirch machli (red snapper with green and red chilies), 350

RICE
- albaloo polow (sour cherry rice), 293
- blueberry risotto, 162
- chirashi zushi (garnished sushi), 314
- garides me feta (shrimp with feta cheese), 329
- lobster maharaja with green rice, 86
- machboos deyay (Emirati rice pilaf with chicken), 218
- paella de marisco (seafood paella), 102
- spicy tuna on crispy rice, 270
- tahta lahem (Emirati lamb pilaf), 67
- tuna tahta (Emirati spiced pilaf with tuna), 175

ROCKET
- roasted pumpkin and feta cheese salad, 253
- Umbrian farro and pearl barley salad, 330

ROMANESCO BROCCOLI
- warm lentil salad with garden vegetables and poached shrimp, 205

ROSE WATER
- lassie – spicy or fruity, 83
- luqamaat (fried dumplings with date syrup), 216
- tuna tahta (Emirati spiced pilaf with tuna), 175

ROSEMARY
- branzino al sale (herb and salt-crusted sea bass), 206
- caramelised onion and fig tart with manouri cheese, 229
- couscous with a trio of flavours, 282
- honey-basted turkey with chestnut stuffing, 128

S

SAFFRON
- albaloo polow (sour cherry rice), 293
- borani kadoo (sautéed butternut squash with saffron and yogurt), 237
- chai karak (cardamom milk tea), 119
- chbaab (Emirati pancakes), 118
- gahwa Arabia (Arabic coffee), 215
- kashk-e bademjan (eggplant and yogurt dip), 290
- lassie – spicy or fruity, 83
- luqamaat (fried dumplings with date syrup), 216
- paella de marisco (seafood paella), 102
- sup-e pesteh (pistachio soup), 289
- tahta lahem (Emirati lamb pilaf), 67
- tuna tahta (Emirati spiced pilaf with tuna), 175

SALADS
- Brussels sprouts with mint yogurt sauce, 246
- cauliflower and roasted beetroot salad with tahini dressing, 238
- fattoush (bread and purslane salad), 99
- fennel, beetroot, and orange salad, 126
- guava and pomegranate salad, 264
- kale Caesar salad with yogurt dressing, 240
- kyuri to wakame no sunomono (marinated cucumber and seaweed with sweet vinegar dressing), 312
- quinoa herb salad, 260
- roasted pumpkin and feta cheese salad, 253
- scallop ceviche with mango, 183
- tabbouleh (parsley and bulgur salad), 364
- Umbrian farro and pearl barley salad, 330
- warm lentil salad with garden vegetables and poached shrimp, 205

SALMON, 263
- Asian glazed salmon, 263
- chirashi zushi (garnished sushi), 314

SAMPHIRE
- branzino al sale (herb and salt-crusted sea bass), 206

SAUCES AND SALSAS
- basil butter sauce, 160
- black peppercorn sauce, 200
- Bois Boudran sauce, 254
- cardamom sauce, 176
- green coconut curry sauce, 161
- hogao (Colombian tomato salsa), 182
- mango avocado salsa, 225
- mint yogurt sauce, 236
- peanut sauce, 339
- ponzu sauce, 313
- salted caramel sauce, 271
- spicy mayonnaise, 270
- tomato sauce, 93
- walnut sauce, 74

SCALLOPS
- scallop ceviche with mango, 183

SEA BASS
- branzino al sale (herb and salt-crusted sea bass), 206

SEAWEED
- chirashi zushi (garnished sushi), 314
- kyuri to wakame no sunomono (marinated cucumber and seaweed with sweet vinegar dressing), 312

SEMOLINA
· channa bhatura (spiced chickpea curry with fried bread), 85
· ma'amoul bil jibn (cheese-filled shortbread pastries), 78

SESAME SEEDS
· chirashi zushi (garnished sushi), 314
· klaichat tamur (Iraqi date cookies), 136
· luqamaat (fried dumplings with date syrup), 216
· spicy tuna on crispy rice, 270

SHORTBREAD
· ma'amoul bil jibn (cheese-filled shortbread pastries), 78
· klaichat tamur (Iraqi date cookies), 136

SHRIMP
(see prawns)

SOUPS
· Afghan aush (Afghan noodle soup with Swiss chard), 321
· chili con carne with daqoos, 344
· chilled beetroot soup with yogurt, 338
· gazpacho (chilled tomato soup), 101
· harira (Moroccan tomato lentil soup), 109
· molokhia (jute leaf soup), 191
· nasu tama miso (eggplant miso), 311
· sup-e pesteh (pistachio soup), 289
· tom yum goong (spicy and sour shrimp soup), 366

SOUR CREAM
· Afghan aush (Afghan noodle soup with Swiss chard), 321
· marbled cheesecake brownies, 303
· a trio of tartines, 150

SPINACH
· couscous with a trio of flavours, 282
· lobster maharaja with green rice, 86
· quinoa herb salad, 260
· trio of smoothies, 142

SPIRULINA
· trio of smoothies, 142

SQUAB
· hamam mahshi bil freek (freekeh-stuffed squab), 68

STEW
· salonat lahem (braised goat and root vegetable stew), 304

STRAWBERRIES
· grilled honey and mint strawberries with mascarpone, 201

SUMAC, 32, 167
· arayes (lamb-stuffed mini pita sandwiches), 168
· beef shawarma with tahini sauce, 170
· fattoush (bread and purslane salad), 99
· musakhan rolls (sumac and caramelised onion chicken rolls), 167
· tabbouleh (parsley and bulgur salad), 364
· Tatar kulaghi (meat dumplings with yogurt sauce), 135

SUSHI RICE
· chirashi zushi (garnished sushi), 314
· spicy tuna on crispy rice, 270

SWEET POTATOES
· spiced sweet potatoes with marshmallows, 127

SWISS CHARD
· Afghan aush (Afghan noodle soup with Swiss chard), 321

SZECHUAN PEPPER-SALT
· bong bong gee (bong bong chicken), 276

T

TAHINI, 143
· beef shawarma with tahini sauce, 170
· cauliflower and roasted beetroot salad with tahini dressing, 238
· fattet al hummus (chickpeas with pita and tahini yogurt), 248
· tahini raw powerbites, 143

TAMARIND PASTE
· channa bhatura (spiced chickpea curry with fried bread), 85
· Portuguese spiced hammour, 160

TARTS
· apfeltorte ohne deckel (apple tart without a lid), 51
· Biscoff cheesecake with salted caramel sauce, 271
· pastiera napoletana (Italian Easter cake), 94

TEA
· chai karak (cardamom milk tea), 119
· istikan chai (Iraqi tea), 134
· trio of smoothies, 142
· za'atar chai (thyme tea), 43

THYME
· blueberry risotto, 162
· branzino al sale (herb and salt-crusted sea bass), 206
· marinated beef tenderloin, 199
· roasted eggplant with avocado, thyme, and green olives, 261
· za'atar chai (thyme tea), 43

TOMATOES
· Afghan aush (Afghan noodle soup with Swiss chard), 321
· borani banjan (eggplant with tomato and mint yogurt sauce), 236
· branzino al sale (herb and salt-crusted sea bass), 206
· chili con carne with daqoos, 344
· couscous with a trio of flavours, 282
· fattoush (bread and purslane salad), 99
· garides me feta (shrimp with feta cheese), 329
· gazpacho (chilled tomato soup), 101
· gemista me feta (Greek stuffed tomatoes with quinoa, capers, and olives), 226
· harira (Moroccan tomato lentil soup), 109
· kale Caesar salad with yogurt dressing, 240
· lobster maharaja with green rice, 86
· mirch machli (red snapper with green and red chilies), 350
· polpette con salsa di pomodoro (Italian meatballs and tomato sauce), 93
· roasted pumpkin and feta cheese salad, 253
· salonat lahem (braised goat and root vegetable stew), 304
· tabbouleh (parsley and bulgur salad), 364
· tahta lahem (Emirati lamb pilaf), 67
· tom yum goong (spicy and sour shrimp soup), 366
· tostadas de platano con hogao (fried green plantains with tomato salsa), 182
· Umbrian farro and pearl barley salad, 330

TUNA
· spicy tuna on crispy rice, 270
· tuna tahta (Emirati spiced pilaf with tuna), 175

TURKEY
· honey-basted turkey with chestnut stuffing, 128

V

VEGAN
· Afghan aush (Afghan noodle soup with Swiss chard), 321
· Chinese 'strange flavour' eggplant, 277
· couscous with a trio of flavours, 282
· fattoush (bread and purslane salad), 99
· fennel, beetroot, and orange salad, 126
· gahwa Arabia (Arabic coffee), 215
· gazpacho (chilled tomato soup), 101
· ginger lemonade, 149
· guava and pomegranate salad, 264
· harira (Moroccan tomato lentil soup), 109
· istikan chai (Iraqi tea), 134
· kyuri to wakame no sunomono (marinated cucumber and seaweed with sweet vinegar dressing), 312
· muhammara (walnut and red pepper dip with flax seed), 73
· nasu tama miso (eggplant miso), 311
· quinoa herb salad, 260
· roasted eggplant with avocado, thyme, and green olives, 261
· sup-e pesteh (pistachio soup), 289
· tabbouleh (parsley and bulgur salad), 364
· toasted pumpkin seed guacamole, 345
· tostadas de platano con hogao (fried green plantains with tomato salsa), 182
· trio of smoothies, 142
· za'atar chai (thyme tea), 43

VEGETABLES
(see specific vegetable)

VEGETARIAN
· Afghan aush (Afghan noodle soup with Swiss chard), 321
· albaloo polow (sour cherry rice), 293
· blueberry risotto, 162
· borani banjan (eggplant with tomato and mint yogurt sauce), 236
· Brussels sprouts with mint yogurt sauce, 246
· caramelised onion and fig tart with manouri cheese, 229
· cauliflower and roasted beetroot salad with tahini dressing, 238
· channa bhatura (spiced chickpea curry with fried bread), 85
· chbaab (Emirati pancakes), 118
· chilled beetroot soup with yogurt, 338
· Chinese 'strange flavour' eggplant, 277
· couscous with a trio of flavours, 282
· dum ki dal (slow-simmered Indian lentils), 159
· fattet al hummus (chickpeas with pita and tahini yogurt), 248
· fennel, beetroot, and orange salad, 126
· fesenjan ba ordak (duck with walnut and pomegranate sauce), 294
· gazpacho (chilled tomato soup), 101
· gemista me feta (Greek stuffed tomatoes with quinoa, capers, and olives), 226
· grilled cheese sandwich with Marmite, 57
· guava and pomegranate salad, 264
· harira (Moroccan tomato lentil soup), 109
· kale Caesar salad with yogurt dressing, 240
· kashk-e bademjan (eggplant and yogurt dip), 290
· nasu tama miso (eggplant miso), 311
· pain perdu (French toast with salted caramel sauce), 363
· quinoa herb salad, 260
· roasted eggplant with avocado, thyme, and green olives, 261
· roasted pumpkin and feta cheese salad, 253
· sup-e pesteh (pistachio soup), 289
· tabbouleh (parsley and bulgur salad), 364
· tortilla Española de patatas (Spanish omelette with potatoes), 100
· tostadas de platano con hogao (fried green plantains with tomato salsa), 182
· Umbrian farro and pearl barley salad, 330
· warm lentil salad with garden vegetables and poached shrimp, 205

W

WATERCRESS
· a trio of tartines, 150

Y

YAMS
(see sweet potatoes)

YOGURT
· Afghan aush (Afghan noodle soup with Swiss chard), 321
· borani banjan (eggplant with tomato and mint yogurt sauce), 236
· borani kadoo (sautéed butternut squash with saffron and yogurt), 237
· Brussels sprouts with mint yogurt sauce, 246
· chapli kebab (Afghan beef patties), 322
· chilled beetroot soup with yogurt, 338
· fattet al hummus (chickpeas with pita and tahini yogurt), 248
· kale Caesar salad with yogurt dressing, 240
· kashk-e bademjan (eggplant and yogurt dip), 290
· keema matar and raita (minced meat with peas and cucumber yogurt sauce), 351
· lassie – spicy and fruity, 83
· machboos deyay (Emirati rice pilaf with chicken), 218
· Tatar kulaghi (meat dumplings with yogurt sauce), 135
· trio of smoothies, 142

YUZU JUICE
· roasted pumpkin and feta cheese salad, 253

Z

ZA'ATAR, 43
· couscous with a trio of flavours, 282
· kale Caesar salad with yogurt dressing, 240
· za'atar chai (thyme tea), 43